The Story of Nigeria

THE STORY OF
NIGERIA

Michael Crowder

Chicago, July 1992

R. YEBOAH-SAMPONG

FABER AND FABER
London · Boston

First published in 1962
by Faber and Faber Limited
3 Queen Square London W.C.1
First published in this non-net edition 1978
Reprinted 1980
Phototypeset by Western Printing Services Ltd, Bristol
Printed in Great Britain by
Redwood Burn Ltd, Trowbridge & Esher

ISBN 0 571 11210 2
Non-net edition available in Nigeria only

For
Laz Ukeje
and
Onuora Nzekwu

Contents

List of Maps

8   *Contents*

Preface to the Fourth Edition

It is now fifteen years since *The Story of Nigeria* was first written, and ten years since it was substantially revised for the second edition. In the preface to the third edition, prepared in 1972, I pointed out that so much new material had become available on the history of Nigeria that meaningful revision of the existing text would in fact involve writing an entirely new book. I therefore contented myself with undertaking minor changes made necessary by the new state structure of Nigeria and added an Appendix on 'Major Contributions to the Study of Nigerian History since 1965'. If that observation was apposite in 1972, it is even more so today as each year brings to the bookshelves significant additions to historical scholarship relating to Nigeria. To write a new full-length history of Nigeria in the light of this scholarship would be a Herculean task for any one historian and certainly one which I would not, myself, care now to attempt.

In response to the continuing demand for *The Story of Nigeria* I have, however, made a number of minor textual revisions and added a new chapter on the years since independence for this fourth edition. I had hesitated to add such a chapter in the last edition, despite requests from my publishers, since the events of Nigeria's tragic civil war seemed still so close in 1972 that it would have been difficult to put them in any kind of historical perspective. I trust such perspective is not too apparently lacking in the new chapter prepared for this edition. I have also updated the Appendix on 'Major Contributions to the Study of Nigerian History since 1965'.

To keep down the cost of the volume, in particular the paperback edition, the prefaces to the first three editions have been omitted. I would, therfore, like to add here a list of all those who have in any way helped me in the preparation of the various editions of *The Story of Nigeria* whilst emphasizing that they are in no way responsible for the end product. Professor Peter Morton-Williams; the late Dr R. E. Bradbury; Professor Akin Mabogunje; Professor James Coleman; Dr P. C. Lloyd; Professor Pierre Verger; Mr Thomas Hodgkin; Mr George Vellacott; Professor I. A. Akinjogbin; Mr Bernard Fagg; Professor J. F. Ade Ajayi; Mr Roland Brown; the late Professor Daryll Forde; Professor

John Hunwick; Professor Thurstan Shaw; Professor J. Desmond Clark; Professor David Brokensha; Professor Lalage Bown; Professor R. G. Armstrong; Professor Martin Dornboos; Professor Robin Horton; Mr Robert Smith; Mr Rex Akpofure; Dr Rita Cruise O'Brien; Mr J. E. Lavers; Professor R. J. Gavin and Dr A. I. Asiwaju.

In conclusion may I express the same hope I did in the Preface to the Third Edition that, despite the vast addition to our knowledge of Nigerian history since *The Story of Nigeria* was first written, it may continue to be of use to those who require a short introduction to the history of this great nation.

MICHAEL CROWDER

University of Lagos,
6 May 1976.

1 The Birth of Nigeria

Nigeria, the most populous country on the African continent, only came into being in its present form in 1914 when the two British protectorates of Northern and Southern Nigeria were amalgamated by Sir Frederick Lugard. Sixteen years earlier, Flora Shaw, who later married Lugard, first suggested in an article for *The Times* that the several British Protectorates on the Niger be known collectively as Nigeria.[1]

Although Nigeria[2] was the creation of European ambitions and rivalries in West Africa, it would be an error to assume that its peoples had little history before its final boundaries were negotiated by Britain, France and Germany at the turn of the twentieth century. For this newly created country contained not just a multiplicity of 'pagan tribes', but also a number of great kingdoms that had evolved complex systems of government independent of contact with Europe. Within its frontiers were the great kingdom of Kanem-Borno, with a known history of more than a thousand years; the Sokoto Caliphate which for nearly a hundred years before its conquest by Britain had ruled most of the savannah of northern Nigeria; the kingdoms of Ife and Benin, whose art had become recognized as amongst the most accomplished in the world; the Yoruba Empire of Oyo, which had once been the most powerful of the states of the Guinea Coast; and the city states of the Niger Delta, which had grown partly in response to European demands for slaves and later palm-oil; the largely politically decentralized Igbo-speaking peoples of the south-east, who had produced the famous Igbo-Ukwu bronzes and terracottas; and the small tribes of the Plateau, some of whom are descendants of the people who created the famous Nok terracottas. Between these very diverse groups there was much more commercial and cultural contact than has usually been appreciated, and only research in the past fifteen years has begun to reveal how much the superficially disparate peoples of Nigeria have in common.

Any country is, in a sense, an artificial creation. In the case of Nigeria, however, union was so sudden, and included such widely differing groups of peoples that not only the British, who created it, but

the inhabitants themselves have often doubted whether it could survive as a political entity. On 1st October 1960, despite many difficulties, focusing mainly on the differences among its various component groups, Nigeria became a sovereign federation and has survived
intact despite a protracted civil war. The pages that follow, starting
with the earliest known history of its various inhabitants, tell the story
of the young nation of Nigeria. They may serve to illustrate some of the
difficulties that impeded progress towards independence, as well as the
common factors in the past of its people which are so vital to its
survival. And if the term Nigeria may appear anachronistic in reference
to Kanem-Borno and Ife, one must remember that Mercia and Wessex
are considered just as much a part of the history of Britain.

The Federal Republic of Nigeria covers an area of 570,000 square km.
and according to the 1963 census has a population of 55,600,000 people,
an increase of 20,000,000 people over the 1953 census.[3] The coastline
stretches for 800 km. from Badagry in the west to Calabar in the
east, and includes the Bights of Benin and Bonny. Its borders are
contiguous with the Republic of Bénin (Dahomey) to the west, Niger
Republic to the north and the Republic of Cameroon to the east.

Nigeria is now divided into nineteen States: Anambra, Bauchi, Bendel, Benue, Borno, Cross River, Gongola, Imo, Kaduna, Kano, Kwara,
Lagos, Niger, Ogun, Ondo, Oyo, Plateau, Rivers and Sokoto States. It
falls more naturally into four geographical regions: a dense belt of
mangrove forests and swamps stretching along the coast and often as
much as sixty miles wide; a forest belt which covers much of southern
Nigeria; the northern savannah and sahel; and the great Jos Plateau
(see map). The northern savannah, which lies on the marches of the
Sahara, stretches from Sokoto to Lake Chad, and in parts reaches as far
south as Oyo. This great plain, punctuated by occasional outcrops of
granite rock, or inselbergs, forms the basis of the wealth of northern
Nigeria, producing groundnuts and cotton. It is densely populated and,
in parts, as heavily cultivated as Holland. In Kano State certain areas
support as many as 1,300 inhabitants per square mile: from the air the
land is a jigsaw of fields and irrigating rivers. The main subsistence
crops of the north are guinea corn, bulrush millet, peas, beans and, of
late, cassava introduced from the south. Specialized crops include
tomatoes, onions, maize, sweet potatoes, sugar-cane, rice, wheat and
tobacco. Groundnuts and cotton are the main crops grown for export.
Goats are reared to provide the superb leather known to the outside
world as Morocco leather, because before the British occupation the
north exported most of its goods destined for the outside world by
caravan across the Sahara to the countries of the Mediterranean littoral. The southern edge of this great plain is bounded for the most part by

the great Jos Plateau, which merges with it in sparsely populated Borno. The plateau is generally poor in agricultural resources, producing mainly subsistence crops. It is, however, rich in tin and also produces columbite.

Below the confluence of the great Niger and Benue Rivers lies the forest belt which covers much of the south. The subsistence crops of this area are yams, coco-yams, cassava, maize, plantains, palm produce and rice as well as secondary crops of citrus fruits, pineapples, bananas, tomatoes and vegetables including sweet potatoes and ochra. The principal exports of the south are palm produce, cocoa, mainly from the south-west, and rubber, timber, oil and some cotton, mainly from the south-east. Anambra State has important coal deposits. Over the past decade there has been rapid industrialization of the country, particularly in the fields of textiles, petrol refining, groundnut-oil extraction, soap manufacture, assembly of vehicles and electrical goods, shoes and clothing. The most spectacular development since independence has been the exploitation of Nigeria's oil reserves, which now account for 90 per cent of the country's foreign earnings.

Nigeria today is inhabited by a large number of ethnic groups ranging in size from a few thousand to many million, speaking between them several hundred languages. Though at first their variety of customs, language and social organization is bewildering they can be classified into a number of linguistic groups which give a fairly good indication of their wider cultural affiliations. Of course linguistic affiliation does not necessarily imply common descent, since contact between two very different groups can result in the assimiliation of the linguistic system of one by the other. The majority of Nigeria's inhabitants speak one of the large group of languages which Joseph H. Greenberg[4] has defined as the Niger-Congo family, which is in turn part of the still larger Congo-Kordofanian family.[5] The Niger-Congo family is divided into a number of sub-families, one of the most important of which as far as Nigeria is concerned is the Kwa sub-family. The Yoruba, the Edo, the Nupe and the Igbo speak languages classified as Kwa, which also includes the Twi-speaking people of modern Ghana. The Ijo, the fishing population of the Niger Delta, speak a language that bears no immediate relationship to any other language in the Niger-Congo group, but which is nevertheless a member of this family. The Ijo include about twenty groups, amongst them the Kalabari, Okrika and Nembe peoples. The Efik and Ibibio of what is now the Cross River State speak languages generally classified in the Cross River group, which in turn falls into a huge sub-family defined as the Benue-Congo. This includes many of the major groups of the present Benue and Plateau States, such as the Tiv, who number

1. Nigeria's major ethnic and linguistic divisions

over a million, as well as many small groups like the Batu who are but a thousand strong. These groups share the common factor that until the arrival of the British their political organization rarely extended beyond the village. The Benue-Congo sub-family includes the Bantu languages predominant in Equatorial Africa and what used to be called the Semi-Bantu languages. The Cameroons foothills in the old Benue and Adamawa provinces are inhabited by small groups most of whom speak languages of what Greenberg calls the Adamawa-Eastern sub-family. The light-skinned, nomadic Fulani who graze their cattle throughout the north and appear to contain a large Caucasoid admixture speak a language of the Niger-Congo family, though it corresponds more closely to the Western Atlantic languages like Serer and Wolof spoken in Senegal where the Fulani first made their home in West Africa. The neighbouring Hausa, who are physically clearly of Negro stock, by contrast speak a language which is connected with the Hamitic languages spoken in North Africa, mainly by people of Caucasoid stock; whilst the Kanuri, who inhabit north-eastern Nigeria, speak a language classified by Greenberg as Nilo-Saharan, linking them with Fezzan and Darfur. With certain qualifications, which will soon become apparent, the ethnographic pattern of Nigeria has remained roughly constant for the past 800 to 1,000 years, and many linguistic experts would say longer.

The story of Nigeria as it is known today goes back more than two thousand years. Much of the earlier history of its peoples is contained in myths and legend, for only in the north, where the Kanuri and Hausa came into contact with the Arabs, are there any extensive written records before the nineteenth century. We can, of course, reconstruct something of the history of Africa and its contemporary political divisions from botanical evidence and the distribution of cultivated plants;[6] from archaeological research, which has made great advances in the last decade;[7] from linguistic relationships and ethnographic distribution. But for the present until archaeological investigation is undertaken on a much wider scale we must rely on oral tradition and on a few chronicles whose veracity we have few means of checking.

A proper appreciation of the difficulties of interpreting oral tradition of African societies is essential to a realization of the approximation which colours most dates and most statements of fact until the beginning of the nineteenth century. In a number of societies which had no written languages, there were certain members of the community whose duty it was to remember its history, or that of its rulers. Thus in a Yoruba court a professional oral historian was retained by the Oba, and he was usually responsible for reciting dynastic lists. In an illuminating article on the problems of recording oral history amongst the Bakuba,[8] Vansina has listed the six sources of oral tradition available amongst these people. These are the commonly available sources among Nigerian ethnic groups: formulas including titles and names; poetry; lists including genealogies; tales; commentaries; and precedents in law. It can be readily appreciated that for a proper interpreta-

tion of oral traditions a thorough knowledge of the indigenous language is necessary. But there are greater difficulties in interpretation
itself. Since so much of oral tradition is intimately bound up with the
socio-political relationships of the ethnic group, it is often in the
interests of factions to distort it. The most common motive for distortion is occasioned by dynastic disputes, and if the party with the
weakest claim to the throne succeeds, it is certain that it or its court
historian will immediately modify history to create an air of legitimacy
around the new régime. There is also the basic distortion of memory,
even though the memories of non-literate people are often less fallible
than those of a literate people. The dynastic list of the Yoruba kingdom
of Ketu in the Republic of Bénin, where an individual was responsible
for reciting the full rote, and suffered death if he made a mistake, is
obviously more reliable than one where no such penalty was imposed.
There is also a tendency to telescope early history. Kings drop out of the
list if they achieved nothing of significance in their reigns, or else a
single heroic act by one may be attributed to another with a fuller list of
memorable deeds. There is thus an immense task before the historian,
who has to compare different versions of the same tradition, and take
into account all these possible sources of distortion, wilful or otherwise.
It will need many years of patient work before more definite statements
on early Nigerian history can be made. Fortunately over the past
fifteen years a great deal of work in the field of recording and analysis
of the oral traditions of many different ethnic groups in Nigeria has
been undertaken, and as a result our knowledge of the pre-
documentary history of the country has been greatly enlarged. It is also
very important in talking of the history of Nigeria to appreciate Vansina's warning: ' "Written sources are better than oral ones," is the
maxim of a non-historian. For the practitioner sources are sources.
They can be good or bad, but there is nothing intrinsically less valuable
in an oral source than in a written one.'[9]

In northern Nigeria we are fortunate in the number of documents
available to us on the history of Borno and Hausaland. But these, too,
are subject to many limitations. Some have been copied and may have
been changed. For instance, in one copy of a treatise by the Muslim
reformer Usman dan Fodio, his attack on the use of titles is tactfully
left out by the copyist in deference to his titled master. Naturally there
were often the same political motives for distorting history as there
were in non-literate societies. The Kisra legend which traces the origin
of many peoples of northern Nigeria to the Near East is supported by
local as well as Arabic documents, which may seem to lend it greater
credibility. However, this may well be an attempt by Muslim Arabs to
rationalize the origin of the peoples they encountered in northern

Nigeria, for the North African Arabs lived in societes in which all relationships with other people were conceptualized in lineage terms. The Kisra legend might therefore be an attempt to place the Negro peoples in relationship to themselves. A more recent example of this can be found among the Tiv, who also place great emphasis on their genealogical relationship with one another. Theoretically all Tiv can trace their ancestry back to Adam, who it is said had one son, Tiv, the ancestor of the tribe, and another from whom all foreigners including white men are descended.

Finally, we find that the early records of traditional history made by British District Officers and anthropologists and published in book form have come to be the 'official history' of a particular people. Thus an investigator is likely to have Meek's, Talbot's or Palmer's version of a people's history given to him as the authoritative version.[10]

All these factors necessarily mean that for the present we must treat the early periods of Nigeria's history with considerable circumspection. The broad outlines may be there, but they may yet be subject to radical changes in the light of research being carried on at the present time.

In Nigeria, as in the rest of Africa, there is evidence of social change and cultural development during the Early and Middle Stone Age which lasted from about one million to about 5,000 years B.C. It is probable that the African continent played a significant role in man's early social and physical development, especially in the Neolithic revolution. One authority, G. P. Murdock, has suggested that there was a spontaneous development of agriculture in the region of the Upper Niger between 5000 B.C. and 4000 B.C.[11] He believes that among other things these West Africans were the first to cultivate cotton. He bases his theory on botanical evidence, but it must be stressed that at the moment there are few botanists who support his hypothesis. Whatever the origin, there is no doubt that during the years from 5000 B.C. to A.D. 1 ethnic groups in the Sahara regions, and probably many of those inhabiting modern Nigeria, started to practise settled agriculture. In the north-east of the continent Egypt developed a powerful monarchy and an impressive civilization. Trade was carried on across the Sahara desert by the Berbers, who introduced domesticated animals and plants of the South-West Asian agricultural complex to the Negroes of the Sahara fringe.

The thousand years before the birth of Christ witnessed some of the major changes of the African continent. The North African coast was colonized by the Phoenicians and the Greeks. At the same time the decline of Pharaonic Egypt was paralleled by the rise of the Meroitic civilization of Nubia in the eastern Sudan. On the south-east coast trade was carried on with Indonesia and crops of the Malaysian com-

Ground Stone Axes of the Late Stone Age from Nigeria

That at the top left has been partly bound with leather for use as a charm, since ground stone axes are widely believed to be thunderbolts and to partake of the power of the deity of thunder and lightning.

(Courtesy: Professor Thurstan Shaw)

plex were introduced. Some, like yams, quickly spread across Central Africa to the Guinea Coast, showing the long distances over which agricultural, if not political, ideas could travel.

Against this general setting we can take up the history of Nigeria, beginning with its prehistory, in particular the Stone Age or the period covering the first appearance of Man till his discovery of how to smelt metals.[12] Little is as yet known about the Stone Age in Nigeria as compared with East Africa, though each year archaeologists are extending our perspectives of the development of early man in the country, especially in the south.[13]

We do not seem to have clear evidence of a pebble tool culture such as was found in the Olduvai Gorge in East Africa and was dated as being a million years old. This pebble tool culture, known as the Oldowan culture after the Olduvai Gorge, is represented in Nigeria by pebble tools found north of old Bussa, now flooded by the Kainji lake. However, these pebble tools were found in association with more sophisticated stone tools, suggesting that they represent a culture of a later date than the true Oldowan culture.

The Earlier African Stone Age is represented by some 'handaxes' found on the Jos Plateau. These handaxes are really stones, either pointed or oval-shaped, which are flaked on both sides, and not axes. They were probably used for cutting and digging. This handaxe culture is known as the Acheulian culture after Chelles-Acheul. They have been found in different stages of sophistication in many parts of Africa, but we only have evidence of their existence on the Jos Plateau and at Ngalda on the northernmost bend of the river Gongola. One Acheulian handaxe from Nok has been dated as being 39,000 years old.

The reason why Acheulian material has been found only around the Jos Plateau and Ngalda is that at the time the desert extended much farther south than it does today, though the northern Sahara was wet enough to support man. The Jos Plateau, being on high ground, as was Ngalda, formed a projection of land with sufficient rainfall to support men and animals, linked with the wet parts of the northern Sahara. That we know about the existence of Acheulian man on the Jos Plateau is due to the tin-mining industry, for the handaxes were revealed as a result of excavation by miners for tin rather than by archaeologists. This should caution us to be careful in our interpretations of the distribution of early man in Nigeria. Later excavations, whether by archaeologists or by miners, may reveal a different picture from that which we have at present.

The Acheulian culture was succeeded by the Sangoan culture, named after Sango on the western shores of Lake Victoria, where it was first identified. Sangoan man typically used stone picks which he used to dig up edible roots. He tended to live in woodland areas and along rivers, but does not seem to have penetrated the rain-forest. In Nigeria evidence of Sangoan man's activities has been found along rivers to the west, north-west and south of the Jos Plateau, in particular in the upper valley of the River Sokoto, near old Bussa, and in the Abuja-Keffi region. It is probable that Sangoan man knew how to make fire. He seems to have penetrated Nigeria from the east, coming down the Benue valley, spreading westwards but limited in the south by the rain-forest. The fact that he followed rivers is accounted for by the dry climate of the period.

Examples of tools used by men living in the African Middle Stone Age, lasting from about 30,000 B.C. to 3000–4000 B.C., depending on the areas in which it flourished, are plentiful in northern Nigeria. At Asejire, near Ibadan in western Nigeria, such tools have also been found. They are much smaller and more delicately cut than those of Sangoan man. Indeed, the men who made them were true *Homo sapiens*, that is 'knowledgeable man', our direct ancestors. Men in this period had bodies not very different from our own.

The Later African Stone Age is represented in Nigeria by microliths found in various parts of northern Nigeria, at Asejire, at Iwo Ileru, in the Mejiro Cave at Old Oyo and at Afikpo. The stone tools of this period are very small and finely made and are known as microliths (micro = small, lith = stone). In some excavations these microliths have been found together with pottery fragments and polished stone tools, in others without. In the Rop rock shelter in the Jos Plateau a layer of microliths with pottery fragments and polished stone implements lies above a layer of microliths without them, suggesting that there were two phases in the development of the Later Stone Age in Nigeria. We are now in a period of Nigeria's prehistory when change was becoming rapid. Men made more and more sophisticated stone implements including finely pointed arrows and sharp spearheads for hunting and defence. The wide distribution of stone axes in Nigeria indicates that there was a wide distribution in Late Stone Age times. On the Jos Plateau there are ancient fortified villages and (possibly) Stone Age footbridges still in use. At Birnin Kudu rock paintings which may be more than two thousand years old have been discovered.[14] In Late Stone Age times major revolutions were taking place north-east of Nigeria, first in the Middle East, then in Africa itself in the Nile Valley.

Some ten thousand years ago, when man in Nigeria and indeed in the rest of Africa and Europe was still hunting wild animals and collecting wild fruits, a major revolution took place in South-West Asia. There men began to keep the seeds of the wild barley and wheat they used for food, and planted them at the beginning of the rains. They also started to keep sheep and goats, and later cattle and pigs in captivity. This meant that instead of constantly moving in search of food, they could settle in one place assured of supplies of grain and meat. This is known in the Neolithic Revolution. This revolution spread to the Nile Valley where the ancient Egyptians began to grow wheat and barley in the fertile lands produced by the flooding of the Nile, which deposited rich silt on them.

The revolution did not stop in Egypt but spread westward into the fertile areas of the Sahara. We know that the Sahara was not altogether desert at this time from the rock-paintings found at Tassili in now arid regions of the Sahara, which depict giraffes, elephants and hippopotami, and later cattle.

In time, however, parts of the Sahara began to dry up and people moved northwards and southwards in search of moister climates where they could grow their grain and graze their animals.[15] Some reached the savannah of northern Nigeria where, because of the different climate, they could not grow the grains that grew in the Sahara. Instead of wheat and barley, they started cultivating tropical grasses which were the ancestors of guinea corn, finger millet, African rice and bulrush millet. Thus agriculture was introduced to Nigeria, though it does seem that men living in the forest areas practised agriculture in the form of planting yams and palm-nuts. The incursion of people from the southern Sahara pushed the original inhabitants farther into the forest, where they cleared areas to grow their yams and palm trees.

Stone implements are unwieldy and likely to fracture. No one today would think of using a stone tool if he had a metal one available. Some five and a half thousand years ago in Asia Minor people discovered how to smelt iron-ore by heating the rocks to a temperature at which the metal separated from the rocks in which it was contained. Already these people knew how to do this with copper. But copper, and bronze, which they made from copper and tin, are not so strong as iron. Also iron-bearing rocks are more plentiful than copper and tin-bearing ones.

The ancient Egyptians knew how to make copper and bronze but the knowledge did not spread southwards because of the natural barrier to communications represented by the swampy Sudd to the south of Egypt.

In 600 B.C. as a result of invasions by the Assyrians who discovered the use of iron, the Egyptians also learnt how to smelt it. Their main source of supply came from their southern neighbour, Kush, which had large deposits of iron-bearing rocks at Meroe, after which the Kingdom later took its name.

The knowledge of iron-making spread to North Africa and from there, probably more precisely from ancient Carthage, it spread southwards across the desert. We know that as early as 300 B.C. iron was being smelted at Nok, in northern Nigeria.

Evidence of the vigorous Late Stone Age Nok culture in northern Nigeria first came to light in the form of two terracotta heads found in the Jos Plateau area. In 1936, a small terracotta head of a monkey was found in a mine in the village of Nok, south-west of Jos; then in 1944 a beautiful mask of a human head, also of baked clay, was found at Jema'a, and was immediately connected with the terracotta found at Nok. Later, the name of Nok came to be given to the culture of the early inhabitants of this region; evidence of this culture has since been found in many parts of northern Nigeria. It is believed to have flourished between 500 B.C. and A.D. 200,[16] and covers an area stretching diagonally from Katsina Ala in the south-east to Kagara in the north-west.

These high-quality terracottas, some of which rank as great works of art, tell us a good deal about the Nok people. They were agriculturists and probably kept cattle. They were fond of ornaments—for many of the little figures wear necklaces and bracelets, and many tin and quartz beads have been found in the tin mines of the plateau. They also knew how to smelt iron though shortage of iron-bearing rocks seems to account for the continued use of stone implements. The Nok culture seems to have developed and continued into the early Iron Age. It is believed that the art of the Nok had long been established and may have influenced the early art of the Yoruba, which has certain characteristics similar to the Nok terracottas.[17] At Taruga, twenty-five miles south-east of Abuja, a Nok-type culture that appears to have used iron implements independent of stone ones has been excavated. There iron-smelting was active in the period c. 300–200 B.C. and its relationship to the Nok culture is proved by the presence of similar terracotta figurines.

At Daima, in the Borno State, evidence has also been obtained for iron-working some time in the first half of the first millennium A.D. Apart from the Nok culture, of the period covered by the first millennium A.D. we do not yet know much that is definite. The evacuation of the Daima mound does, however, show continuous human occupation from the sixth century B.C. into the earlier part of the second millennium A.D., that is well over fifteen hundred years. It was this period that saw the spread of Malaysian food plants throughout the Guinea Coast—among them yams, including coco-yams, certain types of rice, bananas, mangoes, coconut palms and sugar cane. It is also thought that during this period, people from the Nigerian (northern) plateau moved south-east through the Cameroons into Equatorial Africa, where they displaced the local pygmy hunters.

The introduction to North Africa of the camel, which can travel for days in the desert without water, at the beginning of the Christian era made trans-Saharan trade, which had been carried on since Carthaginian and Roman times, much easier. In the seventh century A.D. when the Arabs conquered North Africa, an important new factor in African history, Islam was introduced. The impact of these developments before the ninth century A.D. on Nigeria was very slight. What is clear is that by that time there was a major division between Nigerian peoples as a result of geographical conditions.[18] In the forest belt of the south, the people largely depended on certain varieties of root crops, fruits and a few domestic animals. Weaving was of a very simple kind, but pottery and carving were well developed. Known sources of iron were scarce and smelting was carried on in only a few centres. The peoples of the forest belt were generally organized in small units which seldom exceeded a thousand in number. However, towards the end of the millennium, as a result of incursions from the north or of internal changes, some of these loosely organized groups began to form themselves into state-like societies. In the open savannah of the north, the organization of large political units was much easier than in the dense forests of the south, because communications were simpler. Also, grain grew easily: consequently, there was often sufficient surplus food to allow some members of the community to leave farming for work such as weaving, iron- and leather-working, as well as the various duties of government. This was usually the beginning of state-like organizations. The first state with a form of centralized government in Nigeria appears to have been the kingdom of Kanem-Borno, a section of which comprised present-day Borno State.

2 Sudanese States

From the seventh century there flourished in the Western and Central Sudan a series of states and empires which depended in part on their role as middlemen for the exchange of the products of the forest lands of the south with goods coming across the Sahara desert from North Africa. A number of these states developed in what is now northern Nigeria, the most important of which were Kanem-Borno and the Hausa States. Only Kanem-Borno rivalled in size and power the more westerly states of Ghana, Mali and Songhai. The more southerly Sudanese States of Nigeria, such as Kwararafa and Nupe, were probably at least as powerful as Kano and Katsina, but because none of the Muslim scholars and travellers who wrote about the states of the Sudan visited them, we know much less about them.

Our knowledge of the early history of all these states is still very vague and often dependent on one authority, the reliability of whose evidence we have no means of ascertaining. It seems, therefore, difficult at this stage to generalize about the inspiration for the state-forming process in the Western and Central Sudan as some historians have tried to do in recent years.[1] But it does seem clear that one important factor in the growth of these states was the opening up of regular trade relations with Northern Africa after its invasion by the Arabs at the end of the seventh century.

Trade had been carried on across the Sahara before the Arab conquest. Carthage imported ivory and gold from West Africa, as did the Roman provinces of North Africa. With the introduction of the camel into North Africa around A.D. 100, travel across the desert became easier. Much larger than the donkey, and able to travel several days without water, the camel became the principal carrier of the trans-Saharan trade.

Before the Arab conquest the trans-Saharan trade was in the hands of the Berbers. After their conquest, the Arabs took control of this trade, or rather organized the trade using Sahara nomads as carriers and guides. They were particularly interested in gold, which became vital to the economy of the Muslim world and Europe as the basis of their currencies. The growing prosperity of the states of the Muslim world also increased demands for ivory, leather and ostrich feathers. Once the Berbers of North Africa had been converted to Islam, Arab demand for Negro slaves increased because in Islam it is not lawful to enslave Muslims.

West Africans participated eagerly in the growing trans-Saharan trade, which brought them much-needed salt from the desert, as well as cloths, weapons, horses and beads. The new states of the Western and Central Sudan also traded among themselves. Kano cloth, for instance, was to become much prized throughout the Western and Central Sudan. One of the most extraordinary achievements of these empires, from the accounts of Arab travellers, was their maintenance of security of trading conditions over vast areas of West Africa.

Probably the most important results of the Sahara trade were the penetration of the Sudan by Islam and the introduction of writing. Many of the kings of these states employed Muslims as scribes and advisers in their courts because they could read and write and had a knowledge of mathematics which was useful in dealing with taxation problems. Literacy helped trade not only with North Africa but within the Sudan. Thus Hausa merchants were in contact with traders from Mali, which became a powerful empire in the fourteenth and fifteenth centuries and with traders from its successor Songhai, which rose to its height in the fifteenth and sixteenth centuries. We owe much of what we know about these early states to the introduction of writing in the Western Sudan, for not only did Arab traders and travellers record their impressions of what they saw in these states, but a number of Muslim West Africans wrote their own histories either in Arabic or in their own languages reduced to Arabic script. Since Islam arrived later in Hausaland than in Borno, we know more about the early history of Borno than we do of Hausaland. Even so, this is still very uncertain.

The future empire of Kanem-Borno began to emerge some time in the ninth or tenth centuries A.D. It was situated to the north-east of Lake Chad. The inhabitants of Kanem were cut off from the west by the *erg* or dune country of Tenere and spoke a language of the Central Saharan branch of the Nilo-Saharan language family. This language family extends north and north-eastwards. It bears no direct relation to the Chadic or Afro-Asiatic languages spoken by the Hausa and peoples of the plain of Borno to the south-west, cut off as they were from contact with Kanem by the erg of Tenere.

The origins of Kanem are very shadowy. Arabs writing in the ninth century about the lands to the south of Fezzan refer to their inhabitants as Zaghawa.[2] Today the Zaghawa are represented by a small group of Negro nomads in the Chad and Sudan republics. The Zaghawa to whom

2. States of the Niger-Chad region in the sixteenth century

early Arab writers refer seem to have imposed themselves on the inhabitants of Kanem and established a number of small states. One of these was eventually to dominate the whole of Kanem. In the tenth century the Arab writer al-Muhallabi records that the Zaghawa consisted of many tribes ruled by a 'divine' king who was worshipped by his people, and regarded as the giver of life and death.[3] He was also thought to exist without food. He imposed taxes on the peasantry and was entitled to their goods and animals for use as he wished. This ruler was the King of Kanem.

By A.D. 1000 then, Kanem seems to have emerged as the dominant state in the 'Zaghawa' lands north-east of Lake Chad. We cannot, however, at this stage be clear as to how much territory the ruler of Kanem controlled at that time.

The rulers of Kanem,[4] who took the title Mai, believed that they were descended from Sayf b. dhi Yazen, the great Arab culture hero. He and his followers conquered the Magumi nomads north-east of Lake Chad. He then proceeded to subject neighbouring groups to his authority. He and his descendants ruled them as Mais (lords) of the Sefawa (*Sayfa*wa), the name by which the Kanem-Borno dynasty which lasted till 1846 became known.

We have no means of checking whether the Sefawa dynasty was in fact founded by Sayf b. dhi Yazan, who is credited with many similar achievements in Arab records. It may be an attempt by Muslim Arab or Borno historians to give the Muslim Mais of Borno Arab ancestry. Whatever the truth, the Sefawa dynasty lasted nearly a thousand years and was one of the longest-lived in Africa.

The first capital of Kanem was established at Njimi, whose location has not yet been settled satisfactorily. Palmer places it variously just east or north-east of Lake Chad.[5] Urvoy placed it at Tie, some twenty miles east of Mao in Kanem. Though ruins of some brick buildings remain there, it seems far too small to have been the capital of any kingdom, and was more probably just a desert fort. Urvoy provided the ingenious theory[6] that the nomadic rulers lived outside the settlement in tents, which is a possible answer, but based on no definite evidence. The Kanuri today say that the old capital of Njimi is in Niger not far from N'Guigmi. In fact, there is a large site with walls 800 yards by 1,600 yards (732m. by 1463m.), 10 miles (16km.) south of N'Guigmi, but the likelihood of their story is reduced by the fact that in the reign of Mai Idris, about A.D. 1600, there were several large towns in that region. Other alternatives present themselves. On some contemporary maps there is an Njimi on the south-west end of Lake Fitri. There are three or four ruins of baked bricks in fields round Mussoro in Chad. Possibly one of these marks the site of the ancient capital. Unfortunately Arab historians and geographers who refer to Njimi are not very helpful since their other reference points are unknown to us.[7]

Whatever the location of the capital, by the end of the first millennium the kingdom of Kanem was beginning to take shape.

The Sefawa dynasty followed a deliberate policy of marrying members of the ruling families of states it defeated. This strengthened the dynasty's rule over peoples from different ethnic groups. Kanem prospered from the trans-Saharan trade, and with trade came Islam. Islam had definitely penetrated Kanem by the eleventh century since around 1080 Mai Hume was converted to the faith.[8] Under his Muslim successors in the twelfth century Kanem's power was gradually extended over the Chad Basin. By the thirteenth century, its influence was beginning to spread as far afield as Egypt, Tunis, Fezzan and the Middle Niger, where the Negro Empire of Ghana had flourished, and where its successor Mali was growing rapidly in power. Under Mai Biri (c. 1150–76) contact with the north coast was more frequent and the reigning Prince of Tunis, who belonged to the famous Tunisian Hafsid dynasty, is even recorded as having received the gift of a giraffe sent to him by 'the King of Kanem and Master of Borno'.[9] As the royal title suggests, the empire was already expanding south of Lake Chad to include modern Borno. Indeed one of the chief characteristics of the Kanem-Borno Empire was its military expansionist nature. With its influence stretching north to Fezzan[10] and south into Borno, Kanem was an impressive empire.

It was organized under the centralized rule of the Mai. He ruled through a council of twelve, which had considerable control over his policy. It was made up of both free and slave-born members. His authority was supported by a large army commanded by a Kaigama, or supreme commander. The provinces were ruled by four governors, of whom the two most important were the Yerima, who governed the lands of Yeri, and the Galadima, who controlled the lands of West Borno. These governorships were confined by tradition to members of the royal family. This was the main weakness of the political system. The provincial governors constantly intrigued against the Mai, and were ultimately the cause of the break-up of the empire in the early thirteenth century. Yet, in order to hold sway over the growing territories of Kanem, it was absolutely essential to give a great deal of power to the provincial governors. Secure in their remote strongholds, they were ideally placed to organize rebellions if they were so inclined—and they frequently did so.

Under Mai Dunama Dibbalemi (c. 1250), Kanem reached the height of its power. He pushed the Empire's frontiers north into Fezzan. With his large cavalry force he extended Kanem's control of lands westward of Lake Chad. Mai Dunama was a devout Muslim and went on pilgrimage to Mecca. When he passed through Cairo he founded a *Madrasa* for Kanem students.

But even during Mai Dunama's reign there was unrest in the Empire and he had to put down a number of revolts. For the next one hundred and forty years Kanem suffered from plots against the Mais by members of the royal family and rebellions by subject peoples. Kanem was so severely weakened by this that a neighbouring tribe of nomads, called the Bulala, took advantage of it, expelled the Sefawa dynasty from Kanem and forced it to move south into Borno. Over the previous two centuries the peoples of Kanem had been slowly infiltrating parts of Borno. Here they mingled with the So people whom they met and subsequently either annihilated or absorbed, for we hear no more of them.

In spite of the growing influence of Islamic teachings, certain traditional customs persisted in the Kanem Empire. For example, women remained exceptionally powerful in the state—particularly the Magira, or Queen Mother, despite the fact that in purely Islamic societies all women were kept in purdah. One Magira even imprisoned the ruling Mai for failing, we are told, to enforce Muslim law correctly!

Towards the end of the century, between 1386/7 and 1390/1, Mai Umar ibn Idris finally abandoned Kanem and withdrew west of Lake Chad into the Borno region. It took nearly a century for the Sefawa dynasty to establish itself in its new home. It was harassed by hostile tribes to the south and torn by civil wars within. Nevertheless, by the early fifteenth century Kanem-Borno had foreign relations with Egypt and the states of the North African coast. As early as 1391, Mai Abu Amr Uthman b. Idris was in correspondence with the Mamluk Sultan Barquq in a long diplomatic letter which still survives.[11] It became powerful enough by the middle of the century to exact tribute from Kano, with which it carried on extensive trade.[12] But it was not until the end of the century, during the reign of Mai Ali Gaji (1473 – c. 1503), that the civil wars ended, the occupation of Borno was completed and the new capital at N'gazargamu was built on the south bank of the River Yobe, c. 1470.[13]

While Kanem was being transformed into the new Kingdom of Borno, important changes were taking place in what are known as the Hausa States. These small city-states were growing in commercial power and drawing the attention of the trading centres of North Africa and the Sudan. The Hausa states are supposed to have been founded at different times during the period A.D. 1000–1200. Legend has it that Bayajidda, son of Abdullahi, King of Baghdad, having quarrelled with his father, left home and journeyed into Borno and thence to Daura.[14]

There he killed a dreaded snake which prevented the people from using their only well for water except on Fridays. The Queen of Daura in gratitude married Bayajidda, and their son, called Bawo, succeeded his father and had six sons, who became kings of Daura, Kano, Zaria, Gobir, Katsina and Rano. Another Hausa state called Garun-Gabas, near modern Hadeija, was said to have been founded by Biram, the son of a daughter of a Mai of Borno. Together these states became known as the Hausa Bakwai, or the Seven Hausa States. In addition to these original states, there were the so-called Banza Bakwai, or the 'banza' (illegitimate) states—Zamfara, Kebbi, Nupe, Gwari, Yauri, Yoruba, Kwararafa. They were called 'banza' because they were states which did not descend directly from Bayajidda but were said to have come under Hausa or Borno influence. This is only one version of the legend describing how the Hausa States were formed; other versions differ considerably and the origin of all of them still remains obscure.

These legends no doubt are attempts to explain how states arose in Hausaland. Prior to the rise of states it seems that most of the peoples in Hausaland and the plain of Borno lived in small hamlets and villages, some of which were walled for defensive purposes.[15] The family was the most important element in these communities. But leadership emerged where work that could not be organized by one family alone had to be undertaken. Thus where large-scale farming activities had to be arranged, a *sarkin noma*, king of farmers, would be responsible. Likewise there was a 'father of hunting'.

What factors led to hamlet or village developing into a town, or *gari*? The population of a village situated in fertile land would expand rapidly. A village located near iron-ore reserves would prosper and grow from trade in iron implements with neighbouring villages. If a village was situated on trade routes between other villages it would likewise expand. When there was danger of attack from outsiders people might move into the hamlet or village that was best situated from the defensive point of view. Lastly, since it was believed that certain powerful protective spirits (*iskoki*) lived in the great black granite hills or inselbergs scattered over Hausaland, people might gather near them for protection. The Dalla hill in Kano is one such example.

The size of these towns meant that a permanent leader was needed to organize the activities of the people. He was known as *magajin gari* and under him were the heads of the various wards of the town, the *mai unguwa*.

Some of these towns developed into small cities or *birane* (singular *birni*) surrounded by defensive walls. The reasons for the growth of a *gari* into a *birni* could vary: its situation on a trade route, its access to iron-ore, the fertility of its surrounding land, and in particular its defensive position. Clearly the last factor is the most important for, in times of war, the people living in surrounding hamlets could take refuge behind the walls of the *birni*. These also enclosed agricultural and grazing land so that the inhabitants could cultivate crops and feed their cattle during a siege.

The *birni* was ruled by a king, or *sarki*, assisted by a number of ministers. There would be ministers in charge of the market, of the city gates, of defence, etc. Most important of all the king of the *birni* was also ruler of the surrounding land. In return for his protection people in the city and outside it would pay taxes in produce. When he died, he would be succeeded by a member of his family.

In the new Hausa *birane*, then, a ruling group emerged. People were differentiated between rulers (*sarauta*) and common people (*talakawa*).

We cannot be sure in our present state of knowledge at what date the various city-states of Hausaland emerged. The developments described above seem to have taken place between *c*. A.D. 1000 and 1400. By 1400 the most important city-states were Kano, Katsina and Zaria (Zazzau). Gobir did not rise to importance till after the fifteenth century. No doubt many small city-states developed and were either conquered or absorbed into the larger states like Kano and Katsina. Rano, one of the original Hausa Bakwai, is a case in point and it seems to have been absorbed by Kano and Zazzau not long after its foundation.

Before the mid-fifteenth century we have little information about the way in which Katsina, Zazzau and Gobir developed. However for Kano, we do have more detailed information. Bayajidda's grandson, Bagauda, was not as the legend suggests, founder of Kano, for it was already a large settlement around the Dalla hill ruled by priest-kings, who controlled a large area of surrounding countryside. The rulers of Dalla were backed by the power of the spirit, Tsumburburai, of which they were priests.

Bagauda does not appear to have settled Kano itself. This was the work of his successors, who at first had to share authority with the priest-kings of Tsumburburai. It was only the ninth ruler of the Bagauda dynasty who finally destroyed Tsumburburai's shrine. By the early fifteenth century, when Kanajeji dan Yaji, the fifteenth Bagaudawa *sarki*, came to the throne, Kano had emerged as a major commercial centre controlling a wide area of territory, including Rano.

As a result of trade with Borno and Mali, Islam had begun to penetrate Hausaland by the fifteenth century. In both Kano and Katsina it is said Islam was introduced by Wangara traders from Mali possibly as early as the second half of the fourteenth century. But there is also linguistic evidence that Islam may have penetrated Hausaland from

Kanem-Borno. The Hausa words for reading and writing, introduced by Muslims, are of Kanuri origin.[16]

In Kano, Muhammed Rumfa, who reigned in the second half of the fifteenth century, accepted Islam both as his personal religion and as that of the state. He sought advice from the famous Muslim jurist Al-Maghili, who wrote a book for him on how a true Muslim government should be run. This has been translated as *The Obligations of Princes*.[17] Al-Maghili spent some time in Kano and later other North African Muslims actually settled there. Al-Maghili also advised the Sarkin Katsina, Muhammad Korau. Muhammed Rumfa built mosques and introduced Muslim law. Though we have much less information about Muhammad Korau of Katsina and Muhammad Rabbo of Zazzau, his contemporary who was said to be the first Muslim King of Zaria, it is from their reigns that Islam became a major force in these states.

By the end of the fifteenth century, Kano and Katsina had emerged as the two most important states in Hausaland, with Zazzau a major factor in the south. Trade between Hausaland and North Africa had been opened up. From the point of view of the development of the state, Islam had become an important factor, especially in Kano. There Muhammad Rumfa (*c*. 1466–1493) was considered a Muslim reformer or *mujaddid*. His importance in the history of Kano is emphasized in *The Kano Chronicle*, which declares that he was 'a good man, just and learned; he can have no equal in might from the time of the founding of Kano until it shall end'.[18]

We have seen that before the sixteenth century Hausaland had contacts with Mali to the west and Kanem-Borno to the east. These, however, had not been very important. In the sixteenth century Hausaland became closely involved with the affairs of Songhai, which had succeeded Mali as the most important state in the Western Sudan, as well as those of the re-constituted empire of Kanem-Borno. It also became involved with the growing Tuareg state of Aïr, situated on the caravan routes that linked Kano and Katsina with North Africa. The Songhai Empire, with its capital at Gao, controlled most of the Western Sudan, from the River Senegal in the west to the borders of Hausaland in the east. Its influence extended across the Sahara desert as far north as Taghaza though its southern boundaries did not extend far beyond the River Niger, which was its life-line.

Songhai looked for expansion eastwards to the Hausa States and the Tuareg Sultanate of Aïr. Kanem-Borno, which now that it was firmly based in modern Borno, is more properly called Borno, also looked to Hausaland and Aïr for expansion, and this ambition was to bring it into conflict with Songhai.

It was at this period that the Western and Central Sudan became involved with the politics of the Islamic world. The Sultan of Morocco, who claimed leadership of the Islamic world, was challenged in this claim by the Ottoman Sultan at Istanbul. Both, therefore, tried to obtain acknowledgment of overlordship from the rulers of Songhai and Borno. In particular, the Moroccan Sultan cast envious eyes on the wealth of Songhai, which controlled the trans-Saharan gold trade. At this time, we must remember, Songhai and Morocco had common frontiers.

Hausaland and Borno thus became involved not only with the Western Sudanese power of Songhai but also with the struggle for supremacy in the Islamic world between Morocco and the Ottoman Empire.[19] This involvement became deeper as the volume of trade across the desert from Birnin N'gazargamu and Kano and Katsina increased. And though, as we shall see, Hausaland was ravaged by invasions from both Songhai and Borno, as well as the Kororofa, to the south, it was a period of development and prosperity for the Hausa States.

Throughout the Western and Central Sudan during the sixteenth century there was a considerable expansion both in the number of people who were converted to Islam and in the number of people who could read and write in Arabic. Many mosques were built and many schools were established. Some of the *ulama*, or scholars, wrote down the story of their times, and some of their manuscripts have survived to this day. Thus the contemporary historian has documentary evidence for the events of this period written by the local people. Examples of these are the *Tarikh al Fattash* and *The Kano Chronicle*. In addition the Arab traveller, Leo Africanus, who journeyed through the Western and Central Sudan, recorded his impressions of the area thus providing us with an important outsider's view of the events of those times.

By the opening of the sixteenth century the Sefawa were firmly established in their new capital at Birnin N'gazargamu. Mai Ali Gaji, who had put an end to the civil strife in the Empire, died around A.D. 1503, leaving to his successors an empire able to withstand the Bulala, who continued to harass Borno on many occasions. But Idris b. Ali, known as Katagarmabe (c. 1504–c. 1526), who succeeded his father as Mai, conquered Kanem and defeated the Bulala, who nevertheless continued throughout the century to be a problem for the rulers of N'gazargamu.

To the west of Borno, Kano and Katsina had been conquered by Songhai, bringing its borders very close to Borno. Leo Africanus who travelled in the region in 1526, reported the subjection of Kano and Katsina to Songhai, which was however, short-lived. Of Kano he wrote: 'The inhabitants are rich merchants and most civil people. Their king was in times past of great puissance, and he had mighty troops of horsemen at his command, but he has since been constrained to pay tribute to the kings of Zaria and Katsina.'[20] He considered Borno next in importance to Songhai and Gaoga (Bulala).

Songhai's position in the Central Sudan was undermined by one of its tributary states, Kebbi, which for a while under the leadership of its Kanta[21] controlled all of Hausaland. In *c.* 1561, for instance, it had became so powerful that Borno had to send an army to attack its capital of Surame because Kebbi had launched a campaign against Aïr, which at that time was Borno's tributary. Indeed throughout the century Aïr, strategically placed on the trans-Saharan trade routes, proved a problem for Borno because both Kebbi and Songhai also tried to take control of it.

From the south, Borno suffered attacks from the shadowy power of Kwararafa, which appears to have been based on the Benue River valley. Kwararafa also made long-distance raids on the Hausa States.

Thus while Borno had re-established itself firmly in the Central Sudan, its position was still precarious: it had to contend not only with outside attacks, but also with continued resistance from the peoples it had conquered in order to re-establish itself in Borno.

Borno's frontiers were secured by Mai Idris Alooma, who came to the throne around 1569 and reigned until the end of the century. Mai Idris defeated the Bulala and removed them as a threat during his reign. Similarly he dealt with internal resistance in Borno. In the north and north-west he defeated the Teda and Tuareg and as a result was able to get on with the business of organizing the internal administration of Borno. Mai Idris Alooma is the most famous of Borno's Mais largely because his Imam, Ahmed ibn Fartua, chronicled the first twelve years of his reign and his wars. We thus know more about him than about any other Mai.[22] We should, however, be careful before accepting that his was the most important reign in the history of Sefawa Borno just because we know more about it than any other. Nevertheless it does seem that in the thirty years he ruled he did as much as any other Mai to bring peace and prosperity to Borno. In particular, he seems to have been an innovating Mai. He introduced Turkish musketeers into his army who trained his own soldiers in the use of firearms. We get a vivid picture from Ahmed ibn Fartua's chronicles of his reign. It differed little from other Sudanese armies, except in its efficacy. The vanguard of the army was the cavalry of the nobility, superbly caparisoned, both horse and rider in armour bearing decorated shields, feathered lances, a riot of colour in the fierce Sudanese sun as drummers urged them on and slaves sang their praises to a cacophony of brass trumpets. Behind them followed the infantry, the peasants sparsely armed with bows and arrows or spears. The rear was brought up by women carrying loads, or possibly by some ferocious-looking group of naked pagan warriors, called in from the outskirts of the empire. While Idris Alooma's army benefited by the presence of the musketeers, trained by Turkish instructors and selected from among his household slaves, the army as a whole was ill-disciplined and incoherent, relying as much on numbers as anything else. Its recompense was pillage or slaves, and it was more often deployed against defenceless villages than against formidable enemies like Kanem or Kano. Yves Urvoy, in a brilliant description of this Sudanese army, sums it up thus: 'This braggart and anarchic cavalry, the despised and badly organized plebeian infantry, the surprise raids, the pillaging of hamlets, the rare and brilliant battles, the confused multiplication of individual combats, is our own feudal army of Crécy and Agincourt.'[23]

Idris Alooma was concerned to model his administration on the *Shari'a* or Muslim law. He built many mosques, some in brick, and established Muslim law, administered by *qadis* (Muslim judges) as the law of the land. In the international field, Mai Idris Alooma became a key figure in the dispute between the Sultan of Morocco and the Sublime Porte, as the Ottoman Sultan was known. Whilst he continued his predecessor's policy of maintaining diplomatic relations with the Ottoman Empire, and in particular with Tripoli, which it had occupied in 1551, when the Turks seized Fezzan which Borno claimed as its tributary he decided to exploit the rivalry between Morocco and the Ottomans, who now controlled North Africa from Algiers to Egypt. In order to check Turkish incursions into his territory he acknowledged the Sultan of Morocco, Al-Mansur, as supreme head of the Islamic Community.

When Mai Idris died in *c.* 1600, Borno had become the single most powerful state of the Western and Central Sudan. Songhai had been overthrown, as we shall see, by a Moroccan expedition which had, however, failed to maintain the integrity of the conquered empire. Meanwhile Kebbi had lost its hegemony over Hausaland.

By the sixteenth century Katsina and Kano had emerged as the two most powerful states in Hausaland. But Hausaland as such had no unity other than that of sharing a common culture and a common legend of origin. The Songhai invasion did not bring about political unity for it was too short lived. In 1516/17, however, the ruler of Kebbi, a Hausa-speaking state which was tributary to Songhai, as we have seen, declared its independence. The Kanta or King of Kebbi who had aided the Askia of Songhai in an attack on Aïr was dissatisfied with his share of the booty collected after Aïr's defeat. Kebbi then conquered much of Hausaland and for part of the sixteenth century

Hausaland was united under the Kantas based on Surame, the ruins of whose walls can still be seen today.

This brought Kebbi to the western borders of Borno, and the two states were frequently at war over Aïr. Aïr, with its capital at Agades, was an unusual state, comprising several Tuareg confederations that had agreed to come together to regulate the trans-Saharan caravan trade. Prior to the formation of the state, the Tuareg confederations were often engaged in disputes about the levying of caravan tolls, and had no commonly accepted leader to negotiate with neighbouring states. They therefore agreed to acknowledge as their ruler a Sultan, not chosen from among them, but a man of servile origin, and thus neutral in his relationship to all of them. Because of the importance of Agades as a cross roads for the trans-Saharan trade for Songhai, Hausaland and Borno it was obviously a great prize over which Songhai and Borno, and later Kebbi, were in constant dispute.

In 1590 the Moroccan Sultan, Ahmed Al-Mansur, sent an expedition of 4,000 soldiers and 600 engineers across the desert to occupy Songhai. Already in 1583 Morocco had taken the Songhai oases of Tuat and Gurara which gave Morocco control of an important sector of the Sahara trade. In 1589/90 Al-Mansur demanded that Askia Ishaq II acknowledge Moroccan sovereignty over the Taghaza salt-mines which provided salt for exchange with West African gold. Ishaq refused and as a result Al-Mansur sent out an expeditionary force to conquer Songhai and secure for Morocco control of the sources of West African gold.

While his army succeeded in defeating Songhai, the Moroccans were only able to rule small pashaliks in Timbuktu and Gao, and the Songhai Empire broke up into its component parts. Kebbi lost its hegemony over Hausaland, which similarly broke up into its component states. By the beginning of the seventeenth century Borno was the only state in the Western and Central Sudan that retained its earlier importance. And up until the Jihad of Usman dan Fodio, it was the only state to retain anything like the power it enjoyed in the late sixteenth century.

3 Kingdoms of the Forest

South of the Niger there flourished the related states of Yoruba and of Benin. These may not have been the first states to have developed in this area, but they are the the first of which we have any definite knowledge. Legends of the Yoruba tell of migrations from the north or north-east. It is possible that the growth of the highly centralized kingdoms of the Yoruba and of Benin in the forests of the south were associated with those of the north.[1] The establishment of Oyo and Benin could hardly have been the result of mass migrations from the north, since the Yoruba and Edo (Benin) languages bear no relation to Hausa or Kanuri, It may well have been the result of incursions by small groups who imposed their ways on the indigenous population but were linguistically if not culturally assimilated by them. What does seem clear is that some time during the first millennium strangers from the north-east either invaded or settled at Ile Ife, establishing a kingdom there.

The Yoruba creation myth that probably parallels this event talks of Ile Ife as the origin of life. In the beginning the earth was covered with water. Olorun, the supreme god, let his son Oduduwa down a chain carrying a handful of earth, a cockerel and a palm nut. Oduduwa scattered the earth over the water and the cockerel scratched it so that it became the land on which the palm tree grew. Its sixteen branches represented the sixteen crowned heads of Yorubaland, probably the heads of the main settlements established by the newcomers.[2] Unfortunately we still know very little about ancient Ife, which is revered today as the original home of the Yoruba.

A second version of the myth of origin recorded by Samuel Johnson tells that Oduduwa was an eastern prince driven out of his kingdom.[3] After long wanderings he conquered the local inhabitants of Ife, where he settled. He had seven children who were the ancestors of the Oba of Benin and the six crowned rulers of Yorubaland, namely the Olowu of Owu, the Onisabe of Sabe, the Olupopo of Popo (Egun), the Orangun of Ila, the Alaketu of Ketu and the Alafin of Oyo. In this story the non-Yoruba kingdom of Benin is included and both Benin and Yoruba traditions agree on the circumstances. Oduduwa sent his son or grandson Oranmiyan to rule over Benin, a task which the latter found impossible, deciding that only a prince of Benin blood could rule that kingdom. He therefore fathered a child by a Benin woman and left him as ruler. He then founded a new kingdom at Oyo, which he made his capital. Adimu, who was either a slave or the original ruler of Ife, was left to guard its national treasures.

This myth and its variants seem to describe a second invasion of Yorubaland, and suggest that at the time Ife, and probably Benin, were well-established states. The date of this invasion is usually placed at the beginning of the present millennium.

There are at present no means by which the history of this very early period can be checked, but as Chief Egharevba has shown, there are many traditions and sayings associated with the first period of the Benin 'Empire'.[4] The rule of the Ogiso or early kings was apparently so unsatisfactory that the Bini tried to set up an alternative, non-hereditary 'republican' type of government, but the first of their leaders, Evian, immediately nominated his own son, Ogiamwe, as his successor. It was at this stage that Benin sent to Ile Ife for a prince to rule over them. The coincidence of the decline of the first Benin state and the arrival of Oduduwa is significant, as indeed is the request of the Bini to a foreign people to come and rule over them. This could either be a convenient legend to disguise what in fact was a conquest by Oduduwa's party or alternatively it may represent a not uncommon occurrence in Africa. There are several examples of centralized states ruled over by a chief invested with supernatural powers and surrounded by a large number of small, headless communities, constantly feuding and in daily terror of death and disorder, beset by droughts and other misfortunes. For these people the sacred kingship of their neighbours often seemed the source of good order, regular rainfall and other benefits. So they grouped together and demanded a prince of the royal blood to rule over them or sent a leader to be initiated into the mysteries of sacred kingship.

Though very little is known for certain about the early history of Oyo and Benin, there have fortunately survived from the ancient kingdom of Ife some remarkable and very beautiful bronzes[5] and terracottas, some of which rank among the masterpieces of world sculpture. They give evidence of great technical accomplishments and the elaborate regalia of the Oni or kings of Ife, whom many of the bronzes seem to portray, indicate a complex society.[6] Their naturalism still remains a puzzle for historians of West African art, most of which has been more formalized, more abstract and more symbolic than Ife art.[7]

The bronzes were probably cast some time around the twelfth century or even earlier,[8] though it is not clear whether they preceded or followed the founding of Oyo. Mr Peter Morton-Williams in a paper read to the Historical Society of Nigeria suggests that Oyo was founded at the earliest in 1390 or at the latest in 1440.[9] References in legends to Adimu who was left to guard the national treasures suggest that sacred cult objects already existed, and these were very probably the bronzes and terracottas dug up at Ife. The fact that Benin history records the introduction of bronze casting in the time of Oba Oguola, who probably reigned in the early fifteenth century, would roughly tally with Professor A. W. Lawrence's opinion that if Benin style is derivative of Ife naturalism then the latter must have flourished some three centuries earlier. The conquest of Ife by Oduduwa's party might explain the apparent discontinuance of the Ife naturalistic style. The odds then seem to be in favour of Ife art's preceding the second invasion.

Even though the supposed invasions of Ife and Benin were associated, they would obviously have been invasions of a small group of people, for the languages of Benin and Yorubaland, though related, are very different. The languages of the indigenous people obviously survived that of the invaders.

Oranmiyan must have chosen Oyo as his capital because it was in a fertile sector of the savannah belt, with good access to the Niger and caravan trails leading both from north to south and east to west.[10] It was also strategically placed to defend the new kingdom against the neighbouring powers of Borgu and Nupe, and probably was one of the terminations of the caravan trail from the north. This invasion, then, led to the establishment of twin kingdoms, Oyo and Benin, which until the establishment of the British Protectorate at the end of the nineteenth century were to remain two of the most powerful kingdoms on the West Coast.

Unfortunately little is known about the early history of Oyo, for there was no written language, and unlike Benin which was first visited by Europeans at the end of the fifteenth century, it appears in European descriptions of the coast only as the vague but powerful kingdom of 'Katunga' in the interior. For our information we have to rely on oral tradition especially as contained in *The History of the Yorubas* by the Rev. Samuel Johnson. Not until the end of the seventeenth century are there any definite dates for the history of Oyo. It was during the preceding century that Oyo appears to have begun its expansion into an empire that eventually controlled most of Yorubaland. It was probably at this period, too, that Oyo developed its force of light cavalry which was the key to its military success.[11]

At its height the empire of Oyo covered a huge area, bounded to the north by the Niger, to the east by Benin, to the west by the frontier of modern Togo and to the south by the mangrove swamps and lagoons that form a barrier between the sea and the interior. The kingdom founded by Oranmiyan was based on Oyo, commonly referred to as Old Oyo as a result of its abandonment and transfer in *c.* 1836 to a new site, which lies about 104 km. to the south of Ilorin. The King of Oyo, known as the Alafin, became the supreme ruler of a large area of what is now called Yorubaland.[12] Under him ruled a number of provincial kings, the most powerful of whom was the Onikoyi of Ikoyi. The Alafin, as supreme monarch, ruled over other monarchs whose powers and independence varied according to his calibre and their own proximity to his capital. The Oyo kingdom was divided into a number of provinces, comprising Yoruba proper, and possibly even including the important town of Ife, the traditional birth-place of the tribe. To the south-west lay the Egbado, closely controlled by Oyo, and the semi-independent Egba; to the south was Ijebu, another independent Yoruba kingdom, though one which may have been subject to Benin at various times; and to the east, the Ekiti, who appear always to have been independent of Oyo. In this complex organization only Oyo proper can be said to have been completely under the rule of the Alafin. The remoter provinces were almost completely independent and, despite its early connections with Ife, Benin soon achieved its independence.

It is not clear at what stage the political organization of Oyo developed into that described by Johnson, but from early times Oyo developed a complex political structure of title grades and palace societies through which government was exercised. This differed considerably from the system generally obtaining in other Yoruba kingdoms.

To begin with, it appears that the rule of primogeniture obtained in Oyo, but that it was abandoned in favour of selection from among members of the royal family by the Oyo Mesi.[13] There were seven principal councillors of state, though the number and composition of this group varied over the centuries. They were also the ward heads of the city of Oyo and were presided over by the Basorun, or Prime Minister. The eldest son of the Alafin was appointed Aremo, or Crown Prince, and from the early eighteenth century onwards he was forced to commit suicide on the death of his father,[14] an arrangement that safeguarded the Alafin from plots by an over-ambitious son. The Aremo was placed in charge of the royal children and was also responsible for some of the vassal kingdoms.

The Alafin was considered *Ekeji Orisa*, that is Companion of the Gods, as well as Owner of the Land and Lord of Life.[15] He administered the empire* through three eunuchs, one the Osi Efa, the Eunuch of the Left, who was responsible for political affairs and died with the Alafin,

* See map on p. 85.

one the Ona Efa, the Eunuch of the Middle, who performed the Alafin's judicial tasks, and one the Otun Efa, the Eunuch of the Right, who performed the Alafin's religious duties. The Alafin rarely appeared before the people in person and spent most of his time in his huge palace.[16] The main check on the power of the Alafin was held by the Oyo Mesi who, if they felt the Alafin had exceeded his powers, could divine that all was not well between the Alafin and his spiritual double and force him to commit suicide by presenting him with an empty calabash or parrot's eggs, or more directly by informing him that he had failed to conform to precedent. However, the Oyo Mesi were restrained from abuse of this power by the fact that one of their number had to die with the Alafin. Another restraining influence was the various cult groups, or 'secret' societies, which flourished in most Yoruba kingdoms, though it has recently been shown that the Ogboni, so prominent in nineteenth-century Oyo, was a late importation.

The Oyo Empire was supervised by officials called *ajele* or *Asoju oba*, meaning one who was the king's eyes. The ajele resided in the vassal kingdoms to supervise payment of tribute to Oyo. They had the same status as the kings they supervised, controlling them through the authority of the royal cult of Sango, a deified Alafin. Since Sango was the god of thunder and lightning they could threaten recalcitrant kings with his wrath.

Government at Oyo was a delicate balance of power between the Alafin and his palace administration on the one hand and the Oyo Mesi and the more representative Ogboni society on the other. The division of power in Oyo is nowhere better illustrated than in the composition of the army. The head of the army was an ilari or titled slave called the Are-Ona-Kakanfo, and was directly responsible to the Alafin, whilst the army was raised by the Oyo Mesi as ward heads. The Alafin himself was represented in battle by the Osi Efa.

There was only one Kakanfo at any one time, and if he were to suffer defeat as leader of the Oyo army, then he had to commit suicide, which is certainly one explanation for the success of the Oyo army.

Ife retained its constitutional and spiritual importance for Yoruba-land, and to a lesser extent for Benin, but its power as a state clearly declined, for the important kingdoms of Owu and Ilesha, neither of which owed allegiance to the Oni, established themselves within eighty km. of its city walls. Bradbury has suggested that the rise of Benin and Oyo coincided with the decline of Ife 'as an effective political empire, though it has retained its primacy as a religious metropolis and the source of true divine kingship to the present'.[17] In Benin to this day on the coronation of an Oba, his cheeks are chalked with Yoruba tribal marks, which are subsequently erased, whilst the Oba of Benin were given token burial in Ife. Willett recently excavated the 'graveyard' of the Oba of Benin, in Ife, known as 'the heaven of the kings of Benin'. Even the Alafin of Oyo, as Akinjogbin has shown, was sanctioned in office by the Oni of Ife.

The provincial kingdoms and towns differed somewhat in their organization from that of Oyo. Each town was an entity in itself, ruled by an Oba who was supplied by one of the sections of the ruling lineages. In the smaller towns, all the non-ruling lineages supplied chiefs, who together with heads of various cults and societies formed a council which exercised considerable control over the acts of the Oba. Since most lineages as well as associations, whether political or religious, were represented on the council the people of the town had a voice in their government.[18]

The history of the Yoruba before the eighteenth century is extremely vague, the only available source for it at present being Johnson's *History of the Yorubas*, written at the end of the nineteenth century. It is said that there is a Hausa history of the Yoruba extant in Katsina, but as yet this is not available. It would provide interesting material for checking the validity of Johnson's statements about the period before the eighteenth century, since it was written at that time. What follows is necessarily a paraphrase of Johnson's record of the Alafin of Oyo.

The first period of the Oyo Empire deals with what must be termed the legendary kings. Its history is further obscured by the fact that several of the early Alafin were deified, and new, more dramatic legends woven around them.

Oranmiyan, founder of Oyo, son or grandson of Oduduwa, and direct ancestor of the present Alafin who is forty-third in line of succession,[19] was succeeded by his son, Ajaka, who was so mild a ruler that the provincial kings encroached on his lands, and the people dethroned him. His successor Sango is one of the most glamorous figures in Yoruba tradition. He brought ruin on himself and his family by playing with magic. At the time of Sango's reign the supremacy of Oyo was by no means recognized by the other Yoruba kings, particularly the Olowu of Owu, and it was Sango who apparently subjugated this important monarch. Sango's downfall came through his fascination with magic. One day, so the story goes, he used a preparation to summon lightning, and thereby destroyed his own house and most of his wives and children. Either because of discontent among the people about his dangerous interferences with the forces of magic, or because of his desolation at the loss of his family, he hanged himself. He was then deified as the God of Thunder and Lightning, and today is recognized as one of the most important gods with followers all over Yorubaland.

Ajaka came out of retirement to rule once more. He is said to have waged war against the Nupe, as well as against many of his provincial kings. It is interesting that Yoruba tradition tells of contact between these early kings and both Nupe and Hausa. Indeed there is strong reason to suppose that from an early stage Hausa and Yoruba traded with each other. Johnson himself writes that 'Light and civilization with the Yorubas came from the North . . . the centres of life and activity of large populations and industry were in the interior'.[20]

Johnson writes that the Alafin who succeeded Ajaka can be described as 'historical'. However, we are still very much in the realm of legend. An important successor of Ajaka was Kori, who was responsible for the founding of the large town of Ede. The Ijesha were interfering with his subjects, on the borders of their own territory, so Timi, a famous hunter, was sent almost as a marcher lord to defend the Alafin's interests, which suggests that the outlying Yoruba provinces were far from being subject to the Alafin at that time. Timi established himself successfully at Ede, but refused to send Kori his rightful dues on the caravans trading with Benin. He therefore sent the Gbonka, one of his army commanders and a leading member of the Esho, or praetorian guard, to deal with Timi, in the secret hope that Timi would kill him. However it was the Gbonka who killed Timi and on his triumphal return he forced Alafin Kori to commit suicide.

The first king whose reign can be placed with any degree of probability in relation to other known events in the history of Nigeria is Onigbogi. It was during his reign that Nupe invaded Yorubaland and actually destroyed Old Oyo. Dr S. F. Nadel in his study of the Nupe people suggests that the reign of Tsoede, who conquered and refounded Nupe, can be placed about 1531, though this date has no definite accuracy, especially since he is said to have reigned for 128 years.[21] Mr Morton-Williams has suggested *c*. 1516 on the long scale and *c*. 1549[22] on the short scale for the destruction of Old Oyo by Nupe, which is usually credited to Tsoede, who some authorities believe was an entirely mythical figure. Even before the Tsoede conquest, Nupe appears to have been a powerful state. Tsoede was supposed to have been a son of the Ata of Igala whose captial, Idah, was on the River Niger.[23] Bronze casting is said to have been introduced by him from Idah, where the art had been learnt from Benin. However, the famous Tada (Nupe) bronzes which Tsoede is said to have brought with him from Idah, are stylistically closer to those of Ife, and the seated figure is probably the finest work of art to have been found in Nigeria.[24]

It was left to Onigbogi's successor, Ofinran, to lead his people back towards Oyo. His son, the Aremo, Egunoju, continued the return from exile, for Ofinran died *en route*. It seems fairly evident that Oyo was destroyed by the Nupe, for Egunoju founded a new town called Oyo Igboho, where he buried his father.[25] Four kings reigned at the new capital over a period of some fifty years or more. Evidently life was not very secure there, for these kings were all engaged in continuous wars with the Nupe and Borgu. However, Egunoju's successor, who was his brother, Orompotu (who may possibly have been a woman) defeated Borgu decisively. It was left to his successor, Ajiboyede, a son of Egunoju, to drive back the Nupe in a battle in which the Oyo captured the Etsu Nupe. During his reign there was celebrated the first recorded 'Bere' or festival to mark a long and successful reign after which peace should be maintained for a period of three years in Yorubaland. Unfortunately the king's favourite son died shortly after the end of this festival. Stricken with grief the king received the sympathies of his courtiers and nobles only to find them with hands fresh from eating. He accused them of feigning their condolences, since he, the king, had not eaten for days, and ordered their execution. The people were angered by this tyrannical act and only the intervention of a Muslim preacher from Nupe saved him from insurrection. The impact of the remonstrances of the Muslim preacher was apparently so effective that the king apologized to the people publicly for his wickedness. Reference to the presence of a Muslim preacher from Nupe may be significant, for Islam had first penetrated Hausaland on a large scale in the fifteenth century and was probably spreading southward by the end of the sixteenth century.

Abipa, who succeeded Ajiboyede, was also a son of Egunoju. It was he who moved the capital to Oyo against opposition from those who had by now established themselves firmly on the farms of the new land. But Abipa was adamant, and the capital was transferred to its original site, where it remained until its abandonment in *c*. 1837.

Little of interest is recorded about the Alafin who ruled at Oyo until the reign of Ojigi, ninth Alafin to rule there after the return from exile. It may have been he, or one of his predecessors called Ajogbu, who made war on Dahomey and attacked Porto Novo in 1698.[26] With him we enter a phase of Oyo history about which it is possible to write with more certainty (see Chapter 7).

Like Oyo, the new Benin kingdom developed its own complex administration of title-holders and palace officials. There was undoubtedly contact between Oyo and Benin, if not through their marcher towns, certainly through Ife, which they both treated as their spiritual home. Caravans probably moved from Benin up to Oyo and the north, or westwards along the edge of the forest belt.

The first king of the Ife dynasty in Benin was Oranmiyan's son, Eweka I, whose reign probably commenced in about 1300.[27] At that time Benin was administered by a group of chiefs or Enogie, with direct responsibility to the Oba. This was obviously part of the indigenous system of administration, for the father of Eweka's mother was a powerful Onogie. Eweka consolidated his hold on the land by appointing his children Enogie in the various villages of the Benin kingdom. He also set up a state council of six hereditary members who became, in effect, kingmakers. At first, the principle of succession by primogeniture was not established in Benin as it is today,[28] and Eweka I was succeeded by one of his elder sons, who was in turn succeeded by his brother. It was his son Ewedo who decided to transfer the capital from Usama to its present site, so as to be rid of the councillors of state, whose powers were becoming almost as great as his own. When he reached the city of Benin he was attacked and prevented from entering it by Ogiamwe, a successor of the administrator of Benin who had reluctantly allowed Oranmiyan to rule over Benin. A battle ensued in which the new Oba overcame Ogiamwe. This victory is celebrated in a Benin coronation ritual, where the Oba and the representatives of Ogiamwe do mock battle.[29] This evidence could bear out the theory that the tradition which portrays the people of Benin inviting the Oni of Ife to send over a ruler was mere convenience to disguise conquest as more dramatically represented by the Oba's defeat of Ogiamwe, possibly a later leader of resistance to the new dynasty. Installed in his new palace, the Oba gradually but effectively reduced the power of the kingmakers. It is said that he changed the name of the country from Ile-Ibinnu to Ubini (Benin). Ewedo was succeeded by his second son Oguola. To him is attributed the introduction of the practice of making brass castings for the preservation of the record of events. Little is known of the reigns of his two eldest sons Edoni and Udagbedo. Ohen, his third son, succeeded him. It is said that he was paralysed, and to conceal this from his councillors, he was carried into the council chamber before meetings and always left last. However, the Iyase, through whom he made all communications to his councillors and subjects, discovered this, and since a crippled Oba could not reign the Iyase was murdered lest he divulge the secret. This angered the people, who rebelled and eventually stoned the Oba to death.

Benin reached its apogee in the fifteenth and sixteenth centuries. In A.D. *c.* 1440 Uwaifiokun usurped the throne from Ogun, the rightful heir. Ogun murdered him shortly after, and took the title of Ewuare. He extended the empire to the west banks of the Niger and became known as Ewuare the Great. He also enlarged the city of Benin. His rule was unpopular and many citizens are said to have migrated to other lands beyond his jurisdiction. This is possibly the source of some of the traditions of Benin origin of neighbouring peoples like the Urhobo, Western Ijo, Western Igbo and Onitsha Igbo. An examination of the form of monarchy of these states suggests close relationship with Benin which could have come about through migration, culture contact or through the installation of a ruling class from Benin. Ewuare it was who changed Benin's name to Edo in memory of a faithful slave who had saved him from being murdered when Uwaifiokun usurped the throne. Under Ewuare, carving in both ivory and wood was greatly encouraged. Indeed his reign, the last before the arrival of the Europeans, is remembered in Benin as one of the greatest in its long history. The kingdom was highly organized, backed by a large and efficient army, which gave it control of a large area of the coast.

The Oba was the focus of both the political and religious life of the empire, participating in an incredible number of elaborate rituals,[30] considering that he also had to govern an increasingly more powerful empire. Checks to the Oba's power came from two groups, the Uzama, or hereditary kingmakers, and the Town Chiefs. The Uzama were either descendants of the original chiefs who invited Oranmiyan to become king, or those followers who came with him. The Town Chiefs were led by the Iyase, who acted as the Oba's chief adviser. There was frequent friction between the Oba on the one hand and the Town Chiefs and the Uzama on the other. It appears that the Palace Chiefs were created as a counterbalancing force that would remain dependent on the Oba, though they did not often attend the Council.

It is interesting to note how the Obas of Benin solved the problem of administering the outlying parts of the Empire through chiefs without encountering the problem of disloyalty as did so many other African kings. Chiefs were not given single blocks of territory, but a series of villages scattered in different parts of the Empire, so that they could not build a coherent base for revolt.[31]

Benin's influence extended as far as Idah and Lagos, which was a Benin colony. Its economy was such as to allow not only for the production of sacred carvings such as one finds in the small chiefless societies of Nigeria, but for a great deal of secular art, such as superbly carved ornaments, bells, lamp-holders, doors and pillars, many of which are now scattered throughout the museums of the world.[32] It seems then that Benin city, with its complex system of defensive walls,[33] its large army, its hierarchy of chiefs, its elaborate court ceremonial, must have been based on something more than subsistence agriculture. It probably carried on considerable trade with its immediate neighbours, as well as Oyo and the northern states. Possibly it supplied slaves for the

Hausa markets, though we have no definite evidence of this. What is remarkable about Benin, and indeed Oyo, is that both of them were purely African states, whose growth was stimulated by contact with neither Islam nor Europe.

4 The Atlantic Slave Trade

Ewuare the Great may have been the first Oba of Benin to meet a European. According to Antonio Galvão, Ruy de Sequiera reached Benin in 1472 during his reign. However, it is more likely that the first European to visit Benin was João Affonso d'Aveiro who reached Benin in 1486. Whoever was the first, the encounter marked a turning-point in Nigerian history. Until the arrival of the Europeans the coast had been of little significance in the politics of West Africa. Benin, Ife and Oyo all looked to the interior for their trade. The creeks of the Atlantic littoral had been inhabited only by a few small fishing communities. Contact with the outside world was across the great Sahara desert. Benin, Ife and Oyo were probably the ultimate destinations of the trans-Sahara caravans. The arrival of the Portugese in Benin marked the first stage in the complete reorientation of the economy of Nigeria, culminating in the establishment of the British Protectorate over northern Nigeria in 1900–6 when trans-Saharan trade gave way to the speedier export of goods by road and rail through the ports of the Atlantic coast.

Until the fifteenth century Africa, south of the Sahara, had remained unknown to Europe. Nevertheless, in classical times there are references to voyages beyond Cape Bojador. Herodotus recorded that Phoenician mariners successfully circumnavigated the continent, returning through the Pillars of Hercules *c*. 612 B.C. He also mentions Carthaginian trade in gold with West Africa. There are references made to a visit of Hanno the Carthaginian to West Africa in *c*. 500 B.C.

These voyages are all of historical interest but had little bearing on Portugese decisions to venture beyond Cape Bojador.[1] It was known even before the fifteenth century that somewhere in the hinterland of the Maghreb gold was obtained by the Arabs from Negro peoples. This gold was then sold on the European markets. Not unnaturally Europeans wanted to gain direct access to the source of supply so that they could avoid using the Arabs as middlemen. Furthermore, nations like Portugal and Spain were interested in finding a sea route to India, which would likewise save them from trading for Indian goods through Arab intermediaries. These two economic motives, combined with the

3. Nigeria's slave-trading ports, sixteenth to eighteenth centuries

hope that a Christian king would be found in tropical Africa as an ally in the struggles against Islam and the desire to further geographical understandings, led Prince Henry of Portugal, known better as Henry the Navigator, to equip expeditions to sail beyond Cape Bojador and attempt to discover a new route to India. By 1462 as a result of his enthusiasm and imagination most of the coast from Senegal to Sierra Leone had been opened up to trade with Europe. After his death in 1462 Portugese enthusiasm for exploration lost something of its initial ardour. In 1469, however, Fernão Gomes, a rich Lisbon trader, was granted the exclusive rights of coastal exploration for six years provided he explored 100 leagues (about 400 miles) along the coast each year. By 1471 the gold trade had been opened up at Mina and trade expeditions were sent out each winter. It was during the winter of 1472–3 that Fernão do Po and Pero de Cintra first explored the Bights of Bonny and Benin.

The Portuguese were not the sole explorers of the coast, since their neighbours the Castilians were always on their heels. And they were obviously much more worried by this rivalry than subsequent history shows, since they secured Papal Bulls about their rights on the coast in 1451, 1455 and 1456. Castile only ceased to rival them on the West Coast after Columbus had discovered the New World. By 1480 the Portuguese had completed their exploration of the West Coast and were able to settle down to its fruits, mainly in gold from Mina and peppers from Benin. Between 1475 and 1479 trade was brought almost to a standstill by the war between Portugal and Castile. England also appears to have profited from this, for in 1481 an embassy was sent by John II of Portugal to Edward IV of England to request that he restrain his subjects from trading in West Africa, over which Portugal had a monopoly by virtue of its Papal Bull.

In 1483 John II declared himself Lord of Guinea, but in reality his hold over the lands to which he so proudly claimed title was non-existent. The Portuguese were only established at strategic points on the coast by virtue of treaties with local kings. Apart from hostility on the part of these kings to any penetration inland, there were all the difficulties of climate and disease that were to make later attempts at penetration of the interior so hazardous. Furthermore the Portuguese, hotly rivalled by other European powers, found it easier to concentrate on the erection of stout forts, at which goods could be received and defended against marauders, rather than acquire extensive territory which they were in no position to defend.

Portuguese trade with Benin was largely effected from the small island of São Thomé, where a Portuguese settlement was established. Indeed as early as 1485 John II gave authority to the people of São Thomé to trade with Benin, where peppers were a much-prized commodity. São Thomé, where early attempts at settlement were far from successful, found that Benin could supply its greatest want: a labour force, for it had no indigenous population. Soon Benin was exporting people to work on the plantations of São Thomé. Later it was discovered that by exporting slaves from Benin to Mina huge profits could be made, since gold merchants were prepared to pay for them at twice their original cost. The demand for slaves on São Thomé increased after 1493 when colonization of the island was started with deported Portuguese Jews, exiles and convicts. Thus began one of the most remarkable forced migrations in history, whereby the pattern of the world's population was radically altered. The slave trade which followed close on the first visits to West Africa—slaves were on sale in Lisbon as early as 1441—was to make the Negro race second only to the Europeans in its dispersion over the world's surface.

The Portuguese built a factory, as trading stations on the coast were known, at Gwato, the port of Benin, to handle the pepper trade and to purchase slaves. Fortunately through the establishment of this factory we have some amount of information about ancient Benin, though it is often far from accurate. Benin was quickly recognized by the Portuguese as one of the most important kingdoms on the coast and the King of Benin sent an ambassador to Portugal in the reign of King John II (1481–95). In return Portugal sent missionaries and factors (trading agents), together with many presents for the King. The King himself showed little enthusiasm for the new religion, though he ordered his son and some of his chiefs to become Christians. He also ordered a church to be built.

Pina, a contemporary chronicler, records the visit of the Benin ambassador thus:

'This ambassador was a man of good speech and natural wisdom. Great feasts were held in his honour, and he was shown many of the good things of these kingdoms. He returned to his land in a ship of the King's, who at his departure made him a gift of rich clothes for himself and his wife: and through him he also sent a rich present to the king of such things as he understood he would greatly prize. Moreover, he sent holy and most catholic advisers with praiseworthy admonitions for the faith to administer a stern rebuke about the heresies and great idolatries and fetishes, which the Negroes practise in that land.'[2]

Early optimism about the value of the pepper trade with Benin was damped and by 1510 trade with Benin was almost exclusively in slaves. This was to be the pattern for the next three hundred and fifty years, when trade in the natural products of West Africa finally ousted that in humans. Slaves were normally sent over to São Thomé where they joined large caravels, packed with men from the Congo and Mina, and sailed to their destinations.

From the start, however, there was considerable intercourse between the Bini and Portuguese. The Portuguese taught some of them to read, and in 1553 Captain Windham was surprised to find that the King of Benin 'could speak the Portugal tongue, which he learned of a child'.[3]

To this day a section of the Benin royal palace speaks a language quite unintelligible to the ordinary Bini, which is allegedly derived from Portuguese. That the King of Benin greatly impressed the Portuguese is clear from the report of the Portuguese representative, Duarte Pires, to King Manuel from Benin, 20th October 1516.

'. . . he pays us high honour and sets us at table to dine with his son', and no part of the court is hidden from us but all the doors are open. Sir, when these priests arrived in Benin, the delight of the king of Benin was so great that I do not know how to describe it, and likewise that of all his people; and he sent for them at once; and they remained with him for one whole year in war. The priests and we reminded him of the embassy of your highness, and he would so behave as to give great pleasure to your highness, and he replied to us that he was very satisfied with it; but since he was at war, that he could do nothing until he returned to Benin, because he needed leisure for such a deep mystery as this; as soon as he was in Benin, he would fulfil his promise to your highness, and he would so behave as to give great pleasure to your highness, and to all your kingdom. So it was, at the end of one year, in the month of August, the king gave his son and some of his noblemen—the greatest in his kingdom—so that they might become Christians; and also he ordered a church to be built in Benin; and they made them Christians straightway; and also they are teaching them to read, and your highness will be pleased to know that they are very good learners. . . .'[4]

Some twenty-five years later, a Portuguese navigator wrote that the men taken as slaves were mainly captives of war, or sometimes children sold by their parents in the hopes that they might find a more profitable life elsewhere. He also gives an interesting account of the burial of the King of Benin, though its accuracy cannot be vouched for since he states in the same account that most Negroes live to 100 years old. He was also quick to observe the divine status of the Benin kings:

'The Kings are worshipped by their subjects, who believe they come from heaven and speak of them always with great reverence, at a distance and on bended knees. Great ceremony surrounds them, and many of these kings never allow themselves to be seen eating, so as not to destroy the belief of their subjects that they can live without food. . . .'[5]

After 1520 few Portuguese lived for any length of time in the Nigerian region, and their agencies were held by mulattoes or Africans able to speak Portuguese. The main reason for decline in direct trade with Benin was the growth of Asian trade and the creation of better bases at Fernando Po and São Thomé.

The hazards of West African trade are well brought out in Richard Eden's account of Windham's voyage to Benin in 1553,[6] at a time when Portuguese monopoly of the West Coast trade was already being whittled away by rival European powers. Eden describes a visit to the King of Benin. 'They were brought with a great company to the presence of the king, who being a black Moore (although not so black as the rest) sat in a great huge hall, long and wide, with walls made of earth, without windows, the roofs of thin boorde, open in sundry places, like unto lovers to let in the aire.'

They traded successfully with the king, who straight away offered them the thirty to forty hundredweight of peppers in his own store, and promised to gather enough to fill all their ships within thirty days. He did this, collecting the phenomenal amount of eighty tons. But the crew drank too much palm wine and caught fevers. Most of them died. So Windham sailed without the pepper, full haste to avoid further disaster, leaving several of his crew behind including one Nicholas Lambert, a son of the Lord Mayor of London. This was one of the last of the major pepper expeditions. It also marked the end of Portuguese monopoly of trade on the West Coast.

From then on England was to establish herself not only as a leading trader on the coast, but as one of the chief exporters of slaves, a trade profitable both to Africans and Europeans, though bringing with it untold human misery and degradation.

Some estimates put the total number of slaves exported from West Africa and Angola as high as 24,000,000, of which probably only 15,000,000 survived the notorious Middle Passage across the Atlantic.[7] In the sixteenth century about 1,000,000 slaves were transported to the Americas, in the seventeenth century, some 3,000,000, and in the eighteenth century some 7,000,000 or 70,000 a year. Of these about 22,000 were shipped annually from ports in Nigeria. Benin and its colony of Lagos sent about 4,000 and the ports of Bonny, New Calabar and Old Calabar, which grew up directly in response to European demands for slaves, together with the Cameroons sent some 18,000. Even in the nineteenth century, when many major European powers had abolished slavery, and when the British Navy patrolled the coast of Africa, another 4,000,000 slaves were taken across the Atlantic. Many of these came from Yorubaland, where civil war produced thousands of captives to be sold into slavery.[8]

The stimulus to this colossal traffic in human beings was the discovery of the Americas and the realization of their mineral and agricultural wealth. In 1580 the union between Portugal and Spain opened up the West Coast, hitherto a Portuguese monopoly, to the country with a monopoly of the New World. Spain's policy of settling and developing the New World and her stake in West Coast trade greatly stimulated the sale of slaves in West Africa. Both in the West Indies and on the mainland the Spaniards found that the indigenous inhabitants, with the exception of the Indians of Mexico and Peru, were unable to adapt themselves to the new conditions imposed on them by their conquerors, particularly by succumbing to newly introduced European diseases. In the West Indies the establishment of Spanish rule led to the extinction of nearly the entire indigenous population. This was repeated on the mainland to which the Spaniards moved after the exhaustion of the West Indies mines. There was not enough labour available or willing to leave Europe and live in these new lands, so that when it was found that Africans survived well in the climate, and moreover were adaptable both to working in mines and on plantations, the slave trade that had been carried on in a desultory way at the beginning of the sixteenth century received tremendous new impetus. The settlement of North America and the West Indies in the early seventeenth century by Britain and France led to further demands for slaves, especially with the development of sugar-cane plantations in the mid-century. In 1637 the Dutch, who had thrown off the Spanish yoke in 1572, conquered Brazil, and in order to supply the already established Portuguese planters with slaves, set about capturing West Coast slaving forts. In addition to these major slaving powers, supplying slaves to their own colonies, there were the purely commercial slavers like the Brandenburgers and Danes who sold to the highest bidders. During the seventeenth century the Dutch were the leading slavers, followed by the Portuguese. But after the Treaty of Utrecht in 1713 Britain and France took control of the traffic, the French mainly operating on the upper Guinea Coast. The British who had acquired the Spanish monopoly of the slave trade under the terms of the treaty were rivalled by the Dutch on the lower Guinea Coast. The British were particularly strong in the Niger Delta ports, where a corrupt form of English became the language of the slave dealers. Liverpool and Bristol owe their growth at that time to the profits of the slave trade.

Thus in the seventeenth and eighteenth century the West Coast of Africa became a centre of European enterprise and rivalry with slaves as the prize. There was only one means by which the Europeans could ensure the supply of slaves, and that was to obtain the co-operation of the local population. In certain instances it was feasible to make raids on sea and riverside villages, but the small number of slaves captured by these methods never justified the huge expenditure in fitting up a ship to go to the West Coast. It was impossible for the Europeans to penetrate inland, not only because of the tight control the local rulers had on their territories, but also because of the diseases to which they were subjected. It was also in the interests of the coastal middlemen to prevent the European from penetrating inland and trading direct with the slave-supplying areas. African chiefs were not only reluctant to hand over land to European traders, but were also prevented from doing so by customary law whereby, in most cases, land belonged corporately to the people. In such circumstances the European and African slave dealers soon established friendly relations to further their mutual interests.

The slave traffic raised surprisingly few objections in the minds of either Africans or Europeans. The Europeans, of course, conveniently salved their Christian consciences by suggesting that in fact they were saving 'heathens' for Christendom. Anyway, on many occasions they had profits of the order of £5,000 to £10,000 a trip to dispel any qualms they might have felt. Moreover, the horrors of the Middle Passage were far from the sight of ordinary civilized people. To the African the idea of slavery was not foreign. Most groups had some form of domestic slavery, though this was very different from that introduced by the Europeans. In the African system slaves, though of inferior status, had certain rights, whilst their owners had definite and often onerous duties towards them. In Borno, for instance, the kings often sent slaves out to govern their provinces; Hausa kings often ruled through slaves; and in Yorubaland slaves of the Obas attained great power and were much feared by their subjects. In these states slaves had a special usefulness as recruits to high office, since they had no influential lineages behind them, and hence no pressures on them that could be potentially opposed to their ruler's interest. They were also utterly dependent on their ruler, and as slaves could attract no following among the freeborn. In some states eunuchs held similar positions.

Once slavery had been instituted it was hopeless to expect those Africans who profited from it to have any more conscience about it than the Europeans who bought slaves, especially since in this case the Africans were not usually selling their own people, but members of other ethnic groups whom they often considered not only inferior, but also only fit to be slaves. When they did sell their own people it was usually because they were criminals. Thus thieves in Igboland were usually punished by being sold into slavery. A parallel to this can of course be seen in the English system of transporting convicts to Australia. Normally prices for slaves were high, since demand invariably exceeded supply, though occasionally when there were few ships, the price of slaves dropped. The slavers usually anchored some distance away from the slave port, and most of the negotiations were conducted on board after customary presents had been given to the local chief. Slaves would be brought out by canoe and the traders would then present them to the ship's surgeon for inspection; those rejected were often murdered on the spot.

In exchange for slaves the Europeans brought a large and varied list of goods, whose popularity differed along the coast. James Welsh, who visited Benin in 1588 on a trading voyage, lists the following items they carried for trade: linen, woollen cloth, iron bars, copper bracelets, or manillas, glass beads and coral.[9] This was not a slaving voyage, and they bought in exchange ivory, palm-oil, pepper, cotton-cloth. He also reported that cowries were the local form of currency. A century or so later James Barbot visited Bonny where the rate of exchange for slaves was thirteen iron bars for a male slave, nine for females.[10] In 1703–4 the price of slaves in nearby New Calabar was twelve bars for a man and nine for a woman. Often media for the purchase of slaves were copper bars, beads of various sorts, brass belts, cloths, ox horns for drinking cups, pewter tankards, spirits and blue linen.[11]

On board ship the lot of the slaves was terrible. Crammed into the holds of the ships, men slaves were shackled to each other by chains.

There was hardly room to move. It was almost impossible for them to excrete, other than where they were lying, so that dysentery soon became rife. Each day the slaves were taken on deck for exercise and left there till evening. The women, boys and men were all separated. The ship's officers had the right to use any woman slave. Strongest precautions were made against attempts at suicide by jumping overboard. If conditions were frightful for the slaves they were almost as bad for the wretched sailors, many of whom were press-ganged into service on the slavers with contracts that forbade them to complain subsequently about their ill-treatment. About a sixth of the slaves transhipped died; probably a greater proportion of the sailors did, being whipped for the slightest fault by sadistic captains who seemed to make a speciality of the slave trade. Not all slaving captains were of this character. For instance, Captain Hugh Crow from Liverpool was a more thoughtful master, priding himself on delivering his slaves all fit and alive. He was a close friend of King Pepple of Bonny.[12]

Slaver captains did not always have it their own way. On many occasions slaves revolted on board, for they often out-numbered Europeans ten to one. On the Bonny River a group of slaves just carried aboard an English ship took advantage of the bargaining between the captains and the local chiefs for further supplies of slaves, seized the ship's arms and overpowered the crew. This is one reason for the barbarity of the instruments of torture or discipline kept on the ship. The men were usually all chained together, though on one occasion women, who were allowed the freedom of the deck, saw the armoury unlocked and swiftly passed arms to their men, and together they seized the ship. The lot of the slave was little improved when he reached his destination, especially in the British West Indian colonies, where many of the slaves from the Delta ports were sent. The method of sale today seems almost comic, except when one puts oneself in the place of the slave. Those who looked about to die were quickly sold at cheap prices to surgeons; the healthy ones were often sold at what was called a 'scramble'. They were enclosed in a pen, obscured from the public view. Prospective buyers paid an agreed price, and were then let into the pen to seize the best they could. The terror of the wretched Africans as a horde of white men rushed amongst them, grabbing them as quickly and in as great a number as they could, can easily be imagined. No one ever thought to warn them of the method of their sale, which, compared with that of the African markets, must have appeared utterly barbaric. Indeed the barbarism of the West Indian colonies was incredible; for misdemeanour on these islands the slaves were subject to the most inhuman of punishments. Trivial offences might mean an ear lopped off, a hand axed, a tongue or nose slit. 'No slave to be buried after sunset,' reads one of the laws. 'Nor in any other than a plain deal board coffin, without covering; nor shall scarfs and favours be worn at any of their funerals. The punishment for transgressing to be 50 lashes, and the scarfs, etc., to be forfeited.' Of course, such laws were largely a result of fear of slave revolts such as took place in Brazil, Havana, some of the French West Indian colonies and Jamaica itself.

It is interesting to follow up what happened to the many Nigerians who were forcibly settled in the New World. On the whole they soon lost their ethnic identities, especially in those territories where families were broken up indiscriminately and where no consideration was given to the welfare of the slaves. It was difficult for a group in the British West Indies to retain its identity when, as we have seen, common participation even in a funeral, was forbidden. Different peoples reacted differently to the new situation. Many ethnic groups lost their cultural individuality under the oppressive slave system. This was not the case with the Yoruba, who were not usually captured individually as in the east but as the result of wars, which might cause a large number from the same town to be transported. It must be remembered also that they were shipped through the ports where the Portuguese and Spanish purchased their slaves, and many of them found their way to Brazil, Cuba and Trinidad, where their masters were less oppressive in their attitude, especially with regard to the possibility of slaves practising their own religions. This was far from being an altruistic concession in Brazil, for the government permitted and indeed encouraged the maintenance of cultural traditions, thinking that thus, on the classic formula of divide and rule, they could preserve the ethnic identity of various groups and prevent Africans of various tribes uniting in their misery against them. The Governor of the state of Bahia, writing in the early nineteenth century, said: 'These feelings of animosity between tribes may be regarded as the best guarantee for the security of large towns in Brazil.'[13]

This finds a modern parallel in South Africa, where the official policy of the Nationalist Government has been to emphasize differences to prevent Africans uniting against them.

On the other hand the African as such was not despised by the Latin races, and indeed many slaves attained their freedom and became powerful traders long before the eventual abolition of the trade there in the late nineteenth century. Miscegenation, frowned on in British and French territories, was the general rule in Brazil where, as to a lesser extent in Cuba, traditions of the Yoruba in particular survived, since they were one of the major ethnic groups there. Today there has developed in Bahia and other towns that were based on a slave economy a syncretistic religion combining elements of the Catholic and Yoruba

religion. Yoruba from Nigeria can still recognize the religious ceremonies practised by their cousins in Brazil. In Cuba, Efik and Ibibio
slaves re-created Egbo, whose membership included both black and
white. In Haiti Voodoo is a survival of traditional African religions.[14]

A further feature of this cultural interchange between Nigeria and
Brazil was the repatriation of large groups of slaves who revolted
against the government. Between 1807 and 1813 the Muslims, chiefly
Hausa, revolted against not only their white masters but also fellow-
Africans who were not Muslims. This was undoubtedly an extension of
the Holy War being fought in northern Nigeria at that time by the
Fulani, and is an indication of the close contacts between Nigeria and
the New World. Muslim Africans who had been liberated and had
become wealthy also joined the revolt. The last of these revolts took
place in 1835 and resulted in the expulsion of all the Muslim freed
slaves, many of whom returned to Lagos. This started a more general
return movement which included Christians too. Verger has written:
'These were those who established themselves in those parts of Lagos
still known as the Brazilian Quarter . . . where . . . they built houses
like those they used to build in Brazil. . . .'[15]

5 The Niger Delta and its Hinterland

The slave trade had marked effects on the political structure of the Niger Delta and its hinterland, where a large proportion of the slaves exported from Nigeria were procured. Before the arrival of the Portuguese the Delta seems to have been inhabited mainly by the Ijo peoples, who lived in small, scattered fishing villages in the tidal zone. Most of these Ijo communities have a history of moving down from the north-west, several claiming that they migrated from Benin, or rather away from Benin domination. But these legends refer to a period well before the opening up of coastal trade. These early southward movements, whatever their causes, were unrelated to the slave trade; possibly they referred to some upheaval in the early Benin Empire.

The arrival of slave traders in the Delta stimulated the growth of a number of trading states, which were in effect expanded versions of small Ijo fishing villages that happened to occupy favourable positions on the creeks of the Niger Delta.[1] The most important among these were Bonny, Owome (New Calabar), Okrika, whose origins can be traced to the early seventeenth century, and Brass (Nembe), which only became a major slave-trading state in the early nineteenth century.[2] Farther down the coast at the mouth of the Cross River, the Efik trading state of Old Calabar was also organized to meet European demands for slaves. In the western Delta the Itsekiri kingdom of Warri, closely related to Benin, became another major source of supply for slaves.

Before the arrival of the Europeans the Ijo of the eastern Delta lived in villages ranging from two hundred to about a thousand inhabitants. Their villages were divided into a number of wards or 'houses', each representing a patrilineage. The 'head' of the village was the *amanyanabo*, title to which was usually vested in one particular lineage, though in some villages the amanyanabo was elected by the ward heads. The amanyanabo's functions were largely ritual, though he did preside over the village assembly, which consisted of all adult males. The ward heads were usually chosen on the grounds of age, but ward members of exceptional political or economic ability could aspire to the office over someone of greater age. Cutting across allegiance to the house were such ties as membership of age-sects and dancing societies, and relationship with kin outside the patrilineage.

The Ijo traded with the peoples of the hinterland, who were mainly Igbo and Ibibio. The Ibibio, like the Ijo, lived in villages usually consisting of about five hundred inhabitants. Likewise they were presided over by a ward head whose election was determined by seniority. The Igbo lived in federated village groups numbering some five thousand inhabitants and the head of the ranking village was the 'president' of the group.[3] Some Igbo, however, lived in larger communities with more centralized political structures, such as Onitsha, which had come under the influence of Benin. Some, too, had attained high technological skill to which the beautiful Igbo Ukwu bronzes bear witness. These are associated with the Eze of Nri, or priest-king of the Umieri clan, and have been dated by radio-carbon techniques to as early as the ninth century A.D.

The Ijo exported dried fish and salt, which they panned in the salt water creeks, to the peoples of the hinterland in exchange for vegetables and tools, particularly those made of iron. The pattern of this relationship was radically altered by the advent of the slave trade. The sparsely populated Ijo could not find slaves from among their own communities in sufficient quantitites to satisfy European demands, even if they had been prepared to sell their own kin. They therefore looked to the more populous groups in the hinterland, in particular the Igbo, as a source of supply. They bought slaves from Igboland and beyond not only for export, but also for use in their own communities. One of the most dramatic changes in these fishing villages was the rapid expansion of their population through the importation of slaves who were quickly assimilated into the community. Ijo culture was not, however, markedly affected by these involuntary immigrants because the trading states operated a ruthless system of assimilation whereby those slaves of ability could gain great power and prestige in society by observing its rules, whilst those who were unable to assimilate were relegated to the most menial tasks, were ill-treated and subject to severe punishments. Such arrangements have led Horton to describe Ijo society as a 'carrot and stick society'.[5]

The slave trade also changed the pattern of trade between the Ijo and their hinterland neighbours.[6] In exchange for the slaves the Europeans brought salt, used as ballast on the way out from Liverpool and Bristol, dried fish which came from Norway and new consumer goods such as cloth and tools. Probably most important of all, however, they brought firearms which enabled the Ijo states and their neighbours to dominate the trade. The peoples of the hinterland no longer sent their crafts down the coast in the same quantities as before, since tools from Europe were cheaper and better made. They did increase their sale of vegetables, however, since these were needed in greater quantities by the expanding fishing villages and by the European slavers to feed the slaves on the Middle Passage across the Atlantic.

Those Ijo fishing villages which were successful in gaining control of the slave trade with the Europeans underwent considerable internal changes in their social organization. First, their population expanded from small villages of a thousand inhabitants to sizeable towns of between five and ten thousand inhabitants. The new function of the community as an exporter of slaves in considerable quantities to the Europeans provided an increasing emphasis on individual economic ability as a means of achieving status in the system. Economic achievement rather than traditional status became the basis of political power in the community. While government in the fishing village had been carried on by an assembly of all adult males under the presidency of the amanyanabo, it was now effectively concentrated in the hands of the amanyanabo and the leading traders of the state. The amanyanabo, whose functions in the former order had been largely ritual, was now transformed into a hereditary monarch[7] and leading trader of the state. The most significant alteration in the Ijo community was the emphasis laid on the role of the house. In the fishing village loyalty to the house or ward did not exclude loyalty to other groups. But success in the slave trade necessitated the concentration of the loyalties of the people to their houses, for it was this unit which became the basis of productive activity in Ijo society.

The development of the importance of the house, and of house rule, which according to G. I. Jones[8] crystallized in the eighteenth century, is a striking example of the adaptability of an African society to a new economic and political situation. The house which has been named the canoe house to distinguish it from the house or ward of the fishing village was, as its new name suggests, based on the possession of a canoe, though one equipped for war. The house also possessed ordinary trading canoes for bringing slaves down from the markets of the interior. The canoe house consisted of a wealthy trader who was the head of the house, his children and all the slaves he owned. All his lineal descendants and slaves were members of the house. When he died, preference of succession was given to one of his own children, though a remarkable feature of these Ijo states was that a slave of outstanding ability could succeed to leadership. The new head of house was chosen by all freeborn and slave members of the house. The head of house exacted tax from other traders in the house. With this he was able to run the house and equip the war canoe, paddled by fifty men and with muskets and cannon tied fore and aft. A great deal of capital was

needed to maintain a canoe house because the head of house had not
only to equip this war canoe but maintain the trading canoes which
supplied his income. Because of the large amount of capital necessary
to sustain this canoe house, there was a tendency to the concentration
of economic and therefore political power in the hands of a few. The
financial ability to equip a war canoe allowed a man to found a new
canoe house. The head of an existing house always encouraged his
members to branch off on their own, since this would give him extra
voices in the assembly, for these traders remained politically dependent on him, even though they now had their own voice in the affairs of
the assembly. The head of house had a great deal of authority over his
members, in certain cases even being able to settle cases of homicide.
Any inter-house dispute became a matter for the town assembly.

The amanyanabo was the initiator of policy. He decided on the
conduct of war, and led the battle fleet. He was expected to pay for the
conduct of war, and to defray these expenses the town assembly agreed
that from time to time he should have a complete monopoly of a
particular trading article.

The system of house rule was encouraged by the European traders,
who preferred to trade through a few men with established reputations
who could also vouch for the honesty of their subordinates. Some of
these traders took on trust several thousand pounds' worth of goods to
exchange for slaves in the interior.

This pattern of house rule was the most characteristic feature of
these new trading states, including the non-Ijo states of Old Calabar
and to a lesser extent Warri.[9] The organization of each state, however,
differed considerably. Bonny, New Calabar and Warri were under a
strong monarchical system, whilst political authority in Brass and Old
Calabar was divided.

In Old Calabar, for example, there was no one supreme person, and
ascendancy in the community shifted from the leading house of Duke
Town to that of Creek Town. The real power in the community was the
Egbo Society. This was a secret society to which only those of age and
wealth could belong. Membership cost a considerable sum, but, once
admitted, members shared in the proceeds of payments by other
initiates. It gave out laws, settled disputes between various branches of
the houses and collected debts. It was, thus, Egbo which in 1850, under
European pressure, passed a law forbidding human sacrifices.

As G. I. Jones has written: '. . . Egbo was the sole authority capable of
maintaining peace between the different groups or stopping fights and
disturbances once they had broken out, since it alone could apply
effective sanctions against offenders.'[10] In Bonny and New Calabar, by
contrast, political authority lay with the king in council with his chiefs.

In Bonny the monarchy dated back probably to the fifteenth century, and at the height of slave traffic in the eighteenth century the state was under the remarkably capable Pepple dynasty. However, his power was not absolute and, like most African kings, he was bound by restrictions of other important members of the community, in this case the house heads. The power of the various Delta states depended on their fast large war canoes.

The economy of all the Delta states was based on slaves not only for export but as the workers within the state. However, there was a considerable difference in the attitudes of the various states towards slaves. Old Calabar and New Calabar make a striking contrast in this respect. In New Calabar as we have already noted the main emphasis for membership of the state was acculturation, rather than descent from the founding ancestor of the house as it was amongst the Efik. Thus a slave who was successfully integrated into New Calabar could rise to the highest position of state. It was a capital offence to refer to a man as of slave origin. Again, the competition between the three Ijo trading towns of New Calabar, Bonny and Okrika, forced them to lay emphasis on ability as the major criterion for leadership if they were to survive in the fierce struggle for control of markets. Thus, at a later date in Bonny, when there was strife between two major factions in the state, a slave, Jaja, was able to establish a rival state of Opobo. In the New Calabar state the slaves lived in their masters' compounds, giving them little chance to organize themselves; in Old Calabar they were relegated to plantations, whilst the freeborn stayed in the towns, giving them ample opportunity to organize revolt. In New Calabar there were no slave revolts for only those slaves who were idle or stupid suffered oppression. In Old Calabar there was oppression of the slaves, not only through refusing to admit them to high status in the community, but also by excluding them from any participation in society. In addition once Egbo, the main instrument of government in Old Calabar, had unified the Efik settlements at the mouth of the Cross River the geographical insulation of their route to the markets eliminated the cut-throat competition with other states which would otherwise have turned attention to ability rather than pedigree in the selection of leaders.

James Barbot gives a good picture of trade conditions in the Delta states.[11]

'On the first of *July*, the King sent for us to come ashore, we staid there till four in the afternoon, and concluded the trade on the terms offered them the day before; the King promising to come the next day aboard to regulate it, and be paid his duties. . . .

'The second, heavy rain all the morning. At two o'clock we fetch'd the

King from shore, attended by all his *Caboceiros* and officers, in three large canoes; and entring the ship, was saluted with seven guns. The King had on an old fashion'd scarlet coat, laced with gold and silver, very rusty, and a fine hat on his head, but bare-footed; all his attendants showing great respect to him and, since our coming hither, none of the natives have dared to come aboard of us, or sell the least thing, till the King had adjusted trade with us.

'We had again a long discourse with the King and *Pepprell* his brother, concerning the rates of our goods and his customs. This *Pepprell*, being a sharp blade, and a mighty talking *Black*, perpetually making objections against something or other, and teasing us for this or that Dassy, or present, as well as for drams, etc., it were to be wish'd, that such a one as he were out of the way, to facilitate trade. . . .

'Thus, with much patience, all our matters were adjusted indifferently, after their way, who are not very scrupulous to find excuses or objections, for not keeping literally to any verbal contract; for they have not the art of reading and writing, and therefore we are forced to stand to their agreement, which often is no longer than they think fit to hold it themselves. . . .

'We gave the usual presents to the King, etc. . . . To Captain Forty, the King's general, Captain Pepprell, Captain Boileau, alderman Bougsby, my lord Willyby, duke of Monmouth, drunken Henry and some others two firelocks, eight hats, nine narrow Guinea stuffs. We adjusted with them the reduction of our merchandize into bars of iron, as the standard coin, viz: One bunch of beads, one bar. . . .

'The price of provisions and wood was also regulated.

'Sixty King's yams, one bar; one hundred and sixty slave's yams, one bar; for fifty thousand yams to be delivered to us. A butt of water, two rings. For the length of wood, seven bars, which is dear; but they were to deliver it ready cut into our boat. For a goat, one bar. A cow, ten or eight bars, according to its bigness. A hog, two bars. A calf, eight bars. A jar of palm oil, one bar and a quarter.

'We paid also the King's duties in goods; five hundred slaves, to be purchased at two copper rings a head.

'We also advanced to the King, by way of loan, the value of a hundred and fifty bars of iron, in sundry goods; and to his principal men, and others, as much again each in proportion to his quality and ability. . . .'

By the end of the eighteenth century, as Jones has shown,[12] the pattern of trade between the Ijo and the Europeans had become better regulated. The 'breaking of trade' or negotation of terms had become a ritual since the system had over the years become standardized. Customs or 'Comey', paid by the Europeans to the Delta kings, had also become standardized, and by the beginning of the nineteenth century it had for example at Bonny been fixed at £150 per vessel, and at Old Calabar at £250. Even the ubiquitous dash, payable to various groups involved in the trade, had a fixed rate and was taken into account by buyer and seller when the price of exchange was settled.

Receipts from customs levied were shared among the amanyanabo, his chiefs. The villages along the creeks which connected the state with its hinterland trading market also received a portion. The Ijo states therefore comprised not only the trading town, but also nearby dependent fishing villages, the villages along its trading creek, as well as the hinterland market, which was peopled by the Igbo or the Ibibio.

The supply of slaves to the Delta ports was controlled by the Aro of Arochukwu, and in a land of politically decentralized people, they maintained a highly complex and centralized system of trade, coupled with religious-political domination. The power of the Aro, a sub-section of the Igbo peoples, was based on the universal respect of the peoples of eastern Nigeria for the oracle known as the Long Juju, which was said to be Chukwu, the Igbo supreme deity.[13] Thus the Aro, who controlled the oracle which resided in a cave in their territory, commanded great respect among the Igbo and the Delta states. The Aro as representatives of the oracle settled in small colonies throughout the region, ostensibly as mediators between other tribes and the oracle. These colonies very quickly became trading colonies, hedged with religious sanction. In loosely organized Igboland the Aro were the only people who could safely travel from village to village unharmed. Thus Aro hegemony over Igboland, which was directly founded on the proceeds of the slave trade, provided the mechanism of communication over long distances in Igboland where none had existed before: one could now travel in the company of a recognized Aro agent, a guarantee of safe conduct. The Aro colonies were sited on the main trading routes, and along them passed slaves for the Delta ports. The Delta rulers found the oracle a convenient buttress to community discipline. Slaves would be threatened with being sent to the oracle, where it was believed certain death would follow, though, in fact, the cunning Aro rarely killed a man, but sold him into slavery. In New Calabar it was common for one chief to accuse another of witchcraft, so that he would be sent for 'trial' by the oracle. To avoid certain enslavement the chief would have to pay the oracle keepers most of his fortune, which would consist largely of slaves. He would return a broken man, without followers (i.e. slaves) and therefore without status. The Aro backed up the efficacy of the oracle by hiring mercenaries to raid those who would not respect it. Fines from big men had to be paid in slaves who were supposed to be eaten by the oracle, but in fact were quickly exported.

West of the Aro sphere of influence, the hinterland was characterised by the migration eastward from Benin to the Niger of people who drew the indigenous population together into sizeable states. The classic example is the migration of the Onitsha dynasty to the Niger, which is generally believed to have taken place in the seventeenth century. Though classified as Igbo, the Onitsha, as do many other Igbo groups along the Niger, have strong Benin influences in their political structure. They had a monarch, which most Igbo societies did not; and many of their chiefs bear Benin titles.

Benin was the most important state west of the Niger. The port for Benin was Gwato, where factors of the King exercised his monopoly on trade. Olfert Dapper, writing at the end of the seventeenth century, remarked that: 'As soon as a ship has anchored on this coast, the King is informed, and he summons two or three Fiadors, and twenty or thirty merchants to whom he gives authority to go and do business with the Whites.'[14] Benin traders were interested in cloths of all descriptions, brass armlets, looking-glasses, iron bars, fine coral, cowries from East India, beads and perfumes. In exchange they exported slaves, local cloths, pepper, jasper stones, leopard skins and ivory.

At that time Benin appears to have been very prosperous, with a large well-disciplined army. But at the beginning of the eighteenth century when Van Nyendael visited Benin, he remarked: 'Formerly this village was very thick and close built, and in a manner over charg'd with inhabitants, which is yet visible from the Ruins of half remaining Houses. . . .'[15] Benin seems to have overspent itself by the eighteenth century, its constant wars ultimately impoverishing the kingdom. Van Nyendael was nevertheless impressed by its organization. He describes the honesty of the traders, the just code of law, the lack of beggars, and the civility of his own reception.

By the end of the century, Captain John Adams, writing in the period 1786–1800, remarked the decline of the slave trade in Benin and its concentration farther down the coast in the Delta ports. Significantly for the future he observed: 'Human sacrifices are not so frequent here as in some parts of Africa; besides those immolated on the death of great men, three or four are annually sacrificed at the mouth of the river, as votive offerings to the sea, to direct vessels to bend their course to this horrid climate.'[16]

By the eighteenth century the Itsekiri state of Warri had become more important in the overseas trade than Benin. According to tradition it was founded towards the end of the fifteenth century by a Benin prince. By the end of the seventeenth century it was effectively independent of Benin. 'The King of Ouwerre is the ally and in some manner the vassal of the King of Benin, but in other respects he is absolute in his dominions,' Dapper wrote.[17] There appears to have been considerably more contact between the Portuguese and the Itsekiri of Warri than with Benin, for he records that Antonio Domingo, Olu of Warri in 1644, was a mulatto, his father having been educated in Portugal where he married a Portuguese lady.[18] In 1682 Father Jerome Merolla da Sorrento recorded that the reigning Olu of Warri was married to a Portuguese woman of São Thomé.[19] He had married her according to Catholic rite, and many of his subjects had apparently followed his example in adopting the Catholic faith.

P. C. Lloyd has written that the 'development of the new kingdom . . . and its independence from Benin must certainly owe much to Portuguese influence, for all mission activity was centred here when Benin itself seemed to be fruitless soil for proselytising'.[20] Indeed Warri was the only town connected with the slave trade which came under strong missionary influence. Dapper recorded that 'the King himself and most of his inhabitants have some leaning towards the Roman religion'. Elsewhere slave traders were not concerned with the propagation of their culture.

In Nigeria, as elsewhere on the coast, the first effect of the slave trade was depopulation, though this is exaggerated when one considers that probably during the early eighteenth century no more than 11,000 people were sent abroad annually from Nigeria. Some areas were worse affected than others. For example Captain John Adams estimated in the heyday of the slave trade that between 1800–22 probably some 370,000 Igbo had been sold into slavery.[21] This may seem a very large figure, but it certainly had its economic *raison d'être* since then, as now, Igboland's chief problem was dense population.

The slave trade tended to bring some equilibrium of population to south-eastern Nigeria which, in parts, was intensely overpopulated, in other parts sparsely populated. There is evidence to suggest that in fact most slaves came from the overpopulated areas where there was land hunger, being exchanged with the agriculturally richer areas for yams and other farm products.[22]

The slave trade brought great suffering to many Africans both on their way to the coast where they were roughly handled, and on the Middle Passage to the Americas. To a few, like the Delta traders, it brought considerable wealth. It introduced some new commodities, but for the most part imports were substitutes for locally manufactured objects so that the quality of life was not improved and in some cases indigenous crafts and industries declined. The trade no doubt stimulated the growth of states in Africa but at the expense of the insecurity produced for neighbouring peoples who were the object of their slave raids. The strongest and potentially most productive members of these societies were removed to the Americas where they developed the land for their white masters and provided much of the capital that financed the industrial revolution in Europe and later America. The three centuries of contact between Europe and Africa which were focussed on the slave trade brought to the latter none of the benefits of the technological innovations of the former except in the form of cast-off firearms with which slave wars could be the better prosecuted. As far as this relationship was concerned, then, these were a barren three centuries.

6 The Holy War of Usman dan Fodio (1804–30)

Hausaland and Borno were at first unaffected by the arrival of the Europeans on the coast; their economy remained firmly orientated towards the Sahara desert. Even in the eighteenth century when the Hausa states were sending slaves to the markets of the south, their main concern was still with the desert trade.

By the beginning of the eighteenth century Katsina had won the long struggle for control of the caravan routes from Hausaland to North Africa and for a hundred years she was to remain the leading commercial and cultural centre of the Western Sudan. Borno, alone among the great Sudanese states, survived intact, though it was constantly threatened on its northern borders by desert nomads and on its southern borders by the sedentary peoples that served as its slave reservoir. The standard of learning in the state rose, and a number of Mais, ruling in the second half of the eighteenth century were noted for their scholarship. Intellectuals now played an important role in the court, whose structure had become more elaborate, especially since princes who in ancient days would have ruled provinces were kept under surveillance in the capital or in the nearby summer palace of Gambarou. The new nature of the court appears to have been ideal for court intrigue, and the Mais seem to have lost much of their control of political affairs as a result. The growing weakness of the empire was made clear towards the end of the eighteenth century when the Borno army suffered a disastrous defeat at the hands of the Mandara, a subject people.

The first half of the eighteenth century witnessed the rise to power of Zamfara which, though one of the oldest of the Hausa Banza Bakwai states, was only now becoming of major importance in the politics of the Western Sudan.[1] In 1700, however, Zamfara conquered Kano, and by the middle of the century she was rivalling Katsina's supremacy in Hausaland. At the same time the Hausa state of Gobir which, despite the importance of its frontier position on the desert, had remained rather remote from the general trend of affairs in Hausaland, began to assert its power, and from 1731–43 engaged Kano in a series of hard battles. The Gobirawa were at the time being pressed back on their

4. The Sokoto Caliphate (or Fulani Empire) and Borno, *circa* 1850

northern frontiers by desert tribes and were looking for expansion to
the fertile lands of Zamfara on their southern borders. At first they
infiltrated peacefully into Zamfara, and Barbari, King of Gobir, gave
his own sister in marriage to Marroki, King of Zamfara. A treaty was
drawn up whereby the Gobirawa were allowed to settle near modern
Sabon Birni, for the King of Zamfara welcomed the assistance of the
Gobirawa in his struggle for supremacy in Hausaland.

In 1764, however, Barbari attacked and sacked Birnin Zamfara,
capital of King Marroki, who fled to Kiawa, a Katsina town, where,
with the help of the Katsinawa, he held out against the Gobirawa and
defeated Barbari's successor, Bawa, at the battle of Dutsin Wake.
Ultimately, however, the Zamfarawa were driven out of Kiawa and
established a new capital at Anka in the south of their territories. All
this was achieved by the Gobirawa at the price of continual war not
only with Zamfara but with its powerful Katsina ally. At the end of the
eighteenth century Gobir was superficially the most powerful state in
Hausaland, but internally it had been considerably weakened by these
prolonged wars which prepared the way for the defeat of its ruling Habe
dynasty at the hands of the Fulani.

The Fulani were a light-skinned race of cattle nomads whose original home was in the Senegal River valley. Several Fulani clans, notably the Torodbe, had come under the influence of Islam as early as the eleventh century, and from the fourteenth century onwards they had been proselytes of their religion throughout the Western Sudan. By the end of the sixteenth century both the Torodbe and the cattle-herding Fulani, who had remained animist, were established throughout Hausaland and as far east as modern Adamawa.[2] In the courts of the kings of the Western Sudan, the Muslim Fulani played important roles as administrators, much as the clerics did in the courts of the kings in mediaeval Europe. Some of the kings by whom they were employed were themselves ardent Muslims, but the majority were either avowedly animist or mixed traditional practices with their observances of Islam. After the collapse of the Songhai empire at the end of the sixteenth century and its division into its constituent parts, Islam, in so far as it was upheld by the rulers of the Western Sudan, saw a general decline. Its main standard-bearers remained the Fulani, who found their position in the courts of the traditionalist kings increasingly more difficult, for the kings began to fear the power of this group upon whom they were so dependent for the conduct of the affairs of state. Some even actively persecuted the Muslim minorities in their states.

Under such conditions, the Muslim Fulani were increasingly drawn to the idea of revolt against their 'pagan' masters. For according to the Shari'a or Muslim law, revolt against the state is legitimate if the ruler places obstacles in the way of the practice of the Muslim faith or mixes Muslim and pagan practices. If Muslims are persecuted, a flight from the land of the pagan, or the *hijra* is decreed to be followed by the declaration of Holy War, or *Jihad*.[8] Thus the Fulani rose in rebellion against the Mandingo authorities of the Futa Djallon in the highlands of Guinea in 1725 and the pagan Fulani rulers of the Futa Toro in the upper Senegal valley in 1768.[4]

The aim of these rebels was to establish states governed in accordance with the Shari'a. The importance of these Jihads, taking place so far away from Nigeria, was that they served as inspiration for Usman dan Fodio in his own Jihad against the rulers of Hausaland.

The Fulani were established in Gobir, as in the rest of Hausaland, not only as cattle-herders but also as officials in the courts of the Habe kings, many of them occupying high positions. Others were teachers and traders many of whom became very wealthy. By the turn of the eighteenth century their increasing political and economic influence in the northern states gave the local rulers considerable cause for disquiet, especially since they formed a class at the vanguard of movements for religious and intellectual reform. They openly criticized what they described as the religious laxity and the decadent standards of learning in the Hausa states. In some ares they were openly asserting themselves, as in the Benue where the Fulani were attacking the Jukun even before 1800.[5]

The general unrest amongst the Fulani living in the towns was focused on a famous Muslim scholar in Gobir, Usman dan Fodio.[6] He was born at Marata in Gobir in December 1754, a Fulani of the Torodbe clan which had migrated fourteen generations before from Futa Toro. His education was broad, consisting of the traditional Islamic sciences of Grammar, Law, Exegesis, Theology, Rhetoric and Prosody. He had several teachers, two of whom were inspired by the reformist ideas that were stirring throughout the Muslim world at that time. One of them was his uncle, Binduri, with whom he studied for two years, the other, the famous Mallam Jibril of Agades who had already preached an unsuccessful Jihad against the Hausa kings. On completing his education he returned to Degel in Gobir where he became a teacher and itinerant preacher carrying his message of religious and social reform to the peoples of Gobir, Zamfara and Kebbi.[7] He even travelled beyond the Niger. His sermons appear to have attracted large crowds for his fame was already widespread when Nafata, King of Gobir, sought him out to become tutor to his own children. As a result he gained considerable influence in the court both with the king and the nobility. In 1802 Yunfa, who had been his pupil, succeeded to the throne of Gobir. He was deeply resentful of the power of his old tutor in the court, and particularly concerned about his radical reformist ideas. He even took drastic measures against the further conversion of his people to Islam. The wearing of the turban was forbidden to men, and the veil to women. This interference, as Hiskett has written, was almost entirely political for it was these customs which gave to the Shehu's party the cohesion and sense of common identity which the Habe kings feared.[8]

The Fulani justified their Jihad against Yunfa and the other Habe kings on the grounds that though they professed Islam, in mixing traditional practices with their observance of the 'true faith' they were juridically pagans against whom it was legitimate to rebel.[9] And it is clear that in many respects Islam, as it was practised in Hausaland where it had been established for three hundred years, made concessions to the indigenous religion of the Hausa. Indeed, as far as the Habe monarchs were concerned, they practised a calculated syncretism whereby their authority as Muslim monarchs was boosted by, and to a considerable extent depended on, their respect for Habe religious rites and social practices. Thus the Fulani attack on their 'reversion to paganism' was an attack on the very authority by which they ruled.

Though the Habe kings made such political concessions, Islamic learning flourished in their courts. They maintained around them a small circle of Muslim divines and scholars. At the court of Gobir, Usman dan Fodio had been amongst the most respected of such scholars.

It becomes clear in this light that the attacks of Usman dan Fodio struck at the very heart of Yunfa's power, and Yunfa's anti-Islamic measures were undoubtedly designed to prevent Usman, the reformer, from gaining more adherents. The antagonism between the two was not really that between believer and infidel, even though the Fulani were able by their own definition to depict Yunfa as an unbeliever. It was rather between a radical reformer and a conservative willing to compromise in pursuit of stable government.

In the *Kitab al-Farq*, a work on the Habe kingdoms attributed to Usman dan Fodio, and translated by Hiskett, the writer accuses the Habe rulers of imposing illegal taxation on the population of their states.[10] Taking into account any natural prejudice that might come into the writings of one attacking the established régime, there was no doubt much truth in his charges. In the Habe kingdoms *gaisuwa*, or the giving of bribes to superiors, was common; judges were open to bribery; Muslims were pressed into military service; illegal market taxes were imposed. Undoubtedly the indiscriminate, oppressive and frequently excessive imposition of taxes was one of the sorest grievances of the people against their rulers. In particular the Fulani nomads bitterly resented the taxes on their cattle, and here, as much as in the violation of the principles of the Shari'a, we may look for the motives which brought both the Hausa commoners and the Fulani nomads into Usman dan Fodio's camp.

Usman dan Fodio argued that Holy War became obligatory under three conditions. 'Firstly on the orders of the [Muslim] ruler. . . . Secondly, if the enemy launch a sudden counter-attack on Muslim territory. . . . Thirdly, to rescue captured Muslims from the hands of the heathen.'[11] The latter two of these three conditions were soon fulfilled as a result of actions by Yunfa. First he forced Usman to leave his court for Degel, his home town, where he became so outspoken against the Habe régime that it is said Yunfa even planned to have him killed. Then Yunfa attacked Gimbana where one of Usman's disciples, Abd al-Salam, had refused to bless some Gobirawa troops passing through the town. Yunfa took prisoner some of Abd al-Salam's disciples, who were freed by Usman's troops. Yunfa then threatened to destroy Degel and thus heralded the general persecution of the Shehu's followers. Usman emigrated from Degel to Gudu in February 1804 (i.e. performed the *hijra*), recalling the emigration of the Prophet from Mecca to

Medina. The Shehu's brother, Abdullahi, said at the time, according to Usman dan Fodio in *Tanbih al-ikhwan*: 'Truly this matter has become intolerable; recourse must be had to arms. There can be no doubt that the situation demands a prince to manage our affairs, for Muslims should not be without government'. Usman dan Fodio was therefore elected Caliph and leader of the revolt against the Habe King of Gobir, and his followers did 'homage to the Sheik, as is directed by the Kuran and Sunna[12] in such circumstances, and made him leader of the Holy War'.[13]

Thus in the early months of 1804 the fifty-year-old Muslim scholar and reformist preacher, Usman dan Fodio, found himself at the head of a great Jihad, or Holy War, that within a few years was to sweep most of the Hausa kings off their thrones, and during the next thirty was to establish Fulani hegemony throughout all Northern Nigeria with the exception of Borno and certain non-Muslim areas inaccessible to the Fulani cavalry.

The causes and motives of this Jihad are extremely complicated. As far as it concerned Usman dan Fodio, who was given the title of *Amir al-mu'minin*, or Commander of the Faithful, in acknowledgement of his religious leadership of the revolt, it was a Holy War to establish a purer form of Islam in what he considered a predominantly corrupt and decadent society. This fits into the pattern of reformist movements taking place throughout Africa at that time. As Thomas Hodgkin has written of Usman dan Fodio: 'His ideas and achievements have to be understood in the context of the succession of reforming movements which profoundly affected the Muslim world during the latter part of the eighteenth and nineteenth centuries—beginning with Muhammad Ibn Abd Al-Wahab in Saudi Arabia, and including Muhammad ibn Ali al-Sanusi in Cyrenaica (Barka), Shehu Ahmadu and Al-hajj Umar ibn Said in the Western Sudan and Muhammad Ahmad ibn Abdullah (the Mahdi) in the former Egyptian Sudan. These movements, though differing from one another in many respects, had a common objective—"a return to the pure and primitive faith of Islam, purged of heresies and accretions". This implied the attempt to restore the original model of the Islamic State, as it was believed to have existed in the time of the Prophet and the first four Caliphs: a State in which social justice, administered in the light of the Shari'a by God-fearing rulers, took the place of the arbitrary decisions of irresponsible—and effectively non-Muslim—despots.'[14]

The initial motive force of the rebellion came from a small cultured group of Fulani, mostly religious leaders and teachers who, as Hiskett has written, 'were able to carry their Jihad to a successful end . . . due to their sense of cohesion and intellectual superiority over the surrounding Hausa. This gave them a degree of organizing ability and political acumen above that of the Hausa aristocracy'.[15]

Beyond the primary religous motive lay many political and economic factors. Group feelings were of dominant influence. The Fulani were a small minority amongst the Hausa, and some authorities have sought to explain the Jihad as a war between Fulani immigrants and Habe Hausa rulers, although this is too clear cut an explanation, for many of the Hausa *talakawa*, or common people, joined the Shehu's revolt, whilst as Abdullahi, the Shehu's brother, complained bitterly, many Fulani remained on the side of Yunfa. Certainly the cattle Fulani (*Bororoje*) who joined the Shehu did so largely out of tribal loyalty,[16] for many of them were certainly not Muslims. However, it is again difficult to know whether tribal loyalty or resentment of Habe taxation and raids on their cattle was the more important motive for their support of the Shehu's Jihad.

Most significant was the large number of *talakawa* to join forces with the Shehu, who was preaching not only religious reform but a reform of the political affairs of the kingdom, particularly the oppressive system of taxation and the despotic administration of its ruler. Economic fears were also involved; the town Fulani were in many cases extremely wealthy, and this, combined with their political influence, aroused considerable jealousy. Ultimately it is very difficult to say whether religious or economic motives, class feelings or tribal loyalties, played the largest part in the revolt.

In its later stages the Jihad seems however to have become increasingly political and correspondingly less religious in its character. Zamfara, for instance, had considerable cause to regret its early assistance to the Fulani against Gobir when its towns were sacked by Abdullahi, the brother, and Bello, the son of the Shehu. Later Al-Kanemi who, as we shall see, effected a religious revival in Borno similar to that in Hausaland, was to write to Bello asking him why he should want to carry the Jihad into Borno, which was a Muslim state under himself, a reformist ruler. He also accused the Fulani of seizing political power in the guise of a religious revolt. Al-Kanemi's letter, and the reply made to it by Bello, not only illuminate the arguments for and against a Jihad, especially when this concerned attacking avowedly Muslim states, but serve as an excellent illustration of contemporary diplomatic correspondence.[17]

Perhaps the harshest critique of the revolution came from one of the Shehu's earliest disciples. Abd al-Salam, who it will be remembered had precipitated Yunfa into attacking the Fulani after his refusal to bless the Gobirawa soldiers, had sought refuge afterwards with the Shehu, where he became one of his closest lieutenants. His initial fervour for the Shehu's Jihad declined in later years, and he took up arms against Bello. The reason he gave for this was that the Jihad had lost its early reformist character. He cited the fact that the best posts in the administration had gone to the Shehu's brother and son, whilst he, an early disciple, had been given nothing.

If anything, its complexity of motives gave the Jihad added force. The old régime crumbled before the Fulani armies which fought vigorously though they were hastily drawn up.

The actual history of the Jihad can be divided into three phases: the consolidation of power in Hausaland and the establishment of the Fulani Empire; the attack on Borno; and the southward expansion of the Fulani Empire.

Once it became apparent to the King of Gobir that the Fulani were proving a real danger to his own security, he sent out forces to attack them. The Fulani retaliated by raiding outlying Gobirawa villages. The first engagement between the two forces occurred on 21st June 1804 at Tabkin Kwatto where the Fulani, assisted by the Zamfarawa, defeated the Gobir army. It would seem that this was achieved against great odds, for Bello records that the Fulani had only twenty horse, whilst those of the Gobirawa were 'numberless'.[18] This was decisive in its effect on the discontented Fulani throughout Hausaland. The Shehu had demonstrated that Habe kings could be overthrown, and despite his subsequent defeat at Tsuntsuwa he was able to keep the loyalty of his forces. In July 1804, hot from victory at Tabkin Kwatto, he sent what amounted to declarations of intended war to the Habe Hausa kings, urging them to purify their religion.

In 1805 he built a permanent base camp at Sabongari, twenty miles north of the Zamfara capital of Anka. Here he received delegations of Fulani from all over the north. He gave a flag to the leaders of each delegation, blessing them and calling on them to rid the country of unbelievers and to establish Islam throughout Hausaland. The Shehu himself was no soldier and entrusted the army to his brother Abdullahi and his son Bello. The ranks of his army were swollen by the faithful as well as the usual band of adventurers that followed any Sudanese army. This curious admixture of religious fanaticism and opportunism accounts for the charges of mass slaughter and plunder that accompanied most Fulani victories. The Shehu was quick to condemn such actions on the part of his followers.

Zamfara, which had been alienated by the attacks on its villages by Fulani forces, joined its old enemy Gobir, together with Kebbi and the Tuareg, in an attempt to suppress the rebellion. The alliance very nearly succeeded when it defeated the Fulani at Alwassa and all but took Gwandu, which had become the Fulani headquarters. However, after these initial successes the Habe kings seemed unable to resist the Fulani forces.

What was the secret of the Fulani strength? How was a scattered immigrant minority able to overthrow the powerful Habe states, with their large standing armies? These are questions to which satisfactory answers will not be forthcoming until further research is made into Jihadi documents. One important factor was the lack of unity among the Hausa kings. Even so, it is remarkable how the Fulani succeeded. As Bello wrote, 'We had none of the *Soudanese* on our side except the people of Zamfara, and the reason for their being so was their enmity to the people of *Gobir*.'[19] Yet the town Fulani were able to organize their own army in such a way that they could defeat the formidable alliances of the 'Soudanese' kings. In the first place there was close contact between the town Fulani and the cattle Fulani. The town Fulani were often the representatives of a large clan, acting on its behalf in the capital of the kingdom in which they were accustomed to pasture their herds. Very often the leading town Fulani owned large herds, and therefore indirectly controlled the considerable number of their nomadic brethren involved in their care. Since the cattle grazed right across northern Nigeria it was not difficult for the Shehu in remote Gobir to the north-west to have close contacts with town Fulani in Adamawa far to the south-east.

The call to revolt was quick to spread, for there were stronger loyalties between town and cattle Fulani in those times than is the case today. Granted these close connections, how were these nomads formed into the formidable fighting force they later became? In the eighteenth century, the social organization of the Fulani differed considerably from that of the small groups which we are accustomed to see nowadays wandering freely over Nigeria. In those days the Fulani sacrificed considerations of good pasture in order to live in semi-permanent settlements. In their migrations eastward to Nigeria they had been subjected to frequent attacks by local kings, particularly the pagan Bambara kings and the Tuareg. In Hausaland they were not infrequently the object of cattle raids by the Habe kings. Their encampments were organized on a defensive basis,[20] and each group had its own militia to guard it in times of attack. Thus, when Usman dan Fodio called on the Fulani to join his Jihad he was not calling on loosely organized peoples, untutored in the art of disciplined warfare, but men who had long experience of fighting in their own defence. What is more these nomads had certain advantages over the standing armies of the Habe kings: in particular their light cavalry was far superior to the heavy cavalry of the Hausa.

By 1808 the Fulani army had brought most of Hausaland under

control, though right up to the 1820s there were pockets of resistance to Fulani rule. One of their earliest and most important successes was in Zazzau (Zaria), which at first submitted peacefully. Here the Habe ruler, Isiaka Jatau, Sarkin Zazzau, heeded Usman dan Fodio's call to religious reform and was installed as first Emir of Zaria.[21] His son, Makau, when he succeeded to the throne in *c*. late 1804, did not accept the authority of Usman dan Fodio. According to the Fulani he reverted to the traditional religion, or at least mixed the observance of it with his observance of Islam. Thus as far as the Fulani were concerned he was a 'pagan', a description contested by implication in *A Chronicle of Abuja*.[22] A flag was thus given to a Mallam Musa, who joined forces with a Fulani from Borno called Yamusa, and attacked Zaria either in late 1806 or in early 1807.[23] Almost as soon as they reached the city, the 'pagan' king, Makau, with all his subjects fled southwards to what has since become Abuja. Today the kings of Abuja are still referred to as Sarkin Zazzau, the name of the state of which Zaria was the capital.

In 1805 Muhammad Fodi, King of Kebbi (1803–26), was driven out of his capital at Birnin Kebbi by Abdullahi, though from his new head-quarters at Argungu he offered stubborn resistance that the Fulani were never to overcome. He was eventually killed by the Fulani twenty-two years later, but he succeeded in maintaining the great Kebbi dynasty, descended direct from Kanta, for his brother Karari became the first Kebbi King of Argungu. Hadeija, north-west of Kano and on the borders of Borno, submitted to the local Fulani leader Umaru without resistance. And shortly afterwards the neighbouring towns of Kazaure, Garin Gabbas, Gatarwa and Auyo surrendered.

The great Hausa cities of Katsina and Kano both fell to the Fulani in 1807. The local leader of the Fulani in Kano sent to the Shehu for a flag in that year, and though the King of Kano was able to control his eastern territories, the Fulani conquered the west with ease. When they met in battle at Dan Yahaya the Fulani triumphed and the Habe king fled. The victorious Kano Fulani sent to the Shehu to choose a ruler, since there were several factions among them, making choice difficult. The saintly Shehu asked who was the wisest man among them, and when they replied Sulumannu, servant of their general, the Shehu declared that he should be their Emir.

In Katsina three Fulani leaders, Umaru Dumyawa, Na Alhaji and Umaru Dallaji, went to the Shehu for a flag. All three were given flags, though after quarrels between them Umaru Dallaji took over leader-ship of the Fulani revolt against the King of Katsina, who fled with many of his people to Maradi, some fifty miles north. From there he and his successors were to harass the Fulani for many years to come. Umaru Dallaji became first Emir of Katsina, whilst the son of Na

Alhaji became ruler of the Yandaka area, and Dumyawa overlord of Sandam, to which Maradi paid tribute. All three rulers owed allegiance directly to the Shehu. Throughout Umaru Dallaji's reign, which ended in 1835, he was threatened by the Habe kings of Maradi who had Agades and Zamfara as allies. Indeed, until the separation of Maradi and Katsina by the effective establishment in the 1900s of the Franco-British boundary between Niger and northern Nigeria, there was no peace between the two. In 1808 Yunfa, King of Gobir, died in battle outside his capital of Alkalawa. This marked the end of the Jihad in Hausaland.

With all the important Hausa states under the domination of the Jihadists, the foundations of the great Fulani Empire, or Sokoto Caliphate as it is now better known, had been laid. In the fighting the Shehu had taken little part; he was rather the philosopher of the revolution, whilst Abdullahi and Bello were its executives. The new caliphate was divided into two: the Western Sector with headquarters at Gwandu came under the administration of Abdullahi; the Eastern Sector was placed under Bello, who ruled it from Sokoto which the Shehu had made his home. The administration was devolved on these two men, whilst the Shehu returned to his studies.

The first serious check to Fulani expansion eastward came from Borno. In 1805 the Fulani of the Western Province of Borno rebelled and were attacked by Mai Ahmed, who at first drove back their leader Ardo Lerlima, but finally, when other Fulani groups joined the attack, was defeated at Nguru, the Galadima's capital, which the Fulani sacked. This led to a general uprising of the Fulani and a number of small emirates were carved out of Borno by their leaders. Ibrahim Zaki, who came from an old-established family in Borno, founded the emirate of Katagum on the eastern frontiers of Hausaland. Buba Yero, who was given a flag by the Shehu in return for his help against Zamfara in the early days of the Jihad, set himself up in southern Borno in the emirate of Gombe. The most serious threat came from within Borno. In 1808 the Fulani led by Gwoni Mukhtar drove the Mai out of his capital of N'gazargamu, which they sacked. At that time it seemed as though Borno would quickly fall under Fulani domination.

The Fulani were eventually repelled by the leader of a similar cattle-owning, nomadic people, the Kanembu, who came from the old kingdom of Kanem. Under the leadership of Al-Kanemi they had already formed a small army which attacked the Fulani wherever they seemed strongest. This was a curious situation for their acts were apparently quite unofficial, having no sanction from the Mai of Borno though they were clearly in his interest. It seems that a possible explanation was jealousy between the two nomadic groups. The

Kanembu were as reluctant to be ruled by the Fulani as was the Mai. Al-Kanemi absorbed the remnants of the defeated royal army into his own, and marched on N'gazargamu, retaking it and killing Gwoni Mukhtar. In 1810 Mai Ahmed died and was succeeded by Dunama. A period of peace ensued whilst the Fulani consolidated their position in the small frontier emirates. In 1811 Ibrahim Zaki was given a flag with the right to take whatever parts of Borno he could conquer. In a brilliant campaign he took N'gazargamu once again, but Mai Dunama's forces joined with those of Al-Kanemi and drove him back to Katagum. Despite succeeding wars the *status quo* in Borno was fixed by the outcome of this campaign.

Al-Kanemi had thus become the saviour of Borno. He established himself near Mai Dunama's new capital, enjoying great wealth as well as the devotion of the masses.

In 1814, Dunama, in an attempt to shake off this shadow ruler, undertook what Urvoy has described aptly as 'a flight to Varennes', intending to establish himself at a firm base in some distant province.[24] He was caught and deposed, and though the Saif dynasty ruled until 1846 this marked the real end of their power. Al-Kanemi now exercised all the powers of the old Mai. As Clapperton, who visited Borno in 1821, remarked, 'The Sultanship of Borno, however, is but a name; the court still keeps up considerable state, and adheres strictly to its ancient customs, and this is the only privilege left them. When the sultan gives audience to strangers, he sits in a kind of cage, made of the bamboo, through the bars of which he looks on his visitors, who are not allowed to approach within seventy or eighty yards of his person.' Denham and Clapperton were most impressed by the ascetic Al-Kanemi, effective ruler of Borno. '. . . no one could have used greater endeavours to substitute laws of reason for practices of barbarity, and, though feared, he is loved and respected. . . . Compared to all around him, he is an angel, and has subdued more by his generosity, mildness and benevolent disposition, than by the force of his arms. . . .'[25]

Al-Kanemi's first task after repelling the Fulani was to consolidate the greatly weakened empire. Between 1815 and 1824 he re-established his suzerainty over Kanem and the growing state of Bagirmi.[26] By 1826 Borno was once more a powerful state, deprived only of its former territories of Gombe, Hadeija, Misau and Katagum. Al-Kanemi was succeeded by his son Umar, who like his father took the title of Shehu, and ruled through the puppet Mai Ibrahim. In 1846, after a relatively peaceful reign the small state of Zinder revolted and Mai Ibrahim and his followers took advantage of the situation by calling on the Sharif of Wadai to help them throw off Shehu Umar. The latter so manœuvred his troops that he was able to put down both revolts and Mai Ibrahim was executed, his sons having perished in battle. Thus came to an end one of the longest and most distinguished dynasties in African history.

South of Borno the Fulani were more successful. Buba Yero in Gombe subdued all the surrounding peoples and even made expeditions into Jukun country. Yakubu, Emir of Bauchi, who was the only non-Fulani flag-bearer, likewise subdued all the non-Muslim peoples in the Bauchi area, founding the town of Bauchi as his headquarters in 1809.[27] Friction occurred between him and Buba Yero when the latter pushed his frontiers westwards, and Yakubu had to check him at Beri-Beri. Buba Yero was more successful to the south where for a time even the Fulani of Muri came under his jurisdiction.

The farthest the Sokoto Caliphate extended eastward was Adamawa where two important emirates were established, those of Yola and Muri.[28] In 1806 Moddibo Adama travelled to Sokoto to receive a flag from the Shehu; on his return he quickly rallied around him the many Fulani who had settled in the area. He overcame the local non-Muslim peoples with little difficulty. Meanwhile, the Fulani Emir of Muri made more inroads into the territory of the once powerful Jukun Empire, and hastened its already rapid decline, which had been assisted by the ravages of the invading Chamba people from the south-east.

The Fulani faced much greater difficulties in the southward expansion of their empire into Nupe and Yorubaland. In both areas they gained footholds only after years of patient intrigue in local politics.

At the time of the Jihad, Nupe was involved in bitter civil war. Muhammad, the Etsu or King of Nupe, had just died, and his son Majia succeeded him, only to find himself rivalled by his cousin Jumada, who had established himself with his followers at Rajada on the Niger, opposite the Nupe capital of Rabba.[29] As in all northern territories, the Fulani had settled in Nupe, and a certain Mallam Dendo took up the position of leader of the Jihad in Nupe. He had, however, to work with great care. His opportunity came soon after Etsu Majia had defeated and killed Jumada. Mallam Dendo straightway offered his support to Jumada's son Idris, and together they drove Majia out of his capital of Rabba. Mallam Dendo then established henchmen as emirs of Lafiagi and Agaie. Idris soon found the Fulani an embarrassment and attempted to drive them out. The Fulani, ever skilful at intrigue, then joined forces with Majia who routed Idris, gaining himself recognition as Etsu Nupe at Jengi. The Fulani remained at Rabba.

Mallam Dendo never took the title of Etsu Nupe, though he was effective ruler of much of Nupeland. At his death in 1832 the Fulani were still far from secure in Nupe, and their position was made the

more precarious by strife between their various factions. These disputes necessitated the intervention of the Emir of Gwandu on two
occasions. Eventually the rival Nupe etsus were pushed back to two
small towns, Zuguma and Pategi, whilst the title of Etsu Nupe was
taken over by Mallam Dendo's successors, who ruled from Bida.

In Ilorin, the Fulani gained their foothold by similar methods.[30] The
great Empire of Oyo had since the end of the eighteenth century lost
control of many of its tributary states. Afonja, the Governor of Ilorin
and Are-Ona-Kakanfo of Oyo, had successfully asserted his independence from the Alafin of Oyo, but to achieve and maintain this, he had
to join forces with Solagberu, the leading Muslim of Ilorin, and use
Hausa and Fulani mercenaries. Afonja's revolt, as will be seen in the
next chapter,[31] resulted from internal difficulties in the Oyo Empire,
and was not in its origin an extension of the Fulani Jihad. However,
because he was forced to rely for his supply of mercenaries on a certain
learned Fulani scholar, Mallam Alimi, who arrived in Ilorin around
1817-18, his rebellion was to give the Fulani a foothold in Yorubaland.
Mallam Alimi was not a flag-bearer of the Jihad, nor indeed were any of
his sons, whom Afonja asked him to bring in to assist him in his
struggle with Oyo around 1821. However it was one of these sons, Abd
al-Salam, who, as Ajayi has written, 'converted Afonja's secessionist
movement into an outpost of the Fulani Jihad'.[32] After the death of his
father, Abd al-Salam sought to seize power from Afonja, and teamed up
with Solagberu against him. Afonja was defeated in battle and his
body, pierced with arrows, was publicly burnt in the market-place. One
tradition says that he committed suicide. The victorious Abd al-Salam
soon turned against his ally Solagberu, and made himself sole master
of Ilorin, thus establishing it as the southern outpost of the Jihad. It
seems that he was not confirmed as Emir of Ilorin, that is given a flag
by Sokoto, until *c*. 1829.

By 1830 the Fulani were masters of most of what was the Northern
Region of Nigeria. Only Borno, parts of Kebbi and Gobir, the hill areas
of the Jos Plateau and the Tiv and the Idoma did not come under their
control. Much has been written of the decadence and corruption of the
Sokoto Caliphate in its later years. There is, as we shall see (Chapter
13), some truth in these assertions, which have unfortunately obscured
the real virtues of the early years of the Sokoto Caliphate. Probably its
greatest achievements were first the establishment of a uniform system of government through a vast area of Nigeria which for centuries
beforehand had been torn by internecine wars; and second the stimulation of commerce under what might be called the Pax Fulani; and
finally, and in many ways most significant of all, the literary revolution which it stimulated.

Even though the Fulani were accused of destroying the books of the Habe, a much-debated accusation, there was a great revival of learning under Bello. Muslim divines came from far afield to the court at Sokoto. Al-Hajj Sa'id lists among the learned of his reign several women: 'Of women—Zani Gharka, mother of Al-Bukhari; Inna Gharka, mother of Bello and others.' This was apparently true of the following reigns, for under Aliu Baba he lists 'Nanna son of Fodio, Uthmanu his son-in-law, who had married his daughter Miriam, his mother Ladi, his daughter, Miriam, who knew the Koran by heart. . . .'[33]

One noteworthy aspect of the Shehu's reformist ideas was his insistence on the education of women in the tenets of Islam. One of dan Fodio's accusations against the society of the Habe kings in the *Nur al-Albab* was that 'men treat these beings [women] like household implements which become broken after long use . . . this is an abominable crime. Alas—how can they shut up their wives, their daughters, and their captives in the darkness of ignorance while daily they impart knowledge to their students?'[34] At heart the Fulani revolution was a revolution of radical intellectuals. Inevitably after the first ardour of revolution wore off it became increasingly materialistic in outlook. Slave raiding became more frequent, and certain areas were devastated of human beings. Nevertheless, when the British occupied the north in 1900, they took over the administrative system adapted by the Shehu from the old Habe kingdoms to suit the needs of his vast empire and made it the basis of their system of indirect rule.

7 Yoruba Wars

The collapse of the authority of the Alafin of Oyo over his provincial
kings and tributary states at the beginning of the nineteenth century
was touched off by the revolt of Afonja, in Ilorin, aided by the Fulani,
and resulted in intra-Yoruba wars that were to last throughout the
century. The speed with which the Alafin lost control of the situation
was the result of much deeper causes than this simple rebellion.

It has been suggested that by 1700 the Oyo Empire was already in
decline.[1] This does not appear to be true, for the eighteenth century
marked the height of Oyo's conquests of her neighbours and control of
the trade routes to the coast. Even so, during the eighteenth century
Oyo was dogged by political instability and burdened by excesses of
tyranny for which the unwritten constitution of Oyo did not provide.
King after king was rejected by the Oyo Mesi. The probable cause of
this state of affairs was the increasing rivalry between the Oyo Mesi
and the palace administration which the Alafin was strengthening in
order to secure his control of the expanding empire and its trade routes.
Furthermore, the people themselves were probably in sympathy with
the Oyo Mesi in their attempts to check the growing power of the
Alafin, for the Yoruba expect unchecked power to be oppressive.[2] Thus,
by the middle of the eighteenth century, Oyo was ready for the seizure
of power made by the newly appointed Basorun, Gaha, who proved
equally as tyrannous as the Alafin from whom he snatched control of
Oyo, but who did at least provide some stability for the empire.

During the eighteenth century Oyo's authority stretched south-west
to the Ashanti states and Dahomey, and north-east to the Niger.
Nearly all the towns of western Yorubaland were subject to the Alafin.
These towns, which sometimes numbered as many as 20,000 inhabitants, were each ruled by an oba chosen from the lineage of the founder
of the town by the chiefs of the other lineage groups.[4] The Alafin was
usually represented by *ajele* or intendants, who were frequently
recruited from the *ilari* or titled palace slaves. The ajele supervised the
payment of tribute. In those towns that lay on the Oyo trade routes to
the coast, the ajele had the additional task of ensuring security of
transit for Oyo caravans. Inevitably in a loosely organized empire like

5. Metropolitan Oyo and Yorubaland in the middle of the
eighteenth century[3]

that of Oyo many kingdoms were merely nominal subjects of the Alafin, probably only paying tribute in return for the protection Oyo's
army could afford them. The position of certain kingdoms, particularly
that of Ife, the spiritual home of the Yoruba, is not clear, and there is
still considerable divergence of opinion as to whether Ife was in any
way subject to Oyo, or whether in fact it actually exerted an influence
on Oyo by virtue of its religious position. The main restrictions on the
power of the Alafin in Ondo, Ijebu and Ife itself were the hilly nature of
the countryside and the prevalence of the tsetse fly which made it impossible for him to use his cavalry, which was the basis of his power.
Such was the hilly nature of Ekiti country that it appears never to
have come under Oyo control. It was probably for these reasons that the
Oyo Empire sought expansion westwards into non-Yoruba country.[5]

In Oyo the political authority of the Alafin, as we have already seen,
was considerably restricted by the Oyo Mesi, or council of notables who
exercised right of life and death over him. Should their leader, the
Basorun, declare: 'The Gods reject you, the people reject you, the earth
rejects you'—then the Alafin was forced to commit suicide. This device
was frequently resorted to in the eighteenth century when the rule of
the Alafin became excessively tyrannous. Both the Alafin and Oyo
Mesi were checked by the Ogboni, a secret society composed of both
religious and political leaders and devoted to the worship of the earth.
The head of the society had right of access to the Alafin, and the society
itself judged any case involving the spilling of blood which was considered an offence against the earth. Furthermore, the society had to
sanction certain decisions of the Oyo Mesi, including the rejection of
the Alafin.

The Alafin represented authority only in so far as his decisions were
arrived at after a complicated series of negotiations with the Oyo Mesi
and other factions of society. Thus in no sense could the Alafin be
compared with the Habe (Hausa) kings or the northern emirs as a
fulcrum of power. Attempts to rule on their own, as we have seen, were
the most frequent cause of rejection of the Alafin.

In the eighteenth century Oyo's main problem was the maintenance
of its authority over the young kingdom of Dahomey, founded about
1625. Its authority depended on its formidable standing army, whose
efficacy was described by the Dutch merchant William Bosman in
1698. In that year the Alafin made war on the tributary state of Great
Ardra. Bosman described the army that attacked Porto Novo, the
territory's capital, thus: 'These being all Horsed, and a warlike Nation,
in a short time mastered half the King of Ardra's territories, and made
such a slaughter among his subjects, that the Number of the Dead
being innumerable, was commonly express'd by saying, "They were

like the Grains of Corn in the Field. . . ." This Nation strikes such a terror into all the circumjacent Negroes, that they can scarce hear them mention'd without trembling: And they tell a thousand strange Things of them.'[6]

Dahomey first defied the authority of the Alafin in 1724 when it invaded Great Ardra in an attempt to gain access to the sea. The Alafin promptly despatched an army, backed up by cavalry, which after initial successes was defeated by the Dahomeyans. Dalzell described the ruse by which Dahomey gained this impressive victory: 'In the morning the Eyeos, seeing the enemy fled, secure of victory, began to burn and plunder the town and to indulge themselves very freely with the treacherous liquor: this soon intoxicated and spread the ground with the major part of their army. At this juncture, the Dahomians, who had timely information of the enemy's disorder, fell upon them with re-doubled fury, destroyed a great number, completely routed the rest; and those that escaped owed their safety to their horses.'[7]

The Dahomeyans were nevertheless frightened of the consequences of this victory and sent presents to appease Oyo. However, in 1727, Dahomey attacked Wydah in another attempt to gain access to the sea.[8] Wydah, which had aided Oyo in its attack on Great Ardra in 1698, appealed to the Alafin for help and a second army was despatched against Dahomey. It swept through Dahomey, ransacking its villages, and in 1729 the King of Dahomey sued for peace and promised to pay tribute. This was not paid, and in 1738 Oyo once again invaded Dahomey, laying siege to Abomey the capital. The Dahomeyans tried to make peace, but the Oyo terms were: 40 men, 40 women, 40 guns and 4,000 loads of cowries and corals a year to date with effect from the defeat of 1728. The Dahomeyans would not accept this, but such was the pressure exerted by Oyo that in 1747 Dahomey agreed to pay tribute on these terms.

The subjugation of Dahomey coincided with the appointment of Gaha as Basorun by Alafin Labisi who ascended the throne in 1754.[9] Gaha immediately murdered the new king's two chief supporters, so that Labisi was forced to commit suicide. Each succeeding Alafin came increasingly under the influence of this ruthless but capable Basorun. It was not until the accession of Abiodun as Alafin that Gaha met oppo-sition from his nominal master. At first Abiodun accepted his posi-tion as figurehead, but quietly plotted against the Basorun with the army commander, Kakanfo Oyabi. On a fixed day all members of the Basorun's family in Oyo and its tributary states were murdered, and the Basorun himself was seized and burnt. According to Dalzell, the king's supporters 'ripped open the bellies' of the pregnant women of the Baso-run's family, 'and cut to pieces the immature fruit of their womb'.[10]

Abiodun became Alafin in fact as well as in name in 1774. His reign is remembered by the Yoruba as one of the most peaceful in their history, but with his death in 1789, as Johnson writes, ended 'the universal and despotic rule of the Alafins of Oyo in the Yoruba country. He was the last of the kings who held the different parts of the kingdom together in one universal sway and with him ended the tranquillity and prosperity of the Yoruba country. The revolution ensued, and the tribal independence with the loss to the Yoruba of the Nupe and Bariba, and Dahomey provinces, and the Egun later on, which had continued to our own day. In a word, with Abiodun ended the unity of the Yoruba kingdom.'[11]

In fact, as Akinjogbin has shown, an important part of the empire had already gained its independence.[12] In 1783 the Bariba of Borgu soundly defeated the Oyo army, and Oyo was subsequently never able to bring them back into tributary relationship. Biobaku has suggested that the Egba obtained their independence from Oyo under their leader Lishabi between 1775 and 1780,[13] though it has been suggested that this may have taken place later.[14] Johnson does not mention it as occurring in Abiodun's reign, nor as one of its immediate sequels. Dahomey, under King Adahoozu, whilst not obtaining its independence from Oyo, failed to pay tribute twice during Abiodun's reign, in 1781 and 1784. The Nupe, some of whom living to the west of the Niger seem to have been subject to Oyo control, defeated the Oyo army only two years after Abiodun's death and declared their independence.

Despite these disastrous events, the collapse of the Oyo Empire was staved off for another twenty-five years. If we accept Biobaku's dates for the Egba revolt, then at first appearances no further inroads were made into the authority of the Alafin until 1818 when King Gezo of Dahomey declared his independence. Two years later the outbreak of the Owu wars heralded the impending disintegration of the empire. This was impossible to stave off, for Afonja, the Alafin's own army commander, had already rejected his authority and set himself up in alliance with the Fulani as an independent ruler over the important Oyo province of Ilorin which was virtually at the doorstep of the imperial capital.

The reasons for the break-up of the Oyo Empire are many and complex. One of the chief causes of collapse was that the traditional political institutions were not suited to running an empire as large and prosperous as Oyo had become by the eighteenth century. The elaborate constitution which allowed for maximum participation of all sections of society in the decision-making process had to give way to the concentration of power in the hands of a single person or group that could make rapid decisions. Thus in the late seventeenth and early eighteenth centuries the Alafin became increasingly despotic. Reaction to this was the elimination of the power of the Alafin by the Oyo Mesi led by Basorun Gaha, who, far from returning to the traditional political system of Oyo, likewise concentrated power in his own hands. Nor did Abiodun's deposition of Gaha and his followers resolve the situation. There remained a basic tension in Oyo between on the one hand the need for concentration of power in the hands of one man or group if the empire was to be efficiently managed and on the other the traditional Yoruba dislike of such acquisition of unchecked power by one individual or group.

Furthermore the military strength of Oyo, hitherto unchallenged, had weakened seriously under Abiodun. The defeat of the Oyo army by Borgu and Nupe within the space of eight years was not only a great humiliation but cut off Oyo from her northern trade contacts, and in particular, as Akinjogbin has shown, her main supply of slaves for export to the coast.[15] Since it appears that slave trading was becoming increasingly important for Oyo at the end of the eighteenth century, she had to turn elsewhere for slaves, without which she had nothing to exchange for guns with the European traders, guns which were vital to her army and thus to the maintenance of the empire. She was forced to look towards her tributary kingdoms to the south as a new source of slaves, thus creating increased tension among the Yoruba-speaking peoples. It has been argued that the desire of the provincial and tributary kings to share in the profits made by Oyo from the slave trade was one of the principal causes of the break-up of the empire.[16] However, Ajayi has insisted that there is little evidence for this view, since the great expansion of the slave trade in this area, which only took place in the 1820s, was a consequence rather than a cause of the civil wars.[17] Ajayi's interpretation would seem to be substantiated by the sequence of events between the death of Abiodun and the Owu wars as outlined by Akinjogbin. This interpretation is complemented by the fact that it was not until the 1820s that the British naval patrol was beginning to check the export of slaves from the Niger Delta, forcing the European traders to seek elsewhere to satisfy their needs.

It was therefore not until about the 1820s that the Europeans began appreciably to increase their demand for slaves in the Dahomey ports, through which Oyo exported her slaves. Indeed Akinjogbin points out that at the time when he suggests Afonja, the army commander, and the leading provincial kings were breaking away from the control of the Alafin, there was actually a decline in demand for slaves in the Dahomey ports because of the banning in 1794 of the slave trade by the French, who at that time were the main traders in the area. The law against the slave trade was not repealed until 1802 and French interest in the slave trade in this area never really revived.

It was at the end of the eighteenth century that the effective breakdown in the authority of the Alafin over his provincial kings took place, and not in 1817 as was once assumed. One of the main causes of this breakdown was Oyo's need for an alternative source for the supply of slaves. Her cavalry could not operate in the Ondo-Ekiti area. Dahomey to the west was too powerful and too sparsely populated to be used as an alternative. There remained the densely populated Yoruba provinces to the south: Owu, Ife, Ijebu and the possibly independent Egba. The main problem of raiding in this area, Akinjogbin argues, was that Oyo might come into conflict with Ife, with which spiritually and constitutionally it had a special relationship. The Alafin of Oyo, whilst the ruler of the Yoruba Empire, could not be installed without the formal sanction of the Oni of Ife as king of the spiritual home of the Yoruba.[18] The Alafin-elect had to obtain the *Ida Oranyan* from the Oni, for without it Akinjogbin argues he could have no authority over the empire. In order to obtain this sword he had to promise that he would never attack Ife or its neighbouring territory. This ceremony is still observed by the Alafin today.* Thus in 1793 when Awole ordered the army to take the market town of Apomu in Ife territory, allegedly to avenge a grievance against the Bale of the town, though probably more in order to gain slaves, he violated the terms of his accession. Afonja was reluctant to attack an Ife town in view of the special position of Ife, and thus refused to undertake the expedition. It would seem that all the other important chiefs of Oyo refused to support this attack, and there appears to have been a complete breakdown in the authority of Awole as Alafin. In 1796 when he ordered the army to take Iwere, it killed his supporters and forced him to commit suicide, though not before he had uttered a curse that has become memorable in Yorubaland. From the palace forecourt he shot three arrows, one to the north, one to the south and one to the west, crying: 'My curse be on you for your disloyalty and disobedience, so let your children disobey you. If ye send them on an errand, let them never return to bring you word again. To all the points I shot my arrows will ye be carried as slaves. My curse will carry you to the sea and beyond the seas, slaves will rule over you, and ye their masters will become slaves.' Then he smashed an eartherware dish, shouting: 'Broken calabash can be mended but not a broken dish; so let my words be irrevocable.'[19]

From then on there seems to have been a complete breakdown in the authority of the Alafin, a situation which was to lead to warfare in

* In Oyo, however, today the ceremonies in the Sango shrine are considered much more important.

Yorubaland for nearly eighty years. Afonja, the army commander, and the important provincial kings, such as Opele, Bale of Gbogun, and Adegun, the Onikoyi of Ikoyi, set themselves up as semi-independent rulers within the empire.

Thus, if Akinjogbin's chronology is correct, the Oyo Empire had effectively come to an end by 1797. However it was not until the Owu wars of 1821 that the full impact of the collapse of Oyo authority was felt throughout Yorubaland.[20] Insecurity in Oyo itself, occasioned by the internal political situation, the economic depression that had taken place as a result not only of the decline in the slave trade, but in the loss of traditional sources of supply of slaves, the presence of hostile Nupe and Borgu not far from the capital, together with fear that the Fulani revolution in Hausaland might extend itself southwards towards Yorubaland, led to the emigration of many Oyo to the south. One of the factors in the collapse of the Oyo Empire which it is still difficult to assess is the influence of Islam. The new religion had undoubtedly made its influence felt in Oyo even before the eighteenth century, but it probably only became important as a political factor towards the end of the century, with the preachings of reforms by Usman dan Fodio. The Shehu undoubtedly travelled south out of Gobir. Whether his preachings had any repercussions in Oyo politics is difficult to tell. But the Fulani revolution itself, particularly when after 1808 it began to expand beyond Hausaland, certainly presented itself as a menace to the security of Oyo.

The cause of the outbreak of the Owu wars is not at all clear. Johnson says that the Onikoyi, the leading provincial king, ordered the Owu to attack some Ife towns that had been engaging in indiscriminate slave trading with the Ijebu.[21] This naturally incurred the anger of the Oni of Ife who, thinking that he would easily conquer the Owu, marched against them only to be severely defeated. However, there was some altercation between the Owu and some powerful Ijebu traders, as a result of which the Owu took and destroyed Apomu. The Ijebu then joined forces with the remnants of the Ife army and Oyo refugees fleeing from the Fulani and, armed with guns, drove back the cutlass-swinging Oyo. They laid siege to their own town and destroyed it in 1827.

This would suggest that the Ife were trying to break into the monopoly of Oyo in the slave trade, which as Ajayi and Akinjogbin have stressed, remained intact until after the Owu wars. The war may have been the first open expression in Yorubaland of the breakdown in the authority of the Alafin and the empire, a situation which had been a reality for the past twenty years.

Though the political difficulties in Oyo might of their own have led to the long series of wars that raged through Yorubaland in the

nineteenth century, it is just possible that if the various factions in Oyo
had sunk their differences, the situation could have been saved. But the
fact that Afonja, the Are-Ona-Kakanfo, had, in his attempt to consolidate his secessionist movement, decided to rely on the Fulani meant all
hope was lost for the maintenance of the integrity of the empire, for
Afonja had brought into play a new political force, which it was clearly
impossible for the Alafin to control, with one part of his army in
rebellion under Afonja, and the other tied down in Owu. Normally
Afonja, as Are-Ona-Kakanfo, would have been a slave, which would
have made it difficult to understand how he could, given his servile
status, have mustered sufficient support from the freeborn. However
he was a royal prince through his mother, and, after unsuccessfully
contesting the throne of Oyo, gained the position of Are-Ona-
Kakanfo.[22]

Afonja's rebellion and the Owu wars led to a series of conflicts
between the various Yoruba kingdoms and sub-groups that lasted for
the rest of the century, and saw the obliteration of some of the most
important provincial kingdoms of Oyo.

Owu was laid siege to by the Ife, Ijebu and Oyo forces, and finally
invested in 1820.[23] Oyo was itself taken by a force led by the only
surviving son of the Basorun Gaha, showing how strong the rift between the Alafin and the Basorun had been and how long it had
persisted. Gaha's son, who formed his army in Borgu, might even have
taken Ilorin, had he not been deserted at the last minute by the
Onikoyi. Alafin Adebo died while his army was trying to take rebelli-
ous Gbogun. His successor, Maku, was the author of the famous message to Afonja: 'The new moon has risen', to which the latter replied
impertinently: 'Let that new moon quickly set.'[24] Ironically soon afterwards Maku waged unsuccessful war against Iwo and had to commit
suicide.

The success of Afonja's revolt encouraged every provincial king to
seek his independence from Oyo. Afonja was now the only man with
anything like the power of the former Alafin, but to obtain this he
played into the hands of the Fulani. With the Fulani established in
Ilorin, the Yoruba were completely cut off from their traditional source
of supply of slaves. Oyo, as a result of its defeat by Nupe and Borgu,
had had to turn towards the southern parts of the empire for a new
supply. Now with the collapse of Oyo authority, coupled with the
general increase in demand for slaves both for export and for domestic
purposes, the wars between the various sections of Yorubaland were
given added impetus. The increase in the demand for slaves by European traders in the Dahomey ports and at Badagry and Lagos was a
reflection not only of the rising demand for slaves in the Americas, but

of the increasing difficulty in obtaining them in the Delta ports where the British Anti-Slavery patrol was having some success in controlling export of slaves from Old Calabar and Bonny. The stretch of coast from Lagos to Togo, known as the Western Slave Coast, was more difficult to control.[25] At the same time the development of legitimate commerce in Yorubaland was also to increase the demand for slaves for use as head-porters and farm-labourers.[26] Consequently what had started as civil wars arising from the break-up of the Oyo Empire increasingly took the character of slave-raiding wars. In these circumstances it is at first sight perhaps surprising that during this long and vicious series of wars, whose motives and complexities are often difficult to follow, people managed to carry on farming their land, that the unity of Yoruba culture was not destroyed and that indeed the Yoruba remained the vigorous progressive people they are today. Of course it must be remembered that comparatively few people were involved in the fighting. However, in the case of the sack of Old Oyo, and the obliteration of Owu, Ikoyi and many other important towns in northern Yorubaland, there were thousands of refugees.

For a simpler understanding of the complex wars that lasted up until 1893 it is convenient to name the chief participants. To the north was Ilorin, outpost of the Fulani Empire, intent on carrying the Jihad into Yorubaland. Close by was Oyo, ancient imperial metropolis seeking both to reassert its former authority, and later, after its people were forced to move south, to re-establish itself. To the west was Dahomey, now a great military power, participating in any war which provided opportunities for capturing slaves. To the south were the Awori, the Egba and Ijebu, now placed in a strategic position to act as middlemen for the export of slaves to the coast and for the import of firearms with which to continue the wars. In the east lay many kingdoms, some of which were now independent of the Alafin, some of which had never been under his influence. These, too, became embroiled in the general holocaust, both as slave raiders and sources of supply for slaves. In the course of the war there emerged two major cities, one of them, Ibadan, destined to be the saviour of Yorubaland from the Fulani, the other, Abeokuta, destined to be the stepping-stone for Christian influence in Yorubaland.

After the fall of Owu, its inhabitants were chased into Egba territory, where for nearly ten years there ensued a series of battles, invariably alleged to have begun because of some injustice, but more often than not inspired by the desire for slaves. Egba towns were destroyed willy-nilly as undisciplined freebooting armies rampaged across the countryside and thousands were rendered homeless or taken as slaves.

In about 1828 the Ijebu, Ife and Oyo forces settled at the small

Gbagura town of Ibadan, into which some of the homeless Egba also moved.

The chief of this mixed settlement was Maye, an Ife man. He was a considerable leader but was jealous of the Oyo whose leader, Lakanle, was fortunately able to stand up to him. It is not surprising therefore that civil war soon broke out, and when an Egba leader had shot an Ife chief, the Egba decided to leave for what was to become Abeokuta, of 'the town under the Rock', led by Sodeke, a hunter. The new town, probably founded in 1829 or 1830, comprised several communities: the Egba-Alake, the Egba-Oke-Ona, the Gbagura and the Owu refugees. They set up a federal form of government, in which the chiefs of each community participated, though Sodeke remained their acknowledged leader. Both the Ibadan and the Ijebu did their best to destroy this new settlement, the Ijebu being particularly jealous of this potential rival to their monopoly as middlemen in trade with the coast. In Ibadan itself there were further disputes, from which the Oyo section emerged supreme. Maye was executed and a civil government instituted. From then on Ibadan grew to be the most important town in Yorubaland, closely associated with Oyo, but though it acknowledged the Alafin as titular ruler of the Yoruba and did not demand a crown for its own chief, it was never subordinate to it.

The Yoruba might well have defeated the Fulani and driven them out of Ilorin, if only they had not been so divided amongst themselves. They were never able to unite against the enemy. Indeed, if the three powerful rulers of Ikoyi, Gbogun and Ago-Oja had for once combined they might have stemmed the Fulani menace, but they chose to make alliances where they saw the greatest opportunity of personal aggrandizement. It was not a paying policy, for very shortly Ikoyi, once the premier provincial kingdom, was captured by Ilorin. The succession in Ikoyi was disputed, the Alafin supporting one claimant, the Ilorin the other. The result was that the Ilorin attacked and killed the Onikoyi approved by the Alafin and appointed their own candidate, Soyenbola, as his successor. The only town now powerful enough to resist the Fulani was Gbogun but the Fulani soon took it, forcing Edun, the greatest Yoruba general of his day, to flee.

Ilorin was thus able to subjugate many of the important towns of Yorubaland. Abd al-Salam, the Emir, tried to make inroads into Ijeshaland, but he was unsuccessful, since the Fulani horse could not operate easily in the hilly and wooded country of that area. Refugees from the northern towns and from Oyo flooded south to Ife, and such was the apparent folly of the civil conflict at the time that the Oni of Ife, with the Fulani at his back door, insisted on humbling the Oyo by making them undertake the most menial of tasks and selling them into slavery.

A later Oni however permitted them to settle outside Ife, and there they built the town of Modakeke, defended by a huge wall. With reason, the Ife were furious with their Oni for allowing the Oyo to build a town which they realized might soon become a menace to their own security. They poisoned the Oni and set out against Modakeke, but were repulsed. Once again the Ife attacked, this time to be so severely defeated that Ife, original home of the Yoruba, was deserted.

It is almost impossible to outline the tangled skein of civil strife at this time. The most important event in the decade 1830–40 was the destruction of Old Oyo. Oluewu became Alafin in succession to Amodo who, it is said, died of a broken heart when fire destroyed the Afin (palace) and all its treasures. When Abd al-Salam tried to force Oluewu to become a Muslim, the latter secured an alliance with Borgu in a final and bitterly unsuccessful effort to throw off the Fulani yoke. In c. 1835 Old Oyo was abandoned, and today almost nothing remains of 'Katunga', the great metropolis of Yorubaland.[27] Once again the failure of Yoruba chiefs to support the Alafin in his hour of crisis ruined his chances of success even before he had started fighting. Oluewu, himself, was captured and put to death. The new site for Oyo was chosen by Atiba, son of Abiodun, who, after a successful career as a freebooter, had become too powerful to be denied the crown. He selected Ago Oja (Oja's camp) where he had lived probably since c. 1830. He collected all the Oyo refugees around him, and on pain of death forced all the villages for miles around Ago Oja to move into the new capital. Oluyole, ruler of Ibadan, also an Oyo, was made Basorun out of deference to his city's immense power. The Ibadan were to protect the north and north-east and were given a free hand in Ekiti and Ijesa. Ijaye was to protect the south-west, whilst the Alafin, who was no longer to go personally to the wars, was responsible for Iluku, Igboho, Kisi and Saki, where many Oyo refugees were living. Kurunmi, chief of Ijaye, was made Kakanfo. By thus conferring these important titles on the leaders of what were now the most important Oyo towns, Atiba hoped both to secure their loyalty and lessen their rivalry.[28]

With the foundation of New Oyo, a turn in the fortunes of Yoruba-land became evident. The Ibadan defeated the Ilorin at Gbodo and again at Oshogbo, c. 1838, when the latter were laying siege to that town. This latter victory in fact halted the Fulani advance to the sea, and though there were many battles in the following fifty years, the Fulani were never able to make the easy inroads into Yoruba territory that they had made in the previous decades. The Alafin failed to follow up this success and even in the hour of triumph civil war broke out once more. Finally the only people who had been able to live in peace in these troubled times, the Ekiti, were brought into the war, when Ilorin attacked them. At the same time the powerful Basorun at Ibadan began plotting to wrest the throne from the Alafin. Though the Alafin was apparently not perturbed by this, Kurunmi, the Are of Ijaye,* greatest Yoruba general of the day and a man intent on carving out a kingdom for himself, resented any further increase in the strength of the Basorun, and it was hardly surprising that a move on the part of some Ibadan to occupy a ruined town between Ijaye and Oyo provoked war between the two cities of Ibadan and Ijaye in 1844. This war, known as the Batedo war, lasted two years, and so deep were the internal divisions in Yorubaland that even the Ibadan at one stage called on their enemies the Ilorin as allies.

In the south-west the Dahomeyans, once tributaries of the Alafin, were expanding their vigorous kingdom, whose main source of revenue came from the sale of slaves. They attacked Otta in 1845. Three years later they captured the town, carrying off its inhabitants as slaves. But their first serious invasion of Yorubaland was the 1851 attack on Abeokuta.[29] Taking advantage of Ibadan's preoccupation with the north in a war against the Ilesha that did not finally come to an end until 1854, the Dahomeyans marched on Abeokuta, a column of Amazons at their head. The Dahomeyan Amazons, a unique feature in the history of West African armies, were originally superfluous wives of the king used first as bodyguards and then to swell the ranks of the army.

During the nineteenth century there were usually as many as from 3,000 to 8,000 Amazons, and in the army that attacked Abeokuta 6,000, out of a total strength of 16,000, were women. At the time Abeokuta was not in a particularly good state to resist this impressive army, and without the aid of the cunning Oba of Isaga, an Egbado town on the Dahomey route to Abeokuta, the city might well have fallen. The Dahomey army had been informed by an Egba spy which were the weakest points of the Abeokuta defences. When they attacked Isaga the Oba quickly submitted, advised the Dahomeyans to attack the south-western wall of Abeokuta and then sent a messenger to inform the Abeokuta leaders of the probable Dahomey approach. The Egba immediately set about strengthening this section of the wall and prepared their army of some 15,000 men, most armed with guns, to meet the Dahomey attack.

At first the Dahomeyans appeared as if they would take the town, and it was really only the discovery that they were fighting women that spurred the Egba into the final resistance that drove off the Dahomeyan army. However, the most significant factor in this was the

* Kurunmi was usually known as the *Are* of Ijaye, from his title as Kakanfo, Are-Ona-Kakanfo.

part played by Britain. Not only had the British Consul, Beecroft, visited King Gezo of Dahomey in an attempt to persuade him to give up slaving, but he had also issued ammunition to the Egba army through the missionaries stationed there. Indeed, without the aid of the British Consul and the missionaries it is doubtful whether the Egba could have saved Abeokuta from destruction by the far better equipped Dahomeyans. British intervention in the first Dahomeyan invasion of Abeokuta marked the beginning of a new era in the history of the wars in Yorubaland.

8 The Suppression of the Slave Trade

The abolition of the slave trade by Britain in the first half of the nineteenth century was to make a profound impact on the peoples of what is today Nigeria, for it laid the foundations of her legitimate commercial relations with West Africa. It also eventually led her to establish herself politically along the West African coast, the most important stretch of which was that of modern Nigeria.

The abolition of the slave trade by Britain in 1807 may appear somewhat paradoxical when it is remembered that at the turn of the century she was the chief carrier of slaves from West Africa. The decision of 1807 was the climax of thirty years of agitation in Britain against the slave trade.[1] Before 1772 few people had had any conscience about it. So far removed was the common Englishman from the conduct of the slave trade with the attendant horrors of the Middle Passage and the cruel system of labour in the plantations that it is hardly surprising that he rarely questioned its morality. In 1729 the question of the rights of slaves on British soil had been considered by the Solicitor General and the Attorney General, whose opinion was that a slave did not become free by coming to Britain, and remained the property of his master. However, there were a few people in Britain who were not content with this interpretation of the law. And in 1772, as a result of Granville Sharp's one-man crusade against the institution of slavery, a test case was brought before Lord Chief Justice Mansfield to establish whether a slave had freedom under the laws of Britain. This was the case of *Somersett* v. *Knowles*. Somersett, a Black man, had run away from his master, who recaptured him and clapped him in irons on board a ship bound for the West Indies. Granville Sharp learnt of this and took out a writ of habeas corpus for Somersett, which was heard by Lord Chief Justice Mansfield, who ruled that once a slave set foot on British soil he became free. This was the starting-point of the movement for the abolition of the slave trade which had for years been fundamental to the plantation economies of the colonies of the great European powers.

In 1776 a motion was moved in the House of Commons that the slave trade is contrary to the laws of God and the rights of man'. It failed, and it was left to ardent social reformers like William Wilberforce, M.P.,

Thomas Clarkson and Granville Sharp to carry on the struggle against this long-established trade. In 1787 they formed the Society for the Abolition of the Slave Trade, and with Wilberforce as their agent in Parliament began to lobby for abolition. Though Wilberforce gained the sympathy of William Pitt and Charles James Fox, it took him twenty years to secure a majority in the House.

Before it the society had the formidable opposition of the vested interests in the slave trade. Liverpool and Bristol both depended largely on it for their income, and many members of the government were deeply involved in it. Indeed, eighteenth-century economists believed that the wealth of the West Indies, which depended on the slave trade, was fundamental to the strength of the British Empire. Certainly the triangular trade between Africa, the West Indies and Britain supplied some of the necessary capital to finance the industrial revolution.[2]

How then did the abolitionists persuade Parliament to do away with what was apparently a vital factor in the British economy? The end of the eighteenth century was a time of new ideas in Europe. America had just broken away from England. The foundations of the French Revolution were being laid by the radical and revolutionary ideas of Liberty, Equality and Fraternity. The rights of the individual, as in Thomas Paine's *The Rights of Man*, were being bandied about in pamphlet and newspaper. Not unnaturally a public receptive of such arguments was also likely to be receptive of the idea that "Negroes" were also men and that the slave trade was wrong. Certainly they were shocked to read of its brutality in accounts like that of Falconbridge, who had been a surgeon on a slaver.[3] But even then the entrenched interests seem too great to have been overcome by the zeal of Wilberforce and his small but ardent band of abolitionists. Did Wilberforce really succeed in changing the attitude of a nation? Did he really touch the conscience of Parliament? It hardly seems possible in a nation that carried on public executions of children for petty theft right up till the middle of the century and instituted a system of child factory labour whose conditions, in many cases, were far worse than those for the slave on the sugar plantation. It is not to belittle Wilberforce and the humanitarians to suggest that in fact by the time of his campaign the odds against him were not so overwhelming as has commonly been suggested. The fact is Britain was really economically ready for this change-over from an economy of mercantilism, based largely on the Indian trade and slave carrying between Africa and the West Indies, to that of the first industrial nation in Europe. A good example of this change-over is Liverpool which, at the time of abolition, was already diverting many of her ships to trading in cotton with America. As a new industrial nation Britain had greater interests in the opening of markets for her manufactured goods than in retaining a slave trade that was not necessarily conducive to the expansion of the West African market. Significantly the hostility of the British Government to trading in slaves by other nations did not prevent it from allowing Manchester goods to be used by such nations as their main means of exchange for slaves. Britain had another great interest in stopping the slave trade: she needed palm-oil as a lubricant for her factories, for soap and for lighting. While slave trading continued, production in the oil-growing areas of the interior of West Africa would always be hampered. It was therefore very much in the interests of Britain to check slavery in order to permit the economic exploitation of the coast.[4]

It is significant also that neither Bristol nor Liverpool collapsed as a result of the cessation of the slave trade; and relatively few English ships found it worth while to engage in privateering as slave dealers after abolition. One notorious French slaver, Théodore Canot, complained that the British combined suppression of the slave trade with the promotion of their own commerce in adulterated Manchester goods.[5] Despite these commercial motives, 'the unweary, unostentatious and inglorious crusade of England against slavery', as the historian Lecky has written, 'may probably be regarded as among the three or four perfectly virtuous pages comprised in the history of nations'.[6]

It was one thing for Britain to proclaim the legal abolition of the slave trade, quite another to persuade other nations to follow suit. Britain tried to bring the slave trade to an end both by treaty with other powers and by seizing ships actually carrying slaves. In certain cases other nations followed Britain by abolishing the slave trade. Denmark had actually declared it illegal in 1804. The U.S.A. abolished it in 1808, Sweden in 1813, and the Netherlands in 1814. But official abolition did not stop slavers from operating on the coast. In defiance of the law many American ships crossed the Atlantic with human cargo over the next fifty years. Thus Britain had to undertake the establishment of an anti-slavery patrol on the West Coast to capture slaving ships. In 1817 she secured from Spain[7] and Portugal treaties which agreed to the reciprocal rights of search and the subsequent condemnation of ships if they were found with slaves on board. This often had horrific results, since slavers were liable to discharge their human cargo into the ocean if capture seemed imminent. Later, fortunately, treaties were secured which allowed the condemnation of ships if slaving equipment was found on board. Even so the patrol was largely ineffective in its early years and the figures of slaves exported from West Africa, far from decreasing, actually rose steeply.[8]

Two problems therefore confronted Britain. First was the difficult diplomatic tangle over the right of search; second was the smallness of the patrol for so lengthy a coastline. For operational purposes the coast was divided into three strips: from Senegal to Sierra Leone; from Sierra Leone to Cape Coast Castle; and from Cape Coast Castle to the Line (Equator), beyond which treaty powers ceased. This last was known as the Bights Division. The West Coast was an unpopular station, and to encourage the anti-slavery patrol the 1807 Act provided for generous rewards for the capture of slavers. But by 1824, when abolitionist enthusiasm was waning under the mistaken impression that the slave trade was dying a natural death, the bounty was reduced from £60 for a rescued male slave to £10. In 1830 it was further reduced to £5. Nevertheless, the Navy did capture a large number of slavers, towing them to Freetown where they were brought up before the Court of Mixed Commission which was empowered to condemn them. Freetown had been established by the Society for the Abolition of the Slave Trade as a settlement for freed slaves. Despite the inconvenience of taking ships from the Bights of Benin and Biafra [now Bonny] on the long leg up the coast to Freetown the British government insisted on keeping it as its base for the suppression of the slave trade.[9]

The abolition of the slave trade by the country that hitherto had been its chief practitioner came as a profound shock to many African chiefs who had looked to Britain as their best customer. When the kindly and successful British slaver, Captain Hugh Crow, arrived in Bonny on his last visit, he informed his old friend King Opobo Pepple of Britain's decision to abolish the trade. Pepple replied, 'We tink trade no stop, for all the Ju-Ju men tell we so, for demn say you country can niber pass God A'mighty'.[10] And as late as 1842 Lieutenant Levinge of the West African Naval Squadron said that Africans in the Delta often asked him whether England was at war with the other nations of Europe. 'They cannot understand why we take them [the slavers]. We carried on the slave trade so shortly before ourselves, that I do not think they clearly understand why we should be so anxious to suppress it now.'[11]

It was hardly surprising that few of the chiefs took much notice of Britain's change of heart. There were other customers. Indeed, in the ensuing economic war between the slavers on the one hand and the British legitimate traders on the other, 'what determined the side the Africans took', as Dr Kenneth Diké has written, 'was the importance or otherwise of the trade to the economy of the country'.[12] Certainly the presence of the naval squadron at the various mouths of the Niger did not at first deter Bonny, which had become the leading slaving port on the coast, from dealing with Spaniards, Portuguese and American slavers, as well as a polyglot bunch of pirates and privateers. Bonny was the chief offender, though even she tried to get the best of both worlds. In 1826 12 slavers and 12 British merchantmen were reported in Bonny waters.[13]

Inevitably there was bitter competition between the slavers and the legitimate traders. Life was difficult for the latter, for whenever a slaver arrived, even in Calabar which by the 'twenties had largely devoted itself to trade in palm-oil and timber, everyone rushed to meet the slavers' requirements.[14]

Farther up the coast Lagos and Badagry flourished as they had never done before on the profits of the slave trade. Civil war amongst the Yoruba, wars between Yoruba and Fulani, Egba and Dahomeyans kept a plentiful supply of slaves for the markets of Brazil and Cuba. Even here the rivalry between legitimate traders and slavers was keen.

These attempts at the suppression of the slave trade, despite their early inadequacy, were to bring about a revolution in the economy of the African slaving states. A new economic order based on trade in the products of the West African forests was ushered in. However, in the Niger Delta the old trading organization that was built up to deal with the slave trade was taken over unmodified to cope with the new trade in palm-oil. Many of those who would have been exported as slaves were now employed as porters. While Bonny rose to the position of chief slave port on that part of the coast, Calabar compensated for her loss by exporting palm-oil. In 1828 she exported 2,000 tons whilst Bonny exported almost none. However, by the 1830s Bonny, which was still the chief slaving state, was whittling away Calabar's early lead. Her traders switched from slaves to oil as the markets demanded. New oil markets were developed by the coastal traders, who usually exercised a monopoly over them. In addition to palm-oil these traders sold timber, ivory and bees-wax to the British ships.

Britain's growing interest in the promotion of legitimate trade saw a gradual change of both official and commercial attitudes towards the local rulers, who in the past had been accustomed to having their sovereignty completely respected by the European slave traders. In 1824 Captain Owen, who was significantly given the task of surveying the coast of Africa by the British Admiralty, anchored in Bonny waters, and sent a junior officer to tell King Opobo he had arrived. The King was furious at the breach of etiquette, and resented deeply the fact that British ships had anchored in Bonny waters without his permission. In retaliation he ordered the complete cessation of trade with the British.[15] Though the affair was ultimately settled amicably, it indicated a new trend in British attitudes to West African chiefs. Later in 1836 the Navy, now backed up by the Equipment Treaty which allowed them to take Spanish and Portuguese ships as slavers if they were carrying the appropriate equipment, seized some Spanish ships waiting for slaves in Bonny. A tremendous dispute over this infringement of sovereignty arose between the responsible naval officer, Lieutenant Tryon, and the Regent of Bonny, who was naturally supported by the Spaniards. He ordered the arrest of Lieutenant Tryon and threw him into jail. The Navy promptly sailed into Bonny and forced the Regent to sign a treaty ensuring the protection of life and property of British subjects.[16] This was the thin end of the wedge. Legitimate trade was becoming so important that the British Government in order to make it secure was prepared to usurp the power of the coastal chiefs.

In 1834 Britain's trade in palm-oil was worth £500,000, a huge sum for those days, and she was not going to be without control of its source. Such was the concentration of naval force at the mouth of the River Bonny by the end of the thirties that Bonny was compelled, at least outwardly, to cease her traffic in slaves. Indeed Britain's treatment of Bonny may be taken as typical of her new attitude to African states.

After the death of King Opobo Pepple, the date of which is uncertain but which has been placed in 1830, there was an interregnum in Bonny. There appears to have been a struggle for power between the two main houses of Bonny, the Manila house and the Anna Pepple house. Since they could not agree on a mutually acceptable candidate, there was a regency under the control of the Anna Pepple chiefs. Eventually the Anna Pepple house had to accept William Dappa Pepple, candidate of the Manila house, but it appears they held on to the regency, on the grounds that he was too young to rule on his own. The Regent, as we have seen, had supported the Spanish slavers against the British Anti-Slavery patrol. Though he had signed a treaty with the British assuring them security of trade, the Regent continued to support the Spanish slavers, and within a month of signing the treaty, a British trader was detained by him contrary to Article I. Thus in March 1837 the Anti-Slavery patrol was sent to depose the Regent and install William Dappa Pepple as the King of Bonny in fact as well as name.

The new King, it was felt, would be more favourable to British trading interests. In 1839 a treaty abolishing the slave trade was signed with Bonny; but it was never ratified since the Navy believed that compensation offered for the loss of the slave trade would be used to finance it further. In 1841 a new treaty was negotiated abolishing the slave trade with the important proviso that 'if at any future time Great Britain shall permit the slave trade to be carried on, King Pepple and the Chiefs of Bonny shall be at liberty to do the same'.[17] This treaty, too, was not ratified and King William Dappa Pepple never received his compensation. The existence of the patrol at the mouth of the River Bonny made it difficult for him to carry on the trade openly, but he and his chiefs cunningly diverted their trade to the small, concealed state of

Brass which exported hundreds of slaves to Brazil and Cuba.[18] By 1844 such were British encroachments on Bonny that even King William Dappa Pepple, who owed his position to the British, was complaining of their interference. That same year a treaty abolishing the slave trade was ratified on the spot, the only condition under which he would sign.

It is significant, too, that in 1842 Palmerston tried to reacquire Fernando Po as a base to watch over the oil river ports and to give British traders protection. The earlier settlement there had been abandoned at a time when legitimate trade was not so important.

By the 1840s a large section of the British fleet was engaged in the anti-slavery patrol in West African waters. The ensuing decade, 1840–50, was critical both for the suppression of the slave trade and the establishment of British interests in Nigeria. The growth of legitimate trade during the period in which Britain was busily suppressing slavery is most significant. In 1820 there were 38 British merchantmen trading in the Bights of Benin and Biafra. In 1840 there were 134. Oil exports had increased from 200 tons in 1808 to 13,945 in 1834 and 25,285 in 1845. It is apparent that Britain was looking increasingly towards West Africa as a profitable area for trade.

Despite Britain's growing commercial interest in West Africa, the suppression of the slave trade nearly suffered disastrous setbacks in the decade 1840–50. In 1839 an English captain and ardent abolitionist called Denman actually destroyed a slaver's barracoon in an attempt to attack the slave traders at the very source of their supply. In 1841 Captain Nurse followed suit and razed a barracoon on the Rio Pongos, but in the process he destroyed a considerable amount of foreign property. The foreigners declared themselves legitimate traders, and in England, the country of merchants *par excellence*, there was an outcry against Nurse's action on the grounds that it endangered the growth of legitimate trade. Aberdeen, the British Foreign Secretary at the time, then decided that the Navy should refrain from such actions unless the chiefs in whose waters these barracoons were sited agreed by treaty to their destruction. This, then, marked the beginning of a new phase in the suppression of the slave trade. The Navy started to make treaties with the coastal chiefs to gain their consent to the suppression of the slave trade. Later this system of treaty-making was to be used in the establishment of the British Protectorate over Nigeria.

All was not well for the abolitionists. In 1846 Peel's Tory Government reduced the import duty on sugar which in effect increased demand for it in England and therefore the demand for slaves to work on the sugar plantations of Cuba. Statistics bear this out: it is estimated that in 1842 only 24,800 slaves were exported from West Africa. By 1847 there were 84,356.

In the mid-nineteenth century there was a sharp conflict between humanitarians and traders. All went well when their interests coincided; but when, as in the case of the Sugar Act, they conflicted, humanitarian interests suffered. During the forties the West African Squadron came under frequent criticism, particularly because of its cost. Even those with humanitarian interests attacked it, because at times it apparently worsened conditions for slaves, who would be thrown overboard the moment a ship of the squadron gave chase to a slaver. There was a strong commercial faction that felt that British trade with Brazil would be seriously endangered if Brazil did not obtain the slaves, the main prop of her plantation economy. A Member of Parliament called Hutt led these diverse factions in an attempt to have the squadron withdrawn, and in 1849 his Select Committee decided by one vote that the squadron should be called off and diplomatic pressure and missionary enterprise should be used to check the slave trade in its stead. In the Lords, Bishop Wilberforce managed to set up a rival committee which rejected Hutt's decision. When the reports of both Houses came up before the Commons Lord John Russell made it a vote of confidence in his Government to reject Hutt's motion for the withdrawal of the squadron, so that it was defeated.

The result of the defeat of Hutt's motion for the abolition of the anti-slave squadron was an increase in zeal for the cause of suppression. There were fresh diplomatic approaches to foreign powers and an increasing number of treaties were made with West African chiefs. One naval captain considered that without a naval squadron on the West Coast 'the coast would become a nest of pirates; the number of slaves exported would be enormous; all legitimate trade would cease, and in a very short time we would have to increase the squadron for the protection of what trade remained'.[19]

By the 1850s slave trading had largely been abolished in Old Calabar, with which official treaties had been negotiated. In Bonny, which was increasingly subjected to British political pressure, it had gone under cover. Farther up the coast, Lagos was still a sore spot. By the mid century the slave squadron had completed much of its work. Britain had supplied the slave ports with an alternative trade—that in palm-oil. Between 1830 and 1850 legitimate trade had increased by 87 per cent. But the traders in palm-oil, known as the palm-oil ruffians, were little different from the slavers themselves. They lived the same precarious existence on the fringe of Africa. They never penetrated inland. A great new field of commerce in the interior still remained to be exploited. This was the result of the enterprise of explorers, missionaries, and traders, African and European.

9 Explorers and Missionaries

The movement in Britain for the abolition of the slave trade was accompanied by the desire to find markets for the products of Britain's new industries. At first the marketing of these goods was handled entirely by the African middlemen of the coastal kingdoms, who secured their monopoly on the basis of their exclusive knowledge of conditions in the interior and the fact that the climate was too unhealthy for Europeans to penetrate beyond the coastal fringe.[1] However, as Britain's trading interests grew in Nigeria, so did the desire of her merchants to trade direct with the markets of the interior. Much of the history of Nigeria in the nineteenth century concerns the resistance of African kings and middlemen to penetration of the interior by European traders. That these traders did in fact overcome this resistance was in the first instance largely due to the pioneer work of explorers and missionaries.

It is not surprising when one considers Britain's needs for overseas markets in the first half of the nineteenth century that many of the leading names in the history of the exploration of the West African hinterland should either be British or those of men like the German, Barth, who were sponsored by the British Government. The pioneers of inland trade were the great explorers like Mungo Park, Clapperton, the Lander brothers, Barth and Baikie. Their main problem was to discover an inland highway for trade into West Africa. Their attention was focused on the still legendary Niger.

The exploration of this great river dates from the founding of the African Association in 1788. This association represented a multiplicity of interests, such as politicians, scientists, industrialists and humanitarians. The chief object of the society was initially, as Adu Boahen has shown,[2] the promotion of scientific knowledge about Africa, but it was significant that one of its founder-members was Josiah Wedgwood, an architect of the industrial revolution in Britain. The Association was to show great concern with the opening up of Africa to legitimate trade. However, though humanitarians were strongly represented on the board by Fox, Wilberforce and Clarkson, the Association showed no open concern with abolition as such. As Boahen points out, its founder, Sir Joseph Banks, was against abolition, as were its second secretary, Bryan Edwards and his successor, Sir William Young.[3] There was no direct reference to the abolition of the slave trade in the objectives of the Association. Nevertheless the humanitarians intended to use it to further their own ends, for they believed that promotion of legitimate trade was necessary to fill the vacuum that would be left by the suppression of the slave trade.

The importance of the African Association, which was given the backing of Pitt, must be seen against contemporary political developments in the British Empire. Britain had just lost her American colonies, and was looking to India as an alternative outlet for her economic expansion. Australia had just been discovered and British interests in the Far East were increasing. Geographically Africa lay in the path of the main axis of British trade. It was thus of a high strategic interest, heightened twelve years later by the Napoleonic Wars. It was not surprising, then, that the British Government gave the African Association its unofficial support.[4]

The specific object of the Association was to organize the exploration of the interior of Africa. At the time West Africa was, as far as Europe was concerned, almost a *carte blanche* and had been used as such by the more imaginative pictorial geographers of the preceding centuries, who dotted the land with mythical cities, and often more mythical lakes and seas that were to confuse considerably the determination of the source of the Niger, which, because it was hoped it might prove a major highway of trade into Africa, became one of the chief objects of the Association's attentions.[5] In 1788 it was believed that the Niger flowed to the west, as Leo Africanus had reported over two centuries before.[6] The Gambia and Senegal Rivers therefore appeared as its most obvious outlets. In an attempt to discover the Niger, the Association equipped expeditions to cross the desert, all of which were tragically unsuccessful. Others were sent to the West Coast to attack the problem, as it were, from its southern side. Tragedy also struck the first explorer on this route, Major Houghton, who was either murdered by Moors or died of hunger as a result of being deserted by them,[7] but not before he had sent back sufficient information to suggest that the Niger might flow to the east.[8] It was left to Mungo Park, a young Scotsman, whose two journeys into the interior of West Africa have earned for him next to Livingstone the most celebrated place in the history of the European exploration of Africa, to tell Europe for certain which way the Niger flowed. Inspired by an incredible determination, which allowed him to suffer the unendurable in the firm belief it was predestined by God, he succeeded in reaching the Niger. Even when he had been robbed of all his belongings, and was sick with fever and deserted by his followers, he did not give up his quest for the Niger. Finally, after a hellish journey, he came 'through some marshy ground where, as I was anxiously looking around for the river, one of them called out *geo affili* (see the water); and looking forwards, I saw with infinite pleasure the great object of my mission; the long sought for, majestic Niger, glittering to the morning sun, as broad as the Thames at Westminster, and flowing slowly to the *Eastward*. I hastened to the brink, and having drunk of the water, lifted up my fervent thanks in prayer, to the Great ruler of all things, for having thus far crowned my endeavours with success.'[9]

This information was to set the world of armchair geographers abuzz. Hitherto it had been taken for granted that the Niger flowed to the west.

Major Rennell propounded the theory that the Niger flowed into a great lake—the sink of Africa—where it simply evaporated.[10] However, his theory, which gained wide recognition, was opposed by the German geographer Reichard, who correctly stated that the huge delta of rivers in the Bight of Benin was the Niger's outlet into the sea.[11]

The African Association declared that as a result of Park's discovery 'a gate is opened to every commercial nation to enter and trade from the West to the eastern extremity of Africa'.[12] Therefore when Park, who had subsequently become a doctor in Peebles, volunteered to return to the Niger and seek its outlet, the Association accepted his services eagerly and the British Government put up the money for a lavishly and, as it eventually turned out, farcically equipped expedition. Park set off this time not alone but with a band of forty-five Europeans, fully equipped to construct a boat in which the party would sail down the Niger to its mouth. The expedition was a disaster, a monument to bad organization. Park, brave and capable of much suffering himself, was incapable of understanding the needs of others, and before he himself was killed on the Bussa rapids in northern Nigeria, every man in his party but his Mandingo servant Isaaco had died. Fortunately the devoted Isaaco made his way back to the Gambia and delivered up Park's manuscript to the British Government.[13] At the time Park's achievement of travelling eight hundred miles from Timbuktu to Bussa was not appreciated, since contemporary geographers estimated it at only a tenth of the actual distance.

The problem of the Niger was left aside during the Napoleonic Wars. However, the end of those wars saw a revival of interest in the termination; but an unsuccessful expedition by Major Peddie following Park's old route dampened the British Government's enthusiasm, which only really revived in 1821 when Denham, Clapperton and Oudney left for Nigeria across the Sahara. That same year a West Indian planter named M'Queen became a champion of the theory that the Niger's outlet was in the Bight of Benin, deducing this from reports his slaves had given him.[14] Crossing from Tripoli, the Denham-Clapperton expedition at first seemed to justify Rennell's theory, for in 1823 they discovered Lake Chad, supposedly 'the vast sink of Africa'. However, when they followed the river that fed this lake they found it dwindled to a mere trickle after a short distance.

In Borno, Denham and Clapperton were received by Al-Kanemi, who actually wrote to King George IV saying that he would welcome four or five traders from England in his country: 'The Rayes Khaleel (Major Denham travelled under this name) desired of us permission, that merchants seeking for elephant-teeth, ostrich feathers, and other such things, that are not to be found in the country of the English, might come among us. We told him that our country, as he himself has known and seen its state, does not suit any heavy (rich) traveller, who may possess great wealth. But if a few light persons (small capitalists), as four or five only, with little merchandize, would come, there will be no harm. This is the utmost that we can give him permission for; and more than that number must not come.'[15]

The party was greatly impressed by the vast array of chain-mailed horsemen under the command of the Shehu.[16] Clapperton and Oudney, who died shortly after, moved on into Hausa country. Clapperton arrived at the great metropolis of Kano eager with anticipation. He was extremely anxious to look his best on entering this city which frankly, after the tales he had heard from Arab traders, disappointed him. He dressed in his best naval uniform but 'not an individual turned his head round to gaze at me, but all intent on their own business, allowed me to pass without notice or remark'.[17] In Kano he noted that the only foreign goods on sale were French, German and Italian.

Clapperton moved on to Sokoto, the capital of the Caliphate, ruled over by the scholarly Caliph Bello, who was able to tell him much about the country.[18] Though he would not allow Clapperton to leave for the Niger, he expressed a desire to establish commercial relations with the British, and asked that a consulate be established in Sokoto. Clapperton left a happy man and joined Denham, who had gone south along the Shari River which he confused with the Benue, the main tributary of the Niger. Clapperton had every reason to be pleased with himself. He had been promised commercial relations with Sokoto; he had been told by Caliph Bello that he would have no difficulty in reaching the sea by the Niger; and a consulate had been established in Borno. The party left a Mr Tyrwhitt, who had joined the expedition in May 1824, as consul in Kuka, the capital of the Shehu of Borno.

The British Government was well pleased with the expedition. The prospects of trade with the interior seemed about to be realized at last, for Clapperton had even been told by Caliph Bello the name of the port at the mouth of the Niger. Clapperton's return to England seemed to herald the end of the long quest for the termination of the Niger. The Government promptly equipped a second expedition to be led by Clapperton with the object of reaching the interior from the seaboard, preferably up the Niger.

But on his return to the coast to try and find the port, which Caliph Bello had called Rakah, Clapperton met with disappointment. No one had ever heard of such a place. So he decided to trek overland from Badagry to Sokoto, where instead of friendliness he met with considerable hostility from the Caliph. There was now no question of trade, and certainly no question of giving up slave dealing. It seemed that a rival economic interest, that of Arab merchants from Tripoli and Morocco, had persuaded the Caliph that trade with the Europeans would be foolish. The Caliph also had suspicions about Clapperton's friendly relations with his enemy, the Shehu of Borno.[19] Bitterly disappointed, and making no headway against the Caliph's new position, Clapperton became ill and died in April 1827. Richard Lander, his Cornish servant, tried to reach the coast along the River Niger, but at the confluence of the Niger and Benue he was captured by the local inhabitants and forced to make his way back by land. On his return to England Lander persuaded a reluctant government, which had now come to believe that trade with the interior would never be possible because of the high incidence of disease, to make him a grant to return once more to the coast. He was given £100 for himself and his brother, who was to accompany him, and a further £100 to keep his wife in his absence.

In 1830 the Lander brothers trekked overland from Badagry to Bussa where Mungo Park had met his death.[20] There they were able with much difficulty to secure two canoes. They sailed down the Niger through the confluence with the Benue until at Asaba they were taken captive by local Igbo. Eventually their captors agreed to deliver them to the master of an English brig anchored at Brass on the mouth of the Niger. They were taken downstream and were overjoyed to learn that they had at last discovered the mouth of the Niger. At Brass, Richard Lander was allowed to go on board the brig to negotiate the ransom with its captain, Thomas Lake. At first Lake was most reluctant to pay up, but eventually agreed to do so on delivery of John Lander. No sooner was John Lander on board than he set sail without paying a penny. Thus in 1830, in melodramatic circumstances not untypical of trade in those days, the quest for the Niger was ended by the efforts of Richard Lander, a 'gentleman's gentleman' turned explorer. A new phase of exploration had opened. The route to the interior was known.

Now the great question, of such great import for the future of Nigeria, was whether life was possible for Europeans in the interior.

Once the mouth of the Niger had been discovered, it was not long before this new knowledge was put to commercial use. With British naval supremacy on the coast, the Niger opened up tremendous and unexplored possibilities to British trade. It was significant that shortly after the return of the Landers a Liverpool trader, Macgregor Laird, financed a commercial expedition to the coast in 1832, though at the time he was virtually the only merchant interested in opening up interior African trade. His two ships, the *Alburkah* and *Quorra*, were the first two iron steamships ever to be built as ocean-going vessels. Commercially, however, the expedition was a disaster, accompanied by a heavy death toll from malaria. Only nine of the forty-eight Europeans on the expedition survived. Nevertheless, it did sail up the Niger as far as the confluence and beyond.[21] The failure of this expedition postponed further attempts to penetrate the interior for commercial purposes until 1841.

Now a new element was brought in as the motive force behind the development of internal trade: the humanitarians and their delegates, the missionaries.

The humanitarians had quickly come to realize that the prohibition of the slave trade was not enough. Certainly, as we have seen, the British Navy was not sufficiently strong to prevent traders obtaining slaves for export to the Americas. The answer, they maintained, was not only to increase the size of the Anti-Slavery patrol but to attack slavery at its economic root—that was, to show Africans an alternative method of obtaining money with which to buy European goods. The natural, not the human products of Africa should form the basis of exchange. This was the view put forward by Sir Thomas Fowell Buxton in his book *The African Slave Trade and its Remedy*.[22] The only way to save Africa from the evils of the slave trade, he insisted, would be to call out its own natural resources. At the same time every effort should be made to save the souls of those whom they were rescuing from slavery. Already missionaries had established a settlement for freed slaves in Sierra Leone, and with the growing militancy of Christian sects in England, thoughts began to turn towards the evangelization of the whole West Coast. Africa seemed an excellent missionary target, for it was considered in the words of Eugene Stock in his *History of the C.M.S.*, published in 1897, 'one universal den of desolation, misery and crime'.[23]

Thus early missionaries in West Africa had a dual purpose: to promote legitimate trade between African and European, and to convert Africans to their own religion. This came out clearly in the expedition up the River Niger in 1841. The object of this expedition, sponsored by the Society for the Extinction of the Slave Trade and for the Civilization of Africa, of which Buxton was a leading member, was to promote trade in the interior, to conclude treaties with local chiefs and to establish a model agricultural farm. This farm, originally the idea of Commander William Allen who had travelled with Laird's expedition in 1832, was to serve as an 'exhibition centre' for the surrounding people. The expedition, consisting of 145 Europeans, was given an official send-off at Exeter Hall by no less a person than Prince Albert, Consort of Queen Victoria.

The expedition was the brain-child of men who were almost entirely ignorant of conditions in the interior of the Niger region. One of its members, W. Simpson, carried letters from the Chief Rabbi and the Rabbi of the Portuguese Community in London, in case they were to encounter Jews.[24] The expedition came under heavy fire in England. Robert Jamieson, in *An Appeal . . . Against the Proposed Niger Expedition*,[25] protested to the Government against humanitarian interference in commerce, pointing out that its experiment in Sierra Leone had already proved a failure. Merchants also objected to interference by the Government in trade.

Nevertheless the expedition set sail in three ships: the *Albert*, *Sudan* and *Wilberforce*. On board were two missionaries, the Rev. J. F. Schön and Samuel Crowther, a freed slave who later became Bishop on the Niger.[26] He had been taken as a slave during one of the Yoruba inter-tribal wars in 1822. The slaver in which he was being transported across the Atlantic was intercepted and taken to Freetown. On his release he was sent to the C.M.S. school where his great intelligence soon caught the attention of the missionaries. In 1825 he was baptized Samuel, though he always kept his native name Ajayi, which means one born with his face to the ground and destined for a remarkable future. He was then sent to the Parochial School in Liverpool Street, Islington, in London. He took the name Crowther from a distinguished member of the Church Missionary Society.[27]

Crowther and Schön were charged with pursuing the new policy of 'Bible and Plough' on the expedition. From now on missionaries were to play a major role in the exploration of the interior. Hitherto their influence and interest in Nigeria had been marginal, largely because the local chiefs did not permit penetration of the interior, and also because of the difficult living conditions under which most Europeans succumbed to malaria. Furthermore, European slaving interests had naturally been hostile to missionary penetration.

The 1841 expedition was superficially a disastrous failure and set back the promotion of commercial enterprise ten years, for on the expedition over a third of the members of the expedition died of malaria.[28] Ironically the expedition carried plenty of supplies of the one thing that could have cured them: quinine. But they used it only when a patient showed signs of recovery. The model farm, purchased from the powerful Ata of Idah, was a failure, and the expedition returned to England with little to show for their early optimism and enthusiasm.

The Times and the *Edinburgh Review*, both of which had criticized the expedition, wrote self-satisfied editorials that prevented its repetition for another decade. And though the foundations of the Niger mission had been laid in 1841, it would hardly have survived as a concept had not Henry Venn been made Hon. Secretary of the C.M.S. in that year. He it was who had such faith in Samuel Ajayi Crowther, who became the first black Anglican bishop of modern times. He it was who took the Rev. J. F. Schön's advice, based on his experiences on the expedition, that since Europeans could not easily survive the climate, Nigeria must be evangelized by Africans themselves, of whom there were large numbers ready to offer themselves in the Sierra Leone settlement. As a result of the failure of the 1841 expedition the Niger mission was to start predominantly as an African mission.[29]

Despite the setback which the 1841 expedition represented at the time, missionary penetration of Nigeria really dates from then. As C. C. Ifemesia observes: 'Whatever were the opinions of Buxton's critics, the British missionaries (especially the Church Missionary Society) never believed that the expedition was a total failure.'[30] They believed that as a result of the mission they had learned much, both about the country and its peoples and how best to organize their subsequent efforts. Missionaries were to become latter-day, less spectacular explorers, pushing into the remotest corners of the country to spread the Gospel, and thereby to make the hinterland accessible to government and trading interests. Missionary enterprise in Nigeria took the form of a three-pronged attack: the Church of Scotland mission occupied itself with Calabar; the Church Missionary Society established missions in the Niger Delta and up the Niger; the Methodists, the Church Missionary Society, and the Baptists advanced into Yorubaland. In all three areas freed slaves and Africans played an important role in the evangelization of Nigeria.

Africans were very much in the vanguard of missionary activity in Badagry and Abeokuta. In the late 1830s a number of freed slaves from Freetown returned to their original homes in Lagos, Badagry and Abeokuta. As a result of trade between Badagry and Freetown, some of the Aku (Yoruba) Creoles learnt of the great Yoruba cities of Abeokuta and Lagos and decided to return there. Two parties left Sierra Leone, one for Lagos, the other for Abeokuta. The Lagos expedition finished with all 300 members being robbed of their possessions. By 1842 over 500 returned ex-slaves were resettled in Abeokuta. Their appeals to the Church Missionary Society in Sierra Leone to open a mission in Abeokuta brought down Henry Townsend, who had been preceded in the missionary field in Nigeria by a mulatto, Thomas Birch Freeman, head of the Gold Coast Methodist mission. He had opened a station at Badagry in 1842 and had already established cordial relations with Sodeke, the founder and leader of Abeokuta. Townsend actually met Freeman while he was on his way back from Abeokuta, where the immigrants from Sierra Leone had been well received.

A year later an important event took place in London. Samuel Ajayi Crowther, whose journal of the 1841 expedition had greatly impressed the C.M.S., was ordained a priest. Afterwards he preached before Sir Thomas Buxton. When, later, as a result of Townsend's visit to Abeokuta, the Yoruba mission was established, it was only natural to make the Yoruba-speaking Crowther one of its members. Together with the German missionary Gollmer, Townsend, two catechists and an interpreter, Crowther set off for Abeokuta, only to learn with distress that Sodeke had died. This meant not only that the new mission would be without the protection of this sympathetic ruler, but also that the one unifying force amongst the Egba sub-tribes and immigrants that went to make up Abeokuta had been removed. Matters were further complicated by the dispute over the chieftancy in Lagos, where Kosoko, a well-known slaver, had usurped the throne of his uncle Akitoye.[31] Some Egba war chiefs had given their support to Kosoko, so it became impossible for the missionaries, enemies of slavery, to reach Abeokuta. Further, Gezo, the slaving king of Dahomey, had control of the Badagry–Abeokuta road. The missionaries therefore contented themselves with opening a mission at Badagry. Schools were built, an experimental farm was established and a steel corn mill introduced to stimulate legitimate trade. Not until 1846 were they able to leave for Abeokuta, where they were well received by the people. Again a church was built and schools established. However, their work did not easily survive the death of their first convert in 1848. Funeral rites in most indigenous African religions are of deepest significance to their adherents. When, therefore, on the death of an indigenous convert the mission attempted to bury him according to Christian rites there were naturally many relatives anxious that he should be buried according to native custom. Feeling ran high and riots, together with a general persecution of the Christians followed.

Perhaps one of the most significant results of the establishment of the mission at Abeokuta was the visit four months later of the representative of the large trading firm of Thomas Hutton and Co., with a view to establishing a factory or trading store. Soon afterwards factories were opened at Abeokuta as well as Badagry which had become an important trade centre both for slaves and legitimate commerce.

The prestige of the missionaries in Abeokuta, both Baptists and C.M.S., rose as a result of their close co-operation in 1851 with the Egba in the defence of the city against the Dahomeyans. The Amazon vanguard of the Dahomeyan invaders was repelled with Townsend of the C.M.S. and Bowen of the Baptist mission offering advice. Bowen had in fact been a contemporary of Davy Crockett, fighting Indians in Texas and Alabama, before becoming a missionary.

The C.M.S. in London felt optimistic enough to expand its activities beyond Yorubaland. Hinderer, together with his wife, who became a great missionary in her own right, arrived initially with the intention of going to Hausaland but, because of the civil wars, remained in Yorubaland travelling extensively and gaining warm receptions everywhere except in Ijebuland.[32]

The emphasis in any history of early missionary activity in Nigeria must be on the C.M.S., since as an offshoot of the Anglican Church it had official sanction in days when Nonconformism was still a social disadvantage. No better illustration is given of this than the close interest of Queen Victoria in the mission's work. She sent two Bibles to the mission, one in English and one in Arabic; and Prince Albert, a year before his Great Exhibition of 1851, not surprisingly made it a gift of a steel corn mill. Later, when Crowther went on leave, he was received by Lord Palmerston, the Foreign Secretary, and had an audience of Queen Victoria, at which he read the Lord's Prayer in Yoruba, described later by the Queen as soft and melodious.[33]

The political influence of the Church Missionary Society, therefore, was much greater than that of any other group. Indeed, as we shall see in the next chapter, one of the main factors behind Britain's decision to depose King Kosoko of Lagos in 1852 was pressure from the missionaries at Abeokuta, who found his slave trading prejudicial to the development of legitimate trade in Egbaland. And as they were prepared to lobby the British government in furtherance of their policy of 'Bible and Plough', so too they were willing to interfere in local politics. Townsend, for instance, was largely responsible for the introduction of the new supreme ruler of Abeokuta, the Alake, preferring one sovereign chief, with whom he could deal direct, to a multiplicity of chiefs without real power. Later on, as we shall see, this political interference was to bring considerable tension to both Lagos and Abeokuta.

The second prong of early missionary enterprise in Nigeria was on the Cross River in the old slave-trading state of Calabar. In 1846 Hope

Waddell arrived in Calabar together with a group of Christian Jamaicans to establish the Church of Scotland Mission. In 1834, on the release of all Jamaican slaves from bondage, the Church of Scotland had established a mission in Jamaica, and it was largely through the moving spirits of these freed slaves that the mission to Calabar was organized.[34]

In Calabar conditions were as bad as anywhere on the coast. We have already seen that, by contrast with Bonny and New Calabar, the Efik treated their slaves with scant consideration. Human sacrifice on a large and ostentatious scale, associated with the death of chiefs, was prevalent; twin murder was practised; and widows were often forced to remain in total seclusion without washing or changing their clothes for several years. To abolish these practices and the slave trade, as well as to evangelize the people, was the main aim of the Church of Scotland missionaries. Their mission was granted land between Duke Town and Henshaw Town by King Eyamba V of Duke Town, who with King Eyo Honesty of Creek Town was the most important ruler of Calabar at the time. Shortly after the mission's arrival a leading chief died in Duke Town, and despite the intervention of the missionaries many slaves were killed to accompany him on his eternal journey. In 1847 King Eyamba himself died—this was the signal for large-scale sacrifice.

In Creek Town the missionaries were more sympathetically received. King Eyo Honesty cleared a site for a mission house and school. Pressure from both the missionaries and legitimate traders forced the Calabar chiefs to conduct sacrifices at the death of any of their number more and more secretly. In 1850 ten ship captains, three surgeons and two missionaries met in the mission house at Creek Town to form 'A Society for the Suppression of Human Sacrifices in Calabar'. They wrote to both king and chiefs to inform them that all friendly intercourse with them would cease until the practice was discontinued. As a result an Egbo society law was passed on 15th February 1850, abolishing human sacrifice. This was not always easy to maintain. The real test was to come later in 1858 when King Eyo Honesty himself died after a long reign. Not one man was sacrificed!

The history of the Niger Mission, which was the third prong of missionary attack in Nigeria, once again illustrates the combination of commercial and philanthrophic interests that so often went hand in hand in West Africa.[35] Before the highly successful expedition up the Niger in 1854, led by Dr Baikie, little headway had been made on the Niger. In 1848 an American Negro and the principal of the Fourah Bay Institution in Freetown did lead a mission to the Delta to try to resettle 100 freed Igbo slaves. But the King of Bonny refused them permission and instead they were sent to Calabar. Baikie's expedition was to mark the foundation of one of the most successful missions in West Africa, the Niger Mission, the first to start off with an entirely African-staffed mission, following the earlier recommendations of Schön.

The background to the Niger Mission was the highly successful expedition up the Niger and Benue in 1854. The British Government, whose appetite for expeditions up the Niger had been damped by the 1841 failure, was stimulated to a further trial by despatches sent by the great German explorer, Heinrich Barth. Still interested in the country around the Niger, and hoping that it would be possible to open up trade across the Sahara in sufficient volume to supplant the trans-desert slave trade estimated at 10,000 per year,[36] the British government had sent James Richardson with two Germans, Barth and Overweg, across the desert for reports on the general conditions in these countries on what was known as the Central African Mission. Richardson and Overweg died, but Barth covered hundreds of miles in northern Nigeria and wrote eventually a voluminous and fascinating book describing with remarkable observation and scholarship the geography, history and ethnology of the peoples he encountered.[37]

In 1852 a despatch from Barth informed the British government that he had crossed the Benue. He speculated that this was the same river as the Tshadda that flowed into the Niger at Lokoja. To ascertain this, and to promote once more trade with the interior, the government financed an expedition to sail up the Tshadda to see if in fact it was the Benue. The expedition originally mooted by Barth[38] was of deepest significance for the future of European commercial interests in West Africa, for not one European died on the 900 miles' journey into the interior to Yola.[39] The use of quinine as a prophylactic against malaria showed that life was possible for Europeans in the interior of Africa. From this date, as much as any other, can be traced the growth of effective British interest in the hinterland of Nigeria, which was eventually to lead to the establishment of a British protectorate over Nigeria and the loss of sovereignty by the various African kingdoms and states that comprised it.

While Baikie and other members of the expedition occupied themselves with the more mundane tasks of the expedition, Crowther set about reconnoitring the sites for the future Niger Mission, at Onitsha and Lokoja amongst others. The subsequent history of these missions and their associated trading stations belongs to the next chapter.

The activities of these early missionaries were to have the most profound influence on the future of southern Nigeria. In the north, of course, they came up against the barrier of Islam, and were able to make little progress except in non-Muslim areas.

Before the arrival of these missionaries, traders, the only other representatives of European culture, had made remarkably little impact on the societies with which they conducted their commerce. New consumer habits were naturally developed as a result of both the slave and the oil trade, but even with the new economic régime brought about by the commercialization of palm-oil, the Delta societies remained fundamentally the same. Certainly the traders never sought to alter this situation. The missionaries, by contrast, came out with the deliberate intention not only of changing the economic habits of a predominantly slave-trading society, but of converting it to a completely new way of life: that of Christ. These missionaries came from a society deeply convinced that their religion and their mode of life, especially with its new benefits of industrialization, were superior to anything else in the world.[40] When they arrived in Africa they quickly came to the conclusion that there was nothing good in indigenous African religion. Almost from the start they condemned the indigenous religions in all their aspects, and required of the African conversion not only to a new religion, but to a completely new way of life. For this they have been frequently attacked, for in so doing they destroyed many of the riches of African culture, in particular its ritual art. On the other hand, it must be said in defence of the missionaries that they made a correct appreciation of the fact that West African religions were much more closely integrated with West African cultures than Victorian Christianity with the rest of Victorian culture. To destroy the one effectively it was essential to destroy the other. In this missionaries were later to be opposed by the administrators, with their policy of indirect rule through traditional institutions. The fact that many Nigerians today still largely retain their traditional religious world view even when they are practising Christians is in part due to the fact that the missionaries were never able fully to carry out their policy of effacing not only traditional religion, but the entire culture with which it was so intimately bound up.

The most powerful factor of change introduced by these early missionaries was Western education. In traditional society the wealth and power that education could bring introduced education as a new indicator of status. Later, when the occupation of Nigeria by the British brought about a great demand for indigenous employees for the new administration, the benefits of Christian education were seen to be very great. Christian education and knowledge of the English language also gave common ground to members of many of the widely differing groups of which Nigeria is composed. It was from these early converts that the first African élite to gain the respect of the white man emerged. It was this élite which was to provide the leading members of the professional and commercial world, and which ultimately was to produce the leaders of the nationalist movement for self-government and independence.

10 The Growth of Legitimate Trade

In 1851, Kosoko, King of Lagos, was forced off his throne by the British on the grounds of his slave-trading activities and replaced by his more tractable uncle, Akitoye. Three years later, *The Pleiad* sailed up the Niger without a single European member of the crew succumbing to malaria. Both these events may be taken as symbolic of the increasing attraction to Britain of the Nigerian region for trade.

In the one case the installation of a king not only sympathetic to British interests but also largely dependent on Britain for his authority, in place of one openly hostile to her, was a classic example of nineteenth-century colonial expansion; in the other it was proved that life beyond the coast was possible for Europeans and this diverted attention from the coastal states to the supposed wealth of the interior. Nigerian rulers now faced a Britain openly prepared to interfere in their politics if they proved hostile to her trading interests. This becomes increasingly clear from the activities of the British Consuls in the years between 1850 and 1865, and makes the subsequent recommendations of the famous 1865 Select Committee that the British government should withdraw from the West Coast seem on the surface quite paradoxical.

The gradual opening-up of the interior to direct trading relations between African producer and European buyer, and the consequent breakdown of the monopoly of coastal trade held by the Delta middlemen and the Liverpool traders, were to produce a crisis in Delta politics. In this period much of the thinking of the representatives of the British on the West Coast was on the lines that if trade was to be carried on to advantage, then the highest authority in the land would have to be not the African chief, but the British government. This was a view that evoked considerable opposition in Britain, not only from commercial and humanitarian circles, but also from the government itself. The Treasury and the Colonial Office approached imperial expansion with great parsimony, agreeing to acquire colonies only if it was clear that they could support their administration from locally derived revenues. This opposition to any colonial enterprise that might prove a burden to

6. Niger Delta oil markets in the nineteenth century

the British budget crystallized in the findings of the Select Committee of 1865.[1]

By 1850 British trading interests were being concentrated in two regions of what is now Nigeria: Lagos, the gateway to the rich forests of Yorubaland; and the Delta ports, which were the outlet for the trade of the interior of eastern Nigeria. The chief export was still palm-oil. The slave trade became progressively less important as the African middlemen of the Delta found it more profitable to export palm-oil.[2] Only in the area around Lagos where a steady supply of slaves, mainly prisoners taken in the Yoruba civil wars, continued to reach the coast, was it still of a serious nature. However, in both Yorubaland and the

Delta hinterland the internal demand for slaves rose as a result of the expansion of legitimate trade. Labourers were required to gather the palmnuts, porters to carry oil to the coast. Sir Richard Burton informed the British Parliamentary Select Committee on Africa in 1864 that legitimate trade had led to an increased demand for slaves as porters. Thus legitimate trade, which the abolitionists hoped would prove a substitute for the slave trade, was actually responsible for its increase.[8]

During the fifties the Delta was pre-eminent in the palm-oil trade, and Bonny was its richest port. The oil was prepared in the markets of the interior by boiling the husks in water and skimming off the result-ant oil. It was then transported to Lagos or the Delta ports. In the 1855–6 season the Delta exported 25,060 tons of oil, which was over half the total quantity of oil exported from Africa. Of this quantity, 16,124 tons were sold by Bonny and its rival New Calabar; 4,000 by Old Calabar; and 2,280 by Brass. However, by the end of the fifties Lagos, now under the docile rule of Dosunmu, paid off earlier British interven-tion by exporting over 20,000 tons.[4]

The oil trade was monopolized by the middlemen of the Delta, who prevented any contact between the producers and the white merchants who came mostly from Liverpool. These merchants supplied the middlemen with credit in the form of trade goods, which were taken up to the markets of the interior and exchanged for palm-oil, and to a lesser extent ivory, timber and bees-wax. Credit goods, which were known as 'trust', were often supplied up to the value of £5,000 to reputable middlemen for as long a period as a year. There was no real form of money though Spanish dollars were generally accepted. The value of goods was measured variously in the different ports. In Bonny, for instance, they were equated to iron bars worth about five shillings each.[5] A wide range of goods, particularly cloths, guns, beads, lead and copper rods, were used in exchange. Vast profits were made by the Liverpool merchants through their monopoly. They fobbed off second-rate goods to the Africans who had no standards of comparison, and often sold them bizarre second-hand clothes pretending that they were those worn by the aristocracy in England. We should not laugh there-fore at the amused descriptions by contemporary travellers of the pretentious attire of many African kings, for it was as often as not encouraged by the white traders themselves with high profit as the primary motive.

Basically the control of the standards of trade was in the hands of the African authorities, though this became less and less the case with the interference of the British Consuls. The palm-oil traders were as rough a lot as the old slave traders, and well deserved their title 'Palm Oil Ruffians'. The African chiefs could not actually bring these traders before their own courts, so they resorted to the expedient of imposing collective punishment on the European community through the banning of trade. This was fairly effective, since conditions on the Coast were such that most traders were very anxious to get back to Europe as quickly as possible, and could stomach no delays. The ban on trade was always absolute because of the strict control African chiefs exercised over their subjects. There was no 'scabbing' on the African part, to use a modern trade-union term. On the other hand the Europeans found it difficult to combine effectively, since whenever a European community stuck out for lower prices, there was usually one of their number willing to trade at the African's price.

In 1854 Africans and Europeans in Bonny combined to deal with the problems of local trade by setting up a 'Court of Equity' on which both Bonny middlemen and European super-cargoes were represented. Traders offending against the regulations of the court, which was presided over by a different white supercargo in monthly rotation, were subject to fines, which had to have the approval of the King of Bonny. If such a trader refused to pay, a collective boycott was placed on him until such time as he did. This court was so successful that soon similar ones were instituted at New Calabar, Akassa, Benin River, Old Calabar, Brass and later Opobo. Despite this healthy development in the regulation of coastal trade, the European traders still used the power of their local Consul to force their own terms on African chiefs. Indeed the growth of British consular power is the most characteristic trend in relations between Britain and Nigeria in this period, and is epitomized by the career of the first of Britain's consuls, John Beecroft.[6]

In 1849 John Beecroft was appointed Her Britannic Majesty's Consul for the Bights of Benin and Biafra. As Dr Dike has written, it was he who 'laid the foundations of British power in Nigeria and initiated the politics which were to characterize the consular period of Nigerian history'.[7] His very remarkable career in West Africa began on Fernando Po, when it was occupied by Britain as a base for the suppression of the slave trade in 1827. When it was abandoned by Britain, he stayed on to look after the interests of the liberated slaves who had been settled there. In 1843 he was appointed Governor of the island by Spain. Already he had acquired an unrivalled knowledge of the coast. In 1835 he had travelled as far up the Niger as Idah, and not one of the Europeans on his expedition died. In 1840 he had entered the Benin River and proved that it was not the principal outlet of the Niger. In the following two years he had led further expeditions up the Cross River. He thus came to know most of the coastal chiefs intimately, and was deeply respected by them.

From 1844 to 1849 the British Navy employed him on various political missions, so that he became the obvious choice for appointment as first British Consul for the Bights of Benin and Biafra. During his six years as Consul he was to wield immense influence in the Delta and farther up the coast in Lagos. From the outset he was bent on involving Britain in the affairs of the coastal states, for as he saw it important British interests were at stake. He therefore interfered constantly in local politics and advocated the eventual take-over of the coastal states by Britain.

Soon after he was appointed Consul, English traders in Bonny complained to him about their treatment at the hands of King William Dappa Pepple.[8] Beecroft himself was in favour of putting an end to what he considered to be Pepple's persecution of British traders, some of whom had actually been murdered on their way up the New Calabar River in 1847. Pepple argued that he had nothing to do with these murders nor the insecurity on the New Calabar River, for both were the responsibility of an important priest, Awante, who was 'jew jew' and therefore outside his jurisdiction.[9] Beecroft paid little attention to Pepple's complaints about the series of treaties he had signed with Britain agreeing to the abolition of the slave trade and the protection of British interests; these had not been ratified nor, more important, had the subsidy promised him been paid. In the case of Calabar and the Cameroons, Pepple complained that those treaties had been ratified and the subsidies paid. Why not his? His bitterness was increased by the fact that his rival and neighbour, New Calabar, was still trading in slaves and making a profit out of it. Whereas warships could block the Bonny River with ease, New Calabar, like Brass, was concealed in the creeks.

In these circumstances British traders feared a recurrence of past disturbances, so Beecroft came in to settle the dispute. He summoned Pepple to come on board his warship, which Pepple naturally refused to do, inviting Beecroft to come to his own palace, an invitation Beecroft eventually accepted. Though a treaty was signed between the King and the Consul on 3rd October 1850, regulating conditions of trade,[10] no real improvement in relations resulted from this visit. Rather it made Pepple deeply suspicious of British intentions. He was in a difficult position, faced with threats of British intervention from without, and the hostility of the party backing Alali, the former Regent, from within. Alali was only too eager to exploit any difficulties that might come King Pepple's way. The net result of this show of force on the part of the Consul was merely to increase Pepple's antagonism towards the British.

The following year Beecroft took what was to prove a crucial step in Britain's involvement with Nigeria and deposed Kosoko, the slave-trading King of Lagos. Kosoko's uncle, Akitoye, was placed on the throne after having guaranteed to suppress the slave trade in Lagos. The British government took this dramatic step largely because Kosoko was proving one of the major obstacles to the suppression of the slave trade on that part of the coast. Furthermore his neighbour, King Gezo of Dahomey, had told Beecroft that he would not give up slave trading while Kosoko still indulged in it. The missionaries at Abeokuta had exerted great pressure on the home government in favour of deposing Kosoko, for while he reigned there was little hope of legitimate trade through the port of Lagos.

The Kosoko dispute has usually been painted as one between a bad slave-trading king and his peace-loving Uncle Akitoye whose throne he had usurped.[11] This is an oversimplification of a very complex dynastic dispute, which dates back to 1811 when the Oba of Lagos died and his second son Adele succeeded him instead of Esilogun who, as eldest son, felt himself to be the rightful heir. This led to a series of disputes and the eventual expulsion of Adele by Esilogun in 1821. Adele turned to the British at Badagry, and in 1825 tried to effect his return with the help of the Navy. It was not until 1833, however, that Adele actually became king again, this time with the aid of the Oba of Benin, his overlord. He died the next year and was succeeded by his son Oluwole, who died in 1841 without issue. This led to rival claims, chiefly between Oluwole's cousin Kosoko and his uncle Akitoye. As it was, Akitoye was crowned King of Lagos by the Oba of Benin. Naturally Kosoko resented this and worked hard to undermine the power of Akitoye, and in 1845 he expelled him. Akitoye made an alliance with Abeokuta, in an effort to re-establish himself, and was financed by a well-known slave trader, Domingo José, which, as Ajayi rightly points out,[12] destroys the picture that Akitoye was an anti-slaver. Had he been King of Lagos at the time when the missionaries and British traders were trying to promote trade between Abeokuta and the coast, he would just as likely as Kosoko have been an instigator of the slave trade. As it was, both missionaries and Consul saw in him their main hope for establishing a friendly ruler at Lagos.

The missionaries lobbied Palmerston at home, and in due course instructions were sent to Beecroft to deal with the situation in Lagos. He visited the missionaries in Abeokuta, and then went to Badagry, where he held discussions with Akitoye, who was already growing unpopular with the local chiefs. Indeed by this time most of Badagry's chiefs were on Kosoko's side, so that Beecroft was able to take Akitoye to Fernando Po on the grounds that he would otherwise be attacked by the Badagry people. In Fernando Po, Akitoye agreed that if he were restored he would outlaw slavery in Lagos. In 1851, on Beecroft's return, Kosoko's guns fired on a ship flying a flag of truce, and in retaliation Beecroft attempted to seize Lagos with a small naval force, but Kosoko was too well defended and compelled him to retreat. This premature invasion infuriated the British government, particularly Palmerston, the Foreign Secretary, who had already written: 'If Lagos, instead of being a nest for slave traders, were to become a port for lawful trade, it would become an important outlet for the commerce of a large range of country in the interior, and instead of being a den of barbarism, would become a diffusing centre of civilization.'[13] Instructions had already gone out to the Commodore of the West African Squadron to effect the capture of Lagos, and to have Beecroft instigate a half-cock invasion was humiliating to Palmerston, who was already under fire from Parliament over his West African policy. Fortunately for Palmerston the squadron retrieved the situation by taking Lagos. A month later Kosoko was expelled and Akitoye installed. The latter signed a treaty abolishing slavery, guaranteeing missionary activity and according Britain most-favoured-nation terms. His power was considerably reduced compared with that of Kosoko, and what amounted to a British Protectorate was in fact established. A vice-consul was appointed to supervise the execution of the treaty and the Navy promised support if Kosoko should attempt to recapture Lagos, as seemed very probable at the time.

In the same year Beecroft found cause to intervene in the slave rebellion in Old Calabar. The Efik, unlike the Ijo states, treated their slaves harshly, and excluded them entirely from participation in the politics and commerce of their community. The majority were relegated to plantations in the interior, from which they might be seized at any time for sacrifice. However, the preachings of the missionaries instilled in them a desire for freedom and in one plantation on the Kwa River, to which all in trouble with Egbo fled, a political organization called The Blood Men sprang up among the slaves. Several of its members were arrested in Duke Town in 1851. This was the signal for the first of a number of uprisings. The slaves ravaged the plantations and threatened to invade Duke Town itself unless they were released. The white supercargoes, fearing a stoppage in trade if there were no authority in Duke Town, called in Beecroft, who effected a settlement that modified certain aspects of Egbo goverment, but certainly did not put an end to the slaves' grievances. His contention was that without Egbo there would be chaos, and chaos would of course impede the trade of British merchants. The following year Beecroft even presided over the election of the new King of Old Calabar.

In 1852 an event of momentous importance took place. It was also one that was later to necessitate the increasing attention of the Consul. The

British government agreed to subsidize a small fleet of steamers owned by Macgregor Laird, which were to form the basis of a regular mail service between Liverpool and West Africa. The introduction of this new service had two important consequences. First, it allowed a large number of small traders to come out to West Africa, who would otherwise have been unable to, since they would never have had the capital to finance a ship. Secondly, it introduced into the Delta competition against the great Liverpool houses. The small traders found that they could undercut the established and highly monopolistic prices of the old firms; furthermore the African middlemen found it cheaper to export oil direct to Liverpool on the mailships, rather than through the old Liverpool firms. By 1856 there were nearly 200 firms operating in the Delta in place of the few houses trading before the inauguration of this service. This caused great bitterness amongst the old-established trading houses who had sunk much capital into their West African trade; it also opened the eyes of the African to the extortionate profits and shoddy goods these houses had so long palmed off on them. Relations between the African middlemen and Liverpool traders were never amicable again.

In 1853 Beecroft's jurisdiction as Consul was restricted to the Bight of Bonny, since there was now a Consul permanently resident in Lagos. He soon had business in Bonny again. The story of the exile of King William Dappa Pepple is a long and complicated one.[14] Its broad outlines, in so far as it affected trade relations with Britain, must suffice here, for this incident confirmed that Britain was prepared to use action such as she had employed in Lagos to further or secure her trading interests. In May 1852, King William Dappa Pepple had a stroke. He then appointed the two senior chiefs of the Manila Pepple house, his main basis of support, as regents. The supercargoes agreed to recognize their authority, but the Anna Pepple house immediately protested at this delegation of power. The British Consul was then brought in to settle the dispute and after meeting with the chiefs and the supercargoes, approved the regency. Pepple soon recovered and resumed his powers. However he now antagonized not only the Anna Pepple house, who were naturally hostile to him, but also the supercargoes and some of his own supporters, through his policy of forcing Bonny traders to take goods on trust from him at excessive rates before he would let them trade in the interior, where he himself as a result was able to trade on more favourable terms. This also antagonized the white supercargoes who had lost business through it. Tension rose so high in Bonny that some European gigs were attacked and considerable property destroyed. The supercargoes were now suspicious that Pepple himself had engineered these attacks. Pepple now faced a

divided kingdom and hostile supercargoes. He attempted to divert
their attention by an attack on his powerful and prosperous neighbour,
Amakiri of New Calabar. This attack was a failure, since the Anna
Pepple faction refused to join the war party. The supercargoes, concerned about the effects on trade, sent speedily for Beecroft who at once
came to settle the dispute. Pepple was exiled through the Court of
Equity over which Beecroft presided. The official British version of the
event was that not only did the chiefs want him exiled, but that he
himself had begged the Consul to give him safe conduct to Fernando Po.
A more realistic view is that, however much even the Anna Pepple
faction were opposed to him, they did not want him exiled since it was
usually difficult to replace a deposed monarch, and furthermore, traders in the interior might not trade with them once Pepple had gone.[15] A
convention was signed by the chiefs and the Consul whereby it was
agreed that succeeding Bonny kings should not engage in trade, thus
embodying, as G. I, Jones has put it, 'the consul's conviction that the
king should be concerned with government and not with trade, and
that King William Dappa Pepple's downfall was due to his neglect of
this principle.'[16]

Soon after Pepple's departure for England his successor died and
poisoning was suspected, though an English doctor vouched that he
had died of natural causes. Civil war flared up and the Anna Pepple
factions took over the town, destroying in the process most of the
property of the house of William Dappa Pepple. Beecroft's successor,
Consul Lynslager, in a surprisingly conciliatory tone, treated with the
Anna Pepple faction for the institution of a regency council of four. This
was not a success. As Consul Hutchinson wrote later in his book *Ten
Years' Wandering among the Ethiopians*: 'The experience of years has
taught the British as well as the Native Traders that this government has been no more than a mockery and delusion. . . .'[17] Co-
ordination of government was so weak, and the authority of the regents
treated with such contempt that very soon the European traders who
had sought the removal of Pepple were demanding his return. By 1859
they were acutely aware that no one but the legitimate king would be
accepted in Bonny, and arrangements were made for his restoration. In
1861 he returned to Bonny having been paid compensation of £4,520.
He was accompanied by a number of English men and women who
had accepted positions in his court, but since they were not paid they
soon left. The British Consul and the supercargoes had learnt that
they had to be careful about interfering with the institutions of
African government, unless they were prepared to take them over
altogether.

In 1855 a critical situation developed in Calabar as a result of the introduction of open competition into local trade. The Christian Africans who had come from Sierra Leone to settle there attempted to help the local middlemen avoid the extortionate trading terms of the Liverpool supercargoes, who complained about this to the new Consul Lynslager (Beecroft died in 1854), saying that King Eyo and the Sierra Leoneans were shipping oil direct to England before paying the 'trust' they owed them. Consul Lynslager warned King Eyo to pay off his 'trust' before he shipped oil to England on his own account.

The next year the Consul destroyed Old Town Calabar on the grounds that it had broken the law against human sacrifice. In Old Town, where the Church of Scotland had established a mission station, the Chief, Willy Tom Robins, had ordered a large number of people, including his wives, to be put in chains as hostages for what seemed to be his impending death. When he did die many people were sacrificed, and, since this was a breach of the agreement between Calabar and the Consul, Lynslager effected the complete destruction of the town. This incurred bitter protests from the Church of Scotland missionaries, who believed that the white traders had merely wanted to make an example of Old Town, where they had not trading posts, so as to bring Duke Town and Creek Town into line. However, Lynslager sent despatches to say that he had destroyed Old Town on the invitation of the missionaries.

The situation in Calabar deteriorated rapidly. The antagonism between the supercargoes and the Sierra Leoneans became so acrimonious that the whites took to beating up the 'interlopers'. There was little that the divided authorities of Calabar could do. (It paid to have a centralized monarchy such as Bonny in cases like this.) Matters came to a head in 1857, when King Eyo Honesty actually chartered a boat, the *Olinda*, to ship oil direct to England. Lynslager's successor, Consul Hutchinson, prevented the ship from setting sail on the grounds that Eyo owed the equivalent of £18,000 in trust. Significantly the trust was owed to the Consul's former employers, Messrs. Hearn and Cuthbertson. The Foreign Office was annoyed by this incident, and three years later, with evidence of Hutchinson's corruption mounting, it ordered a Commission of Enquiry into his conduct, as a result of which he was transferred. This was a severe blow to Liverpool interests in Calabar.

Despite these dramatic shows of force, the British Consuls had considerable difficulty in enforcing the punishments they chose to inflict on people who interfered with trade. The local rulers did not consider that the British Consuls had any right to force free trade on them, and merely recognized that when warships were around the safest policy was to bow to British demands. Without warships the Consuls found it virtually impossible to obtain payment of fines, as in 1862, when some

Benin River groups refused to pay a fine for damaging a trader's store. It was clear that effective regulation of trade in their favour could only be secured if some form of protectorate were established over the Coastal states. However much the Consul might desire this, there was still considerable opposition in Britain to any extension of overseas responsibilities.

So far, both in the Delta and in Lagos, European trade had been restricted to the coast. Trade with the interior remained almost exclusively in the hands of the African middlemen, and in the case of the lands beyond the Niger and Benue, no effective trade relations had been established. Baikie's voyage of 1854 changed this situation.[18] Not only did he prove that European life was possible in the interior, but he travelled as far as Yola on the Benue, a distance of over 1,400 km. from the coast. In 1857 the British Government made a contract with Macgregor Laird to maintain a steamer on the River Niger for five years. A subsidy of £8,000 was offered for the first year, diminishing annually by £500. Laird placed Baikie in charge of this expedition, which was in fact a failure, since the *Dayspring* in which they sailed was wrecked on the Juju Rock at Jebba. Nevertheless, as Dike has written: 'Just as 1854 marked the end of the era of exploration, so in 1857 the traders took over where the explorers left off. Seen in this light the voyage of the *Dayspring* marked the beginning of an era in Nigerian history.'[19]

Factories or trading posts were established at Aboh, Onitsha and Lokoja on the confluence of the Benue and Niger. Laird even issued small copper coins, very popular, to replace cumbersome cowries. Trade was not brisk to begin with, amounting to less than £9,000 in the third year. Laird had to contend with much opposition. His ventures were resented by the Liverpool supercargoes as much as they had resented his earlier introduction of the mail steamers. But whereas the latter venture benefited the African middleman, his attempts to trade direct with the markets of the interior were a deadly threat to the livelihood of the middlemen themselves. Thus Laird had ranged against him both African middlemen and Liverpool supercargoes, who now combined to wreck his commercial adventures. Attacks on the steamers by hostile 'natives' were often alleged by Laird's traders to have been instigated by the Liverpool supercargoes acting through the Delta middlemen, who had long-standing contacts with the peoples of the interior. Heavy guns were positioned at strategic points on the river, and the steamers frequently came under severe fire. Sometimes the steamers were even stopped and boarded, despite punitive measures taken by naval gunboats. In 1859 a number of villages 100 km. inland were shelled for their part in the attack on the *Rainbow* on her return from a successful voyage up the Niger.

By 1860 Laird had largely convinced the Government that inland trade could pay, and the Government in return offered to escort his ships up the Niger. The instructions to this effect were not carried out by the local naval commander, who felt that the risks were too great to justify such a convoy. As a result Laird's expedition was a disastrous failure, involving heavy loss of capital. From then on until 1870 escorts were provided.

In the meantime Baikie, who had been wrecked in the *Dayspring* on Juju Rock at Jebba, installed himself at Lokoja near the site of the model farm, where he took on the role of unofficial consul, and set about exploring the possibilities of trade with the north.[20] His intentions are best described in his own words: 'The position I have now selected may possibly prove a permanent British Commercial site; and it is most favourably placed both as a convenient rendezvous and as a centre for trade. A direct route to Nupe is now being opened, and other roads lead also to Zaria and the interior of Hausa. As soon as I get a little settled I shall see about the possibility of a direct route to Lagos.'[21] With the assistance of Lieut. Glover he did establish a direct route to Lagos and won the friendship of Masaba, King or Etsu, of Nupe. Baikie demonstrated clearly that the Niger was the real highway to the interior, including Hausaland, of whose potentials Clapperton and Barth had already written. Baikie conceived his task as helping to secure for Britain a commanding position in Africa, and when the Foreign Office ordered his return home, he refused, both because he felt his work was not then complete, and also because he was in debt to King Masaba. In 1862 he trekked to Bida, Zaria and Kano, and died two years later on his way back to England.

Throughout the lands of the Niger valley there was a growing hostility to the new-style traders, stimulated by their enemies the middlemen and Liverpool traders. Though Laird's factories were attacked and destroyed, by the early sixties trade with the interior was well on its way to supplanting the old coastal trade. By 1865 the executor of the will of Macgregor Laird, who had died in 1861, promoted a new Company of African Merchants to trade with the interior. The British government even promised a subsidy. The ferocity of the attacks by Liverpool traders on this Government decision are a testimony to the seriousness of the economic threat this company and those like it represented to them. After 1865 the pattern of trade in the Delta changed radically, and British penetration of the interior became more and more systematic.

Intimately bound up with this expansion of trade with the interior was the founding of the Niger Mission. The 1857 expedition led by Dr Baikie in the *Dayspring* was again a combination of trading, govern-

ment and evangelical interests. On board was the by now well-
travelled Rev. Samuel Crowther, together with the Rev. J. C. Taylor
and a party of catechists, bearing a commission from the C.M.S. to
found the Niger Mission.[22] At Onitsha both trader and churchman
negotiated with the Obi or King for land, and the Rev. J. C. Taylor, a
freed Igbo slave, was left in charge of the new Onitsha mission station.
Crowther sailed upstream founding small stations at both Gbebe and
Lokoja, after which his work was called to a halt for a year when the
Dayspring ran aground on Juju Rock at Jebba. The only mission station
to be really successful was Taylor's mission at Onitsha where a school
was opened. Soon delegates from many parts of Igboland were asking
for stations to be opened in their own towns and villages. The difficulties of the early years of the Niger Mission, which is remarkable as an
almost exclusively African enterprise, were largely the result of its
close association with trading interests. The Mission was dependent on
the interior traders for both transport and supplies, and inevitably in
the minds of the local people it became identified with the traders they
so hated. Thus, in 1859 and 1860, attacks on the trading posts at
Onitsha brought the mission's work to a standstill. Attempts were
made to make it independent of the traders, but this was almost
impossible, since the mission relied on them for both supplies and
communication with the outside world.

Despite these early vicissitudes, Venn, the Secretary of the C.M.S.,
did not lose faith in Crowther and in 1864, against considerable opposi-
tion from the Yoruba Mission under Townsend, he nominated him as
Bishop of 'Western Equatorial Africa beyond the Queen's Dominions'.
Crowther had been reluctant to accept this great office, but Venn was
insistent despite the irate and threatening letters of a disappointed
Townsend who had long coveted the episcopate now given to Crowther.
Venn was convinced that, with the heavy mortality of Europeans, an
African mission was the only solution. Unfortunately Townsend's disappointment at not being selected brought into mission affairs an early
element of racial bitterness. Thus whilst the Queen's Dominions such
as Lagos and Freetown were excluded from Crowther's diocese, so too
was the Yoruba Mission at Abeokuta as a special concession to Townsend and the European missionaries.[23]

The fifteen years from 1850 to 1865 saw a general expansion of
missionary activity throughout southern Nigeria. Though the Church
of Scotland had been unsuccessful in its earlier efforts to open a mission
at Bonny, it established stations up the Cross River. The Yoruba
Mission opened stations at Oyo, Iseyin, Saki, Ogbomosho, Ijaye, Oke-
Odan and Isaga. The study of indigenous languages had reached
impressive proportions: by 1851 most of the New Testament had been

translated into Yoruba; in 1862 Bowen of the Baptist Mission supplemented Crowther's earlier work by publishing a *Grammar and Vocabulary of the Yoruba Language*. The Reverend S. W. Koelle of the C.M.S. published in 1854 a *Grammar of the Bornu or Kanuri Language*. In 1849 Hope Waddell published his vocabulary of the Efik language which was supplemented by further studies by his colleague Goldie. In 1862 Schön revised his *Grammar of the Hausa Langauge*, helped by a Hausa youth whom Barth had brought back with him from northern Nigeria. In 1864 Crowther published his *Grammar and Vocabulary of the Nupe Langauge*. The role of missionaries in promoting Western education was cardinal in the history of Nigeria. As early as 1859 the Yoruba Mission had published a newspaper called *Iwe-Irohin*, giving news in Yoruba.

In Lagos the overthrow of Kosoko in 1851 had been motivated largely by the exigencies of suppressing the slave trade on that part of the coast; the later annexation of the town was undoubtedly the result of Britain's need for a stable base from which to regulate her trade with the interior. Only against the background of the internal instability of Lagos and the inter-tribal warfare in Yorubaland, which continually interfered with trade, can this expansion of British territorial interests, despite severe opposition at home, be understood.

In 1853 a full-time Consul was appointed for Lagos: Benjamin Campbell, the first to hold this office, was certainly more than a consular representative of the British government; he had a large say in local affairs, in which Akitoye acquiesced since he owed his position to the British. Indeed, on his arrival, Campbell found Lagos on the verge of civil war. Kosoko, through his strong faction in Lagos, was preparing insurrection against Akitoye. Campbell promised naval protection, should Kosoko attack. Cunningly Akitoye precipitated the crisis by attacking Kosoko's men, so that the Navy in effect gave support to aggression by Akitoye, when their instructions had been to offer defensive protection only. Though censured by the Admiralty, Campbell decided that the best way of defending Lagos against Kosoko was attack, and he even sent an expedition to seek out Kosoko in his retreat at Epe. A further indication of the new Consul's power was the fact that in 1853, when Akitoye died, he arranged the installation of Dosunmu, who was likely to prove tractable, before any of the other chiefs even knew of Akitoye's death.

Trade with the interior prospered, though Kosoko proved a major problem through his constant interference with trading canoes plying between Lagos and Abeokuta. Such was Consul Campbell's insistence on the priority of trade that in 1854, against severe opposition from the missionaries at Abeokuta, he completed a treaty with Kosoko, allowing

him the port of Palma and a subsidy of 1,000 dollars on condition that
he gave up his slaving activities. He installed two pro-Kosoko chiefs at
Badagry by force, despite the bitter opposition of the Egba who used the
port as an outlet for their own trade. The missionaries, remembering
the former role of Kosoko, could not easily contemplate any treaty
made with him, especially one as advantageous to him as this. But
Campbell had his reasons—Kosoko alone was sufficiently influential
to extend legitimate trade beyond its present restricted frontiers with
Egbaland. The C.M.S. mission lobbied against Campbell at home;
Campbell in retaliation despatched a petition against the missionaries
signed by leading traders and the local Methodist missionary.[24] The
dispute was certainly not one-sided. Campbell, with some justification,
felt that the C.M.S. under Townsend interfered too much with the
politics of Egbaland and Lagos, which he considered his own proper
province. The missionaries felt that their own ideal state, which was to
lead the way for the regeneration of Africa through legitimate commerce, should not be sacrificed to the interests of men like Kosoko.

In Abeokuta, too, the missionaries had their own troubles. They had
a slaving faction to deal with, and felt that any compromise of principles in Lagos would facilitate the slave trade. By 1856, however,
relations between the missionaries and the Consul became closer,
when Campbell forced Dosunmu to expel Madam Tinubu, a powerful
middleman operating between Lagos and Abeokuta, who was suspected of being a surreptitious slave dealer as well as a party to the
1856 rising against Dosunmu. Moreover, the missionaries had so
encouraged the growth of cotton and palm-oil in Egbaland that trade
boomed in Lagos to Campbell's considerable satisfaction. In 1856
alone, 15,000 tons of oil were exported from Egbaland.

In 1857 the French launched a scheme whereby 'free' labour was
exported from Ouidah to Martinique in the French West Indies. A
contract had been granted by Napoleon III of France to the House of
Régis Aîné allowing it to obtain labourers for work on its plantations on
the condition that they should be volunteers who would be paid for
their work. Payment was made to local chiefs for each labourer
enlisted, and no questions were asked about his provenance. To the
African this was indistinguishable from the slave trade. Both Consul
Campbell and the missionaries associated this scheme with the
deterioration of the situation in the interior: tension increased between
the Egba and Dahomey, and in 1858 war broke out once again between
Ibadan and Ijebu. On 18th April 1859 Atiba, Alafin of Oyo, died and
was succeeded, contrary to custom, by his son, Adelu, the Crown
Prince.[25] Are Kurunmi, the powerful provincial ruler of Ijaye, refused
to recognize Adelu as Alafin, protesting that he should have committed

suicide on the death of his father in accordance with tradition. Ibadan, anxious to curtail the power of its rival, Ijaye, took up Oyo's cause and recognized Adelu as Alafin. It seemed clear that war would soon break out again, with Ibadan and Oyo facing a grand alliance of Ijaye, Abeokuta, Ilesha and Ilorin. As Ajayi has shown, the issue at stake was the claim of the Are that he controlled the provinces west of the upper reaches of the Ogun river. In 1859 there had been a clash in this region in the important town of Saki, which declared its loyalty to the Alafin. When the Are sent troops to assert his authority they were defeated by the people of Saki, and a number taken prisoner. Then in January 1860, the chief of Okeho, again in this region, agreed to pay tribute to the Alafin rather than to Ijaye. The Alafin and the Are both sent troops to establish their authority in the town, and Ijaye, after initial defeat, took the town and with it several dozen prisoners, whereupon Oyo called on Ibadan for help. Ikorudu and Ijebu Remo, both placed strategically on the trade route to Lagos, declared for Ibadan, thus giving it access to the coast and supplies of arms. Fearing that this civil war would completely disrupt trade in the interior, the new Consul, Brand, sent a Lieutenant Lodder to mediate between Ibadan and Ijaye. This mission was a failure and soon afterwards Ibadan made overtures to Dahomey to support them and thereby avenge their defeat by the Egba in 1851. War broke out at the end of March 1860.[26]

Kosoko naturally took advantage of the situation and was only kept under control by the presence of a gunboat. Trade dwindled and Consul Brand, who succeeded Campbell on his death in 1860, suggested to the Foreign Office that Britain should take over Lagos as a protectorate. The Foreign Office was not unfavourable to this suggestion, fearing that the French, who had sent a delegation to Dosunmu, might try to take over Lagos themselves. Brand survived only a year in Lagos, and his successor Foote went even farther by suggesting that the only ultimate solution to peace would be the introduction of troops, and the stationing of consuls at strategic towns in the interior. This was opposed by the Foreign Office, which was not prepared to undertake such large territorial commitments. Nevertheless, vice-consuls were stationed at Badagry and Lagos. When, soon afterwards, Porto Novo placed an embargo on trade in oil, Foote promptly ordered its bombardment, thereby gaining a treaty guaranteeing freedom of trade for Britain.

The situation for the Egba was serious. On their western flank the Dahomeyans threatened; to the north-east the military power of Ibadan was preparing for another attack, though ominously quiescent. Abeokuta was still the main source of trade for Lagos so that plans were even mooted to supply armed defence for Abeokuta. But McKoskry, the

Vice-Consul for Lagos, who succeeded Foote that same year, had a somewhat different approach to the problem, believing that trade should be extended without favour to any one section of Yorubaland. Thus when a contingent of ten men and one officer arrived in Lagos to teach the Egba the art of military defence in pursuance of Foote's policy, they were diverted to the consular guard in Lagos.[27]

Shortly afterwards the Foreign Office sent the Consul instructions to annex Lagos 'to secure forever the free population of Lagos from the slave traders and kidnappers who formerly oppressed them; to protect and develop the important trade of which their town is the seat; and to exercise an influence on the surrounding tribes which may, it is hoped, be permanently beneficial to the African race'.[28] Comparatively little was made of Britain's interest in trade which had been paramount in the actions of all the consuls from 1851 to 1861 and which had led up to the annexation of Lagos.

Thus, on 30th July 1861, Dosunmu ceded Lagos to Acting Consul McKoskry in return for a pension of £1,030 a year. The handing-over ceremony was concluded by the singing of the British National Anthem by three hundred local schoolchildren, conducted by two missionaries.[29] A Governor of the Colony of Lagos, Henry Stanhope Freeman, was appointed and there began a new era in the history of British relations with that part of the coast, an era which inaugurated the new territory of Nigeria. British interests were firmly established in the town. By 1862 there were sixteen British merchants to one French, two Italian, three German and five Brazilian traders. Half in the guise of humanitarian motives, Britain had gained her first foothold on the Nigerian coast primarily to secure her trade.

The history of Lagos subsequent to its annexation in 1861 is closely bound up with the opening up of the interior, largely because of its most able and aggressive administrator in the sixties, Glover, who had accompanied Baikie on the 1857 expedition organized by Laird, and shared the ideals of both concerning the penetration of the interior and its accessibility to trade.[30]

The annexation of Lagos was accompanied by a deterioration of conditions in the interior. The Ijaye wars flared up once more. Ibadan, with the assistance of Oyo and Borgu, surrounded Ijaye and cut off its supplies from the south. In this situation Freeman, as Governor of Lagos, was placed in a dilemma. He had been instructed not to extend British territory, yet he was also to look after trade interests. Freeman, who was strongly influenced by Glover, his right-hand man as Administrator, was led to believe that much of the blame lay with the Egba side, since they refused to let Ibadan have a road to the coast. He tried to force a vice-consul on them, a move that was quickly rejected by the Egba, who had already seen what happenened to Lagos when a consul took up residence. The missionaries complained to the Colonial Office about this interference, and that department made it known that it was against coercion of the Egba. Freeman however pursued a contrary policy, instituting a blockade on Egba trade and annexing Palma and Lekki from Kosoko in return for a pension. He also annexed Badagry so that he could exact a 4 per cent import duty on all goods to help pay for the administration. In the interests of free trade he even destroyed Epe, where the ruler, Posu, had established himself with the rest of Kosoko's followers who had opposed the cession of Palma and Lekki to the British.

In the interior the situation had become very tense. Are Kurunmi of Ijaye had died, thus depriving that town of its most able leader when it was in the direst of straits owing to the successful siege by the Ibadan. Such was their condition that people from Ijaye were even selling themselves to their allies the Egba in order to obtain food. The Ibadan attacked the Awaye people for the help they had given to besieged Ijaye; whilst the Egba attacked the Ijebu Remo for their help to the Ibadan in the Ijaye war. The Egba captured the important Remo town of Iperu, which gave its name to these new wars. They had the singular advantage of having an American sharpshooter called Pettiford, who had fought in the Ijaye wars, and was reserved for picking off Ibadan chiefs in battle. The war was only settled by the intervention of the Alafin, whose influence in Yorubaland was being rapidly reduced by the civil wars. A curious sidelight on this war was the press battle between the missionaries. Townsend championed the Egba through his *Iwe-Irohin*,[31] whilst Hinderer took the part of Ibadan in the *Anglo-African*.

Trade came almost to a standstill during these wars. The new Lieutenant-Governor, Glover, hoped to expand trade in the interior to the friendly country of Masaba, the Etsu of Nupe. But the inter-tribal wars made this impossible. A further threat came to the Egba from Dahomey in 1863, and at the instigation of Townsend and the C.M.S. prayers were uttered for their deliverance in churches as far afield as Switzerland and Syria. In 1864 the Dahomeyans did attack but were repulsed with great losses.

Peace between Ibadan and the Egba was shortlived. The Egba were jealous of and afraid of the growing power of the Ibadan. The Ibadan likewise resented the heavy tolls exacted by the Egba. In March 1865 the Egba attacked and besieged Ikorodu, a Remo town strategic for Ibadan's supplies from the coast. This was one of the most important incidents in the long history of the Yoruba civil wars, for it was the first time the British from Lagos actually intervened in them. The Ikorodu traders appealed for help to the Governor in Lagos, who had pressures placed on him by Lagos traders to the same end. Glover had come round to the view that the only way to end civil strife and thus promote trade in the interior was armed intervention. He was also convinced that the Egba were at the root of the trouble, since they were determined to prevent Ibadan trading with the coast. On 29th March 1865 he gave the Egba twenty-four hours to withdraw from Ikorodu, then despatched West Indian troops to deal with them. In a quick action, using screaming rockets, the Egba were defeated and British authority was by implication extended far beyond the frontiers of the colony. Not long after, the King of Dahomey sent Glover an embarrassing gift of a flag on which Dahomey was represented as about to pounce on a deer (Abeokuta), held down by Lagos and Ibadan.[32] Soon Glover found occasion to chastise the oft-bombarded King of Porto Novo. As in the Delta and in the interior, Britain was becoming inextricably involved in Nigerian affairs.

It must come therefore as something of a surprise that in 1865 the Select Committee on West Africa recommended the gradual reduction of British commitments on the coast, and declared itself against any further territorial expansion. To understand this one must look to the history of both the West Coast and Britain. In England anti-imperialist sentiment was strong. It was backed up by missionaries like Townsend who resented the intervention of Lagos in the affairs of Abeokuta. Free trade was an article of faith for many traders, both in England and on the coast, though often the first trader to call in the gunboat when his interest was affected would be the most convinced advocate of free trade. Liverpool trading interests were hardly happy as a result of their experience of government interest in the coast. Finally there was still a great gulf between the realities of life on the coast and what the government and parliamentarians imagined it to be. If the years 1850–65 proved nothing else, they convinced Britain's representatives on the Nigerian coast that if the interior were to be opened up to legitimate trade with Britain, then British authority would have to be paramount.

11 Prelude to Alien Rule

From 1865 until the proclamation of the British Protectorate over the Niger Districts in 1885, British interests in Nigeria were concentrated in three separate areas. In Lagos the trading requirements of the merchants of the Colony led to constant interference by the Governor in the affairs of Yorubaland. In the Delta bitter competition for the oil markets between the various states and European traders pushed further the local consul's intervention.

It was however expanding trade in the hinterland of the Delta, with its superb river highway, the Niger, that eventually led Britian to proclaim a Protectorate over the Niger Districts, and thus lay the foundations of modern Nigeria.

Although Britain's official sentiments were against any further commitments in her West African settlements, let alone extension of them, Glover was left in charge of Lagos as Lt.-Governor, and on his past record he was hardly likely to stand aloof from Yoruba politics.[1] Under his rule Lagos became increasingly important in the disputes between the Yoruba states, and Glover soon assumed the role of mediator-in-chief. The peace between Ibadan and her enemies, the Egba and Ijebu, was very uneasy. Glover certainly believed that the Egba bore chief responsibility for tension in the interior because of their persistent blocking of the roads from Ibadan to Lagos. He seemed to have little time for Egba complaints that if the warlike Ibadan received arms, they would be the sufferers. And it hardly seemed to the advantage of either the Egba or the Ijebu middlemen to keep the roads closed. Obviously their fear of arms reaching the Ibadan outweighed the economic advantages of keeping the roads open. In an attempt to force the Egba to open the roads Glover blockaded their supply lines in 1865. This policy was to suffer a reversal the following year, when the various West African settlements were amalgamated under a Governor-in-Chief in Sierra Leone to whom Glover was made responsible as Administrator. Blackhall, the new Governor-in-Chief, was much more in tune with official attitudes in Britain and called off Glover's blockade on the grounds that it constituted interference in affairs beyond the province of the Lagos Administrator. Glover went on leave that same year but returned in the autumn. In 1867 the Igbajo war broke out with Ibadan fighting its vassal town of Ilesha. Glover managed to persuade the Ibadan to withdraw from Ilesha. But for this, that town might well have been totally destroyed.

In 1867 the long-standing dispute between Lagos and Abeokuta came to a head. The Egba United Board of Management, a quasi-government of Abeokuta, in which Mr Secretary Johnson, a coloured British subject, was the most important figure, informed Glover that it was going to set up a customs post on the Ogun River. The E.U.B.M. had been established in 1865 in an attempt to form a compromise government in which both chiefs and educated elements would be represented. 'In fact', as Biobaku has written, 'the Board was little more than an empty bureaucracy, parading sovereign pretensions, and issuing largely idle threats. Its single positive achievement was that it established a short-lived Customs Department for levying export duties instead of customary tolls at the gates'.[2] It was this preoccupation with raising revenues from customs that was to bring Abeokuta and Lagos into conflict. Glover tried to use the decision of the E.U.B.M. to set up customs posts as the occasion for the settlement of the boundaries between Lagos and Abeokuta, but this move was rejected by the E.U.B.M. who demanded that Glover withdraw the policemen he had placed at certain points on the frontier. Shortly afterwards a messenger from Glover's old friend, Masaba, the Etsu Nupe, was murdered by the Egba *en route* for Lagos. Glover demanded an explanation, and this only accentuated feelings against European interference, which were running high in Abeokuta. At the time Glover even feared an Egba invasion of Lagos and moved troops up to Ebute Metta. However, the Egba vented their resentment on locally stationed missionaries and European traders who were expelled from Abeokuta on 13th October 1867 after the riot called *Ifole*, or housebreaking. Several factors influenced this outbreak. The Egba still resented their defeat by Glover at Ikorodu. There was increasing resentment against European penetration in Yorubaland, and it was hardly surprising that Glover's oppression of Abeokuta should be associated quite wrongly with the missionaries. Anyway, there were factions in Egbaland which wanted the missionaries out of the way: would-be slave traders; influential Muslims; and the Sierra Leone immigrants. In the end the Colonial Office reprimanded Glover for provoking the crisis through his expansionist aims, which ran contrary to both official British policy and the wishes of the Governor-in-Chief in Sierra Leone.

The expulsion of the missionaries from Abeokuta marked the beginning of a period of stagnation in missionary work in Yorubaland. C.M.S. headquarters were moved to Lagos Island and the Egba Christian refugees settled on the mainland. Lagos itself prospered despite the setbacks to trade brought about by the civil wars of the interior. By 1870 the colony was almost self-sufficient. Over half a million pounds' worth of goods passed through the port annually. The administration recorded a very slight excess of expenditure (£42,379) over revenue (£41,684). Furthermore it occupied a key role in the affairs of the interior; for instance, in 1868, only a year after *Ifole*, the supporters of the two rival claimants for the position of Alake of Abeokuta both sought Lagos's support in their dispute.

However, there seemed no foreseeable end to the civil wars. Indeed the Alafin of Oyo feared that they might soon lead to the extinction of the Yoruba people. After nearly fifty years of fighting, antagonisms ran very deep. The Egba and Ijebu both feared the loss of their position as middlemen. Glover was determined to secure, if not peace, at least a free road from Lagos to the interior unhampered by the interferences or exactions of the Egba and Ijebu. To this end, in July 1871, he presided over a conference of the rulers of the interior in an attempt to secure a permanent and free road for the Oyo and Ibadan. Delegates from Oyo, Ijebu, Ibadan and Abeokuta were joined by representatives from Benin, Ijo, Ilaro and Ketu. There were five major routes to the interior: the Egba route, i.e. Lagos via Abeokuta to Ibadan; the Remo route—Lagos–Ikorodu–Ibadan; the Ijebu-Ode route—Lagos via Ijebu-Ode to Ibadan; the western route—Lagos–Igbessa–Ilaro–Ketu–Ibadan; the eastern route—Lagos–Ijo–Ondo–Oke-Igbo–Ibadan.[3] Glover's aim was to persuade the Egba and Ijebu to keep their roads open by threatening to open up an alternative route through Ijoland and Ondo to Ibadan, which would in effect deprive them of their monopoly. He was not successful in this and in 1871 the Ibadan and Egba were once again at each other's throats over the road to Lagos. Glover offered his mediation in vain, and decided to blockade Porto Novo, the main source of Egba arms supplies. If he could annex this port, so much the better, for then he could cut off all supplies for the Egba and force them to open the road. So exasperated did Glover become that he even considered closing all roads and forbidding any exports through Lagos. This naturally angered the Lagos merchants, who quickly expressed their anger to the visiting Governor of the West African settlements, Pope Hennessy, when he arrived. He was instinctively hostile to Glover. Glover left Nigeria finally as a result of his alienation from the merchants. Dr Biobaku concludes: 'Glover's departure marked the end of an era of unauthorized expansionist policies which the Egba, supported by the missionaries and later by Sierra Leone immigrants and their Ijebu allies, frustrated.'[4]

The first five years of the seventies were relatively peaceful in

Yorubaland, though in 1875 the Ibadan slave-raided into Ekiti country
and reached Nupeland. The Ibadan were then at the height of their
power, but they still depended on Benin for their supplies of gunpowder
since the direct routes to the coast through Ijebu and Egbaland were
closed. In 1877, however, a caravan under military escort was sent to
Porto Novo to collect gunpowder, purchased by the Alafin Adelu
shortly before his death. The expedition, which passed through Egba
territory, was successful, encountering neither Dahomeyans nor Egba
on the way. On receiving news of this the Egba retaliated by closing
their roads completely to the Ibadan, forbidding even the passage of
salt. Despite protests from some of his advisers, the Are of Ibadan
closed the gates of the city to the Egba and declared war on them, with
these words: 'I am going to perform a task which God has allotted me to
do, and those who say that they shall see that I do not accomplish it will
not live to see it done, as done it shall be, and when I have finished there
shall be no more wars for ever in the Yoruba country.'[5] The Are then
sent out raiding parties to ravage the Egba farms on the grounds that
the best way to harass the Egba was to destroy their food supplies.

The war between Ibadan and the Egba had some of the elements of
the strife in eastern Nigeria between the Delta middlemen and the
interior traders. Essentially what the Ibadan wanted was direct trade
with Lagos. The Egba naturally wished, like the Ijebu, who soon joined
them, to preserve their monopoly as middlemen and to ensure that the
already considerable military power of Ibadan was not increased by the
free supply of arms from the coast. They attempted to get the Ondo road
closed to the Ibadan, and to cut off their supplies of firearms and
ammunition. The Ijesha who could control this route, and resented the
oppressive rule of the Ibadan, their overlords, gladly joined the Egba
together with the Ekiti and Ilorin in the north, who also feared
the growing military might of Ibadan. By the end of the year, then,
the Ibadan were surrounded by hostile armies—the Egba and Ijebu
to the south; the Ijesha and Ekiti to the east; and the Ilorin to the
north.

Ibadan did not succumb to this formidable opposition, but in fact
drove off the members of the alliance with surprising ease, which lends
credence to Egba fears of its increasing power. By 1879, however, the
strength of Ibadan's enemies seemed overwhelming. The Ekiti,
together with the Ijesha, Effon, Yagba and Akoko, formed the Ekiti-
Parapo or Ekiti Confederation against Ibadan. Ife helped both parties,
but in reality favoured the confederation. Ibadan was cut off from any
source of firearms and ammunition, except through Oke-Igbo and
Ondo. The chief of Oke-Igbo, the Oni-elect of Ife, tried to cut off this
route, but the Oyo inhabitants of Modakeke, near Ife, managed to get

supplies to them. Soon even the Dahomeyans from the west started to attack the Ibadan.

Trade between Lagos and the interior was by now at a standstill, so it was not surprising that the Governor of Lagos welcomed the Alafin of Oyo's appeal to him to try to reconcile the warring parties. However, the Governor had no success since, when messages were sent to the various war camps, the Ekiti refused to give any firm reply. In 1882 the Ife came out openly against Ibadan and attacked Modakeke, but were repulsed. The combined Ibadan and Modakeke army then took Ife and destroyed it. It is remarkable how well the Ibadan survived these constant attacks. In 1882 they were engaged in battles with the Ilorin, the Ekiti, Egba, Ijebu and Ife. To the west were the Dahomeyans, ready to take advantage of Ibadan's plight and doing so by raids on their farms.

In December 1882 overtures for peace were made between the various participants. The Ijebu, contrary to the wishes of their ruler, the Awujale, actually made peace with Ibadan, and trade was opened up again with the Ilorin. But no general peace could be arranged. In 1884 the Rev. J. B. Wood of Abeokuta attempted to secure peace between the Ekiti-Parapo and the Ibadan but failed, and the following year fighting broke out again at Modakeke and Offa.

As far as Lagos was concerned the trade of the interior was by 1885 completely disrupted, though the wide area of the war did not make life impossible for the people of Yorubaland. Governor-General Rowe wrote in 1883: 'In the so-called war but little actual fighting occurs, few are killed; capture is the object of the warrior on either side. Man hunting is the real business of these fights. . . . All these tribes trade more or less with the Ibadans, notwithstanding they are at war with them; the most saleable produce the Ibadans can bring to market is slaves; to the Egbas they sell the slaves caught from Ijeshas; to the Ijeshas those caught from the Egbas.

'The Egbas, the Ijebus, the Ijeshas are middlemen. When these tribes talk of making peace with Ibadan—they mean a peace on which Ibadan shall bring its produce to their frontier market on the interior side, but no farther—no Ibadan trader must come beyond that market. On the seaboard they will exchange this produce with the Lagos traders for European goods, but no Lagos trader must come into their country beyond the market place on the seaboard. The Ijebus pay a high price for slaves. They use them for farm labourers, and if the Ibadans cease to catch slaves, the Ijebus must cease to import them. The Ibadans find that the most profitable trade article they can take to market is a slave.'[6]

By 1885 it had become abundantly clear that if the Colony of Lagos were to survive, an end to the inter-tribal wars would have to be achieved. This would necessitate direct British interference in Yoruba affairs, implying a reversal of official policy on the part of the British Government.

Events in the Delta and along the Niger were, however, to place Britain in a much better position for dealing with the problems of Yorubaland, for it was there that competition between British and French merchants, and the increasing need to maintain peace in order that trade might be encouraged, led the British government to reverse its policy of non-interference and proclaim a Protectorate over the Niger Districts.

In 1865 King William Pepple died and was succeeded by his son George, a man of weak personality. Control of affairs in Bonny thus rested with an ex-slave, Oko-Jumbo, who became chief adviser to King George. Opposing him was another ex-slave, Jaja, who became head of the Anna Pepple house on the death of Alali, the former regent. For the next twenty years Jaja was to dominate Delta politics.[7] He was a man of exceptional ability, combined with a ruthlessness that alone could ensure survival in the cut-throat competition of the palm-oil trade. He had been an Igbo slave, who, by his quick identification with Ijo customs, was readily accepted in the Anna Pepple house. From an early age he showed considerable ability as a trader and mixed well with the European supercargoes. Thus, when Alali died in 1863[8] with debts to the tune of £10,000 or more, it was difficult to find a successor to the headship of the Anna Pepple house, which also involved assuming leadership of the opposition to Oko-Jumbo. Certainly none of the senior chiefs wished to fill it, and it was with a sense of relief that they saw Jaja take the burden on. Jaja quickly paid off Alali's debts and appeared to Oko-Jumbo's party as a potentially more serious rival than Alali had been.

In Bonny the quarrels between the two factions became so intense that in 1867 King George asked the Consul to intervene on his behalf. This the Consul refused to do, reprimanding him for supporting Brass and Okrika in their attacks on New Calabar. In 1869 the supercargoes sent a message to the Consul that civil war was imminent. Oko-Jumbo was itching for an early outbreak of hostilities since the Anna Pepple house would be at a severe disadvantage because of heavy losses they had sustained in a fire the year before. On 13th September 1869, civil war broke out but came to a sudden halt when Jaja and his followers decamped to one of the outlying colonies of Bonny. Realizing his weakness he had wisely retreated to a position from which he could counter-attack with much more devastating results than the heavy guns of Oko-Jumbo could inflict on him. Jaja had chosen as his retreat a place in Andoni country from which he could cut Bonny off from its richest oil-producing areas. Jaja had been planning this manœuvre even before he succeeded to leadership of the Anna Pepple house. He did so for several reasons which G. I. Jones points out.[9] First, he saw there was little prospect of the Anna Pepple house dominating the Manila faction. Even if it succeeded in doing so there was no possibility that Jaja would be accepted as king since he did not come from royal lineage. Therefore the only alternative was to set off and found a new state. Second, now that Europeans were resistant to malaria, and ships of shallow draft, driven by steam rather than sail, could negotiate the Delta rivers, the advantages of proximity to the interior oil markets were becoming apparent. Bonny had had the advantage of being a sea-port, but was far removed from her markets. Jaja could profit from the discovery of quinine and the use of steamships by founding a new state close to the traditional markets of Bonny, to which he could deny her access. By 15th February 1870, Jaja felt strong enough to declare himself independent of Bonny. Despite warnings from the Consul and from Bonny, the supercargoes traded openly with Jaja. Bonny war canoes retaliated by firing on British ships. Consul Livingstone tried to settle matters by procuring Jaja's return to Bonny. Having failed in that, he sent a man-o'-war to Opobo, as Jaja had named his new state, to force him to open the interior markets to Bonny. After forty-eight hours' bombardment Jaja agreed to treat with Bonny under the arbitration of the kings of New Calabar and Okrika. He delayed as before until once more hostilities broke out. Earl Granville, the British Foreign Secretary of the day, wrote to Livingstone: 'It appears to me, as it did to Lord Clarendon, that the continuance of the present state of affairs is as much owing to the rivalry of the British traders as the quarrels of the natives, and that if it were not for the interference of Europeans the dispute might be easily settled.'[10] The pro-Bonny and pro-Jaja supercargoes both ensured a continual supply of arms to their respective allies. Glover in Lagos was consulted and characteristically advocated direct influence. By Christmas 1870, however, since the Foreign Office refused to countenance interference, Jaja was able to proclaim his new kingdom, which was made up of fourteen of the eighteen houses of Bonny. Jaja had broken Bonny and established what was to be the most important Delta state, until Britain finally declared its protectorate. In 1873 a peace treaty was secured between the two states by Commodore J. E. Commerell, V.C., C.B., with the aid of five warships. Britain recognized Jaja as King of Opobo, who in turn made a few small concessions to Bonny.

The Benin River and the western Delta did not present such dramatic hazards to peaceful trading. There security of trade was guaranteed,

though not always achieved by the Itsekiri Governor of the Benin
River, whose authority was sanctioned by the British Consul, and
recognized by the British traders.

The Governorship of the Benin River had been established in 1851 as
a result of a treaty signed by Diare and other leaders of the house of
Ologbotsere and Consul Beecroft, who was anxious to regulate trade
conditions on the river for the British.[11] Two years later he had failed to
obtain a similar treaty with the other main house of Itsekiri, the royal
house of Emaye. The house of the Ologbotsere, a senior Warri chief, was
established on the north bank of the River Benin with its headquarters
at Jakpa. Under the leadership of the Ologbotsere Eyinmisaren it had
broken away from Warri at the end of the eighteenth century after a
rebellion of some of the leading Itsekiri chiefs against their king. The
secessionist movement was successful and as a result the royal house
now only controlled the south bank.

The abolition of the slave trade had brought hard times for the
Itsekiri. The oil trade was slow in developing and illicit slave traders
were unwilling to risk trading with the Itsekiri because there was a
great deal of difficulty involved in crossing the bar to the Benin River,
behind which they might be temporarily trapped and thus become easy
victims of the British Anti-Slavery patrol. With the development of the
oil trade in the forties came the demands of the British traders that
there be some form of regulation of trade conditions on the river. Thus
Beecroft agreed with Diare and the leading chiefs of the house of the
Ologbotsere, who seemed to him to control the river at that time, that
they choose from among them a Governor of the Benin River, who
would be responsible for securing favourable trade conditions. Diare, a
rich trader, was selected, and ruled until 1870 with a short interruption
when he was unsuccessfully deposed in 1858 by Consul Campbell for
failing to take action against a nephew who had seized a launch belonging to one of the leading British traders. He was succeeded by Chanomi,
a member of the royal house, rather than by Olumu, the richest trader
on the river and also a member of the house of Ologbotsere. Lloyd
suggests that he was either 'reluctant to assume office, or else it was
strongly felt that the office should be held, in rotation, by the House of
Emaye'.[12] Chanomi was deposed in 1879 by the British for stopping
trade on the river, and was succeeded by Olumu, who had transferred
his headquarters from Jakpa to Ebrohimi. Olumu ruled for only four
years before being succeeded by his son, Nana, whom he had effectively
designated as his heir from the time he assumed the Governorship. In
1884 Nana signed treaties with Consul Hewett bringing the Benin
River, Warri and certain parts of Western Ijo under British protection,
and thus establishing paramountcy of British trade in the area.

British gains in the western Delta were paralleled by the advance of British interests in the interior. Despite the decisions of the Select Committee of 1865, a consulate was established in Lokoja and the new Consul J. M. Macleod set sail in H.M.S. *Investigator* the following year. His ship was attacked by local inhabitants and ran aground. This seemed a signal for local people to give general vent to their resentment against the incursions of the European traders. Bishop Crowther, who was busy extending the scope of the Niger Mission, was arrested by an African chief who demanded £1,000 for his ransom. He was, however, rescued in a brilliant sortie by the assistant consul at Lokoja who was himself killed in the fighting. Lokoja was blockaded for six months by hostile tribes, who were ultimately beaten off by allies of the Consul. The following year, 1869, the consulate was closed, but the Foreign Office, betraying continued interest in river trade, in 1871 sent W. H. Simpson to negotiate with Etsu Nupe Masaba for protection of all British traders on the river. Masaba, unlike the chiefs along the river, sought the promotion of trade with the Europeans, since they could provide him with much-needed arms to ward off the many rivals to his throne,[13] and assure for him a monopoly of trade up the Benue and Niger beyond Lokoja.

The Lokoja incidents illustrate both the determination of the British to secure trade in the Niger hinterland, even if it meant placing themselves under the protection of a friendly local ruler, and the equal determination of most of the river-side peoples to keep the European traders away. Considering the vast investments of the British companies on the Bight of Bonny and along the Niger, which together accounted for over £1,000,000 worth of trade annually, it was unlikely that the British, despite the temporary setback at Lokoja, would give in to their opponents. In 1871 hinterland trade suffered another blow when the government abandoned the naval escort for vessels trading up the Niger, and the steamer *Nelson*, having decided to go it alone, was fired on and sank in retreat. Yet in 1872 the consulate in Fernando Po was transferred to Old Calabar, and in 1873 the Courts of Equity, which until then had enjoyed no other sanction than the power of the local chiefs and supercargoes to enforce their decisions, and had at times had those decisions reversed by properly constituted British Courts in Accra, were regularized by an Order in Council. By this Order the consul was empowered to inflict fines of up to £200, imprisonment for 21 days, or order banishment for a year for any breach of regulation between natives and the British. It was clear that, if the British were to protect trade in the hinterland, a more stable form of administration would have to be maintained in the Delta. In 1875 and 1876 the *Sultan of Sockatoo* was so fiercely attacked that no steamer dared enter the river. Behind this concerted attack on the British was the influence of the African middlemen of the Delta ports, particularly the Brassmen, who resented these incursions into their traditional monopoly of the palm-oil markets. Slowly it was slipping into the hands of European traders, who had long since realized that direct trade with the hinterland was inevitable. Thus the temporary alliance between Liverpool traders and African middlemen in the Delta was broken, and the middlemen faced a fairly solid combination of European interests. But the general interest of the British traders was often seriously damaged by the cut-throat rivalry between the various firms. In some small trading stations as many as five firms had established themselves. By 1878 there were four major companies trading along the Niger: Messrs. Alexander Miller Brothers and Co. (Glasgow), James Pinnock and Co. (Liverpool), West African Company (Manchester) and the Central African Trading Company (London). They maintained trading posts along the river and brought in over £300,000 trade a year between them. Their main problem was the hostility of the interior peoples and their lack of common policy and direction. The old cut-throat competition characteristic of the Delta was spreading to the interior. By 1878 the three main companies had established an identical chain of trading posts on the river. Great losses were also sustained as a result of attacks by neighbouring peoples, who during the dry season took advantage of the fact that no steamers could ascend the river to execute punitive bombardments.

The worst of these attacks was on Onitsha when the trading houses and the mission station were burnt down. Bishop Crowther had had a difficult task in maintaining the work of the Niger Mission.[14] Though he had some success in the Delta, especially in Bonny where the worship of monitor lizards was officially abandoned in 1867, his missions had been subject to frequent waves of persecution. Yet by 1880 the Niger Mission, which was entirely in the hands of Africans, had eleven stations. The mission at Calabar had also extended its work. Two missionaries had reached Oban, Uyanga and Ibami in 1879; and in 1884 the Rev. Goldie established a mission station at Ikotana on the Cross River.[15] Thus whilst traders were pushing the boundaries of trade farther into the interior, missionaries were penetrating remote villages and spreading the Gospel. Most important of all, they were bringing education to an ever-increasing number of people. Traders who had for long treated missionary activity with suspicion, were soon to be thankful for the supply of clerks that the missionaries produced from their schools.

Until the 1870s trade in both the hinterland and the Delta had been almost the exclusive province of British merchants. Indeed, surprisingly little interest had been shown in West Africa by other colonial powers. But in the 1870s both Frenchmen and Germans were looking to the West Coast for expansion. Indeed the French were already developing their master plan for Africa whereby they could link their protectorates of the north with the West Coast and, almost more important, extend their territory from Senegal to the Horn of Africa. The contemplation of such vast possessions had been made feasible by the success of railways in Australia and America.

Thus the firms trading in the interior were threatened not only by the hostility of Nigerian traders and interior peoples but, though they did not realize it at that time, by the possibility of foreign competition. Just at this stage in Delta politics there arrived in Nigeria a man, later called 'the Founder of Modern Nigeria', who dealt successfully with both these threats to the British monopoly of trade along the Niger. First he set about amalgamating the various Niger companies, impressing erstwhile rivals with the advantages of co-operation through sheer force of personality. This was George Dashwood Goldie Taubman, who had already travelled in north-east Africa, and had been fired with imperial zeal from an early age.[16] He had a shrewd appreciation of the ambitions of the French in Africa[17] and was determined that they should not carry off what he considered the main prize: the lands of the Niger basin. By November 1879 Goldie (he was later knighted as Sir George Taubman Goldie) had welded all the major companies trading on the Niger into the United African Company, having persuaded their directors that the only cure for over-competition was monopoly. All ships, stores and staff were pooled. But this monopoly was soon to be challenged by the French.

In 1878 the Comte de Semellé had visited Umoru, the successor of Etsu Nupe Masaba, with a view to acquiring land for a trading station for his Compagnie Française de l'Afrique, Équatoriale. But though Umoru granted the British a monopoly in 1879, the help given to him against the rebels by the French secured for the latter his goodwill. By 1882 this company and the Compagnie du Sénégal et de la Côte Occidentale d'Afrique, were almost of equal strength to the United African Company. Goldie tried to ward off their threat in two ways. First, he proposed that his company should become a chartered company so that Britain would establish a protectorate over the Niger through his agency. In this way the British government could secure its interests in the area without incurring the expenses of an administration that might have to be borne by the British budget. In 1882 the National African Company was formed with a view to receiving a charter, though the British government refused at first to contemplate such a move. Secondly, he tried to persuade the French companies to join with his own. When they refused, he undertook a drastic price war against them, using most of his personal fortune and undercutting their prices by as much as 25 per cent. He forced them out of business in 1884. Goldie did not under-estimate the French menace. In 1883 Jules Ferry, with known imperialist ambitions, became Prime Minister of France, and in 1883 annexed Cotonou, Agoué, Great and Little Popo and Porto Novo, driving a wedge between the Lagos and Gold Coast settlements of Britain. The French even sent a gunboat to Bonny in an attempt to secure a treaty by which they could establish a protectorate on the mouth of the Niger.

The Germans were active, too. G. L. Gaiser, founder of the present well-known firm, purchased Mahin beach west of Badagry, though he was later forced to return it. Goldie anticipated these threats with remarkably clear foresight. The Delta he considered no problem, for with easy access to British gunboats the local chiefs and kings could easily be controlled. The hinterland was a different problem. Since it was inaccessible to warships, it would, he believed, always be possible for another power to gain the interior. Though the British government refused to grant Goldie a charter, it conceded him to be the right man to make treaties with local chiefs. By 1884 he had concluded thirty-seven such treaties. He formed a fleet of twenty gunboats, which proved very valuable as opposition to his company's monopoly increased. Akassa, Brass, Patani and Asaba were all bombarded for attacks on the company's trading factories. On the other hand, when Africans like the Etsu Nupe proved friendly and willing to co-operate, the company was prepared to offer its assistance, and indeed it did give him very substantial help in putting down rebellions in 1881 and 1882. Goldie, in fact, behaved as though he had already been granted a charter by the British government. In 1884, when the Germans sent Herr Flegel to gain treaties with the Caliph of Sokoto and the Emir of Gwandu, it was Goldie through Joseph Thompson who forestalled him.

The Foreign Office also gave Consul Hewett grudging permission to make treaties in the Oil Rivers. Sometimes Consulate and Company competed for the same treaties. More serious was international competition: in July 1884 Germany hoisted her flag over the Cameroons a few days before Hewett arrived to declare a British Protectorate. The growing atmosphere of 'scramble for Africa' brought the European powers to the Conference table at Berlin to agree on their respective spheres of influence. It was here that the value of Goldie's work for Britain, on whose behalf he attended the conference as an official delegate, having broken the rival French company only a fortnight before, and armed with a sheaf of treaties with local rulers, was seen. Goldie almost saw his work ruined when Germany proposed the estab-

lishment of an international commission to ensure free trade on the
Niger, whatever power controlled the territory through which if
flowed. However, in exchange for Britain's promise to recognize
Leopold of the Belgians' Congo Association, Bismarck supported a
revised Niger Navigation Act, which, while it insisted on the principle
of international free trade, made no provision for a commission to
ensure its observance.

As a result of Goldie's work, Britain had little difficulty in laying
claims to the area around the Niger. She formally proclaimed a Protectorate over the Niger Districts, thus reversing her declared policy of
1865. The Niger Districts were proclaimed 'the territories on the line of
coast between the British Protectorate of Lagos and the right or western bank of the Rio del Rey' and the 'territories on both banks of the
Niger, from its confluence with the river Benue at Lokoja to the sea, as
well as the territories on both banks of the River Benue, from the
confluence up to and including Ibi'.[18] From now on Britain was deeply
involved in the affairs of Nigeria. Any hesitation about interfering in
the affairs of Yorubaland and the more remote Sokoto Caliphate was
cast aside as trading and government interests fused as a result of
threatened foreign competition. No consideration to African interest
was given either by Britain or by the other powers attending the Berlin
Conference. West Africa was parcelled out in terms of European political rivalry.

12 Company and Consuls

The states of the Oil Rivers found the new British Protectorate little more effective than the consular rule that had looked after British interests until the Berlin Conference. It was rather the Niger Company which showed the chiefs of the Delta states that the Berlin Conference had changed irrevocably the *status quo* in Africa. In 1886, as a result of Goldie's determined work over the preceding eight years, the Niger Company was granted the Royal Charter that it had been refused in 1881. Under the terms of this charter the company obtained political authority over those territories with which the company's agents had signed treaties whilst those territories which had been brought under protection by the Consul became the new Oil Rivers Protectorate. The company was to 'discourage and, as far as may be practicable, abolish by degrees any system of domestic servitude existing among the inhabitants'. On the other hand the company was enjoined to interfere as little as possible in the affairs of native chiefs. Most important of all were the words, 'Nothing in this Our Charter shall be deemed to authorise the Company to set up or grant a monopoly of trade.'[1] The company's subsequent failure to observe this injunction was to incur the animosity of both African and European traders.

The charter was quite explicit about freedom of trade: 'and subject only to customs duties and charges hereby authorised, and to restrictions on importations similar in character to those applicable in our United Kingdom, trade with the Company's territories under Our protection shall be free and there shall be no differential treatment of the subjects of any power as to the settlement or access to markets, but foreigners alike with British subjects will be subject to administrative dispositions in the interests of commerce and good order.' This conformed with the condition laid down by the Berlin Conference that, while Britain had demonstrated clearly her occupation of the lands along the mouth of the Niger, that river should be free to navigation by other powers. The history of the administration of the Royal Niger Company, over whose territories British Protection was officially placed in 1887, is largely that of bitter rivalry with its African, British and foreign competitors who all justifiably complained that the com-

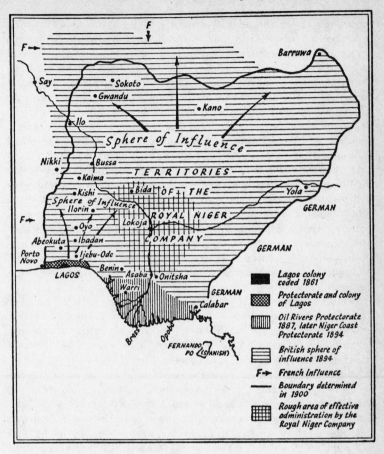

7. The growth of British influence in Nigeria

pany was using its political authority to secure a monopoly of commerce.[2]

The company straightway established its headquarters at Asaba on the Niger, setting up a constabulary, a High Court of Justice and the necessary administration to run both the territories under its control and its numerous trading posts along the Niger. The northern limits of the Royal Niger Company's territories were not in fact marked. To the south they were bounded by the Oil Rivers Protectorate. A thin strip of land connected Asaba and the hinterland with the company's port at Akassa. Economically the company now controlled the trade of the hinterland where the middlemen of the Delta states as well as the Liverpool traders used to make their living. This would have been acceptable if the company had not exercised monopolistic powers. Indeed the extent of this monopoly was not realized in England until the publication of Sir John Kirk's report on the disturbances at Brass in 1896. Under the regulations of the company, Brassmen were considered as foreigners since Brass lay outside the company's territory. Brassmen were therefore required to pay £50 a year for a licence to trade and £10 for each station they traded in. A further £100 a year had to be paid if they required to trade in spirits, 'without which', Sir John Kirk added, 'trade in the Delta is at present impossible'.[3] On top of this the Brass traders had to pay company duties, which it was permitted to levy under the terms of the charter in order to defray the cost of the administration of the territory.

Remembering the value of £100 in the 1880s, it is not surprising that African traders unfortunate enough to live outside the company's territories bitterly resented its policy. Furthermore, by insisting that all trade within its territories pass through Akassa, it dealt a fatal blow to the Delta ports.

No less resentful were the Liverpool merchants in the Delta, as Mary Kingsley, who knew them well and was equally a friend of Goldie, revealed in her *West African Studies*.[4] French and German complaints not unnaturally tended to be biased since merchants of both powers were busily extending their interests in other parts of West Africa and regarded the company's territories with covetous eyes. Sir George Goldie had good reason to be suspicious of them. Free navigation of the Niger for foreign powers was all very well if such powers respected the patently tenuous hold of the company over its territories. This it was clear neither the Germans nor the French were prepared to do. In 1887 a German merchant called Hoenisberg entered the Niger with a cargo of salt, with the deliberate intention, it is said, of annoying the company and of 'busting up their Charter'. He had apparently infringed the customs regulations, so his cargo was seized. He then travelled on to Nupe, where it is alleged he intrigued against the company. He was arrested, tried at Asaba and deported. A year later Von Puttkamer, a nephew of Bismarck and German Consul in Lagos, went to Nupe to investigate the case. In fairness to the foreign traders it must be admitted that as with African and Liverpool traders, the company deliberately obstructed their activities. However, the German threat was not the most serious, and indeed boundary agreements were drawn up with Germany in 1886, 1890 and later in 1893. The constant threat to the company came from the French, still fired with the ambition of creating an enormous African empire. Indeed Sir George Goldie himself declared in an interview with Reuters in 1899: 'The only stroke of fortune that we have had throughout was the reaction of France in 1884 against colonial enterprises in consequence of those disasters at Tonking, to which M. Jules Ferry, the great Colonial Minister, owed his downfall and the nickname "Le Tonkinois". But for this reaction in France, which lasted until the Paris Exhibition of 1889, and which she had long and rightly deplored, we might have been pushed out of Nigeria.'[57] The more arbitrary interpretation of the charter by the company as regards its monopolistic control of the territory may better be understood when it is realized just what a threat to the Niger territories the French were.

The French were establishing themselves on the frontiers of the territories in which the company was interested, both to the west and the north. Technically they also had free access from the south by sea. From their base on the coast of Dahomey they were already trying to establish themselves in Yorubaland.

In 1887 a French mission visited Abeokuta and alleged that it had secured a treaty, never put into effect, permitting it to build a railway from Porto Novo to Abeokuta, and thus drain away the palm-oil trade that was the life-blood of Lagos. There were indications that they were intent on securing a similar treaty with the Alafin of Oyo, so the Governor in Lagos hastened to draw up a treaty of friendship with the Alafin in 1888. In 1889 a Lieutenant Mizon, with a party of Frenchmen and Africans, actually sailed up the lower Niger on a warship armed with a Hotchkiss gun. The party was attacked by the Patani and finally gained succour at Akassa. They then sailed on to Yola, where Mizon attempted to make a treaty with the Emir of Yola. On his return to France, Mizon became a national hero as a result of the attack by the Patani, which was not unnaturally attributed to the machinations of the company. Two years later he returned amidst violent protests by the company, but with permission from the British Foreign Office, to take an armed party through the company's territories. He reached Muri, where he drew up a treaty with the Emir. As an expression of gratitude, Mizon, against protests from his officers, shelled the nearby non-Muslim town of Kwana, which the Emir then raided for slaves to sell in the markets of the north. France conquered Dahomey on Nigeria's western borders in 1892, and was rapidly taking the Western Sudan under control. To stave off French colonial expansion, particularly towards the Fulani Empire which he had secured by treaty for the company, Goldie put forward the idea that a narrow triangle of hinterland extending to Lake Chad, the modern Cameroons, should be given to Germany. But the real crisis in Anglo-French relations in West Africa came in 1894 with Lugard's famous race to Nikki.

Whilst the Royal Niger Company was established firmly on the Oil Rivers, and as far up the Niger as Jebba, there was a very fluid position in Borgu. Though France and Britain had made treaties agreeing the boundary between Dahomey and Lagos, this boundary did not go effectively much farther than 100 miles (160 km.) inland. Far to the north a boundary marking the southernmost limit of France's North African possessions was drawn from Say on the upper Niger in a straight line eastwards to Barruwa near Lake Chad, much the same as the present boundary between northern Nigeria and Niger. A large area of indefinition existed in Borgu, bounded to the north by the Niger, to the east by Nupeland and to the south by Yorubaland. To the west it stretched into modern Dahomey. It was not at all clear which power had rights in this area. It was also not clear whether the Say-Barruwa line merely determined the northern limits to British territory. France chose to read into it that she could expand wherever possible to the south of the line.

The Royal Niger Company was particularly anxious that France should not get a foothold in Borgu since, if she could claim territory to the south of Bussa, she could have a port on the Niger; for the Bussa rapids were the last obstacle to navigation on the river. In 1892 France had declared a protectorate over Dahomey, a development which caused Goldie considerable concern. He claimed Borgu belonged to the company since he made a treaty with the Caliph of Sokoto, who in turn claimed he was suzerain of Borgu. The French, with historical justification, denied that Sokoto controlled Borgu. Goldie countered this by producing two treaties made with the King of Bussa, who styled himself 'Lord of all Borgu'. The French quickly replied that the King of Nikki was the real suzerain of Borgu. In this there was again some truth for although Bussa was the ancestral home of the Nikki rulers, who had to acknowledge spiritual overlordship from its King, in terms of real political power Nikki was the more important.[6] At that time no European had visited Nikki or knew its exact location. It was even a possibility that the Germans, busily establishing themselves in Togoland, might make a dash to Nikki. The French rushed off an expedition under Decœur to gain a treaty with Nikki; Goldie was not caught unawares and arranged for Captain Lugard, who had already distinguished himself as a pioneer of empire in East Africa, to make the treaty with Nikki on Britain's behalf.

Although the exact location of Nikki was unknown, the French expedition had the easier task for their base in Dahomey was a straight march to Nikki. Lugard, who arrived in Nigeria in August 1894, had to start off at a great disadvantage from the company's base at Akassa several hundred miles down the coast. (His task would have been easier if he could have left from Lagos.) With a small caravan of Hausa and Yoruba soldiers, he sailed up to Jebba thus starting what was to become a very long association with Nigeria.[7] Lugard made a quick call on the King of Bussa, feeling that if he were really the 'Lord of all Borgu', he would be able to provide an excellent introduction to the King of Nikki. After some delay Bussa promised to send envoys and letters to the kings of both Kaiama and Nikki in exchange for gunpowder. Lugard returned to Jebba to make preparations for immediate departure with a caravan for Nikki, hoping that Decœur would be delayed because of the rains which made travel extremely difficult at that time of year. On 28th September Lugard, with a caravan of 320 carriers and soldiers, set out on what was later to be called the Nikki Steeplechase. Under appalling weather conditions, more often than not low with fever, Lugard pushed westwards to Borgu. At Kishi in the very north of Yorubaland, and but a few yards from the frontier of Borgu, he made a treaty with the local sovereign where a chief remarked to Lugard that 'the British had introduced law and order into all Yoruba and at last it had come to them'.[8] Despite descriptions of the wildness of Borgu, Lugard was given a very friendly reception by the King of Kaiama, with whom a treaty was drawn up. Kaiama warned Lugard of the dangers of Borgu, and advised him on no account to travel beyond Nikki. As he neared that town a messenger arrived to say that the King had been told that if he looked at a white man he would die within three months. Lugard replied that if he did not receive a favourable message within two days he would move in another direction. The loss would be Nikki's not his. This ruse seems to have paid off, for two days later the messenger returned to say that the King would admit the strangers. His reception of them was very unfriendly. Lugard, however, was relieved to find that he had beaten the French. Eventually after much procrastination Lugard obtained the treaty, five days before the arrival of Decœur's party.

Lugard returned to London to find that his treaty was fast becoming the cause of an international incident. The French hotly contested its validity. In her biography of Lugard, Margery Perham has written of the international background: 'The European nations at this time were not unlike a lot of greedy, quarrelsome children in a school playground; none quite big enough to dominate all the others, kicking and then making up to each other, sulking, coaxing, telling each other secrets and then "splitting", combining for a moment and then breaking up. Britain was the rather aloof child in the corner, a little superior, unwilling to join wholeheartedly in the rough games and yet warily watching lest too many of these quarrelling school mates combined against her.'[9] The Nikki question very nearly developed into an international incident. Both Chamberlain, the British Colonial Secretary, and his French opposite number indulged in what had by then become determined brinkmanship to ensure that they retained as much of Africa as possible.

The Royal Niger Company under Goldie extended its frontier northwards by its conquest of the Etsu of Nupe, who had been slave raiding into the company's territories. To the west it also conquered Ilorin, which had aided the Etsu and had been a constant thorn in the flesh of the British administration in Lagos. Ilorin lay just to the south of Borgu, where France still had ambitions. The French then stationed a Resident at Illo, on the Niger, with instructions to occupy territory as far south as Bussa giving them a port on the stretch of the Niger navigable to the sea. They placed Kaiama under their protection. It thus became imperative for Britain to stop France's advance along the Niger. But Britain was severely handicapped by the fact that the government had delegated its authority to a chartered company, whilst the French could bring down the full weight of governmental administration behind their ambitions. It was clear that sooner or later a stand would have to be made against the French. Chamberlain favoured conceding the right bank of the Niger to a point thirty miles south of Bussa, which would have allowed the French their port. This Goldie hotly contested, citing his treaty with Bussa. Eventually Chamberlain decided on the creation of a military force under the command of Lugard, which would hold the position of the Royal Niger Company in the hinterland. Lugard returned to Nigeria in the spring of 1898. By 16th April he was at Lokoja where the 1st Battalion of West African Frontier Force paraded before him.

Lugard immediately set about organizing his small force to deal with the French, who were by then established at both Illo and Bussa. Lugard's task was to take as much of the territory in this area of undefined sovereignty as he could without precipitating actual fighting. The French had been given roughly the same order—so that both sides were really playing an elaborate game of political chess. While this tense campaign of non-violence, in which any single false move might have meant war, was played out in the dry savannah of Borgu, negotiations in Paris and London were bringing settlement closer. Chamberlain eventually secured a favourable agreement with France, gambling on the strength of Lugard's force and French reluctance to start a war. On many occasions there were very real dangers of fighting, yet by his brilliant brinkmanship Chamberlain, against the opposition of his own Prime Minister, Lord Salisbury, secured a most favourable treaty with France. The French did not get access to the navigable stretch of the Niger, although the British were pushed down the Niger 160 km. from Say to Illo. The French were given Nikki and the northern boundary of Nigeria was determined as a slight variation on the Say-Barruwa line.

British encroachments on Nigerian territory did not go unresisted by the local population. The Delta middlemen in particular demonstrated their resentment of the increasing power of the Royal Niger Company. This opposition was epitomized by the actions of Jaja, King of Opobo. The year before the Treaty of Berlin, Jaja had made his own treaty with the British by which he placed his country under the protection of the British Crown, but he ensured that the usual clause guaranteeing freedom of trade was omitted. He had suspiciously asked for a definition of the word Protectorate. Hewett, who as Consul had negotiated the treaty, defined it thus: '. . . the Queen does not want to take your country or your markets, but at the same time she is anxious that no other nation should take them. She undertakes to extend her gracious power and protection, which will leave your country still under your government: she has no wish to disturb your rule . . .' (Letter 8th January 1884).[10] This concession was probably made because the French and Germans were also attempting to gain a foothold on territories already under British Protection.

Jaja had at first been treated with considerable sympathy by the British Consul. In 1875 he had even sent a contingent to the Ashanti war, as a result of which he was given a sword by Queen Victoria. On the other hand he was a bitter opponent of free trade, preventing any European trader dealing direct with his sources of supply. Indeed any group that dared to trade direct with the European merchants was punished swiftly, as the Kwa Igbo learnt in 1881 when Jaja captured and executed hundreds of their number. His men fell on the group of villages known as Ibuno (Ibeno). Mr Holt, the Liverpool trader, writing to Earl Granville, described the incident thus:

'. . . at daylight on the 11th April last he suddenly invaded them with a force of about fifty fully manned canoes, armed with breech loading cannon and rifles, by means of which he bombarded seven of their villages, which he plundered and afterwards burnt, destroying their crops and stores of food, and taking prisoners upwards of 100 people, whilst the natives of Qua Eboe, unable to protect themselves, and without any means of defence, took to the woods, where many of them greatly suffered from want and exposure.

'Jaja's canoe remained in the river several days, broke into Mr Watt's Factory, scattered his goods about, and either took away or destroyed a number of barrels and hogsheads of oil belonging to him which were in the native towns that were looted. With their plunder and their prisoners, consisting chiefly of women and children, they returned at length to Opobo, where their unhappy victims were cruelly slaughtered, Jaja's own children being made to cut off the heads of some of the Qua Eboe children, to entitle them to wear the "eagle plume" a mark of distinction bestowed only on those who have slain an enemy.'

Whatever the terms of Jaja's 1884 treaty, the international Treaty of Berlin, made far from the sombre creeks of the Oil Rivers, had handed over his country to Britain, and inevitably there was soon to be a clash. Jaja was already involved in a major trade dispute during which European traders had formed the Amalgamated Association to break his monopoly. Oil prices had risen very favourably in England in 1883 and 1884, and this had led to a rise in prices in the Delta, which trimmed the extra profits the English traders had hoped to make. Their boycott to force down Jaja's prices failed since the firm of Alexander Miller Brothers and Co. of Glasgow agreed to trade at his prices. In June 1885 Consul Hewett, who supported the Association, explained to Jaja that as a result of the 1888 Berlin Treaty freedom of trade in the Oil Rivers was now guaranteed. This encouraged the excluded firms, who bitterly resented the fact that Jaja was now shipping oil direct to England, to seek markets up-river. However, Jaja was well prepared and his agents threatened vengeance on any tribe that traded with the Europeans. This was no idle threat to anyone who remembered his expedition against the Kwa Ibo in 1881.

In 1887 the Acting Consul, H. H. Johnston, by way of retaliation, forbade Jaja to exact his 'Comey', or customs duties, on the grounds that his direct shipment of oil was unjust competition with those who paid the duty. Jaja protested to the Secretary of State for the Colonies, and sent a delegation of chiefs to Britain. Johnston decided to take drastic action against Jaja whom he believed to be the instigator of the attacks on English merchants in July. He threatened Jaja with gunboats unless he called off his trade war. Under such a threat Jaja agreed to open trade, but in fact did little to alter the situation. On news of trouble in the markets Johnston sailed up river only to find a boom blocking his way. He then telegraphed London for permission to deport Jaja, and on receiving what he considered an affirmative reply, which was in fact probably the reply to an earlier and quite unrelated telegram, he arranged for Jaja's expulsion. Johnston sailed to Opobo in H.M.S. *Goshawk* and invited Jaja to meet him on the beach of Messrs Harrisons, which Jaja refused to do unless he had the Consul's pledge that he would go free after the meeting. Johnston agreed to this in these words: 'I hereby assure you that whether you accept or reject my proposals tomorrow no restraint whatever will be put on you—you will be free to go as soon as you have heard the message of the Government.'[11] But once there, Jaja was told that if he did not go to Accra for trial he would be considered an enemy and Opobo would be bombarded. Under the cover of H.M.S. *Goshawk*'s guns, there was little Jaja could do, so he sailed for Accra where he was found guilty of blocking the highway of trade, and of failing to honour Article V of his treaty with Britain whereby:

'The King and Chiefs of Opobo hereby engage to assist the British consular or other officers in the execution of such duties as may be assigned them, and further to act upon their advice in matters relating to the administration of Justice, the development of the resources of the country, the interests of commerce, or in any matter in relation to peace, order and Government and the general progress of civilisation.'[12]

He was deported to the West Indies on a pension of £800 a year, and when at last in 1891 he was allowed to return home he died on the way.

Though it was not until 1891 that an effective government was instituted by Britain for her new Oil Rivers Protectorate, from the British point of view much progress had been made. The energetic Acting Consul felt that the deposition of Jaja was a major breakthrough in Britain's attempt to break the power of the African middlemen who lay between her traders and the markets of the interior. Elsewhere, as Cook points out, Johnston felt that progress had been made.[13] Johnston was on good terms with Nana, Governor of the Benin River, and he had secured an understanding with Benin. Furthermore he had avoided a clash between the Royal Niger Company and the British traders of the Oil Rivers. Thus, in 1891, when Sir Claude Macdonald, and not he, was appointed Commissioner and Consul General of the Oil Rivers Protectorate, Johnston felt justifiably disappointed. Macdonald had already gained first-hand knowledge of the Delta when he headed an inquiry into allegations made against the Royal Niger Company in 1889. His policy as Commissioner General and Consul General was to avoid the inclusion of his Protectorate in that of the Royal Niger Company. He believed firmly in free trade, and rightly deduced that the Delta kings would not tolerate government by the Company. Unlike Johnston, he believed the Delta middlemen could be used to advantage.

Thus, on 1st January 1891 Britain established an effective government for her protectorate, with a revenue in the first years of nearly £90,000 derived from import duties. In 1893 the Oil Rivers Protectorate became the Niger Coast Protectorate and included all those areas that had made treaties with Britain and were not included in the Royal Niger Company Protectorate. It was governed by a Consul General responsible to the Foreign Office, under whom served a number of vice-consuls responsible for individual areas. Its administration included customs, postal, marine and medical departments as well as a small army of 200 men. But the extension of this power, even under an enlightened administrator like Macdonald, did not go unchallenged. In 1893 an Akuna chief on the Cross River brought trade to a standstill by deliberately provoking an inter-tribal war. He had murdered some Igbo traders who had been trading with his own people. As a result the newly formed constabulary was sent to end the war, and bring the chief to trial. He was found guilty and hanged. A much greater challenge to this newly constituted authority came from Nana, Governor of the Benin River whom the British ceased to recognize as Governor of the River after they had extended the control of the Oil Rivers Protectorate over Itsekiri country in 1891. 'However, the Itsekiri still regarded him as their leader', Lloyd writes, 'and Nana contrived to use his title.'¹⁴ At first, as we have seen, Nana co-operated with the Protectorate government. But he also created a monopoly on the Benin River and carried on a surreptitious trade in slaves. In 1894 Acting Consul General Moor informed the Foreign Office that Nana had strangled trade on the Benin River and that he had continually defied his authority. Moor sent despatches to Nana summoning him to answer charges against him, but Nana made excuses. Moor then forbade Nana's men to trade on the river, and once again summoned Nana, who not unnaturally refused to go, remembering what had happened to Jaja.

Nana defied all edicts that the river should be made free to traders and placed a bar across the creek leading to his headquarters at Ebrohimie. The gunboat *Alecto* was sent to blow up the barrier, but while it did so it was fired on by Nana's troops.

H.M.S. *Phoebe* came to the rescue of *Alecto* with 200 men and 150 members of the constabulary. Nana put up so strong a fight against this new party that H.M.S. *Philomel* and H.M.S. *Widgeon* had to be brought up in support. On 25th September 1894 a strong attack was made on Ebrohimie, which was captured without casualties, the explanation for this being that Nana had seen the red light and tried to escape. He had even made an ingenious, if desperate, effort to cut a canal from Ebrohimie to a creek behind the town to evacuate all his goods. These, as the attackers found, consisted of thousands of pounds' worth of merchandise, including 8,300 cases of gin. The town was a veritable arsenal with 106 cannon, 14 tons of gunpowder, 445 blunderbusses adapted for use on war canoes, and a machine-gun. Nana gave himself up to the authorities in Lagos, where he was tried and deported to the Gold Coast. The importance of Nana at this stage of Nigerian history was considerable. Like Jaja he stands out as one of the few who were able to offer serious resistance to the encroaching British power, and, as Cook has pointed out, this led to the British practice of removing native chiefs who opposed British penetration, rather than seeking their co-operation.[15]

The real bitterness felt against the Royal Niger Company by those it deprived of trade did not come to a head until 1895 when the Brassmen raided Akassa, the company's port. After years of ineffective resistance to the company's authority, the Brassmen resorted to violence. This had been contemplated before, and the British government was sufficiently aware of the fact to have sent Macdonald to investigate certain allegations made about the company's monopolistic practices. Though he sympathized with the Brassmen, he found that the company had acted within the terms of its charter.[16] The Brassmen took every measure to evade the stringent rules of the company, but by 1895 the situation had become so intolerable to them that they made a direct attack on the company.[17] On 27th January the Vice-Consul at Brass received an anonymous letter informing him that the Brassmen were to raid the company's port at Akassa. The Vice-Consul, who did not give much credence to the warning, nevertheless sent the letter on to the company's Agent General at Akassa, who likewise thought the whole affair far-fetched.

He took the precaution of sending off a patrol and setting a machine-gun at a commanding position on the river. Under cover of darkness, and cloaked by the heavy evening mists of the river, the Brass canoes by-passed the patrol, and attacked Akassa. They destroyed the stores and captured sixty men whom they took to Nembe, for which Brass was the port, killing forty-three of them. None of the European traders was taken.

Though the attack had been made on the company, Brass fell within the jurisdiction of the Niger Coast Protectorate and the Consul General was left to deal with the situation. The Brassmen, who were asked to surrender all their chiefs and armaments, refused to do so, stating that their quarrel was not with the Queen, whom the Consul General represented, but with the company. All they wanted was free access to their old markets. In effect they were complaining as bitterly about the company's monopoly as the Protectorate administration had complained of Nana's.

The Consul General then informed the Brass chiefs that if they did not obey his orders they would be punished. They played for time whilst they prepared their defences. A naval force with a contingent of Protectorate troops broke the barrier on Nembe creek, landed on Sacrifice Island and, despite fierce resistance by the Brassmen, captured it. Another ultimatum was issued to say that the town would be destroyed if the chiefs did not comply. They continued to hedge, so the punitive force attacked Nembe and against stiff resistance captured and burnt it.

The Protectorate government had now established its authority over all the traditional centres of trade except Benin. That proud and ancient kingdom had withdrawn increasingly from overseas trade and its king had actually issued a decree forbidding his people to trade with Europeans. Furthermore, the old kingdom had gained a notorious reputation because of the prominent role human sacrifice had played in its religion in recent years. In 1862 Sir Richard Burton, the Consul at Fernando Po, had tried to persuade Oba Adolo to abolish human sacrifice, but he did not fully appreciate the very deep religious role sacrifice played in the life of the Bini. Gods had constantly to be propitiated through human sacrifice, for if this were not done disaster would follow for the kingdom. However, in 1892 Gallwey, Vice-Consul for the Benin River District, did visit Benin and persuaded Oba Ovenramwen to sign a treaty by which Benin was placed under British protection and human sacrifice and slavery were abolished. Trade was also opened. This did not last for long and in 1896 Acting Consul General Phillips decided to visit Ovenramwen to press his compliance with the treaty. Early in 1897 Phillips set off for Benin at the time of the great Ague festival during which the Oba should see no man who was not a Bini. For the Bini this was a festival of the greatest importance for it marked the time of rededication by the Bini to their king.[18] It was also a time for extensive human sacrifice.

Phillips informed Oba Ovenramwen of his intention to visit him. Ovenramwen was considerably embarrassed, for he knew that to refuse would be to incur the wrath of Britain, but to accept would be to incur the even more dire wrath of the gods. Phillips did not wait for a reply and set off from Gwato, the port for Benin, and was met by the Oba's messengers, led by Ologbotsere, who ordered him and his party to turn back. In the ensuing dispute tempers appear to have been lost, and six of the British party of nine, including Phillips, were killed, together with most of their escort of about 200 men.

Within six weeks of the massacre a punitive expedition of 1,500 was sent to Benin. Ovenramwen had feared this outcome and human sacrifices were increased in a desperate attempt to ward off the inevitable. This, at least, would explain the otherwise staggering number of sacrifices described by Ling Roth, surgeon to the expedition, in *Great Benin*.[19] The Bini were conquered, the town burnt and nearly 2,500 of its magnificent bronzes taken by the British back to Europe. Ovenramwen fled, but after threats by the British he was delivered up six months later. He was tried on 1st September 1897, and deported to Calabar. The fall of Benin was the last major act in the British occupation of southern Nigeria and marked the end of one of the greatest and most colourful of West African kingdoms.

In Lagos the Governor still viewed with considerable concern the strife in the interior which caused constant interruption to trade. By 1888 palm-oil trade was worth £1,172,840 in the first six months, three-fifths of it was in British hands and much passed through Lagos. Moreover, the French were active in Dahomey, and threatened to interfere in Yorubaland if he himself did not. In January of 1886 Lagos was detached from the Gold Coast and became self-administering. Governor Moloney almost straightway sent delegations to the various parties warring in the interior. The two delegations, led by the Rev. S. Johnson, author of the *History of the Yorubas*, and the Rev. C. Phillips, were initially successful. A cease-fire was arranged between the Ekiti-Parapo and the Ibadan, but the Ilorin were still reluctant to call off battle unless the Offa, with whom they were fighting, did so first. Johnson and Phillips then went south-east to Ife where they negotiated peace between that town and its Oyo rival and neighbour, Modakeke.

The various factions then sent representatives to Lagos where a peace treaty was signed including all Yorubaland except Ilorin, which still refused to negotiate. Under the terms of the treaty Ibadan was to be independent of Oyo, and the various members of the Ekiti-Parapo were to have their independence. The Alafin of Oyo and the Owa of Ilesha should be as an older to a younger brother; Modakeke was to be rebuilt within Ibadan territory; and the two war camps should be disbanded. A small Hausa force, led by the Acting Colonial Secretary, Henry Higgins, and Mr Oliver Smith, Queen's Advocate, as Special Commissioners, set off to supervise the dismantling of the war camps. Here is how the Commissioners described the last major act in the long drama of the civil wars:

'The rains ceased before the meeting took place and, the mist clearing away, the sun shone brilliantly on the scene. Thousands of people were to be seen posted on the huge boulders of rocks which were scattered through the Kiriji camp, and crowned the summit of the mountain (the Oke Mesin camp was not visible from the place of meeting, there being a slight rising in the ground between) and, as we learned afterwards, the sound of the gun which was to announce that peace had been concluded, and that the people could go to their homes, was most anxiously awaited in both camps and received, when heard, with cheers and hurrahs.'[20]

The main problem of the peace settlement was Modakeke, the Oyo refugee town near Ife. This had by now grown into a huge town of 60,000 inhabitants, difficult enough to disband at the best of times, let alone at the height of the rainy season. Yet this was what the treaty implied, and it is little wonder that the Modakeke refused to move.

Peace was still not finally restored to the harassed Yoruba, for in the north the Ilorin were fighting with the Offa who were in alliance with the Ibadan. The Ibadan themselves tried to mediate a settlement, but failed, and after their withdrawal the chiefs of Offa submitted to the Emir of Ilorin who had them all murdered. He then raided south to Ikirun in search of slaves. Meanwhile, the Dahomeyans were still a menace on the western frontier, invading Oyo territory in 1887. To the south the Ijebu tightened their control over the roads once again. All Oyo and European traders were forbidden to enter Ijebu territory. The situation was further complicated by the arrival of a French mission in Abeokuta, where arrangements were made for a treaty whereby France would build a railway from Porto Novo to Abeokuta. The apparent advantages of the peace arrived at between the Ibadan and the Ekiti-Parapo must have seemed completely lost to the Lagos Governor, especially when he heard that the French intended securing a treaty with the Alafin himself. Thus, as we have already seen, the Governor hastened to make a treaty with the Alafin by which it was agreed Oyo should cede no territory, open trade to all and levy no tolls, except with the agreement of the Governor in Lagos. All this was to be granted in exchange for 200 bags of cowries a year. Even so the war between the Ibadan and Ilorin appeared to have no end in sight. Ibadan became even more loth to call a cease-fire when she caught some Egba traders carrying arms to the Ilorin. In 1890 Governor Moloney despatched yet another mission to the Ilorin, and Samuel Johnson was sent off to see the Alafin, who gave him little co-operation. But the other Commissioners, in an attempt to get the Ibadan to agree to be more loyal to the Alafin, obtained the consent of the Ibadan that any dispute over the limits of their territory should be settled by the Alafin and the Governor. As Samuel Johnson observed, the Alafin, by agreeing to such an arrangement, was in effect conceding part of his sovereign rights to the Governor.[21] The Alafin became more co-operative with the Lagos government in his attempts to stop the war as a result of the Dahomeyan menaces on his western frontier. He approached the Ilorin who indicated initial interest but carried on their raids, thereby making a settlement impossible. In the south the Egbado, long oppressed by the Egba, appealed to the Governor to place them under British protection.

Not trusting the French, who were dangerously near Egbado territory as a result of the delimitation of French and British spheres of influence reached in the 1890 agreement, Moloney established a small British garrison at Ilaro, an important Egbado town. For the first time Britain had a foothold in the Yoruba hinterland. So furious were the Egba that they embargoed all trade with Lagos, and for a time the city came to a commercial standstill, though eventually the Egba themselves recommenced trade, due to economic pressures in Abeokuta. Following closely on the Egba decision to reopen the roads came more trouble with the Ijebu, who closed their roads in an attempt to prevent the British in Lagos trading with Ibadan, via Shagamu, which they foresaw would deprived them of their position as middlemen. This position the Ijebu abused cruelly: Johnson, who it must be remembered was an Oyo himself, described at great length the injustices inflicted by the Ijebu on the Ibadan and Oyo trading through their territory to Lagos. They were able to do this with impunity since they knew that Ibadan depended on them for its supply of arms. The Ijebu position remained intact under Governor Moloney, who, Johnson assures us, was not a man of action. 'It was said that he was too fond of writing letters to and drafting treaties for men who hardly appreciated the one or comprehended the other nor knew the force or value of their marks or signature.

'During his five years of administration he never once visited the people and scene of which he so much writes: a single visit from him would have cleared up many difficulties in his way and enabled him to understand much, and he would have acted more to the purpose. No wonder then that matters remained *in statu quo*.'[22]

On Moloney's retirement, Denton, the Colonial Secretary, became acting Governor and attempted to visit the Awujale of Ijebuland to secure a peaceful solution to the problem. The Awujale agreed to the visit, but on Denton's arrival at Ijebu-Ode he was roughly received by the chiefs, and though the Awujale showed some signs of friendliness the chiefs did not attempt to hide their deep hostility to the interference of the Lagos government, and refused to accept the customary presents the acting Governor brought them. This Denton rightly diagnosed as a calculated insult.

This incident led the British Government to decide on coercive measures against the Ijebu, and Sir Gilbert Carter arrived as next Governor, determined to bring peace to the interior once and for all. He demanded an apology from the Awujale for his treatment of acting Governor Denton. This was agreed to, as well as a treaty abolishing human sacrifices and opening trade routes in return for a subsidy of £500 a year to cover loss of revenue from tolls to the Awujale. As we have already seen, the chiefs of Ijebu-Ode were deeply opposed to any form of treaty with the British, and under their influence the roads were soon closed again, especially since the ordinary Ijebu did not benefit from the £500 paid to the Awujale in lieu of tolls. The Awujale then took action that may be construed as seeking to placate the Ijebu chiefs. The Awujale, picking a quarrel with the Ibadan, accused the Rev. D. Olubi of the C.M.S. of bringing the Europeans into the interior, and passing European goods through Ijebu-Ode by means of his son.

The Awujale demanded the heads both of Olubi and of the Rev. T. Harding, his English colleague. The Ibadan were so frightened by the Awujale's threats that it seems clear that both Olubi and Harding would have lost their lives had not Sir Gilbert Carter decided to send a military expedition against the Awujale in May 1892. The punitive force landed at the port of Epe on the 13th and with difficulty battled its way through to Ijebu-Ode, which was found deserted except for the Awujale and a few chiefs. The speedy defeat of the Ijebu was the most significant step in the British occupation of Yorubaland. As Johnson wrote: 'The people felt instinctively that a new era was about to dawn on them. A new and foreign power had entered into the arena of active politics in the country, and everyone was exercised in mind as to how the country would be affected by it.

'To the vast majority of the common people it was like the opening of a prison door: and no one who witnessed the patient, long-suffering, and toiling mass of humanity that week by week streamed to and from the coast with their produce could refrain from heaving a sigh of gratification on the magnitude of the beneficial results of the short and sharp conflict.'

For the first time in years caravans passed freely through Ijebu-Ode. 'They brought cloths of native manufacture, cotton, indigo, palm-oil, palm kernels, beads, cattle, poultry, yam flour, pots and plates of native manufacture, calabashes in large quantities, turkeys and pigeons, rubber, etc., and took back mostly salt, cloths and other articles of European manufacture, trade rum, gin, matches etc.'[23]

The speed with which Ijebu was subjected was not lost on the rest of Yorubaland. The Egba sent emissaries to the Governor to present their apologies for their closing of the roads in the past. Early in 1893 Sir Gilbert Carter set off on his famous trek in which he effectively brought Yorubaland under British influence if not control. At Abeokuta he made a treaty with the chiefs whereby all disputes between the Egba and the British were to be settled by the Governor, human sacrifice was to be abolished, and roads were to be closed only with the consent of the British. In effect a British Protectorate had been established. On the other hand a special clause was inserted in the treaty to stipulate that as long as the terms of the treaty were observed there would be no question of annexation without the consent of the Egba.

From Abeokuta Sir Gilbert Carter trekked north to Oyo where, after certain difficulties, the Governor was able to draw up a treaty with the Alafin. The British were given free access to all parts of Yorubaland (i.e. under the Alafin's control) and the roads to Lagos were to be kept open. Christianity would be tolerated and human sacrifice abolished. There would be no agreement made by the Alafin with other powers unless by permission of the Governor as representative of the Queen of England. Any disputes between the parties to the treaty were to be referred to the Governor in Lagos. This treaty clearly compromised the Alafin's sovereignty in favour of Britian. From Oyo the Governor continued what was to be a triumphal trek through Ogbomosho to Ilorin, where he succeeded in persuading both Ilorin and Ibadan to break up their respective war camps. Thus ended sixteen years of bitter war.

The only check to this progress through Yorubaland was in Ibadan. The Ibadan refused to sign the agreement Carter drew up for them on the grounds that most of them as warriors had been absent from their town for many years and found it impossible to negotiate such a treaty without giving it deeper consideration. Furthermore, they objected to the idea that they should have a European Resident stationed in their town.

Carter returned to a triumphal reception in Lagos, for his brilliant diplomatic tour had brought an end to nearly a century of fighting, and had once and for all secured the trade of the interior for Lagos. But he could not resist a few words of bitterness about his failure at Ibadan. He even suggested that it was due to the machinations of someone in his own retinue. Johnson rightly dismisses this: 'His Excellency might have allowed such men as govern a town like Ibadan and all its dependants some credit of knowing their own minds and not be swayed by a mere clerk in his office.'[24] Ibadan accepted the treaty, however, in August 1893, after careful assurances by the Governor that he had no intention of interfering with the government of Ibadan.

The treaty with Ibadan declared that although the Álafin would continue to be recognized as 'the King and Head of Yorubaland' Ibadan should become its headquarters; the treaty made with Oyo should be recognized; land should be provided for a railway; and a Resident plus a small constabulary should be appointed. After this treaty there was peace in Yorubaland. A small fracas with Oyo was quickly dealt with by the first Resident, Captain Bower, when he had to take a punitive expedition to Oyo after the Alafin had carried out the emasculation of a man found guilty of a crime for which that punishment was normally meted out. But only Ilorin really remained a thorn in the flesh of the Lagos administration. As we have seen, that problem was finally settled by a punitive expedition despatched by the Royal Niger Company.

The peace Carter achieved was followed up by measures to promote the trade which Britain had always avowed was her main reason for interfering in the politics of Yorubaland. Roads were built and the railway from Lagos to Ibadan was started. Whatever the motives of the

British in interfering in Yorubaland, there is no doubt that at the time the Yoruba must have been one of the few African peoples who really welcomed such intervention, for it brought them peace after a century of some of the most complex and seemingly futile wars on the African continent.

13 Emirs and Maxims

The system of administration employed by Britain over its various protectorates in Nigeria had so many defects and so many anomalies that it was inevitable that some change should be made. The unpopularity of the Royal Niger Company in the south, and the difficulties of establishing administrative competence over those territories of the north assigned to Britain, led to the withdrawal of the company's charter. In a letter to the Secretary of the Treasury on 15th June 1899, Lord Salisbury gave these reasons for his change of policy:

'The Marquess of Salisbury has for some time past had under consideration the question of approaching the Niger Company with a view to relieving them of their rights and functions of administration on reasonable terms. . . . There are, however, other cogent reasons for the step now contemplated. The West African Frontier Force, now under Imperial officers, calls for direct Imperial control; the situation created towards other firms by the commercial position of the Company, which, although strictly within the right devolving upon it by Charter, has succeeded in establishing a practical monopoly of trade; the manner in which this commercial monopoly presses on the native trader, as exemplified by the rising in Brass, which called for the mission of inquiry entrusted to Sir John Kirk in 1895, are some of the arguments which have influenced his Lordship. . . .'[1]

Probably much more important in Lord Salisbury's reasoning was the critical international situation that had arisen on the Niger, culminating in the French occupation of Bussa in 1897. It became clear that direct governmental control would have to be exercised over the area if the situation was not to get out of hand.

The Niger Company was fully compensated for the loss of its privileged position. The administrative buildings were bought up and a sum of £450,000 was paid as compensation. What is more, the Government undertook to impose royalties on all minerals won in the region bounded by the Niger and a line drawn from Zinder to Yola, and to pay half of these royalties to the company for ninety-nine years. In return the British government took control of all the company's territories on 1st January 1900. The whole of Nigeria was then reorganized into

three administrative areas under the Colonial Office instead of the
Foreign Office. The Niger Coast Protectorate, which had been trans-
ferred to the Colonial Office in April 1899, was included in the new
Protectorate of Southern Nigeria, which absorbed former company
territory as far north as Idah; Lagos remained an official colony
together with a small Protectorate; and a new Protectorate of Northern
Nigeria was established bounded by the frontiers agreed at the
Anglo-French Convention of 1898. The name Nigeria was chosen by
the British government in preference to such suggestions as 'Niger
Sudan', 'Negretia' and even 'Goldesia' in honour of Sir George Taubman Goldie.[2]

In the south the new Protectorate was sufficient of a reality for the
administration to set about establishing itself in earnest, though a
series of punitive expeditions had to be made before the administration
became effective in certain areas. The Protectorate of Northern
Nigeria was nothing but a cartographical claim. As Margery Perham
wrote of Sir Frederick Lugard's appointment as High Commissioner, 'a
colonial governor can seldom have been appointed to a territory so
much of which had never even been viewed by himself or any other
European'.[3] The British held positions along the banks of the Niger
alone and, as the cunning Emir of Kontagora slyly assured his people,
were really a species of fish unable to live away from the Niger. It fell to
Lugard to prove to the powerful emirs like Kontagora that the white
invaders could indeed live a mammalian existence.

Northern Nigeria had been profoundly influenced by the Holy War of
Usman dan Fodio, and because of the coherent organization of the
Sokoto Caliphate presented a formidable opponent for the small forces
at Lugard's disposal. In the years that followed the death of the Shehu,
the Fulani administration had inevitably lost some of its reforming
zeal. Conditions varied from emirate to emirate. Some, like Kontagora,
lived entirely on the proceeds of slave raiding, and in the process
depopulated vast tracts of land. Others, like Kano, lived mainly on
their commercial and agricultural activities. There has been a strong
tendency, particularly among those who sought to justify British occupation of Northern Nigeria,[4] to talk of the decadence of the Fulani
administration in its later years. Certainly it fell from the high standards set by Usman dan Fodio and his son Caliph Bello. In cases like
that of Kontagora, often used as a justification for British intervention,
affairs were indeed lamentable. In 1880 Ibrahim Nagwamatse, son of
the founder of the small emirate of Kontagora, set out on a ruthless
campaign to expand his lands. In the course of his conquests he captured thousands of slaves for sale in the northern markets and devastated hundreds of villages, killing anyone unsaleable as a slave and

leaving a once populous land so desolate that even today it is one of the most sparsely populated areas of the north. When later he was captured by the British and asked to renounce the slave trade, he taunted: 'Can you stop a cat from mousing? I shall die with a slave in my mouth.'[5]

Certainly the example of Kontagora did much to colour British views of Fulani administration. Major Sharpe, Resident of Kontagora, described his province as denuded of all its inhabitants except old men and babies.[6] It is a contrast therefore to read the notes made by Major Burdon, an early Resident in the north, which show a marked enthusiasm for the Fulani and their administration.[7] He writes: 'What is the attitude of the British Administration towards these states? Briefly it is construction not destruction. Our aim is to rule through existing chiefs, to raise them in the administrative scale, to enlist them on our side in the work of progress and good government. We cannot do without them. To rule directly would require an army of British magistrates . . . which both the general unhealthiness of the country and the present poverty forbid. My hope is that we may make of these born rulers a high type of British official, working for the good of their subjects in accordance with the ideals of British Empire, but carrying on all that is best in the constitution they have evolved for themselves, the one understood by, and therefore best suited to the people.'[8]

These are not the words of a man who has recognized an empire about to collapse. Unpopular it may have been, but the system of administration was still effective and developing. The materialism of later years should not be confused with inefficiency.

The Sokoto Caliphate was organized by Bello and Abdullahi on the pattern outlined by the Shehu in his *Kitab al-Farq*.[9] (See Chapter 6.) The provinces, ruled by emirs, were grouped into an Eastern and a Western Sector, responsible to Gwandu and Sokoto respectively, with Sokoto supreme, since it was at Sokoto that the Shehu, as Commander of the Faithful, resided.

For the first time since the brief rise of Kebbi to ascendancy in Hausaland in the early sixteenth century, all the Habe kingdoms, with the exception of parts of Gobir, Zamfara and Kebbi, were united under one rule. The old kingdoms were transformed into emirates, with their rulers owing both political and religious allegiance to the Commander of the Faithful at Sokoto. As D. M. Last has pointed out, the Sokoto Caliphate was not properly speaking an empire, since its unity depended not so much on force, as on the religious obedience the emirs or provincial governors owed the Commander of the Faithful or Caliph at Sokoto. To disobey Sokoto was tantamount to apostasy.[10] The provincial rulers paid tribute to Gwandu or Sokoto, and referred matters of administration to the imperial capitals. The viziers of Gwandu and

Sokoto made regular tours of their respective provinces, reviewing administration and settling disputes. Those emirates like Katsina, Kebbi, Gobir, Zamfara and Nupe, where the Fulani administration was not established over all the inhabitants, called frequently on their respective imperial capitals for troops in time of crisis.

In 1817, the Shehu died and there was a brief struggle for power between Bello and Abdullahi for the succession to the religious leadership of the Caliphate. Bello was quickly recognized as his father's successor, taking the title Commander of the Faithful. Administratively, however, the Caliphate remained divided into the two sectors of Sokoto and Gwandu, with Bello continuing to rule Sokoto as Caliph and Abdullahi ruling Gwandu as Emir. Under Bello the Caliphate was distinguished by its just administration, although it was harassed by a long series of wars with those who were still reluctant to accept the new régime, particularly the Gobirawa and Zamfarawa. Al-Hajj Sa'id wrote of Bello in his *History of Sokoto*: 'He gave all of them their just place, for he was upright and pious. He spent from his own earnings and did not spend from the public purse. He had already said of his father at the start of the Holy War, "Shaik, lawful resources are lacking, and it is necessary that you should spend for necessary expenses this money, but, as for myself, I will earn my own living for I am a young man." He was apprenticed to a craft by which means he became independent of the treasury. . . . He was kind to his subjects, most merciful to them, patient, self-controlled, scrupulous concerning their property in possession of the people, and a good administrator. He scrutinized the judges, reversing their judgements which were dictated by their own interests, nor did he give them free rein in their posts.'[11]

Bello was in political terms architect of the Caliphate, but his achievements as an administrator are the more remarkable when one considers that during his reign as Caliph (1817–37), he personally led the Caliphate forces into battle against rebels, or against dissident Hausa or Borno, some forty times. He found time not only to supervise the government of metropolitan Sokoto but of the provinces as well. In addition he wrote a large number of books on a variety of subjects ranging from theology to diseases of the eye, and the history of the Sudan.[12] Clapperton, when he visited Bello in 1824 at Wurno, his fortified frontier camp, was very impressed by his learning, particularly his knowledge of early Christian doctrinal disputes. On his second visit in 1826 he gave an Arabic copy of Euclid to Bello, who remarked that his family's copy, brought by a relative from Mecca 'was destroyed when part of his house was burnt down last year' and that he was 'very much obliged to the king of England for sending him so valuable a present'.[13]

It is from the death of Bello that some authorities trace the decline of

the Sokoto Caliphate, asserting not only a loss in the religious moti-
vation of Jihad and a corresponding increase of wars inspired by the
desire for slaves, but also a falling off in standards of learning.[14] They
further assert that the Hausa were restive under 'alien' rulers and that
the imperial capitals of Sokoto and Gwandu had lost control of the
provinces, which were effectively independent political units acknow-
ledging only a nominal allegiance to the Commander of the Faithful.
This picture has been much influenced by the eye-witness accounts of
Barth in the 1850s.

This is, however, a picture that is not borne out by the facts, as
Boahen has insisted.[15] So far as administration of the empire was
concerned it is clear that this remained under the control of Sokoto and
Gwandu right up until occupation by the British. Indeed after the
death of Caliph Bello there appears to have been a tendency towards
greater centralization on the twin capitals of Sokoto and Gwandu. The
Emirs of Zaria, for instance, were selected by the Caliphs of Sokoto,
who usually chose them from among the three families in Zaria, on the
recommendations of the electoral council of Zaria. The Caliph was even
able to depose the Emir of Zaria in 1860, substituting his own nominee,
a man who was not even a member of the families that had so far
provided the rulers of Zaria.[16] The Emir of Zaria paid homage as a
vassal at the court of Sokoto twice a year, bringing tribute in the form of
slaves, Zaria cloth, horses and cowries. When Zaria's own vassals had
complaints they could always seek the intervention of Sokoto. The
Waziri (Vizier) of Sokoto, as head of the imperial administration, made
frequent tours of Zaria and other vassal emirates, assessing tribute,
regulating disputes and checking internal administration.

It is clear from the history of Adamawa and Hammaruwa (Muri),[17]
the two provinces most distant from Sokoto, that neither of their emirs
could rule without the sanction of the Commander of the Faithful, to
whom, on the death of an Emir, rivals for the succession were sent for
his selection. The Waziri of Sokoto toured both Emirates, which continued sending tribute to Sokoto until the moment of British occupation.

There were of course exceptions to this general rule. A number of
emirs tried to break away from control by Sokoto. Thus Emir Sidi of
Zaria, who was deposed by Sokoto in 1860, had forbidden the entry of
the Waziri of Sokoto into his city in an apparent attempt to repudiate
his allegiance to the imperial capital. However, when the Caliph summoned him to the court at Wurno to explain his action, he dutifully
complied only to be told that he was deposed and a more tractable
successor chosen to replace him. He remained in Wurno as a prisoner
until he died.[18] Barth, despite the picture he drew of a breakdown in

imperial control over the provincial governments, nevertheless himself records a similar incident. In the Maradi area, where the former
Habe rulers of Katsina had established themselves outside Fulani
control, he recorded the following: 'I then rode to Sadiku, the son of the
famous M'allem 'Omaro of Ghomaro, who had been eight years Governor of Katsina, after the death of his father, till exciting the fear or
wrath of his liege lord in consequence of calumnies representing him as
endeavouring to make himself independent, he was deposed by 'Aliyu,
the second successor of Bello, and obliged to seek safety among the
enemies of his nation (i.e. Maradi).'[19] Whilst in Katsina Barth also
encountered the Galadima of Sokoto, who was concluding a tour of
inspection of Zamfara and Katsina, where he had been collecting tribute. But it is clear that Barth was unwilling to recognize this authority of Sokoto as meaningful, for when he sought negotations with
Lawal, Lamido of Adamawa (1848–72) in 1851, the latter refused on
the grounds that 'he was nothing but a slave of the Sultan of Sokoto', to
which Barth replied that Emir Lawal, 'far from being a slave of the
Sultan of Sokoto, was almost an independent governor of a large province'.[20] Yet on the death of Lawal, the two claimants to succession both
journeyed to Sokoto to seek the choice of the Caliph.[21]

It is not clear why Barth painted the picture of the Fulani empire he
did. In a note to the British government in 1853 he wrote 'it cannot be
denied that the Empire of Sokoto if going in the present way, will soon
be dissolved, and thrown into pieces'.[22] Clearly, as Boahen has
suggested, he over-emphasized the importance of the attacks on
Sokoto authority by dissident Zamfarawa, Gobirawa, Kebbawa,
and Maradi. These were the dissidents that had preoccupied
Caliph Bello for so much of his reign, and whilst they did create
insecurity in an important part of the Caliphate, there was a vast area
that was secure for traders and travellers, as the accounts of travellers
like Clapperton and Lander in the twenties, and Vogel in the fifties,
bear witness. Also these wars, it must be remembered, did not involve
the total population, unless of course they were initiated specifically for
slave raiding. Despite the reports of Barth, these rebels never got the
better of Sokoto and Gwandu, and it can be justifiably claimed for the
Fulani that they did succeed in creating a large area of peaceful
administration covering the greater part of northern Nigeria in which
trade was able to flourish on a much larger scale than it did under the
Habe. Barth himself in his account of Kano, which once again had
become the leading centre of commerce in the Central Sudan, gives an
excellent picture of the improved state of trade under the Fulani
régime. No longer involved in the constant wars of the eighteenth
century, the former Habe states could now trade easily with each other.

Kano quickly regained its former position as terminus of the Sahara caravans, and became the chief emporium of the Sokóto Caliphate.

'The principal commerce of Kano consists in native produce, namely, the cotton cloth woven and dyed here or in the neighbouring towns, in the forms of tobes or *rigona* (sing. *riga*): *turkedi*, or the oblong piece of dress of dark blue colour worn by the women; the *zenne* or plaid, of various colours; and the *rawani baki*, or black litham (Tuareg veil).

'The great advantage of Kano is, that commerce and manufactures go hand in hand, and that almost every family has its share in them. There is really something grand in this kind of industry, which spreads to the north as far as Murzuk, Ghat and even Tripoli; to the west, not only to Timbuktu, but in some degree even as far as the shores of the Atlantic, the very inhabitants of Arguin dressing in the cloth woven and dyed in Kano; to the east, all over Bornu, although there it comes in contact with the native industry of the country; and to the south it maintains a rivalry with the native industry of the Igbira and Igbo, while towards the south-east it invades the whole of Adamawa, and is only limited by the nakedness of pagan *sansculottes*, who do not wear clothing.

'As for the supply sent to Timbuktu, this is a fact entirely overlooked in Europe, where people speak continually of the fine cotton cloth produced in that town, while, in truth, all the apparel of decent character in Timbuktu is brought either from Kano or from Sansandi. . . . Besides the cloth produced and dyed in Kano and in the neighbouring villages, there is considerable commerce carried on here with the cloth manufactured in Nyffi or Nupe. . . . The chief articles of native industry, beside cloth, which have a wide market, are principally sandals . . . tanned hides ("kulabu") and red sheep skins, dyed with a juice extracted from the stalks of the holcus, are not unimportant, being sent in great quantities even as far as Tripoli. . . . A very important branch of the native commerce in Kano is certainly the slave trade; but it is extremely difficult to say how many of these unfortunate creatures are exported, as a greater number are carried away by small caravans to Bornu and Nupe than on the direct road to Ghat and Fezzan. . . .'[23]

Whilst it is true that the Sokoto Caliph lost much of its early reforming zeal, there is little justification for the picture of decadence of religious standards and learning given by so many authorities. Though the intellectual brilliance of Bello's court was not paralleled by any of his successors, the histories of Sokoto and Adamawa, to take two examples, make reference to the religious zeal and learning of a number of their rulers including those who reigned in the second half of the century. Thus the Emir Lawal of Adamawa, whom Barth met, is today in Yola 'often regarded as the *beau idéal* of the Fulani administrator: warrior, scholar, and religious ascetic. He enforced a strict code of moral conduct and even of dress. . . .'[24] Lawal also founded many schools in his province. Whilst his successor, Sanda (1872–90), appears to have been weak and indolent, devoted more to affairs in the harem than in the state, Zubeiru, who came to the throne in 1890 and opposed British occupation of his territory, immediately imposed a puritanical régime on the province. A number of Bello's successors were also noted for their piety and learning, in particular his immediate successor Atiku I (1837–42) and Attahiru Ahmadu, who was deposed in 1903 by the British after only one short year's reign.

There is another aspect of the Sokoto Caliphate that must not be forgotten. Since, like its predecessors, the Habe states, it depended, as indeed did Borno, on slaves for much of its foreign exchange, large numbers of peoples on the periphery of the empire suffered greatly at their hands. The case of Kontagora is notorious, but there were many other areas which also lived in perpetual fear of Fulani raids for slaves to be sold to North Africa or for use as agricultural labour. The insecurity of those areas subjected to these raids is well brought out in Mary Smith's *Baba of Karo*.[25] It was such slaving activities that the British used as one of their main justifications for the conquest of the Caliphate, effected by Lord Lugard between 1900 and 1906.

The Niger Company had made a number of treaties with the Caliph of Sokoto and the Emir of Gwandu which they claimed gave rights of Protectorate over the Caliphate. However, it seems clear that the Caliph of Sokoto believed that all he was conceding to the British traders was a monopoly of European trade with his empire which was granted in return for an annual payment that he must have considered as a form of tribute.[26] Though the Company used these treaties as a basis for their claim to the Caliphate and as a means to keep out the rival French, no effective administration had been established in Fulani territory before 1897. In that year the Royal Niger Company constabulary was sent against both Nupe and Ilorin on account of their persistent raids into company territory. A force of 500 men and 25 officers quickly subdued the Nupe forces and a new Emir, likely to be favourable to the company's interests, was installed. The force then marched on to Ilorin, where a treaty was signed whereby the Emir recognized company sovereignty in his state. The Emir of Nupe was forced to concede to the company the southern half of his emirate which became the province of Kabba. This was the first inroad made by the British into the great Sokoto Caliphate.

It was not until the 1st January 1900, however, when the British flag was hoisted at Lokoja, that real attempts were made to establish British control over those territories north of the Niger and Benue assigned her by the Berlin Conference. Though both the Sokoto Caliphate and Borno came within this sphere, the company had control over neither. True, they had drawn up treaties with Sokoto and Gwandu, to whom all other emirates were politically subordinate, but these were mere scraps of paper useful only for the purposes of international diplomacy. At first the new administration headed by Sir Frederick Lugard was in a difficult position, since the bulk of its defence force, the W.A.F.F., had been seconded to the Ashanti campaign. Only Ilorin, Borgu and Kabba were under effective occupation and even there Lugard had continually to assert British authority.[27] To the north lay the slave-raiding emirate of Kontagora and the emirate of Nupe, Lugard was equally engaged in trying to assemble an administration for the vast country he was about to take over. The old company plans to attack the W.A.F.F. troops in their Wushishi garrison.

At the same time as he was preparing to deal with Kontagora and Nupe, Lugard was equally engaged in trying to assemble an administration for the vast country he was about to take over. The old company administration was at his disposal but, as Lugard himself complained, this was very rudimentary and certainly not equipped to administer a huge country of nearly 15 million people. Furthermore, nothing he could prepare on the small sum of £135,000 available to him would be sufficient to cope with the administration of so vast an area. To deal with this seemingly impossible situation he formulated his famous policy of indirect rule, that is, rule by the colonial administration through the existing indigenous institutions.

From the very outset Lugard decided that indirect rule was the only method by which the country could be governed, and as a result he has often been credited as its originator. This is an incorrect assumption. It had been used in India and Fiji. His close friend Goldie had already propounded it as a suitable method for governing Nigeria. But Lugard ennobled indirect rule from being just an expedient in times of financial hardship and lack of staff to a complete philosophy of government for Britain's colonial peoples.[28] Before he even reached Nigeria he had decided that his political officers should be called Residents, thereby giving them the status of diplomats rather than administrators. In his first annual report he outlined his system: 'The Fulani rule has been maintained as an experiment, for I am anxious to prove to these people that we have no hostility to them, and only insist on good government and justice, and I am anxious to utilize, if possible, their wonderful intelligence for they are born rulers. . . .'[29] In later years he and his successors were to embroider this makeshift policy into a complete theory of administration.

The immediate problem, as Lugard saw it, however, was still the establishment of an effective administration and the promotion of trade. In 1900 he was already advocating the building of a railway, without which the north could never be commercially developed. Such a railway would also facilitate the movement of troops. A campaign was therefore first undertaken against the hostile Emirs of Kontagora and Nupe, the main obstacles between him and the conquest of the rich northern emirates. Nupe and Kontagora, having failed to bring Ilorin in on their side, put up stiff resistance against the British, until a full-scale campaign was launched against them in 1901 after the return of the W.A.F.F. troops from the Ashanti campaign in the Gold Coast, where they had fought with great distinction. Willcocks, Lugard's right-hand man and commander of these troops, was highly impressed by them. In a letter, to Lugard, he wrote: 'I never served with such fellows. How I love them! Always cheerful, plucky, brave and uncomplaining.'[30] With these well-trained troops Kontagora and Nupe were quickly conquered. Abu Bekri fled northwards and the old company Emir was reinstated. Lugard, at the same time, wrote to the Caliph of Sokoto, Abdurrahman (1891–1902), informing him of this and asked him as overlord of Kontagora to nominate a successor to Nagwamatse.[31] To this letter the Caliph did not reply. By April 1901 eight provinces were established and brought under Lugard's control: Borgu, Ilorin, Kabba, Kontagora, Bida, Zaria, Lower Benue (Nassarawa) and Upper Benue (Muri).

In Yola, the Emir Zubeiru, whom Lugard described as 'a fine type of the Fulani ruler, well educated, but possessed with a religious fanaticism, which rendered him entirely intolerant of European "infidels"',[32] ordered the representative of the Niger Company to haul down the Union Jack, despite his earlier treaty with the company. An expedition under Colonel Morland was therefore sent to deal with him. The Emir put up such resistance as he could with the aid of two cannon, but the British forces with their Maxim guns were too great for him. The Emir fled and was murdered by non-Muslims in Adamawa, after attacking German forces in Kamerun. Lugard wrote regretfully of his death: 'I should have wished, had it been possible, to have afforded domicile to this brave though fanatical chief, but he was wholly irrecoverable. . . .'[33]

North of Yola lay Borno, most of which had been assigned to the British under the terms of the Berlin Conference, though no treaty had been drawn up with the ruler of the thousand-year-old state. After the final abortive revolt of Mai Ibrahim against the Al-Kanemi dynasty in 1846, Borno enjoyed nearly fifty years of comparative security internally. Externally she had arrived at a *modus vivendi* with her enemy, the Sokoto Caliphate, which still controlled lands that once had belonged to Borno or been tributary to her. But in 1893 Borno suffered a great upheaval with the invasion of a Sudanese adventurer, Rabih, who defeated the Borno army in 1893, occupying the state in the name of the Mahdi, though he did not acknowledge the latter's authority.[34] By 1896 he had brought the whole state under his control. Rabih had had a chequered career in the Egyptian army and later in the service of the notorious slave raider, Zubair Pasha, who was imprisoned by the Egyptians for fear of the growing power of his private army. Half of this army was taken over by Rabih, who set off on a whirlwind career of conquest and slave raiding. Before he won the great prize of Borno, he had conquered Wadai, Dar Kuti and Bagarimi. In Borno he proved himself as competent an administrator as a general, dividing the newly acquired state into strictly controlled districts which paid him fixed tribute. His army consisted of 20,000 men, nearly 5,000 of whom were equipped with firearms. In 1892 he attacked Bagarimi, disturbed by the presence of the French officer Gentil in that kingdom. In 1899 he massacred a column led by a Frenchman Brettonet, and ordered the strangling of a Frenchman on a mission to Dikwa, which he had made his headquarters.

Rabih was fervently anti-European and advocated Holy War against Europe.[35] Well he might have been, for just as he was about to found a third Borno dynasty, under a much improved administrative system, the final partition of Borno between the colonial powers of Britain, France and Germany was determined by the Anglo-French Convention of 1898. Zinder, Kanem, Bagarimi and the lands east of the Chari were to be given to France; Dikwa and the territories between the Chari and the Yesderam to the Germans; and the rest to the British.

In 1900 the French sent columns to make good their claims to Borno, and engaged Rabih in a fierce battle in which he was killed by one of his former soldiers now serving the French. Gentil then restored the Kanemi dynasty to Dikwa. However, Rabih's son, Fad-el-Allah, still claimed the throne of Borno, and appealed to the British for recognition, promising that he would co-operate fully with them. Major McClintock, who had visited Borno on Lugard's behalf in 1901, was in favour of recognizing Fad-el-Allah, though Lugard doubted whether it would be politic to recognize an avowed enemy of the French. Any indecision on this matter was brought to an abrupt end by a French raid against Gujba, 150 miles within the borders of the agreed British sector of Borno, in which Fad-el-Allah was killed. The French then demanded 80,000 dollars from Abubakar Garbai, the legitimate Kanemi Shehu, for defeating Rabih and his son. Only 6,500 dollars remained to be paid when a British task force arrived to take over Borno. On the way this force subdued Bauchi and established a garrison in the town, hindered only by a self-proclaimed Mahdi, Jibrella of Gombe, who put up extremely brave resistance against the British. In Borno the British did not have to fight, since they promised Abubakar Garbai the throne of Borno if he would cease paying the indemnity demanded by the French and submit to their rule, a proposal he gladly accepted. He was eventually established as Shehu at Maiduguri where a British garrison was installed.

The occupation of Northern Nigeria was slow. An expedition had to be undertaken in 1902 against Abuja, where the Emir, descendant of the Habe rulers of Zaria, had closed the trade route to the north. The Magaji of Keffi was the next to be attacked. As the Emir of Zaria's representative and most influential member of the ageing ruler of Keffi's court, he slaved openly, refusing to recognize the validity of the laws abolishing slavery promulgated by Lugard in April 1901. He actually killed Captain Moloney, the local Resident, with his own hands when the latter tried to persuade him to stop his nefarious practices. He then fled to Kano by way of Zaria, whose Emir still wavered between declaring allegiance to the invading power, or affirming that to his overlord in Sokoto. At the end of the expedition against Keffi, Lugard confidently predicted in his second *Annual Report* that there would be a great increase in trade owing to the pacification of Borno, Yola and the Benue provinces.[36] But two tasks still confronted Lugard: to render trade routes safe from raiders and to conquer the emirates of the far north. As Lugard remarked in the *Annual Report* for 1902: 'Trade cannot, indeed, be established on a satisfactory basis until the northern Hausa States are included in the "Provinces" of the Protectorate and the trade routes rendered safe for small traders.'[37]

Both Sokoto and Gwandu, the imperial capitals of the Caliphate, remained hostile to the new administration. When Abdurrahman, the Caliph of Sokoto, eventually communicated with Lugard, he did so in terms which Lugard chose to consider tantamount to a declaration of war. Grave doubts have recently been expressed about the validity of Lugard's interpretation of this letter as an outright declaration of war.[38]

(Translation of Arabic Letter from Sultan of Sokoto to the High Commissioner, seal undecipherable)

"From us to you. I do not consent that any one from you should ever dwell with us. I will never agree with you. I will have nothing ever to do with you. Between us and you there are no dwellings except as between Mussulmans and Unbelievers,—War, as God Almighty has enjoined on us. There is no power or strength save in God on high.

This with salutations."

'Received about May 1902.'

Whether or not the Caliph's letter was an authentic declaration of war, Lugard used it as such, and decided the north would have to be taken by conquest, despite the disapproval of the Colonial Office which hoped for a negotiated occupation. He decided first to attack Kano where the Magaji of Keffi had been given asylum by the Emir Aliyu, who observed hopefully, 'If a little town like Keffi could do so much, what could not Kano do?'[39] Lugard was well aware that the whole of the Fulani North, including those states already captured, was awaiting his trial of strength with Kano and Sokoto. As long as Kano retained its reputation for invincibility, and Sokoto remained independent as spiritual overlord of all Fulani Emirs, so long would there be hope of escape from the new administration. If Lugard, who had pathetically small forces at his disposal, showed any sign of wavering, he might have a general uprising on his hands, which it would be impossible to contain.

Lugard considered he had two things in his favour. First, in the words of Hilaire Belloc:

> *Whatever happens we have got*
> *The maxim gun and they have not.*[40]

Secondly, Lugard firmly believed that once the Hausa peasantry saw that he was the real master, they would not put up much of a resistance on behalf of their Fulani rulers. Even so Kano presented a formidable objective. The great city, encircled by enormous walls, deep thorn-filled ditches and cunningly constructed gates, could, under a determined leader, withstand almost indefinite siege. Kano was first to show its cards. The Emir despatched a force against Lugard's garrison at Zaria, only to withdraw on the news of the death of the Caliph of Sokoto. Lugard then sent a force of 1,000 local troops and 50 Europeans, commanded by Colonel Morland, against Kano, despite the strong reservations of the Colonial Office about such an expedition.

Thus, in January 1903, after shelling Bebeji, the first town they came to that offered resistance, Lugard's forces marched in triumph to the gates of Kano, each town capitulating without struggle having seen what happened to Bebeji. The test came at Kano, whose defence had been entrusted to two slaves of the Emir, who had himself gone to Sokoto to consult with the newly elected Caliph, Attahiru Ahmadu, and to raise another army. The city was quickly taken, and it appeared that the inhabitants, who were Hausa as distinct from their Fulani overlords, were barely concerned about this change of masters. The army brought up by the Emir of Kano was of little effect since his brother, the Wombai, detached his half and refused to fight. The Emir fled across the French border, leaving his army under the command of the Waziri. On 26th February, the Wombai submitted to the British and was installed as Emir. This was the beginning of the end of Fulani resistance. Katsina's intention of submission was then received and *en route* for Sokoto the British took over Gwandu, the eastern capital. On the 14th March the Sokoto army was defeated. When the British occupied the town they found that the Caliph had fled. Lugard, arriving on the 19th, called together the Waziri and chiefs and asked them either to recall the fleeing Caliph, Attahiru Ahmadu, or elect a new one in his stead. In the event, they decided to choose a new Caliph, Muhammad Attahiru (1903–15). In a speech approving Attahiru's appointment Lugard made it clear that the old empire of Usman dan Fodio was now at an end.

'The old treaties are dead, you have killed them. Now these are the words which I, the High Commissioner, have to say for the future. The Fulani in old times under Dan Fodio conquered this country. They took the right to rule over it, to levy taxes, to depose kings and to create kings. They in turn have by defeat lost their rule which has come into the hands of the British. All these things which I have said the Fulani by conquest took the right to do now pass to the British. Every Sultan and Emir and the principal officers of State will be appointed by the High Commissioner throughout all this country. The High Commissioner will be guided by the usual laws of succession and the wishes of the people and chiefs but will set them aside if he desires for good cause to do so. The Emirs and Chiefs who are appointed will rule over the people as of old time and take such taxes as are approved by the High Commissioner, but they will obey the laws of the Governor and will act in accordance with the advice of the Resident. Buying and selling slaves and enslaving people are forbidden. . . . All men are free to worship God as they please. Mosques and prayer places will be treated with respect by us. . . . It is the earnest desire of the King of England that this country shall prosper and grow rich in peace and in contentment, that the population shall increase and the ruined towns which abound everywhere shall be built up, and that war and trouble shall cease. Henceforth no Emir or Chief shall levy war or fight, but his case will be settled by law, and if force is necessary Government will employ it. . . . You need have no fear regarding British rule, it is our wish to learn your customs and fashion, just as you must learn ours. I have little fear that we shall agree, for you have always heard that British rule is just and fair, and people under our King are satisfied. You must not fear to tell the Resident everything and he will help and advise you.'[41]

Meanwhile it was essential for Lugard to effect the capture of the ex-Caliph of Sokoto and Aliyu, the 'ex-Emir' of Kano, both of whom were potential focal points for opposition to his régime. The Emir Aliyu was captured shortly after Lugard left Kano, having fled to the north where he had been seized by the King of Gobir, ancient foe of the Fulani, who was only too glad to deliver up this scion of the empire to the European conquerers. This was fortunate for Lugard since had Aliyu been able to join forces with the ex-Caliph Attahiru Ahmadu, as did the Magaji of Keffi, Lugard might have been faced with a more difficult task in consolidating his gains in Northern Nigeria than he actually did. The ex-Caliph's flight was undertaken as a *hijra*, or flight from the infidel. When Usman dan Fodio conquered the Hausa kings in the early nineteenth century, he prophesied that in the future, at a given sign that would be clear to all, the faithful would be called upon to undertake the *hijra* towards the east. This prophecy was made known through his daughter, Nana Mariam, and his son, Abubakar Atiku, who reigned as Sultan from 1837–42. As Muffet has shown, the Emir Aliyu, when he travelled to Sokoto on the election of the Attahiru Ahmadu as Caliph in 1902, actually suggested that the time for the *hijra* had come, and that they should abandon the country.[42] Throughout the century there had been a number of occasions when the Muslims had believed the time had come for the *hijra* prophesied by the Shehu. But as Muffet records, when one Emir of Kano in the middle of the century wrote to Nana Mariam to ask whether people who had begun the *hijra* were justified, she answered that the time was not yet come:

'By Allah's wish, it is better to remain. It is better and safer to remain where you are, in spite of other longings. . . . The Shehu, my father, stated that we shall migrate from Hausaland, but he did not decree the time that this would be. He only defined the *hijra* for us. . . .'[43]

The ex-Sultan's call to the faithful to follow him in the prophesied *hijra* to the east gained a response that Lugard had not bargained for. He had considered the alienation of the Hausa peasantry from their Fulani rulers an essential factor in the political situation in the Sokoto Empire; yet a large number of chiefs and peasants abandoned their lands for the long trip eastwards under the leadership of the man they still regarded as their Caliph and perhaps 'had his roots deeper in the hearts of his people than was admitted in the hour of his defeat'.[44] Clearly the exodus, as the *Annual Report* for 1903 stresses, was having a profound effect on the peasantry[45] and it became evident that it was essential to capture Attahiru Ahmadu if British authority were to be firmly established in the area. The Sultan was finally defeated in a battle after a flight of over 900 km. from Sokoto to Burmi, in the course of which he and his followers beat off the British expeditionary force on some six occasions. At Burmi, where Attahiru joined forces with the local Mahdi, and with the Magaji of Keffi and a large number of chiefs from all over the empire, he was finally defeated and killed by the British in a hard fought engagement. Nevertheless his preaching of the *hijra* still inspired many of his followers. As many as 25,000 people led by his son and Ahmadu of Misau migrated to the Sudan, settling on the Blue Nile where the Fulani-Hausa settlements are still in existence today.[46]

After the conquest of Sokoto, Lugard was able to get down to the more fundamental task of administration. One cannot but be impressed by the meticulous annual reports he submitted each year, showing how much thought he gave to every problem of administration. Slavery was abolished, but rather than upset the whole social structure of the country, only those who ran away from their masters were deemed free. A dual system of British and Muslim law was instituted. The organization of the provinces was streamlined. Roads were pushed through the bush. Every effort was made to stimulate trade. All this was the more remarkable since for the first three years of his office Lugard was tied down by military expeditions, and handicapped for the whole period by acute shortage of funds. Nevertheless, his policy of indirect rule seemed to be maturing well.

Suddenly, in 1906, it seemed that all Lugard's work was to be destroyed overnight, when news arrived by telegram from Sokoto:

'. . . whole of C Company Mounted Infantry, defeated and annihilated in Satiru. . . . Hillary and Scott, Residents, Blackwood, West African Frontier Force, are I fear killed. Dr Ellis severely wounded, Sergeant Slack, R.A., and myself and doctor only men remaining most urgent. Signed, Gosling, Sergeant.'[47]

This was a severe blow to Lugard. At a time when his administration seemed to have taken root, white men had been murdered in the heart of the former Caliphate. Would this be a general signal for revolt? Would the emirs, especially those like Gwandu and Hadejia who had never really accepted the new administration, now try to overthrow it? They all knew that his forces were tied down suppressing rebellion among the Tiv, who had come to the aid of their neighbours the Jukun in a quarrel with local Hausa traders, many of whom had been enslaved. Most serious of all, Major Burdon, the highly competent Resident of Sokoto, was trekking southwards on his way home for leave. What was more, the Sokoto rebels had captured a precious Maxim gun.

It was only later that Lugard learnt the full story of the rising. Two years before, the chief of Satiru, a town some 32 km. distant from Sokoto, had declared himself the Mahdi. He had been arrested and had died in prison. However, an outlaw from across the border, Dan Makafo, had now persuaded the chief's son, Mallam Isa, to proclaim himself the prophet Jesus. In their excitement the people of Satiru had risen against neighbouring enemy villages, so the Acting Resident went with a small force to quell the rebels. When he tried to treat with them, they rushed his troops, inflicting the casualties outlined in Sergeant Gosling's telegram. It was a touchy moment for British Imperialism in Northern Nigeria. For the first time the white man had been conquered, and a general rising, if led by the Caliph of Sokoto, could well have broken the hold that Lugard had maintained so effectively till then with his shoe-string army. Indeed everything depended on Sokoto. 'Had he shown the slightest indecision', wrote Burdon later, 'I have no doubt that the bulk of the "talakawa" (peasantry) would at once have joined the enemy.'[48] As it was, Sokoto remained loyal, possibly because he realized that ultimately the British could always draw on more reserves, possibly because he saw that the success of a revolt led by a 'prophet' would be a threat to his own religious pre-eminence. Maybe he really did feel some loyalty to Lugard. M. G. Smith has suggested that this revolt emphasized the interdependence of the Fulani and British administrations and that therefore a 'tacit agreement grew up that force would not be used'.[49]

With Sokoto's decision to support Lugard, the rising was as good as quashed. A military expedition defeated the rebels, whose ringleaders were put to death. The village of Satiru was razed to the ground, and cursed by the Caliph. The Emir of Gwandu, who had wavered on the side of the rebels, was deposed, and an expedition was led against the long recalcitrant Emir of Hadejia, who died in the fighting.

Shortly after the Satiru rebellion, Lugard was appointed Governor of Hong Kong. He left behind him a country now firmly under British control. In a final trial of strength the emirs had proved remarkably loyal. Undoubtedly this had much to do with Lugard himself, for he held them in deep respect. It was for his successors to consolidate the vast gains he had made and to regularize the makeshift administration he had so rapidly and successfully established.

14 The Unification of Nigeria

On the withdrawal of the Royal Niger Company's charter, the Niger Coast Protectorate and all the company's territories as far north as Idah were, as we have seen, amalgamated into the new Protectorate of Southern Nigeria. The Lagos Protectorate, like the Protectorate of Southern Nigeria, was brought under Colonial Office jurisdiction, and comprised all of Yorubaland except the Emirate of Ilorin, which was included in the Protectorate of Northern Nigeria. By 1900 the major areas of resistance to British authority had been overcome, but in some areas of the eastern provinces British authority was only extended with great difficulty. Yorubaland, with the exception of Ijebu, had been brought under British rule by treaty, Benin had been conquered and the Delta states had all been subdued in the interests of trade. However, it took many punitive expeditions to bring the whole of Igboland effectively under British administration.

The first major operation undertaken by the new Protectorate government was against the Aro, guardians of the famous Aro Chukwu oracle, which still retained its political influence over most of the peoples of the Niger Delta and its hinterland. The Aro bitterly resented the extension of British authority over an area in which for more than two centuries the religious and political supremacy of their oracle had remained unchallenged. They therefore did as much as they could to frustrate the alien administration, particularly by using their religious authority to place embargoes on trade with the Europeans.[1] At first the British had hoped to avoid using force in dealing with the Aro. However, when in June 1901 the latter attacked some Ibibio villages, carrying off a number of their inhabitants for sale as slaves on the domestic market, the British decided to take action. As Anene has put it, 'there were no doubts . . . in the minds of the Protectorate administrators that the one remaining obstacle to the consolidation of imperial rule was the Aro.'[2] The attack on the Ibibio was considered by the Protectorate government as having been aimed at the frustration of trade in the interior. This, together with the continuing role of the Aro in the internal slave trade, gave them the excuse they needed to mount an expedition against the Aro and their oracle. However, as Anene has pointed out, the Colonial Office, while sanctioning the expedition, was not happy about extending the Protectorate by conquest.[3] The expedition met with comparatively little resistance, and entered Arochukwu itself on 24th December 1901. A number of Aro chiefs were hanged, and the oracle was burnt. Though the destruction of the basis of Aro authority represented a major step forward in the extension of British authority over south-eastern Nigeria, numerous columns, named after the areas they patrolled, were kept on a standing basis. In Ogoja, Owerri, Ibibio, Urhobo and Western Igbo the new government had its most difficult task, often extending control village by village.[4] The local people had the initiative despite their primitive weapons. Great rain forests, meshes of streams and rivers merging into swampland, made rapid communications almost impossible and put the villagers at a great advantage over their well-armed enemies. Thus for the first six years of the Protectorate's life the new administration, particularly in the eastern provinces, was concerned primarily with the assertion of its authority.

Though some parts of Igboland were not finally brought under British control until as late as 1918, the year 1906, when the Lagos Protectorate was merged with the Protectorate of Southern Nigeria and the north was finally pacified, can be taken as marking the beginning of effective British administration in modern Nigeria. Before then cultural contact with the European, with the exception of the coastal ports and certain towns in Yorubaland, had been of marginal significance. During the three centuries that Europeans had been visiting Nigeria they had made remarkably little cultural impact on the bulk of the local population. This is in marked contrast to the trans-Saharan contact in northern Nigeria, which resulted in extensive changes in religion, law, architecture, technology and concepts of social stratification. It was only after 1906 that the way of life of the invaders had any appreciable effect on Nigerian society. From then on can be traced the rapid breakdown of the structure of traditional society, as the various peoples of Nigeria were brought under an administration which if not uniform in its application was at least controlled by a single power. Before then the British had been but a handful and their main interest in Nigeria had been economic. With the exception of the missionaries they had neither deliberately nor unconsciously attempted to alter Nigerian society except in so far as customs hindered trade, or where practices such as human sacrifice were openly repugnant to them.

The period 1906–12, which preceded the amalgamation of the Northern and Southern Protectorates, is one of the most crucial in the history of Nigeria, for it marks both the beginning of effective administration and the beginning of the rejection of standards and customs that had endured almost intact for many centuries. It was the first time that Nigerians were subjected in any large measure to Western influences, which in the next fifty years were to have such a great effect on Nigerian society. A whole new economic world was to be opened to Nigerians. Christianity, as the official doctrine of the colonial masters, began to spread throughout Southern Nigeria and the non-Muslim areas of Northern Nigeria. New forms of administration and justice were introduced. Finally, education in the Western way of life was made available to a wide range of Nigerians as a result of the spread of missions. So although this period appears from the annual reports as a static one, it was in effect the beginning of major changes in Nigeria.

Since Britain's overriding interest in Nigeria was economic, it is not surprising that one of the dominant factors tending towards the disintegration of traditional society was the growth of Western-oriented trade. A comparison between trade figures in 1908 and 1910 gives an indication of the extent of this growth in Southern Nigeria. In 1908 exports were valued at £3,094,175 as compared with £4,320,000 in 1910, whilst the figures for imports were respectively £3,076,309 and £5,122,000. Exports consisted mainly of palm products. Trade figures for the North were substantially lower, amounting to little more than £200,000 worth of exports in 1910. Yet significantly in 1911, when the railway reached Kano, figures for groundnut exports were 19,288 tons compared with a mere 1,179 tons the previous year.[5]

The rapid growth of the Nigerian economy was to have profound effects on the trading structure of Nigerian societies.[6] The installation of the British administration created a huge free trade area, eliminating the dangers that had beset most traders in the past, and depriving many societies of their occupation of exacters of trade tolls. Under British protection traders could move about the country freely with the result that not only did the volume of internal trade rise steeply, but exporting and importing became easier. The most significant innovation by the new administration was the introduction of a new communications system. The slow caravans that trekked from north to south and back, passing along narrow footpaths, often heavily armed against attack, were now replaced by the railway, which if not fast by modern standards cut days off the old journey, and reduced the cost in human carriers. This growth in the internal market was facilitated by the introduction of a common system of portable currency, which, though in many areas it took a long time to replace traditional forms of currency like cowries and iron bars, necessarily overcame many of the obstacles previously presented for inter-ethnic trading. Systematic taxation gave Nigerians motives for producing more than was normally necessary to maintain the family.[7] The introduction of European goods soon stimulated new wants so that in many parts of the country people were beginning to produce a surplus for exchange.

The new money economy brought with it many changes, more marked in smaller societies than, for example, in Hausaland where a developed export trade had been conducted across the desert for many centuries. Wealth soon began to compete with traditional status. Heredity began to give way to acquisition of riches as the arbiter of influence in the community. New towns began to spring up, or else traditional towns expanded in response both to the demands of trade and the new administration. Here peoples of many different ethnic groups mingled, dealing in the same markets, living side by side, and dropping former ethnic hostilities and differences in the interest of trade. However, the traditional corporate life was slow to be replaced by a life of economic individualism, and it was not undermined to nearly the same extent as in the German Cameroons or certain French territories where efficient plantations were established by alienating indigenously owned land and transferring it either to expatriate individuals or companies. In Nigeria traditional land laws were observed and Europeans were unable to purchase land. Since corporate ownership of land by lineages was fundamental to the traditional structure of most Nigerian societies, the observance of customary land law proved a bulwark against the disruptive elements of the new economic order. At the same time it prevented the economic exploitation of the land by individual Nigerians.

Western economic forces have contributed to the unity of the arbitrary block that is modern Nigeria, and the various ethnic groups comprised within its frontiers have necessarily become more and more dependent on each other as the economy has expanded. Superficially, however, unity was given to the new Nigeria by the establishment of the British administration. Nevertheless, after the amalgamation of the Northern and Southern Protectorates in 1914, the administrative distinction between the two was maintained. However many local variations there may have been in the administrative system, there was one ultimate factor: there had been a diversion of power from the traditional authorities to the incoming colonial administration. Even in the Northern region where the principles of indirect rule were applied most intensively, the Emir was no longer sovereign and held power by grace of the colonial government. His authority was reduced by the knowledge that, if he stepped over the uncertain boundary of rules for good government laid down by the British, he could be deposed. On the other hand his overlord at Sokoto or Gwandu had exercised a similar restraint on his exercise of power. In one sense his position was made more secure in that the presence of the British reduced threats of deposition from within by rivals.[8]

In the North, Lugard's successors, Sir Percy Girouard and Sir Hesketh Bell, consolidated his policy of indirect rule, though not exactly along the lines he had advocated.[9] The regularization of the Native Courts and the reorganization of the Native Treasuries, known as Beit-el-Mal, whereby the Emir had to submit annual budgets for approval by the administration, both fitted in with Lugard's concept of indirect rule as a dynamic process whereby the Native Authorities would become the instruments of modernization themselves. On the other hand under Girouard and Bell the concept of indirect rule came increasingly to mean a policy of minimal interference by the administration in the affairs of the Native Authorities. Thus while in one sense the Emir, now a salaried official of his own Native Authority, had his power implicitly curtailed by having to submit annual budgets for approval by the British administration, the *laissez-faire* attitude of the latter meant that provided the Emir committed no flagrant abuses of his power he remained very much master in his own house. In the South the Yoruba oba and his courts were similarly subjected to the new concepts of what good government constituted and in a certain sense a diminution of authority inevitably ensued. On the other hand, the focusing of attention by the British on the executive role of the oba gave him authority that he never possessed in the traditional context.[10] In the south-east of Nigeria the British appointed local administrations assumed much greater importance than in any other part of Nigeria, and must have proved a revolutionary concept for societies which had conceived political organization at the village level on a largely democratic basis where no one man or group had exclusive power. Furthermore, the introduction of the British system of justice for a large number of matters in the south naturally detracted from the authority of traditional chiefs and broke down many of the sanctions of traditional society. It also provided a place for appeal outside the traditional social system.

Neither the economic nor administrative policy of the government set out deliberately to upset the traditional social structure. Indeed the core of the philosophy of indirect rule as it came to be practised in Nigeria from 1906 onwards was the ensurance of minimum interference with 'native society'. It attempted only to create favourable conditions for trade and to ensure what it considered the basic essentials of human behaviour. By contrast the missionaries, who were excluded from the Muslim areas of the North by Lugard's agreement with the Caliph of Sokoto that he would not interfere with Muslim religion, approached Nigerian societies with a very different attitude.

They were convinced that their own society was superior, and also that conversion of the local people would have to be not only from the traditional religion but from the whole way of life which was intertwined with it and supported it. They therefore deliberately set out to change the very structure of traditional society. Until the beginning of the twentieth century they had made only comparatively small inroads into Nigerian society.

Something of the ardour with which the early missionary pursued his self-chosen task is indicated by the career of that remarkable woman missionary Mary Slessor, who is remembered vividly to this day by many of the peoples of Cross River State. Like her fellows she saw almost nothing that was good in African society, though she never treated the African himself as a man of inferior quality as many other missionaries did.[11]

Mary Slessor left her home in Scotland, where she had worked as a mill girl and had seen the most sordid sides of nineteenth-century industrial life, to serve the Presbyterian mission in Calabar. She arrived there in 1876, and soon became interested in the conversion of the Okoyong people of the Cross River. For the nineteenth-century missionary they presented a considerable challenge: they practised twin murder and human sacrifice. Their country was some of the remotest in Nigeria. Nevertheless, against the advice of the other missionaries, Mary Slessor went to live among these people, eating their food, sharing their life so completely that after many setbacks she was able to persuade them of the undesirability of their practices. Such was her standing with the Okoyong that in 1890 she was appointed Vice-Consul for Okoyong by Sir Claude Macdonald, since it was felt that no official could gain their co-operation. In the years that followed she worked in many different parts of the Cross River, earning the deepest respect of the people, for although she was uncompromising about those practices she found repugnant, she had a deep love and respect for the people she was trying to convert. When she died she had made a great impression on a very large number in the area, many of whose children and grandchildren are amongst the best-educated Nigerians today.

The career of Mary Slessor not only shows what missionaries were fighting, but also how they appreciated that total conversion was necessary. Such an attitude was bound to be disruptive of both those elements which were undesirable on the European scale of moral values and those which gave cohesion to society. The impact of missionaries was more intimately felt by Nigerians than that of administrators. Like Mary Slessor they penetrated the most remote regions, bearing with conditions that would have been intolerable to any other than one who was so whole-heartedly dedicated. In every case they hacked prodigiously away at the very roots of society. Since chiefs or elders were invariably resentful of these intruders, missionaries were often forced to turn to the socially low placed or outcast, who had no deep vested interest in traditional society. Thus a slave, or mother of twins, would be more receptive than a young man destined for important position in the community. Conversion implied for the African a complete rejection of his society. Dancing and drumming were even included in the list of undesirable associations with traditional life. Marriage payment, forming a great bond between two families, polygamy, initiation ceremonies, the basis of a man or woman's education into adulthood, ancestor worship which symbolized the continuing existence of the community, all these were rejected by the true convert. This naturally tended to undermine the structure of the old community. Parental authority, social sanctions were broken down. The convert was necessarily alienated from his community, and indeed was taught to look on its every aspect with contempt. In accepting Christianity he accepted the individualism implicit in its doctrine, which conflicts radically with the corporate concept of African life. He was also taught to believe in the fundamental equality of man before Christ, and the Christian of slave status could use this in argument against his traditional superiors. Later, of course, the Christian convert was to use the same argument in demands for equality with the Europeans. Christianity, whose influence was in the early years restricted to the south, and today affects little more than 30 per cent of the population, had a profound influence on the attitude of the convert towards his own society, for as James Coleman has written, in a searching analysis of missionary impact on traditional society: 'Once the genuine African convert had embraced Christianity, the difficulties of individual adjustment to a socio-political structure incapable of realizing Christian ideals became insuperable.'[12]

Whether the break need have been so dramatic is open to doubt. Subsequent missionaries have felt these early endeavours were too unaccommodating, and implied too great a rupture with the past. Bishop Crowther, who headed the first major experiment in an Africanized mission, believed, like Muslim proselytes, in converting 'the men with influence in the old town so as to win the whole community for the new religion'.[13] But most early missionaries felt that conversion was purely a personal matter, and that no wholesale conversion could be a true conversion. They were not prepared to compromise principles in the light of particular situations. The Muslim proselytizers, on the other hand, probably approaching the problem a little more sceptically, and with a greater appreciation of the realities of African society, made a bee-line for the chief, realizing that once he was converted, the rest of the community would the more readily follow suit. However nominal the conversion might be for the first generation, the succeeding generations would be more likely to be devout Muslims. Bishop Crowther, whilst he never took so calculated an approach as this, undoubtedly as an African realized the difficulties confronting men when asked to give up all their past ways. It was not surprising that his episcopate ended with the Society criticizing him for laxity in supervision and for tolerating heathenish practices amongst his clergy. The mission was purged by a European bishop, and led to a secessionist movement in the Delta, which established the United Native African Church in 1891.[14]

The most radical influence on Nigeria introduced by the British was the Western system of education. Until the end of the nineteenth century education had been conducted at various levels in Nigeria. In the Muslim societies of the north academic education of the Koranic type was fairly widespread. In other societies education of children was essentially directed towards enabling them to take their proper places in the community. There were no societies in the south where reading and writing were understood, so that traditional education was primarily directed towards the acquisition of skills in crafts and agriculture. But since the missionaries were not prepared to modify their educational programmes to suit African needs, academic rather than technical education was given to children. Early suspicion of education was naturally overcome when it was seen that education was the key to success in the new economic order. The revolutionary effects of education were widespread: English was established as a *lingua franca* so that different ethnic groups now had a common means of communication. Education soon came to be seen as a means not only of economic betterment but of social elevation. It opened doors to an entirely new world, the world of the white man. Since missionaries had a virtual monopoly of schools, they were able to use them as a means of further proselytization, and continued to warn their pupils of the evils of their former way of life.[15]

The north was almost entirely insulated against the revolutionary effects of education by Lugard's promise that missionaries would not be allowed in any Muslim emirate without the Emir's consent. Since the government was neither interested in nor had the money to provide education, for the first years of British administration the only form of education available in the north was that of the Koranic school, except for small schools provided by the C.M.S. missions in Zaria and Bida, and the government school opened outside Kano in 1912.

These forces of change were essentially let loose between 1906 and 1912, a period that in terms of events is really rather dull. They were to influence the subsequent development of Nigeria very profoundly. But one man, in a short but dramatic governorship, was to provide the mould in which the jelly of upheaval was to set. This was Sir Frederick Lugard who, because of his previous experience in Northern Nigeria, was nominated in 1912 as Governor-General of Nigeria with the task of amalgamating the Northern and Southern Protectorates. The decisions he made in those years were to influence the canalization of these new forces until, after the Second World War, control of government was slowly taken over from the British administration by the Nigerian nationalists themselves.

The immediate reason for the decision to amalgamate the two Nigerias was economic expediency.[16] The Northern Protectorate was running at a severe deficit, which was being met by a subsidy from the Southern Protectorate, and an Imperial Grant-in-Aid from Britain of about £300,000 a year. This conflicted with the age-old colonial policy that each territory should be self-subsisting. Apart from the fact that it seemed logical to amalgamate the two territories, the one land-locked and the other with a long seaboard, it was felt that the prosperous Southern Protectorate could subsidize its northern neighbour until such time as it became self-supporting. Furthermore, there was the pressing need to co-ordinate railway policy, which at the time was practically non-existent. The Southern track from Lagos had been started in 1901 and reached the River Niger in the Northern Protectorate at Jebba in 1909. It was to continue to Minna, where a Northern line was being constructed to reach Kano. At the same time, Sir Percy Girouard, the Governor, was intent on extending the Northern line to Baro on the Niger, where goods would be shipped down to the sea on barges. By 1912, then, there were two competing systems, the Minna-Baro-Niger system rivalling the Minna-Jebba-Lagos system, though the former proved less effective than was originally hoped. Ironically Girouard's railway had been built with Southern revenues. Since a new line was envisaged from Port Harcourt through Enugu to the North it was essential that there be more effective co-ordination of railway policy and this could best be ensured through amalgamation.

Amalgamation was finally achieved on 1st January 1914. But in preparing for this day Lugard took a number of decisions that were to influence the whole future of Nigeria. Though the two territories were to be amalgamated, Lugard chose to maintain the distinction between North and South, against the better judgement of men who knew Nigeria well. E. D. Morel, at that time editor of the *African Mail* and a persistent critic of colonial policy, advocated the division of the country into four large provinces.[17] It is essential to take careful note of the schemes proposed to Lugard, for much of the politics of Nigeria before

8. Proposed administrative reorganizations of Nigeria, 1914

the creation of the twelve states in 1967, and the addition of a further
seven in 1976, was coloured by dissatisfaction with the then political
division of the country, which might have been different if Lugard had
listened to Morel or Temple, his Lieutenant-Governor for the North,
who himself advocated the division of the country into seven provinces.[18] Morel suggested that the four provinces should comprise a
Northern Province, consisting of Kontagora, Sokoto, Katsina, Kano,
Zaria and Borno; a Central Province corresponding roughly with the
Middle Belt state which used to be advocated by the Action Group party
and consisting of Bauchi, Plateau, Adamawa and parts of Niger and
Benue provinces; a Western Province consisting of the former Western
Region, Mid-West State, Ilorin and Borgu; and an Eastern Province
that would take in Benue Province as far as the Benue River, together
with the former Eastern Region. Temple, who as Lieutenant-Governor
of the North was virtually doing himself out of a job by advocating the
breakdown of the country into seven provinces, suggested the division
of the North into three provinces, and the maintenance of the existing
provincial system in the South—Lagos Colony, Western, Central and
Eastern Provinces. Neither of these plans was adopted by Lugard, who
preferred the existing division partly because he really did not want
the break-up of the administration he had devised for the North, partly
because he did not want too great an administrative burden thrown on
himself. With two responsible Lieutenant-Governors in command of
day-to-day administration, he as Governor-General could carry on
with general reform. Furthermore, Lugard planned his administration
as a continuous one, uninterrupted by leave. During his first tour he
spent six months in Nigeria and six months in London at the Colonial

Office, and afterwards eight months in Nigeria and four in London, thereby never once letting slip the reins of government.[19] To achieve this unique type of government he had to delegate the main burden of day-to-day administration to his Lieutenant-Governors.

The Northern and Southern Provinces of Nigeria together retained their status as British Protectorates, whilst Lagos, the capital, remained a British Colony and its inhabitants had the rights of British citizens. The treaties made with the various Yoruba rulers, except for that with the Alake of Abeokuta, were considered void; for the Chief Justice had found that 'His Majesty had now acquired such complete jurisdiction throughout the Protectorate, with the possible exception of Egbaland, as to be able to legislate in any direction, not only for Europeans and resident non-natives, but for the natives themselves.'[20] Lugard, as we shall see, soon had occasion to bring the semi-independent enclave of Egbaland into line with the other Yoruba kingdoms.

In the general reorganization of Nigeria great powers devolved on the person of the Governor-General. Lugard reduced the already limited powers of the Legislative Council, which in 1906 had been extended to all Southern Nigeria, to a mere cipher by restricting its authority to Lagos Colony alone, and in its place set up an unwieldy Nigerian Council with a majority of officials, and only three nominated Africans from the North and three from the South. As an advisory body, meeting but once a year, it could hardly act as a check on Lugard's powers. Lugard centralized only those departments that he felt necessary for control of overall policy. At every turn he avoided acquisition of a large administration, so that administration was effectively regionalized under the Lieutenant-Governors, a process that only exacerbated the growing differences between the two regions. He amalgamated the Treasury, Railways, Survey, Judiciary, Military, Posts and Telegraphs and Audit. Otherwise everything was left to the Lieutenant-Governors, who merely referred to Lugard any matter that seemed to affect Nigeria as a whole. Their budgets were prepared locally and then incorporated in the general budget for the territory. By centralizing the Treasury, Lugard was able to divert revenue that earlier had been properly the South's to balance the Northern deficit.[21] He had few qualms about this since the bulk of the revenue of the South came from a liquor duty, of which he disapproved and which could not be raised in the Mohammedan North. He even hoped to shift his government headquarters from the South to the North, which was his spiritual home.

The administration of the North remained intact, but the Southern provinces, which had been acquired piecemeal in widely differing circumstances, were reorganized to bring them in line with the North. The three large provinces of the South, where the Provincial Commissioners seemed to have too much power, were broken down into nine provinces with roughly the same population as their northern counterparts. A Resident was placed in charge of each. Bringing the South even more in line with the North, Lugard completely remodelled the judiciary, which had until then been theoretically independent of the executive, though administrators had been commissioners in the district courts of the supreme court, and up till 1914 had presided over native courts, which subsequently they supervised. A supreme court for the whole of Nigeria was established with two divisional courts for the South, one for those provinces west of the Niger and one for those east of the Niger. Under the divisional courts came the provincial courts presided over by the Residents. A Native Court Ordinance introduced native courts for the South in which cases of indigenous law were heard. Admittedly this system sorted out the judicial chaos that had reigned in the Southern Protectorate before amalgamation, but it raised great objections both in Britain, where the separation of executive and judiciary was held fundamental to good government, and in Nigeria, where Lugard's ruling that barristers could not appear in the provincial courts angered the small but vocal group of Nigerian lawyers. Lugard gave as his reason for this ruling that it was designed to restrict 'the fomenting of litigation by lawyers' touts which, by a concensus of opinion, has become a public scandal in the Southern Provinces, with a natural corollary of rendering litigation extremely costly, to the detriment of litigants and the benefit of lawyers'.[22] The greatest objection to Lugard's new scheme was that while it regulated law in the South, it put an end to the attempt to develop a legal system based on that of Britain.

The greatest impact of Lugard's governorship on Nigeria lay in his development of native administration. Having successfully applied indirect rule in the North, he tried to work out a similar system for what he regarded as the chaotically administered South. Let us look first at the development of Native Administration in the North.

In his *Amalgamation Report*, published in 1920 just after his retirement as Governor-General, Lugard defined indirect rule in Northern Nigeria: 'The system of Native Administration in the separate Government of Northern Nigeria had been based on the authority of the Native Chiefs. The policy of the Government was that these Chiefs should govern their people, not as independent but as dependent Rulers. The orders of Government are not conveyed to the people through them, but emanate from them in accordance, where necessary, with instructions received through the Resident. While they themselves are controlled by Government in matters of policy and of importance, their people are controlled in accordance with that policy by themselves. A political Officer would consider it as irregular to issue direct orders to an individual native, or even to a village head, as a General commanding a division would to a private soldier, except through his commanding officers. The courts administer native law, and are presided over by Native Judges (417 in all). Their punishments do not conform to the Criminal Code, but, on the other hand, native law must not be in opposition to the Ordinances of Government, which are operative everywhere, and the courts . . . are under the close supervision of the District Staff. Their rules of evidence and their procedure are not based on British standards, but their sentences, if manifestly faulty, are subject to revision. Their prisoners are confined in their own gaols, which are under the supervision of the British Staff. The taxes are raised in the name of the native ruler and by his agents, but he surrenders the fixed proportion to Government, and the expenditure of the portion assigned to the Native Administration, from which fixed salaries to all native officials are paid, is subject to the advice of the Resident, and the ultimate control of the Governor. The attitude of the Resident is that of a watchful adviser not of an interfering ruler, but he is ever jealous of the rights of the peasantry, and of any injustice to them.'[23]

The basic pattern laid down by Lugard was developed by his successors, who extended it to the non-Muslim areas of the North. Here, of course, its application was more difficult, for in the absence of a powerful emir some petty chief or influential elder was raised to the status of local ruler and agent for the British administration. Inevitably this meant that the local District Officer or Resident had considerably greater power than his counterpart in the emirate. As we have seen, Lugard's successors developed indirect rule in directions that Lugard did not feel desirable. Indeed he quarrelled bitterly with Temple, his Lieutenant-Governor in the North, over the question of the independence of Native Treasuries. Lugard felt that the revenues of these treasuries should be included in the general budget for Nigeria, since this would give him control over them. Temple and the Colonial Office opposed this, believing that the essence of indirect rule was minimal interference on the part of the British government. Inevitably, treasuries that did not come under the control of some central authority gave greater autonomy to individual native authorities, and lessened central control over the Emirs.

The approach of many Northern officers to indirect rule was a static one, which resented any alteration in the system of government of the emirates, whilst Lugard's approach was essentially dynamic, believing as he did that the native administrations could be developed into more and more efficient units of government. Miss Perham, Lugard's official biographer, rightly considers this a fundamental issue in the development of indirect rule in Northern Nigeria and concludes that 'Lugard's policy was at least well worth attempting since, if the new direction he tried to give to policy had been steadily followed by his successors, the Northern region today might have been more uniform in its administration, more centralized, with more fully developed central services. Secondly, it would have presented today rather less of a political contrast with the Southern regions. Thirdly, as the system which many British governments in Africa and elsewhere soon came to regard as the archetype of native administration, it would have been a little less remote both in spirit and form from the more modest realities of these other colonies.'[24]

When Lugard toured Yorubaland and Benin it seemed clear to him that the answer to what he considered the administrative chaos of Southern Nigeria was the introduction of indirect rule on the Northern pattern. The Oba and his court surely corresponded to the Emir and his council. Lugard, of course, misconceived the position of the Oba in Yoruba society. Whilst the Emir was to a certain extent limited in powers by his counsellors, he was effectively ruler of his emirate. On the other hand, as we have seen, the Yoruba Oba was circumscribed in his authority by a large number of checks and balances, effectively only giving voice to a decision that had been arrived at after an intricate process of negotiation and consultation. Certainly he did not possess traditional executive authority that could in any way be construed as measuring up to that possessed by an emir. No Yoruba Oba had ever collected taxes from his people on a regular basis, whilst the Hausa had accepted his ruler's right to taxation for several centuries.[25] Since the levy of taxation was fundamental to the Native Authority system it meant Lugard had not only to translate his Oba into an Emir, but also ask him to levy taxation, hardly a popular measure for a people unaccustomed to it. Lugard sent Richmond Palmer, a trusted Northern Resident, on a tour of the Western Region to report on the feasibility of introducing taxation. Despite protests from Southern officials, which he dismissed as conservatism, Palmer recommended the introduction of taxation to Oyo, Benin and Abeokuta.[26] Lugard received this report with pleasure, though the Colonial Office, bearing in mind the disturbances that followed the introduction of taxation in Sierra Leone, opposed it.

Lugard's first experiment in indirect rule in the South was a success, but the circumstances were rather special. Since the exile of Ovenramwen, after the 1897 massacre, Benin had been without a ruler.

When, in 1914, Ovenramwen died in Calabar, his son was installed Oba under the name of Eweka II. Lugard took the opportunity of instituting a native authority for Benin with the Oba at its head. Direct taxation was introduced and accepted by the people. This success is hardly surprising when one remembers how complete the British subjection of Benin had been, and that for over fifteen years they had been without their ruler, the repository of tribal customs.

This early success was not repeated in 1916 when Lugard introduced his native authority for Oyo, with the Alafin at its head. As Miss Perham points out, there were particular difficulties in making an Emir of the Alafin.[27] In the first place, despite his immense spiritual, political and judicial authority, the Alafin was in no easy position to head a native authority. His decisions were always voiced through an intermediary. He never appeared except behind a veil of beads, and only emerged from his palace three times a year. Thus he was virtually *incommunicado* to his people and yet had to run a system of local government that needed his intimate daily attention to every detail of their life. Secondly, though the great city of Ibadan acknowledged the authority of the Alafin, in fact this was more an act of respect than acceptance of political subordination. This city's inclusion in the Native Authority of the Alafin marked the beginning of many years of tension, ended only in 1934 when Ibadan was made independent.

The first open opposition to the new régime came from the Oyo town of Iseyin, where in October 1916 two representatives of the Oyo N.A., a district head and a native court judge, were murdered. The rebellion of which these incidents were a focus was put down with great speed, which avoided their repetition in other parts of Yorubaland.

Much more serious was the opposition to Lugard's new policy in Abeokuta, where the Native Administration system proved particularly irksome. Until 1914 Abeokuta had been a semi-independent state, guaranteed by the treaty of 1893. The Egba United Government, under its Secretary Edun, aided by a British commissioner and missionaries, had developed an administration roughly modelled on the British colonial system. When Lugard became Governor in 1912 he viewed this anomaly with an administrator's distaste. But it was difficult to find an occasion for bringing Abeokuta into line with the other Yoruba states. In 1914 the opportunity came when one of Secretary Edun's opponents, Ponlade, was arrested and died in prison. This led to demonstrations against the Egba United Government, which were sufficiently serious for the Alake and the British Commissioner, P. V. Young, to call on Lagos for troops. As a result tension was increased to such an extent that the troops were ordered to fire on the demonstrators, an incident remembered as the Ijemo massacre. This gave

Lugard the excuse to suggest that the Egba United Government's independence could hardly be called a reality if they depended on the Lagos government for support. With the agreement of the Alake he therefore abrogated the treaty and brought Abeokuta into the Protectorate under the same conditions as the other Yoruba states.

The legacy of bitterness from the Ijemo massacre came to a head with the extension of Lugard's system of indirect rule to Egbaland. In June 1918 the Egba tore up the railway line and looted stations and trains. A number of people were killed, including a chief and one European. The Alake narrowly escaped with his life; 1,000 troops were rushed in and in the ensuing battle over 500 rebels were killed. Indeed, if Nigerian troops had not just returned from the East Africa campaign, the situation might have become extremely serious. The rebellion was essentially a protest against the introduction of a system of government quite alien to the traditional form. There was bitter resentment against the powers of the district heads, the levying of taxes and the elevation of the Alake to a position of supreme authority where in the past he had merely been *primus inter pares* of the four quarter chiefs of Abeokuta. When the people showed their anger at these innovations they were threatened with troops, a flashback, it seemed, to the Ijemo massacre. A Commission of Inquiry, with one member, a Nigerian barrister, Eric Moore,[28] investigated the riots and laid the blame on the new policy and its unwise application. This was a severe blow to Lugard.

If Lugard had difficulties in applying indirect rule to the West, he found it almost impossible to introduce it in the East. Except for the Delta states there were few chiefs of consequence in the area. A system that depended intimately on a fulcrum of authority obviously had no application in so loosely organized a society as that of the Igbo and Ibibio. In the Delta earlier administrators had attempted to use the trading house as a vehicle for administrative edicts, but this meant that they had to acknowledge the existence of slavery, and in effect give support to it, since the houses were based on domestic slavery. Indeed runaway members of houses, under the House Rule Ordinance, might be arrested and restored, and none could employ a member of a house without the consent of the head of the house. Lugard was immediately antipathetic to anything that smacked of slavery, and abolished House Rule, a system which anyway had lost much of its economic and political *raison d'être*. It is, however, significant that in the Delta there was no difficulty in collecting taxes, for before the British administration the house chiefs had imposed tax on their members. The other parts of the East were ruled through courts, which dispensed not only justice but administrative orders. In certain cases individuals with some apparent authority were raised to the status of warrant chiefs, a class that was to incur great unpopularity. Lugard was quite unable to devise any alternative system for the East. This is not surprising when one remembers that all the time he was occupied with the war and the many other problems of administration. Furthermore, the East was still not entirely subjected to British authority and in the years from 1912 to 1918 it was still necessary for the Government to despatch punitive expeditions against certain groups.

All these reforms were undertaken during the First World War, in which Nigeria, because of her common frontier with the German Cameroons, played no small part. Until the outbreak of war, Germany had occupied a significant place in Nigeria's external trade. She took 44 per cent of Nigeria's exports and accounted for 14 per cent of her imports. War cut off Nigeria from this important source of trade and the situation was made more serious by shortage of shipping. This, however, was only a temporary phase, for provisions-starved Britain soon found that she needed as much of Nigeria's palm-oil as she could get, and trade revived, though towards the end of the war submarine activities off the West Coast made export and import increasingly difficult.

Surprisingly the war was not taken by and large by the Nigerian peoples as an occasion to throw off the colonial yoke. In the Muslim North the Emirs made deep protestations of loyalty and did not waver when Turkey, the leading Muslim power, came into the war on the side of Germany.[29] They were not even affected by the disturbed state of French Niger immediately to the north when, in 1916, the Ouil-liminden Tuareg revolted and besieged Filingué, or when the Tuareg chief Kaossen, in league with Senussi chiefs from Tripolitania, besieged Zinder. The Kaossen revolt, which assumed the character of a *jihad*, gave the British administration considerable cause for concern that it might evoke response from Muslims under its administration. So serious was the situation that Nigerian troops were sent across the border to help the French relieve Zinder.[30]

The only disturbances that could be construed as an attempt to take advantage of the war were the revolt of the Kwale Igbo, which was said to have been aggravated by Germans, and was certainly motivated by pro-German sympathy, and a revivalist movement in the Delta, where the Christian 'breakaway' prophet who called himself Elijah II secured a huge following by taking advantage of rumours that Britain was leaving Nigeria because of the war. He claimed to be helping the Germans and promised the Delta peoples independence. This promise had an appeal in the Delta that it might not have held elsewhere because of the temporary collapse, immediately after war broke out, of the palm-oil trade on which most of the people of the eastern Delta were dependent. The local European traders and administrators were blamed for this collapse. As soon as the palm-oil trade revived the movement faded away.[31]

Nigerian troops played an important role in the war. On 27th August 1914 a detachment of the Nigeria Regiment was sent to help the Gold Coast Regiment and French troops in German Togo, but arrived after the Germans had been defeated. On the 29th of the same month the Mounted Infantry detachment of the Nigeria Regiment occupied the German post of Tepe in the Cameroons and attacked the important river port of Garua on the Benue. They were defeated the next day in a German counter-attack. In the south of the Cameroons Nigerian forces suffered similar setbacks, a hundred soldiers being killed in an engagement at Nsanakang. It was clear that larger forces were needed to fight in the extremely difficult country of the Cameroons, with its mountains and thick forests.

A combined army, consisting of two battalions of the Nigeria Regiment, French and Belgian African troops, the Gambia Company, the Sierra Leone Battalion and the Gold Coast Regiment was formed. They invaded the Cameroons after the successful naval bombardment of Duala on 27th September 1914. By Christmas they had driven the Germans back to Yaoundé, and the important town of Edea had been taken together with the capital, Buea. The northern campaign lasted throughout 1915. In June Garua and N'gaounderé were taken, but attempts to capture Mora were unsuccessful. It was not finally until February 1916, after most of the German forces had retreated from Yaoundé to the Spanish territory of the Rio Muni, that it fell to the British.

This long and difficult campaign earned high praise for Nigerian troops from many quarters, but their achievement was perhaps best summed up by one of their officers, Colonel Cunliffe: 'They have been called upon to take part in a great struggle, the rights and wrongs of which they can scarcely have been expected dimly to perceive. They have been through the, to them, extremely novel experience of facing an enemy with modern weapons and led by highly trained officers. Their rations have been scanty, their barefoot marches long and trying, and their fighting at times extremely arduous, yet they have not been found wanting either in discipline, devotion to their officers, or personal courage.'[32]

There was to be no rest for these troops, for almost immediately four battalions were sent off to East Africa together with a large auxiliary carrier corps. No one was more pleased with their performance than the veteran campaigner in Africa, Sir Frederick Lugard. Nevertheless, he wrote to his wife of the Nigerian soldier: 'He also knows how to kill white men, around whom he has been taught to weave a web of sanctity of life. He also knows how to handle bombs and Lewis guns and Maxims—and he has seen white men budge when he stood fast. And altogether he has acquired much knowledge which might be put to uncomfortable use some day.'[33] In fact Lugard's forebodings would have been more appropriate as a commentary on the impact of the Second World War on Nigerians. Fortunately, in the later war, it was not knowledge of weapons that impressed them so much as the realization that they and the white men were fundamentally the same and equal and that they too were quite capable of running their own affairs.

15 The Rise of Nigerian Nationalism

The years that followed on Lugard's governorship are superficially some of the quietest in Nigerian history. Yet they mark the emergence of a new class of Africans who began to think of themselves as Nigerians rather than Igbo, Hausa and Yoruba. And it was to be this group, initially confined almost exclusively to Lagos, that wrested control of affairs from the British government and attained independence for Nigeria in 1960. So, though there are no dramatic upheavals to record during the period between the world wars, though there are few administrative changes to describe, there was the slow, but all-important development of national consciousness amongst peoples of widely varying religious and cultural backgrounds.

When Lugard finally amalgamated the Northern and Southern Protectorates of Nigeria, it might have seemed, as it often did to him, that he was merely lumping together under the same administration groups of mutually incompatible peoples.[1] Certainly his decision to keep the administration of the North and South separate was guided by such thinking. But the British had created a new political unit, and whether they or the peoples under their administration liked it or not, it was inevitable that a certain number of Africans should begin to identify themselves not with their old tribal allegiances, but with the new political entity known as Nigeria. Thus, whilst Lugard's system of indirect rule tended to preserve tribal consciousness, the needs of the new administration were to produce a new class of Africans—clerks, teachers, traders, parsons, doctors and lawyers—who could no longer think in purely ethnic terms. By and large they were excluded from office in the native administrations, so that they tended to look towards the central administration for an outlet for their natural desire to have some say in their own affairs. Even if they had been assimilated into the running of local government, it is unlikely that their horizons would have remained for long restricted to the administration of the village or the town.

At first Nigerian nationalism was largely promoted by non-Nigerians, and its focus was on Africa as a whole, rather than on the seemingly artificial units drawn up by the European colonial powers.[2]

Men like Edward Blyden from the West Indies, who sought the cultural emancipation of the Negro, or J. P. Jackson, a Liberian, who edited the *Lagos Weekly Record* and constantly attacked the British administration, were at the spearhead of nationalist activity until the twenties. Even Herbert Macaulay, revered today by many as 'the father of Nigerian Nationalism', was a member of the family of that most famous of all freed slaves, Bishop Crowther, a family which had ties all along the West Coast. Indeed Macaulay was agitating against the government in Lagos even before Lugard became Governor-General, organizing effective mass protests against the levy of the Lagos water rate which he said was designed to benefit Europeans at the expense of the Lagosians' purse.

But while outbursts like this were of a parish pump character, these early nationalists had a wider aim. As Diké had put it: 'After amalgamation in 1914, what the nationalists fought was the exclusiveness and racial basis of the Crown Colony system of Government. At the beginning, the fight was not so much for self-government, but for a measure of participation in the existing government.'[3]

To this end the National Congress of British West Africa was founded in 1920 in order that peoples of African descent should participate in the government of their own country, an aim in part inspired not only by the writings of New-World Negroes like W. E. Du Bois and his antagonist, Marcus Garvey,[4] but also by the declaration of the American President himself on the right of all peoples to self-determination. After its inaugural conference at Accra, led by Casely-Hayford, a well-known Gold Coast lawyer, and attended by representatives of the four British West African colonies, it was decided to send a delegation to the Secretary of State for the Colonies to demand, amongst other things:

1. A legislative council for each territory, with half the members elected Africans.
2. Control of taxation by African members of the Legislative Council.
3. Appointment of and deposition of chiefs by their own people.
4. Abolition of racial discrimination in the Civil Service.
5. Establishment of a university in West Africa.[5]

The delegation was treated peremptorily by the Colonial Secretary, Lord Milner, and after encountering certain financial difficulties returned to Africa, so to speak, empty-handed. This hardly put the Nigerians in a bargaining position *vis-à-vis* Sir Hugh Clifford, the new Governor, who roundly denounced them in the Nigerian Council on 29th December 1920, in terms that showed how little sympathy the British official had towards the aspirations of the new African élite.

'It can only be described as farcical to suppose that . . . continental Nigeria can be represented by a handful of gentlemen drawn from a half-dozen coast towns—men born and bred in British-administered towns situated on the seashore, who, in the safety of British protection, have peacefully pursued their studies under British teachers, in British schools, in order to enable them to become ministers of the Christian religion or learned in the laws of England, whose eyes are fixed, not upon African native history or tradition or policy, nor upon their own tribal obligations and duties to their Natural Rulers which immemorial custom should impose on them, but upon political theories evolved by Europeans to fit a wholly different set of circumstances, arising out of a wholly different environment, for the government of peoples who have arrived at a wholly different stage of civilization. . . .' He was equally critical of the concept of West African unity: 'That there is or can be in the visible future such a thing as a "West African Nation" is as manifest an absurdity as that there is, or can be, an "European Nation", at all events until the Millennium.'[6]

But perhaps the most significant attack was on the idea that there could really be a Nigerian nation: 'Assuming . . . that the impossible were feasible—that this collection of self-contained and mutually independent Native States, separated from one another, as many of them are, by great distances, by differences of history and traditions, and by ethnological, racial, tribal, political, social and religious barriers, were indeed capable of being welded into a single homogeneous nation—a deadly blow would thereby be struck at the very root of national self-government in Nigeria, which secures to each separate people the right to maintain its identity, its individuality, its own chosen form of government, and the peculiar political and social institutions which have been evolved for it by the wisdom and by the accumulated experience of generations of its forebears.'

The author of this violent attack on early African claims to participation in the determination of their own affairs was also the author of the 1922 constitution, which for the first time in British Africa provided for elected African members on a Legislative Council.

As we shall see, this was to be one of the main stimuli to the growth of Nigerian nationalism in the inter-war period.

It has been suggested that Sir Hugh Clifford's apparent change of heart was the result of the activities of the National Congress of British West Africa.[7] But this seems unlikely both from the attitude Sir Hugh himself manifested towards it and its failure to evoke any substantial support when it sent its delegation to England. Anyway, the principle of election had already been introduced for the Lagos Town Council in 1920, before the Congress had produced its Accra resolutions.

Sir Hugh's constitution provided for a new Legislative Council, which would consist of forty-six members, twenty-seven of them officials, and nineteen of them unofficials. Of these unofficials, three members were to be elected by all adult males in Lagos with a residential qualification of twelve months and a gross income of £100 per annum, and one in Calabar. He even went as far as to say that the introduction of the elective principle was but the first step towards eventual self-government and the extension of elections to the backward parts of the Protectorate. Clifford himself declared that he had abolished the old Nigerian council and introduced this more liberal constitution because he liked 'a thing to be real and effective or not to have it at all'.[8]

The first thing the new constitution did was to provide an official outlet for the ideas of those coastal gentlemen Clifford had so strongly attacked. With the prospect of three seats on the Legislative Council, several parties were formed in Lagos, and newspapers were produced to champion their respective causes. In the subsequent election of 1923, Herbert Macaulay's party, the National Democratic Party, took all three seats, as it did again in 1928 and 1933. But the limited application of the new elective principle inevitably restricted nationalist activity to Lagos, since there was little scope for political activity in towns which had no seats on the Legislative Council.[9]

Thus most of the issues that concerned Macaulay in the twenties were essentially Lagos issues. Indeed he devoted almost all his energies in the twenties to what was known as the Eleko question. In 1915 the Eleko, or hereditary ruler of Lagos, was asked by the government to persuade the local people to pay the water rate, a commission he refused to undertake since, though paid a salary by the government in recognition of his special position, he was in fact denied all political power. Piqued, Lugard deprived both him and his white-cap chiefs of their salaries. In 1919, official recognition of the Eleko was withdrawn because he took sides with a Lagos faction that opposed payment of the water rate. Finally in 1920 recognition was withdrawn altogether from Eshugbayi as Eleko, and he was later deported. The 1920 Annual Report records: 'Political intrigues in Lagos resulted in the withdrawal of all official recognition of Eleko, the titular "Prince" of Lagos, who had allowed his position to be exploited by political adventurers.'[10] The foremost amongst these so-called adventurers was Macaulay, who conducted an almost fanatical campaign on Eshugbayi's behalf that seemed at times to monopolize all his political thought.

Nevertheless, he sometimes turned his attentions to larger issues, and the ceaseless attacks on the colonial government in the *Lagos Daily News* did much to inspire others with nationalist zeal. Officially his party did have a national programme, and on occasion he castigated the administration for alleged errors far from the confines of the coastal capital.

The British administration was certainly not greatly worried by Macaulay's activities, especially as they did really only touch on events in Lagos. As far as they were concerned, their main problems lay outside the restricted arena of Lagos politics, particularly in south-eastern Nigeria where indirect rule was not proving a success.

In the North Lugard's policy, as we have seen, worked smoothly, though not along the lines he had envisaged. Indeed in the North the path indirect rule followed can only be described as retrograde. The emirates were treated more like the Native States of India than as the administrative conveniences they had been for Lugard. Officials emphasized more and more the differences between the North and South, and sought whenever possible to dispense with the services of Southern clerks. This drift did not go unchallenged. In 1924, an article in the *National Review* by a Captain Fitzpatrick, a former political officer in Northern Nigeria, received considerable publicity for the stinging attacks it made on the administration of indirect rule.

'Before the British took over the country, an Emir was an Emir just so long as his hands could guard his head. The system was one of autocracy tempered by assassination. The Emirs today are maintained by British bayonets, so that there are men holding these positions at this time who would not last one week if the bayonets were to cease. . . .' He accused the emirs of corruption and extortion, describing the native authorities as instruments of oppression that were hated by the people. He feared they would be 'fruitful soil for pernicious, seditious, underground propaganda from Egypt'.[11]

One critic of Fitzpatrick asked why he himself had not done anything about the situation.[12] The answer to this—one does not know if Fitzpatrick gave it—demonstrates clearly the character of native administration at that time: official policy, particularly under Sir Graeme Thomson, Governor of Nigeria from 1925 to 1931, was that political officers should interfere as little as possible in Nigeria's 'Indian states'. Nevertheless, Thomson's predecessor, Clifford, had taken measures to tighten up control of administrative policy. The Lieutenant-Governors of both Northern and Southern Nigeria were placed under the Chief Secretary, who was given overall responsibility for the machinery of administration. However, it was not until the appointment of Sir Donald Cameron as Governor in 1931 that any attempt was made to check the growing separatism of the Northern administration and the ever-increasing autonomy of the emirs.[13]

The system of indirect rule, however, had proved impossible to apply in Eastern Nigeria and the Igbo, Ijo and Itsekiri areas of the present Bendel State. Lugard, as we have seen, had been quite unable to devise a satisfactory version of indirect rule for the largely decentralized societies in these areas. When Clifford became Governor in 1919, one of the first things he did was to order his Secretary for Native Affairs to investigate the situation in the south-east. In 1922 the Secretary of Native Affairs issued his report strongly criticizing administration there.[14] It had failed to introduce effective indirect rule there. Despite superficial trappings, the area was in effect administered directly. The warrant chiefs were exceedingly unpopular with the people and were backed up by little, if any, traditional authority. They were generally corrupt. Worse still, the native courts, the main agencies for British administration, were deeply resented. The court clerks and court messengers abused their positions of power so blatantly that they were described in the report as 'licensed libertines'. Despite this early interest in the problem of administration in south-eastern Nigeria and the constant references in annual reports to the difficulties it represented, for the rest of Clifford's governorship no action was taken to change it. However, in 1926, after long discussions, it was decided that those people who did not pay taxes, mainly in south-eastern Nigeria, should be forced to pay tax in the form of a poll tax based on a $2\frac{1}{2}$ per cent assessment of their rough annual income. This, however, was to be levied on adult males only.

In 1927 assessment was begun, and sparked off disturbances in the Warri and Kwale areas of the Western Provinces which were said to have had the connivance of certain Lagos leaders. Patrols of up to 300 men were needed to quell them and at one time the police had to fire above the heads of the crowd to disperse the rioters. Elsewhere assessment and collection provoked no open trouble.

However, late in 1929, a certain warrant chief, Okugo, whilst reassessing the taxable wealth of the inhabitants of a village called Oloko, near Aba in present-day Imo State, began counting women, children and animals. Rumour quickly spread that this heralded the introduction of taxation of women, for the original poll tax had been preceded by a census, whose purpose had not at the time been divulged to the people. In this densely populated area of Eastern Nigeria, rumour spread quickly and soon the women of Aba and Owerri divisions were up in arms against the administration. Stores were sacked, native courts burnt down and unpopular warrant chiefs attacked. The riots spread to Calabar and Opobo, where, on 17th December 1929, a riot of such ferocity took place that the police opened fire on the crowd and killed 32 people, wounding a further 31.

The greatest significance of these riots was that they were almost exclusively the acts of women, who were able through their age-grade societies to organize themselves far more effectively than any of the local administrators, who were largely ignorant of the structure of indigenous societies, could have imagined. Furthermore, these women were spurred on by the low prices for their farm products because the depression in Europe was already having its effect in Africa.

An official Commission of Enquiry was immediately held on the riots to apportion responsibility for loss of life. It gave speedy exoneration to the officials concerned, but this seemed a vastly unsatisfactory verdict when the scope of the riots was considered.[15] A new Commission, with wider membership, was therefore set up to investigate the causes of the riots. Two of its members were African barristers—Sir Kitoyi Ajasa and Mr Eric Moore. The Commission was asked to discover 'the origin and causes of, and responsibility for the disturbances—and measures taken to restore order, and to make such recommendations as may seem fit.'[16]

As Margery Perham has written, 'whatever view is taken of the findings of this Commission, its activities probably helped to prevent a wedge of bitterness and distrust being driven between the government and the people'. Most remarkable of all was the spectacle of European officials justifying their actions to a Commission on which sat two Africans, a situation not a few of them bitterly resented.[17]

The report of the Commission in particular condemned the way the administration had concealed the purpose of the census of 1926 which had preceded the introduction of taxation. For this reason, the Commission maintained that it was barely surprising that women should have associated the actions of Warrant Chief Okugo with the introduction of tax on themselves, especially at a time of economic hardship. They also reiterated a number of the criticisms made earlier by the Secretary of Native Affairs against native courts and warrant chiefs. The Commission made it clear that there was considerable need for the reorganization of native administration in those areas. In sum the report was a condemnation of the whole system of administration in south-eastern Nigeria, which was effectively one of direct rule. Theoretically the system of administration was one of indirect rule through the indigenous political institutions, in this case the warrant chiefs, but these warrant chiefs were mainly men who appeared to have traditional authority in communities which in fact were not accustomed to invest executive authority in a particular individual. It was clear that if indirect rule was to work in south-eastern Nigeria, then the government would have to discover what in fact were the political institutions of the peoples of the areas. To do this, intensive anthropological investigations were undertaken in the years 1931 and 1932, so as to ensure that any future reorganization would take into full account the natural social organization of the people. By 1935 some 200 reports had been produced, and as a result of the information contained in them a 'very great variety of units of Native Authority' were recognized, which only in a few instances consisted of a traditional Chief or Chief in Council . . . 'and for the most part consisted of Group or Clan Councils or Village Councils'.[18]

Just after the report of the Commission of Enquiry was published Sir Donald Cameron became Governor of Nigeria, and having been responsible for the introduction of indirect rule in Tanganyika, he began to examine closely the whole working of Native Administration in Nigeria. He was extremely shocked, not so much by developments in the East, as by the character of Native Administration in the North. This had been taken a step farther on the road towards the creation of 'Indian States'. Legislation had been mooted whereby *all* inhabitants of an emirate would be brought under the jurisdiction of the Native Authority courts, meaning in fact that Christian Southerners, expatriate Europeans and Lebanese would be tried before local Alkali, or Muslim courts instead of under British law. In a speech to the Legislative Council on 6th March 1933, the new Governor suggested that the administration in the North had departed from Lord Lugard's conception of Native Authority and that they had made feudal monarchy 'the be all and end all' of indirect rule. He attacked the administration for sheltering their Muslim rulers from contact with the outside world:

'I doubt sometimes whether we have done a great deal to impress on the minds of the Native Authorities concerned that the amelioration of the social and economic conditions of a people is one of the primary duties of an administration and that the inspiration to improvement must come from within, from the Native Administration itself.'[19]

Later, Cameron enunciated his own policy for the reform of the Native Authorities of the North.[20] Nigerian emirs should be encouraged to travel not only abroad but in other regions of non-Muslim Nigeria. The areas of the North should be developed along their own lines and not as pseudo-emirates. He also abolished certain practices in the Native Authority prisons such as chaining.

Cameron did not restrict his attention to the North. In the West he made Ibadan independent of Oyo, and suggested that the Native Authority should have a mixed council in which the educated elements could play their part. As we have seen, the exclusion of the educated Nigerian from participation in both central and local government was one of the main stimuli to early nationalist activity. In 1932, on the installation of the new Oba of Benin, Cameron stressed the fact that the duty of political officers was to train chiefs for the increasing burdens of local administration and to that end he insisted that the Resident sit in on the council and advise on day-to-day conduct of affairs. In the south-east it was no time for dramatic changes, but for slow and thoughtful reorganization of a system that had been a blatant failure. For the first few years after the Aba riots, the administration spent most of its time collecting information about the people they had been trying to govern, in some parts for nearly thirty years. The 1932 Annual Report admitted: 'It has moreover been emphasized that in the case of primitive communities with European influences, it is necessary that the process of reorganization should be with comparatively small units.'[21] By the end of 1934 no less than 199 reports on local groups had been submitted, and in the light of these and subsequent reports, the Native Authorities were reorganized to correspond with what were described as live units of government, which were often merely small collections of hamlets and villages.

Cameron's major reform was the abolition of Lugard's system of administrative justice. Cameron was particularly critical of a system of law administered by the administration. 'Change the system of law, if you will, and punish the people by administrative officers exercising a kind of parental correction because the people are primitive; but remember always, pray, if you do so you will thereby be depriving the natives of any judicial court and any judicial system of law.'[22] Lugard himself had justified the administration of British law by political officers on the grounds that they knew the natives better than British-trained lawyers could.[23] Cameron's decision to abolish the provincial courts and limit the powers of the native courts was particularly popular amongst the educated elements. In place of the provincial courts he substituted a High Court for the whole of the Protectorate, under which operated magistrates' courts where lawyers could practise. The introduction of the High Court returned once again to the well-established British principle of the separation of judiciary and executive, though Cameron did envisage that administrative officers with legal experience would act as magistrates. Finally, to emphasize the unity of Nigeria, he abolished the post of Lieutenant-Governor in Northern and Southern Nigeria.

Economically, the period between the wars was a dull one, for the effects of the severe and prolonged depression in Europe made themselves felt on most primary producing countries like Nigeria. A comparison between the export and import figures for 1921, just after the post-war boom had slackened, and those for 1938, just before the demands of a Europe at war made themselves felt in Africa, shows that relatively little economic development had taken place.

	Imports	Exports	Total Trade
1921	10,237,000	8,258,000	18,495,000
1929	13,219,000	17,075,000	30,294,000
1935	7,804,000	11,615,000	19,419,000
1938	8,632,000	9,702,000	18,334,000[24]

On the other hand cotton, which had been grown for local use before the advent of the British and was to be of immense importance to Northern Nigeria in later years, together with groundnuts and cocoa, became increasingly valuable. General wants increased as lists of imports during these years show: they ranged from disinfectant to glassware, ammunition, drugs, china, enamelware, fancy goods, furniture, jewellery, leather goods, rubber goods, textiles, tobacco, cars, soaps, oil, etc.

Perhaps the greatest economic achievement of the administration in the inter-war period was a negative one. In many African countries, notably the Belgian Congo and the German Cameroons, part of which had been attached to Nigeria after the First World War, large banana and oil-palm plantations had been set up, proving themselves economically far more efficient than the rather haphazard farming of bananas and palm trees in Nigeria. However, in Nigeria it had been a principle never to alienate indigenous land, and the establishment of palm plantations in days when government interference in economic affairs was marginal necessarily involved alienation of land to foreign companies. In the Belgian Congo the firm of Lever Brothers had extensive and profitable plantations, and their chairman, Lord Leverhulme, had his eyes on Southern Nigeria for the establishment of similar plantations. In 1924 Lord Leverhulme, at a dinner held by the Liverpool Chamber of Commerce for the Governor of Nigeria, Sir Hugh Clifford, pressed him to permit his company to acquire land and declared:

'I am certain that the West African races have to be treated very much as one would treat children when they are immature and underdeveloped. We have excellent materials. I don't know better materials anywhere for labour in the tropics than the natives of West Africa, but they are not organized. . . . Now the organizing ability is the particular trait and characteristic of the white man. . . . I say this with my little experience, that the African native will be happier, produce the best, and live under the larger conditions of prosperity when his labour is directed and organized by his white brother who has all these million years' start ahead of him.'[25]

Fortunately for Nigeria, Clifford resisted all such attempts to impose Congo paternalist economic theories on Nigeria. But the pressures on

Leverhulme's behalf were considerable. Nevertheless, both the Governor and the Chief Secretary assured the people that Lord Leverhulme's views were diametrically opposed to the declared policy of the government. The criticism made by Captain Fitzpatrick of the system of indirect rule in the North was vaunted by the plantation owners as proof that the present system of government had little to recommend it.

The threat to Nigeria seemed greater when, in 1925, Sumatra emerged as a producer of superior palm-oil by plantation methods. Clifford's successor, Sir Graeme Thomson, looked on Leverhulme's policies with a gentler eye. But at the same time the British government sent out to West Africa Ormsby-Gore, the Parliamentary Under-Secretary for the Colonies, who had backed Clifford partly on the grounds that the introduction of the Congo system would involve government in finding compulsory labour for capitalist profit. In 1926 the matter was effectively closed when the House of Commons gave its support to the system of indirect rule as practised in Nigeria, though educated Nigerians remained fearful of the possibilities of the introduction of a foreign-dominated plantation economy for some time to come.[26]

The nationalist energy generated by Herbert Macaulay for the 1923 elections dissipated in a tangle of Lagos politics from which it was not rescued until the late thirties, when a new generation of Nigerians who looked beyond the narrow political horizons of the capital took over control of the nationalist movement. They were to be the first Pan-Nigerian nationalists, and the outbreak of war in 1939 was to give immense stimulus to their movement for self-government and eventual freedom.

Until the 1930s, most educated Nigerians came from Creole families or from Yoruba families that had been in long contact with Europeans. It was only by the thirties that a wider selection of Nigeria's varied peoples emerged sufficiently educated to compete intellectually with this closed aristocracy.

Appropriately enough, therefore, student organizations were the main instrument in arousing the new spirit of nationalism. Foremost amongst the student organizations abroad was the West African Students' Union, founded in 1925, with the object not only of providing a centre for West African students in London, but also of promoting the understanding of African culture. The founder, a Nigerian called Ladipo Solanke, is often neglected in the annals of Nigerian nationalism. But by providing such a centre, and by his own uncompromising spirit of nationalism, he added a new fire to the movement for colonial emancipation that kept it alive in Nigeria until the return of Dr

Azikiwe from America in 1937. He was an ardent critic of the conduct of administrators in Nigeria, a champion of the glory of the Negro past, a constant writer of letters to the press on subjects concerning West Africa. He made extensive tours of Nigeria and other West African territories to obtain funds for the union, seeking the co-operation of traditional rulers such as the Alake of Abeokuta, who was the patron of W.A.S.U., and the Emir of Kano, who was patron of the Kano branch. By providing this focus for African activity in London, 'from a historical standpoint', as James Coleman has written, 'Solanke was an out-standing figure in the nationalist awakening in Nigeria.'[27]

But it was in Lagos that the next concrete development in nationalist organization took place. In 1936 the Nigerian Youth Movement was formed with Samuel Akinsanya, H. O. Davies, Ernest Ikoli and Dr J. C. Vaughn at its head. It had grown out of the Lagos Youth Movement, organized to protest against the alleged inferior status of the new Yaba Higher College, which they felt should have been of university stan-dard. One of its early members was Obafemi Awolowo, who sub-sequently became leader of the Action Group.[28] At first the Nigerian Youth Movement was restricted in its outlook, but on the return of Dr Nnamdi Azikiwe from America in 1937, it was geared up into a genuine national movement with a broad representation that justified its title 'Nigerian'. Dr Azikiwe, or 'Zik' as he has always been known to both followers and enemies, was an Igbo who had been educated in America, having collected there an impressive array of degrees, which made him one of the first of his people who could seriously compete with the entrenched Yoruba aristocracy of Lagos. He had proved himself a dynamic personality, running a successful paper in Accra with I. T. A. Wallace-Johnson, and narrowly escaping imprisonment on a charge of sedition. When he arrived in Lagos he founded a paper called the *West African Pilot* which was to be the main outlet for his nationalist activities for the next twenty years. As an active politician he brought something new to Lagos politics: the interest and participation of the immigrant Igbo and Ibibio people. With Zik's support the Nigerian Youth Movement could genuinely be regarded as representing more than a mere Lagos faction.

Another important spur to this new outburst of nationalist activity was the Italian invasion of Ethiopia, a country which naturally sym-bolized African independence for all African nationalists. In 1935 a mass meeting was held in Lagos to protest against the Italian action and the Abyssinian Association was formed. Unfortunately, apart from its successful attack on the Cocoa Pool, a monopolistic buying agree-ment arranged by the major European commercial houses, the Nigerian Youth Movement achieved little that could be called con-

crete, being rent by internal quarrels. But this was in a way coun-
terbalanced by the outbreak of war in Europe in 1939, which acted as
an immense stimulus to nationalist activity. Until the 1939–45 war
most Nigerians had been entirely cut off from the outside world. Only
the small élite of students who travelled abroad for their studies had
any effective contact with the current of ideas of the Western world, or
indeed the Communist world. For most Nigerians, the European
remained a special kind of being, destined to command, surrounded by
apparent wealth in the form of large houses and numerous servants.
Few Africans ever attained these heights, and then it was observed
they rarely if ever entered into the exclusive domains of the white
reservations and were rarely employed in the higher posts of the
administration.

One of the most important determinants of the character of the
nationalist movement in Nigeria in the inter-war period, was the
almost total lack of dialogue between the British administration and
the growing educated élite.[29] The majority of British officials, including
those responsible for the formulation of policy, believed that there
could be no such dialogue. Many officials, particularly those who
worked in the provincial administrations rather than the secretariat,
were quite blunt in their contempt for the educated African. Not that
they all considered the African an inferior being. But most of them
were ill at ease with the educated African and felt like Sir Alan Burns,
a former Chief Secretary of Nigeria, that '. . . the worst effect of education in Nigeria has been the manufacture of bad imitations of Europeans instead of good Africans'.[30] The more liberal officials subscribed
to the view of Lugard that even if one accepted the equality of the
African with the European, their cultural and environmental background was such that even when the former were educated, it dictated
the social segregation of the two groups.[31] Thus Africans were excluded
from the European clubs right up to the early fifties. One coloured
official of senior standing in the Colonial Office was refused accom-
modation in the Old Bristol Hotel in 1947, thus causing a great outcry
against the administration in the nationalist press.

At the same time the British had to recognize their dependence on
the educated classes for staffing the subaltern ranks of the administration. Yet they were not prepared to accept that the more capable
members of this class, even those who possessed the requisite educational qualifications, should assume senior posts in the administration
which would in any way put them in a position of directly governing
their uneducated fellow men. They agreed with Lugard that it should
be 'a cardinal principle of British colonial policy that the interests of a
large native population (should) not be subject to the will . . . of a small

minority of educated and Europeanized natives who have nothing in common with them, and whose interests are often opposed to theirs. . . .'[32] This same sentiment accounted for the reluctance of the British to allow Nigerians any role in the executive or decision-making process of government. It was only in 1943 that Nigerians were appointed to the Governor of Nigeria's Executive Council, and even then the two so appointed were in the eyes of the nationalists 'safe' government men.[33] The argument that the educated African could not be safely entrusted with the government of his illiterate brothers cut little ice with the nationalists. Many of them came from families with two or three generations of European education. They could remember the day when the senior Bishop of the Anglican Church in Nigeria was an African and the time in 1875 in Lagos when the Head of Police, and Head of Posts and Telegraph, the Registrar of the Supreme Court and the Collector of Customs were all Nigerians.[34] They did not see any merit in the argument that the alien ruler was more likely to be impartial in his dealing with the illiterate masses than the so-called 'alienated' educated African. This situation was the more aggravating to the Nationalists, for whilst the British denied the educated African's ability to govern his fellow men, at the same time they held out, as Coleman has remarked, 'the vision of ultimate control' by allowing a number of them to sit on the Legislative Council to deliberate over the Governor's policy, albeit in a minority position.[35]

How far the demands of the expanding educated classes for greater participation in their own affairs affected the thinking of the Governors of the inter-war period we shall not know until their papers become available for inspection. It appears that Lugard and his successors of the twenties, Thomson and Clifford, did not consider this educated group as in any way presenting a problem in the formulation of overall policy for Nigeria. However, the Governors of the thirties, Cameron and Bourdillon, both devoted thought to the role of the educated African in the country. As Miss Perham wrote in 1936, after talking with Cameron, and observing his administration: 'He has done much to gain the interest and support of educated natives for his policy.'[36] Bourdillon, writing towards the end of the war, shortly after he had relinquished his governorship, reflected: 'If there is one lesson which the writer has learned thoroughly in the course of thirty-five years spent in trying to manage other people's affairs for them, it is that on the whole they prefer to manage them themselves.'[37] At the opening of the Yaba College, Sir Donald Cameron declared that future government policy would be to employ more Africans in government, a policy which was applauded by Miss Perham at the time, with one major reservation. Africans could be employed in the service branches of government, they 'should not enter . . . the Administrative service'. Rather they should be encouraged to enter into the 'growing structure of native self-government', i.e. the Native Authorities.[38] Miss Perham, whose ideas on colonial policy did not go unheeded by British officials at the time, had strong reservations about the extension of the powers of the Legislative Council over the administration of Nigeria as a whole. She shared the views of those that feared that the educated African could not be entrusted with the government of those from whom he was supposed to be alienated as a result of his Western education.

Thus she suggested: 'In so far as the political ambitions of the educated are centred upon the Legislative Council, they should be met not by giving them an extension of power over the more backward masses, but by increasing their responsibilities, and therefore their sense of political realities, in urban and other advanced areas.'[39]

Under Cameron and Bourdillon there was growing concern with the role of the educated African and a recognition that his demands were important. But it remained in the realm of discussion rather than of practical policy. It was the war which was finally to prepare the climate for the acceptance by the British administration of the real facts of the situation, so bluntly stated by Awolowo in his *Path to Nigerian Freedom*.

'It must be realized now and for all time that the articulate minority are destined to rule the country. It is their heritage. It is they who must be trained in the art of government so as to enable them to take over complete control of the affairs of their country. Their numbers will increase, but, like the articulate and politically conscious group in every civilized country, they will always remain in the minority.'[40]

The failure of the British administration to solve the problem of the educated élite by offering it increased participation in the running of the country's affairs in large measure accounts for the virulence of the nationalist attacks on the British administration after the war.[41]

Possibly the greatest effect of Nigeria's participation in the world war was the sudden realization by a large number of ordinary Nigerians, as distinct from the educated élite, that there were Europeans who were different from the privileged colonial administration, who were farmers and private soldiers, traders and shopkeepers, boot-blacks and servants like themselves. Nigerian soldiers served alongside white soldiers of their own rank. Allied troops came to Nigeria with no more privileges than Nigerians themselves had. Many Nigerians have testified to the immense impact made by this contact between white and black of similar class. The World War projected Nigerians out of a colonial backwater into a modern world in which,

because of the exigencies of war, Nigeria became suddenly important—important as a strategic link in allied defences, as a producer of
primary goods essential to feed the starved allied nations, and also as a
provider of indispensable troops for the Burma campaigns. Indeed the
distinguished anthropologist Meyer Fortes, writing about 'The Impact
of the War on British West Africa', said: 'It may well be that the war
will prove to have been the outstanding instrument of social progress in
West Africa for fifty years.'[42]

Abroad, attitudes towards colonial problems were changing rapidly.
The right to empire was being challenged, and within British government circles themselves there was a certain concern about the
administration of the colonies. In 1938 riots in the West Indies had
prompted the British government to set up a Royal Commission to
investigate conditions there. One of the main causes of unrest proved to
be the very backward economic state of the islands. As a result the
British government established a fund for the West Indies and passed a
more general Colonial Development and Welfare Act for her other
colonies. Under it, £5 million a year was set aside for colonial development projects together with £500,000 for research.

On the other hand the British government, headed by Mr Winston
Churchill, seemed impervious to American criticisms of colonialism.
The third clause of the Atlantic Charter assured 'the right of all peoples
to choose the form of government under which they live. . .'. This was
not unnaturally taken by African nationalists to mean that Nigeria
would have eventual self-government. But Churchill and his Colonial
Secretary, Colonel Oliver Stanley, denied that this clause applied to
African dependencies, Churchill declaring that he had no intention of
presiding over the break-up of the colonial empire. But American
criticisms of colonialism were strong. For instance, *Life* wrote in an
editorial: 'Great Britain had better decide to part with her Empire, for
the United States is not prepared to fight in order to help her to keep
it.'[43] Such criticisms gained some support within the wartime coalition
government in Britain from Labour members, whose Fabian Colonial
Bureau kept them up to date on colonial affairs and, in particular, on
nationalist aspirations. It was to such organizations as this that West
African students in Britain directed their attentions.

Despite early intransigence on the part of the Colonial Secretary,
Labour pressure was able to elicit from the government the promise
that British policy in the colonies would be directed towards their
political, social and economic development, though no indication was
given of a time-table for constitutional advance.

In Nigeria, however, the Nigerian Youth Movement was unable to
concentrate the various anti-colonial pressures because of the internal

dissensions. Rivalry between Ernest Ikoli and Dr Azikiwe in 1941 over who should stand for the vacant Legislative Council seat led to the effective demise of the party. Partly this was the result of press rivalry, for Ikoli edited the *Daily Service* which rivalled Zik's *West African Pilot*; partly it was the result of the character of Zik himself who had never been a man to play second fiddle in a political organization. The occasion for the break-up came when Ikoli was put forward for the seat by the party, and Zik counter-proposed Samuel Akinsanya, an Ijebu. Unfortunately for the future of Nigerian nationalism this introduced an element of tribalism that had been largely subdued till then. Ijebu Yoruba were on the whole disliked by other Yoruba, and Zik said that this was the reason why Akinsanya's candidature had not been accepted. Since Zik had all the Igbo solidly behind him this led to a tribal rift in the party, and despite efforts by Obafemi Awolowo to revive the party between 1941 and 1944, it never again rose above petty quarrels. On the other hand, the climate created by the World War and the current of ideas in Lagos was opportune for the creation of a nationalist movement and, on 26th August 1944, Dr Nnamdi Azikiwe founded the National Council of Nigeria and the Cameroons with himself as Secretary and Herbert Macaulay as President. The N.C.N.C. was not a party in the ordinary sense, but a confederation of trade unions, smaller parties, tribal unions and literary groups. In January 1945 it held its first constitutional convention in which it declared amongst its aims that it intended: 'To achieve internal self-government for Nigeria whereby the people of Nigeria and the Cameroons under British Mandate shall exercise executive legislative and judicial powers.'[44] When a few months later the new Governor of Nigeria, Sir Arthur Richards, presented his constitutional proposals for the country, it was the newly founded N.C.N.C. that led the criticism of its various inadequacies.

16 Three Constitutions

The constitutional proposals of Sir Arthur Richards in March 1945, though they were attacked on almost every side by Nigerian nationalists, mark the real turning-point in Nigeria's progress towards independence. The constitution, which came into effect on 1st January 1947, had, according to the Governor, three objects: 'to promote the unity of Nigeria, to provide adequately within that unity for the diverse elements which make up the country and to secure greater participation by Africans in the discussion of their own affairs'.[1] The new Legislative Council was enlarged to forty-four members with a majority of unofficials, twenty-eight as against sixteen officials. Of these twenty-eight, however, only four were elected, the rest being nominated or indirectly elected. The most important feature of the new constitution was the inclusion of the North in the central legislature, a move that in itself could do nothing but further the unity of the country. However, at the same time regional councils were created for the North, East and West. Though they were mainly confined to discussion, their creation has subsequently been severely criticized as being the foundation of tribalism in Nigerian politics. Diké has written: 'Undoubtedly the Richards Constitution is a dividing line in Nigerian Constitutional development. Before it the keynote in Nigerian politics was unification towards a centralized state and the realization of a common nationality. . . . But with the Richards Constitution this tendency towards unification was on the whole arrested. . . .'[2] Sir Arthur Richards might have agreed with these sentiments as far as the two Southern provinces were concerned, but he would have argued that the inclusion in the central legislature of the North, so long excluded from participation in national politics, necessitated some degree of regionalization to allow for its very obvious differences from the South. On the other hand, it has been argued that if Sir Arthur really wanted to contain regional and ethnic differences he would have been wiser to have followed the earlier divisions proposed by Morel and Temple, and later advocated by Zik, which would have allowed for regional differences but would also have permitted the creation of a strong central legislature. As it was, he established the basis of a very unwieldy federation with one region twice the size in area and population of the other two.[3]

Sir Arthur obviously conceived of the constitution as allowing for the maximum participation of all sections in the national legislature. In theory there was a link between the smallest Native Authority and the national representative, since the Native Authority sent delegates to the regional assembly which, in turn, selected from among its members a delegation to the central Legislative Council.

The constitution was attacked both for its content and for the way in which it was introduced. The newly formed N.C.N.C. regretted 'the unilateral way the whole proposals were prepared without consulting the people and natural rulers of the country. . . . We respectfully suggest that a more democratic approach could have been made to avoid any possible misunderstanding. . . .'[4] Sir Arthur Richards's predecessor, Sir Bernard Bourdillon, himself criticized the peremptory way in which the constitution was introduced,[5] for he had promised Nigerians that they would have a full opportunity to discuss any new constitution, though it must be noted the concept of regional councils was originally his.[6] The particular criticisms, which might not have been so vehement if consultation had taken place, were diverse. The unofficial majorities in the central and regional assemblies were attacked as false since many of the so-called unofficials were nominated or quasi-officials like chiefs and Native Authority members. The Executive Council, to which African members were first appointed during the war, remained under British control. The principle of election, far from being extended, had only been maintained for Lagos and Calabar on the direct intervention of the Colonial Secretary. Curiously enough, in the light of its later policy, attacks were made by the N.C.N.C. on the lack of power delegated to the regional assemblies.

These criticisms which were supported, only less ardently, by the N.Y.M., were accompanied by an effective demonstration of popular discontent. The year of the publication of the new constitution was also the year of the general strike in which Zik played an influential role. The wartime expansion of the economy, following on the increased demand for Nigeria's primary goods, led to a rapid growth of labour unions. In 1940 there were only twelve unions with 4,337 members, by 1944 there were eighty-five with some 30,000.[7] British policy during the war had been to encourage the unions, and in 1942 the Nigerian Trade Union Congress was given official recognition. However, the steep rise in prices during the war led to real economic hardship for wage-earners, many of whom belonged to unions. After complaining bitterly about the regular adjustments of European salaries to the rising cost of living, the Railway, Ports and Telecommunication work-

ers all went on strike, effectively paralysing many of the country's
essential services. Though the new constitution was in no way responsible for the strike, the two became associated since Zik, the most ardent
critic of the constitution, also backed the strikers through his two
papers the *Pilot* and the *Comet*. In certain quarters it was even maintained that he engineered the strike. On July 8th his papers were
banned, and shortly afterwards Zik declared that there was an officially backed plot to assassinate him. This was received con-
temptuously in government circles, but in the country it was widely
believed and had the effect of making him a martyr. When, in fact, at
the end of the strike a Commission of Enquiry recommended an
increase in the cost of living allowance to workers, Zik naturally
emerged in the eyes of the public as the champion of a successful strike.
He was thus in a strong position to make an all-out attack on the new
constitution and the so-called obnoxious ordinances that had been
introduced with it. These vested mineral rights and publicly purchased
lands in the Crown, and gave the government powers to depose and
appoint chiefs. Since land rights and the appointment of chiefs were
close to the structure of almost every Nigerian society, Zik could add
fuel to his campaign against the constitution, which was little understood by the ordinary people, by warning them that their land and their
chiefs were threatened by the government.

During a triumphal tour of the country Zik and his party collected
the considerable sum of £13,000, though the tour was marked by
tragedy when one member of the entourage, the veteran nationalist,
Herbert Macaulay, fell mortally ill. Nevertheless, when the party
returned to Lagos it was to a massive reception, and with the money it
had collected the N.C.N.C. was able to send to London a delegation led
by Zik and composed of men from every part of Nigeria. The Labour
Colonial Secretary, Arthur Creech Jones, paid little attention to the
delegation, merely advising them to give the constitution a try. Unfortunately there followed financial squabbles, and when the delegation
returned home with no definite achievement and a backlog of disputes
over money, the N.C.N.C. suffered a real though, as it proved, only a
temporary setback.

Meanwhile the Richards constitution had come into effect at the
beginning of 1947 and it was envisaged that it would last for nine years
with revision after six. It was accompanied by the introduction of an
ambitious £55,000,000 ten-year development plan for Nigeria,[8] sub-
sidized from the Colonial Development and Welfare Fund to the tune of
£23,000,000. This provided for the extension of rural and urban water
supplies, education, communications, town planning, hospitals and
agricultural and veterinary research. Under it a department of com-

merce and industry was set up. At first the application of the plan suffered from lack of qualified staff, for the Nigerian administrative service had been very much depleted as a result of the war.

Though Sir Arthur Richards had envisaged that his constitution would last for nine years, the new Governor, Sir John Macpherson, appointed in April 1948, said, after only a few months in the country, that progress had been so good that it was time for a change. He did not make the mistake of his predecessor in foisting a new constitution on the country without consulting the people; if anything he went to the opposite extreme by indulging the country in two years of protracted negotiations on the form the new constitution should take. Macpherson, a young Governor, together with Hugh Foot, his young Chief Secretary, proved very much a new broom in Nigeria. He was responsible for the democratization of local government in the East, and in 1948 appointed a Commission to make recommendations about the recruitment and training of Nigerians for senior posts in the government service. Eight Nigerians, including Dr Azikiwe, sat on the commission, which recommended that no expatriate should be recruited where a suitable Nigerian was available.[9] Macpherson also appointed four Africans to his Executive Council, and with the appointment of Dr S. L. Manuwa as first Nigerian Director of Medical Services, this made five, since his post gave him a seat ex-officio.

The people were consulted on their new constitution at every level; a concession, no doubt, strongly influenced by events in the Gold Coast, where riots in February 1948 had forced the government into studying constitutional reform for that country.[10] In Nigeria village councils sent delegates to divisional councils, then to provincial and regional councils, and finally to a general conference at Ibadan.

The decisions made at the Ibadan conference must be seen in the context of the great increase in ethno-centrism that had followed the introduction of the Richards constitution. The origin of this tribal feeling was the source of much bitterness and recrimination by Nigerian political parties.

Fundamentally, as we have seen, there were very considerable differences in the history of the various groups of Nigeria, as well as more points of contact than have generally been supposed. There were latent differences and antagonisms that could be called up by anyone so inclined. The argument over tribalism has been between those who believe that these differences were fixed, and that anyway Nigeria was an arbitrary colonial creation, so that any political settlement should take these factors into account by devolving government on the ethnic groups, and those who believe that politics should be worked out in terms of Nigerians rather than Igbo, Hausa and Yoruba, and that this could be achieved if no one resorted to tribal politics.

In fact originally, the increase in tribal feeling, as Ezera showed,[11] was caused by circumstances rather than design, and only later was it seized upon by politicians. When the British occupied Nigeria they had almost no contact with the large Igbo and Ibibio population of the east, whilst already many Yoruba had received English education and provided a small intellectual *élite* in Lagos. Population pressures and land hunger in the east forced many Igbo and Ibibio to migrate to the cities of the west and north, where they proved remarkably successful as clerks, railway workers and storekeepers. Nearly always they settled in discrete communities, realizing that the key to success under the new administration was Western education, and seeing how far behind the Yoruba they were in this respect, they formed mutual benefit associations in order to give some of their number the advantages of higher education. This tendency to group together was intensified by the close family ties that exist in most African societies and by the fact that in Northern towns Southerners were forced to live outside the walls, in Sabon Garis, or strangers' quarters. Soon these unions began to federate. In 1944, following on the Ibibio State Union, the Pan-Igbo Federal Union was formed. In 1948 Dr Azikiwe, who had already protested against the Yoruba domination of Lagos politics, became President of this Union. Naturally his opponents retaliated by accusing him of being a tribal politician. Later he even made statements that seemed to confirm this view: 'It would appear that the God of Africa has created the Igbo nation to lead the children of Africa from the bondage of ages. . . .'[12]

Tribal feeling had first come to the fore in the quarrel between Zik and the older members of the Nigerian Youth Movement over the candidature of Samuel Akinsanya for a seat on the Legislative Council. This quarrel resulted in Zik leaving the N.Y.M. with all his Eastern followers, so that the party became effectively a Yoruba-controlled organization.

It was not surprising, therefore, that these tribal unions also interested themselves in political affairs and the Pan-Igbo Union itself was one of the founding members of the N.C.N.C. In 1945 some Yoruba students in London formed the Egbe Omo Oduduwa, or Society of the Descendants of Oduduwa, a cultural organization which soon took on the character of a political party. One of these students was Awolowo, who had already enunciated his own political ideas in *The Path to Nigerian Freedom*, which he completed in 1945, though it was not published until 1947.[13] In 1948 the inaugural Conference of Egbe Omo Oduduwa was held at Ife, when Sir Adeyemo Alakija, the President, declared that the 'Yoruba will not be relegated to the background in the future'.[14] Among its objectives was to 'create and actively foster the idea of a single nationalism throughout Yorubaland' and to 'co-operate with existing ethnical and regional associations and such as may exist hereafter, in matters of common interest to all Nigerians, so as thereby to attain to Unity in federation'.[15] The N.C.N.C., at least in theory, always looked to a unitary Nigeria, partly because of the fact that Igbo migration to other parts of the country would be served by a unitary constitution, and partly because its leaders wished to minimize the differences between the various ethnic groups. But the party's policy was never very fixed on this matter.

In 1948, the intense feelings between Yoruba and Igbo, particularly in Lagos where there was severe danger of communal disorders from July to September, furthered the cause of those elements in the N.C.N.C. who wanted a federal form of government in Nigeria based on small states, and the Igbo State Union was founded as the basis of one of these states.

Until the Richards constitution the North was largely isolated from the South, and since its traditional form of government had largely been preserved there was little opportunity for Western-style politics. However, a few Northerners had received Western education and in 1943 a group of them, including Mallam Abubakar Tafawa Balewa, future Prime Minister of Nigeria, Sa'ad Zungur, the first Northerner to go to Yaba Higher College, and Aminu Kano, subsequently leader of the radical opposition in the North, formed the Bauchi Improvement Association. In 1949, Aminu Kano and Abubakar were among the founders of the Northern People's Congress, a cultural Congress which, like the Egbe Omo Oduduwa, was converted into a political organization to meet the requirements of the new Macpherson constitution.

The three years during which the new constitution was negotiated were dominated by ethnic and regional nationalism with the N.P.C. taking the part of the North, the Egbe Omo Oduduwa, which with elements of the old Nigerian Youth Movement became the Action Group, taking the part of the West, and the N.C.N.C., whilst it outwardly preserved its pan-Nigerian aims, taking the part of the East.

At this time, possibly only the extremist Zikist movement could legitimately call itself a pan-Nigerian party. Comprising members from all parts of Nigeria, it was violently anti-colonial, calling on workers to strike and to refuse to pay taxes. In February 1949 ten of its leaders were tried and imprisoned on charges of sedition, and the movement went to earth and might even have petered out but for the notorious Enugu shootings. The miners of the Enugu colliery had staged a go-slow strike in the erroneous belief encouraged by the

Zikists that arrears of pay had been withheld from them. The government sent in a detachment of police to collect the dynamite stored in the mine, fearful that either the miners would use it or that it might find its way into Zikist hands. The miners in turn feared that the police had been sent to break up the strike and rioted. The European in charge of the detachment ordered his police to fire on the strikers and twenty-one were killed. The news of the massacre was received with great horror all over Nigeria, and the Zikists, whom the government strongly suspected of engineering the strike, seized the opportunity and provoked riots in Aba, Calabar, Onitsha and Port Harcourt.

In the ensuing Commission of Enquiry the police officer responsible for the shooting was adjudged to have acted in all honesty, but to have 'made an error of judgment which fell short of that standard that might be expected from one of his rank and seniority'.[16] To nationalists this seemed too small a penalty for him to pay, and in the Legislative Council Zik demanded unsuccessfully that he be brought back from England to stand trial. The Zikist movement reached a dramatic end when, on 18th February 1950, a Zikist attempted to assassinate Mr Hugh Foot, the Chief Secretary. Zikists were rounded up and in April 1950 the movement was proscribed.

Meanwhile all over Nigeria discussion of the new constitution was taking place. From March to September 1949 the divisional, provincial and regional conferences had been considering the future constitution, and between October 10th and 21st the drafting committee prepared a preliminary constitution for discussion by the general conference which was convened at Ibadan with all but three of its fifty-three members Nigerians. The drafting committee proposed a federal system of government with a fairly strong central legislature and executive, though considerable powers were to be delegated to the Regions. The central executive or council of state would have six *ex officio* and twelve unofficial members who would be ministers. The composition of the House should be twenty-two from the East and West respectively and thirty from the North by virtue of its larger population. The North, however, insisted on representation equal to that of both the Southern Regions since its population was greater than that of both combined. It also asked that distribution of grants from the central government be made on a *per capita* basis. It wanted no change in the regional boundaries though the drafting committee had recommended that these should be re-examined.

Four minority reports were presented to the general conference.[17] All of them were very important for they contained the seeds of some of the major political disputes of subsequent years. The first minority report, signed by Eyo Ita, Vice-President of the N.C.N.C., and Mazi

Mbonu Ojike, attacked the regional basis of government, suggesting that Nigeria should be divided into a larger number of ethnic states. They opposed the creation of Houses of Chiefs, as well as the electoral college system, advocating in a second report that this be replaced by universal adult suffrage. A third minority report opposed the denial of franchise to Southerners resident in the North, whilst a fourth, signed mainly by Western Region members, attacked the proposal that Lagos should be separated from the Western Region.

When the conference's recommendations were sent to the Colonial Secretary, he gave them his general approval and referred the outstanding issues back to the Legislative Council for final solution. A select committee of the Legislature decided that the North should have equal representation with the South, but made no concessions on the major issues raised by the minority reports. In January 1952 the new constitution came into effect, with a central legislature of 148 members, half of them from the North, and an executive council of eighteen members, comprising six officials and twelve ministers, four nominated by each regional assembly. In the regions the assemblies were enlarged and given legislative and financial powers. Each had its own executive council with a majority of African over official members. But neither in any region nor in the central government was provision made for the post of premier or prime minister. Revenues were to be distributed to the regions on the principle of need rather than derivation.

In the dry season of 1951–2, Nigeria's first general election was fought by the three major parties: the N.C.N.C., whose dominant policy was the achievement of a unitary Nigeria; the Action Group, which at first was mainly intent on securing Western Region interests and only later took on a national character; and the N.P.C., which was transformed half-way through the election from a cultural organization into a political party, determined to secure the North for Northerners.[18] The N.C.N.C. won the East with a large majority; the Action Group won the West with 49 out of 80 seats (a number of the A.G. members had stood as N.C.N.C. candidates but subsequently crossed the carpet); and the N.P.C. swept the North.

Dr Azikiwe was elected to the Western House as one of the five members for Lagos, but because of lack of party discipline he was not elected as a member of the Central House. Since the other N.C.N.C. members for Lagos refused to stand down for Zik, this left the Action-Group-dominated Western House in the position of selecting which two of the five N.C.N.C. Lagos members they would elect as representatives to the Central House. Naturally they did not choose Zik, since they were only too pleased to be able to exclude the national leader of the N.C.N.C.

The Macpherson constitution, though much more liberal in its outlook than its predecessor, and much more in keeping with the desires of Nigerians themselves, was destined for a short life. Partly this was because of its own deficiencies, partly because of the political situation at the time. From the party point of view there was a fundamental difference between the N.C.N.C. on the one hand, in which important elements wanted a constitution that would give greater powers to the central government, and the Action Group and N.P.C. on the other, both of which wanted to retain as much power in the regions as possible. This was particularly true of the N.P.C. where long administrative separation from the South and relative political backwardness made their leaders genuinely afraid of Southern domination, a point which the leader of the N.P.C., the Sardauna of Sokoto, makes very clear in his autobiography.[19]

In effect, the Macpherson constitution was a compromise between these two positions and apportioned power effectively neither to centre nor to region. And since, on its promulgation, it was stated to be only a step towards further constitutional development, the various parties, despite an initial willingness to make it work, all the time had their eye on future change. Its particular defect was the position of the ministers. There was no real ministerial responsibility under the constitution since ministers were not directly responsible for their departments, but merely acted as spokesmen on departmental affairs in the Legislature and Council of Ministers, where they were charged 'when a decision had been taken . . . (with) . . . ensuring in association with the appropriate official that effect is given to the decision'.[20] They had no responsibility for the formulation of policy in their own department. Furthermore, ministers were held collectively responsible for all decisions made in the Council of Ministers. In an ordinary party or coalition government this would be a reasonable proviso; but in a council where ministers were elected not by the national legislature but from the regional Houses, and where four African ministers from one region together with the six European officials could outvote the eight ministers from the other two regions, there was definite possibility of political deadlock.

The actual breakdown resulted largely from party antagonisms. The N.C.N.C. from the outset was disappointed with the constitution, especially since its own leader had been excluded from the national legislature. In the party there was sharp disagreement between the members holding ministerial office in the Eastern and Central Houses, who wanted to make the constitution work, and those who were disillusioned by Zik's exclusion from the Central House and wanted to withdraw their support. At an N.C.N.C. convention in Jos in December

1952, three N.C.N.C. central ministers were expelled from the party (the fourth, Dr Endeley, the Cameroons representative,[21] was not) and when it became apparent that most of the Eastern ministers sympathized with their colleagues at the centre a meeting of the Eastern parliamentary committee of the party asked for the resignation of all nine ministers so that a cabinet reshuffle could take place. The ministers duly signed resignations, but when six of them learnt they were not to be included in the new cabinet they withdrew their resignations. The Legal Secretary accepted their right of withdrawal and so they were able to remain in office only to have every Bill they introduced, including the annual Appropriation Bill, defeated by large majorities. To pass the latter the Lieutenant-Governor, Sir Clem Pleass, was forced to use his reserve powers. The East thus had a minority government, led by the National Independence Party, formed by the dissident Eastern Region ministers and the expelled central ministers.

As far as the N.C.N.C. was concerned the position was intolerable, yet it was the Action Group that precipitated the final breakdown of the constitution. On 1st April an Action Group backbencher, Anthony Enahoro, introduced a private member's Bill demanding self-government in 1956. It was clear that the Northern members would not support this motion,[22] as they did not feel themselves ready for self-government, and in the Council of Ministers the four Northern ministers, together with the six European officials, voted that no minister should participate in the debate. This was opposed by the four Action Group members who felt that they could hardly dissociate themselves from so important a motion by a member of their own party. The N.I.P. ministers abstained. However, according to the doctrine of collective responsibility the Council had to present a united front in the house, so the Action Group ministers resigned. The North tried to push a milder motion asking for self-government as soon as practicable, but both Action Group and N.C.N.C. walked out of the house.

The Northern members were booed by the Lagos crowds and many of them returned to their homes resolved never again to involve themselves in Southern politics, and seriously contemplated secession from the Federation.[23] The position deteriorated when the Action Group, whose leader, Awolowo, had called the Northern leaders despots and British stooges, announced a tour of Kano, heart of Northern Nigeria. Though the Resident banned it at the last minute, the publicity in its favour had been sufficient to excite deep resentment by local people against the South, though in fact the Northern opposition party, the Northern Elements Progressive Union, welcomed the tour which many have criticized as being an extremely tactless undertaking in the circumstances.[24] The situation was particularly tense in Kano because of the large Southern minority in the Sabon Gari, or strangers' quarter, and from 15th to 19th May there were serious communal riots with an official death roll of 36 killed and 277 wounded,[25] though it is almost certain that the numbers were much larger. Tribal and regional antagonism came to a vicious head in those unhappy days and it seemed that Nigeria would split in two.

Shortly after the riots the Northern House of Chiefs and the Northern House of Assembly passed an eight-point programme which in effect demanded the dissolution of the Federation. It wanted government devolved on the regions, which were to be linked only by a central agency, of a non-political character, appointed jointly by regional governments. This would be responsible for Defence, External Affairs, Customs and West African Research unions, and any other matters the regional governments cared to refer to it.[26] The long separation of North from South seemed to have left too deep an impression for their recent political marriage to succeed. The immediate result of the riots and the motion in the Northern House was the realization by the Colonial Secretary, Mr Oliver Lyttelton, that his earlier complacent statement that what Nigeria 'needs is a period of reflection to let the dust die down'[27] was far from the truth, and almost at once he announced that the Nigerian constitution would be 'redrawn to provide for greater regional autonomy and for the removal of powers of intervention by the centre in matters which could, without detriment to other Regions, be placed entirely within regional competence'.[28]

The various parties sent delegations to the conference in London with many misgivings and with provisos that made its success seem almost impossible. The N.P.C., led by the Sardauna of Sokoto, had already made it clear that the only form in which they would co-operate with the South would be a loose, non-politicized union. The Action Group and the N.C.N.C. in temporary alliance at first refused to go if the N.I.P. attended, and stipulated that if the North were intransigent about the question of self-government they would ask for the creation of a Southern federation which would take self-government in 1956, come what may. Both, however, were agreed on the delegation of residual powers to the regional governments, and as allies they remained tactfully reticent about the question of the status of Lagos. The N.I.P. however opposed self-government in 1956, but advocated the creation of a strong central legislature and the breakdown of the regions into states.

Against this unpromising background it is remarkable how much agreement was in fact reached by the delegates to the London conference.[29] The three major parties agreed to a federal constitution in which residual powers would be transferred to the regions as distinct from the centre as had been the case under the old constitution. Nevertheless, much wider powers were given to the centre than had been envisaged by the Northern delegation. The all-important question of self-government in 1956 was cleverly side-stepped by offering self-government to those regions that wanted it in 1956, but not to the federation as a whole, thus leaving it open for the North to decide for itself when it was ready for self-government. At the time few had believed that the British government would make this important concession on a fixed date for self-government.

The most bitter issue of the conference, which broke up the N.C.N.C.-Action Group alliance, was whether Lagos should remain part of the Western Region or become federal territory. The N.P.C. pressed for the latter solution, since it was anxious to ensure that the main outlet for its goods should not be under the control of any other part of the federation. The N.C.N.C., which had many members in Lagos, also felt that a federation should have a true federal capital. The Action Group, however, argued that Lagos was a Yoruba city, and did most of its trade with the Western Region, and as far as the North's fears were concerned both the railways and the ports were under federal control. In the end the three parties agreed to arbitration of the issue by the Colonial Secretary, who decided that Lagos should become federal territory. Despite its agreement to his arbitration, the Action Group bitterly attacked his decision, and for a while it seemed that the resumed constitutional conference in Lagos proposed for January 1954, at which the fiscal arrangements of the federation and the position of the judiciary and civil service were to be decided, would founder over the future of Lagos. However, when the conference opened the Action Group did not raise the Lagos issue but demanded instead that the right to secession be included in the constitution. This was again rejected by the Colonial Secretary, and the Action Group acquiesced in his decision.

Once again a conference about which most people had been very pessimistic was a striking success. The rules for the actual functioning of the federation were settled by the delegates, in particular the delicate problem of distribution of funds between the centre and the regions.[30] At the 1953 conference Sir Louis Chick had been commissioned to devise a system of revenue allocation based on 'the need, on the one hand, to provide the Federal government and Regional governments with an adequate measure of fiscal autonomy within their own sphere of government, and, on the other, the importance of ensuring that the total revenues available to Nigeria are allocated in such a way that the principle of derivation is followed to the fullest degree compatible with the reasonable needs of the Federal government and the Regional governments'.[31] The conference accepted his basic proposals: that all import, excise and export duties should be federal matters; that all import duties on motor spirits and half the import duty and excise on tobacco should go to the regional governments on the basis of consumption; that half the net proceeds of all other import duties should be distributed to the regional governments on the basis of 40 per cent to the West and 30 per cent each to the East and North; that mining taxes should be collected federally and distributed to the regions on the basis of derivation; that income tax should also be collected federally and distributed on the basis of derivation. As *West Africa* wrote in its editorial at the time: 'Endorsement of the Chick report means economically as well as politically there will be three Nigerias.' In addition the marketing boards were regionalized, and their combined reserves of £74 million were distributed on a basis of £34 million to the West, £24 million to the North and £15 million to the East. The tendency towards the creation of three Nigerias was consolidated by the regionalization of the civil service and the judiciary, though provision was made for appeals to a Federal Supreme Court. The latter move was bitterly opposed by the Lagos Bar, whilst the former was necessitated by the increase in government responsibility devolved on the regions.

The constitution agreed on by these two conferences is essentially the constitution under which Nigeria was governed till the military take-over in 1966. Nigeria became a full federation of three Regions, a federal capital, and the quasi-federal territory of the Southern Cameroons, which by agreement of the conferences had been allowed to break away from the Eastern Region. A national legislature of 184 members, half of them representing the North, was to be elected every five years. However, the elections were to take place region by region, and the system of election varied from one to the other. The appointment of ministers to the central executive council was not now made by the regional assemblies, but by the leader of the party which gained the majority of seats in each regional federal election. Each region had the right to three seats on the council. The principle of full ministerial responsibility for departmental affairs was settled though no provision was made for the post of leader of government business. However, in the regions provision was made for the post of Premier and an all-Nigerian Executive Council with the exception of the Governor, who remained President. Residual powers were now transferred to the regions. It was finally promised that the new constitution would be reviewed before August 1956. But the 1954 constitution, despite subsequent changes, had laid down the basic pattern of government for a self-governing Nigeria.

17 Independence Achieved

The 1954 constitution marks the effective end of the nationalist struggle with Britain; for the next six years, until the achievement of independence on 1st October 1960, Nigerian leaders were preoccupied not so much with wresting power from the colonial government as dealing with the day-to-day administration and development of their country as well as settling the basis on which they would co-operate with each other. It was hardly surprising therefore that the year after the new constitution came into effect was a quiet one with ministers taking over departments and learning the basic mechanics of the services for which they were now fully responsible. In the regions their responsibility was even greater since with the exception of the North there was only one expatriate official in the Regional Executive Council—the Governor. In the federal elections that followed the introduction of the new constitution, the N.P.C. and its allies won 84 of the 90 seats in the North, where the elections were still indirect, though everywhere else they were now direct. The biggest surprise came in the West where the N.C.N.C., having triumphed in the East, won 23 seats to the Action Group's 18, showing the Nigerian politics were not entirely dominated by ethnic factors, though it must be pointed out that the N.C.N.C. gained much of its support in the minority area of the Mid-West.[1] In Yoruba areas it gained support because of the unpopularity of the Action Group's taxation policy. However, since the N.C.N.C.'s close ally, the Northern Elements Progressive Union, won no seats in the North, there was still no party with truly national support. The curious situation arose that whilst the N.C.N.C. had the right to choose six federal ministers, having won both the East and West, the N.P.C. had the largest number of seats in the Federal House. This fact curbed the N.P.C. from its original intention of going it alone in the Federal House, for the presence of six N.C.N.C. ministers made coalition between the parties inevitable, if there was to be a government at all. The Action Group, supported by N.I.P. (now U.N.I.P.), formed a small but active opposition.

The agreement of the N.P.C. and the N.C.N.C., whose political views were diametrically opposed on many issues, to work together in the

Federal government was perhaps the most significant development in post-war Nigerian politics since it proved to be the basis of co-operation in the first five years of independence. It made national unity possible, even if it meant that both parties had to compromise their political views.

In 1955 Sir John Macpherson, who had been ultimately responsible for Nigeria during its period of greatest political upheaval and progress, retired. Though the constitution named after him had proved a failure, he left praised by even the most extreme nationalist elements who recognized that Nigeria's accelerated constitutional progress was in no small measure due to his enthusiasm and understanding of the young federation's needs.[2] His successor, Sir James Robertson, turned out to be the ideal man to represent Britain during the final phase of self-government, and happily the improved relations between Nigeria and Britain were crystallized the following year by the royal tour of Queen Elizabeth and the Duke of Edinburgh.

The visit of the Queen seemed somehow to symbolize the unity for which Nigeria was striving. Indeed, as the editorial in *West Africa* remarked at the time, 'the enthusiasm and devotion that the visit has aroused have gone beyond expectation'.[3] The three main leaders called a political truce for the visit, and a bond of goodwill was created not only between Nigerians but between Nigeria and Britain, a bond that seemed far away from the months of 1953 when the N.C.N.C. banned the Coronation ceremonies.

Whilst Nigerian leaders were absorbed in the mechanics of government they also had one eye on the review of the constitution scheduled to take place in September 1956, when it was assumed that both the West and the East would take up the British promise of self-government in 1956. Indeed the Action Group had published in December 1955 a White Paper, which was approved by the Western House of Assembly, outlining the form self-government would take.[4] However, because of events in the Eastern House of Assembly, the conference had to be postponed.

The N.C.N.C. had long been dogged by instability in the second ranks of its leadership. On 30th April 1956 Mr E. O. Eyo, the chief whip of the Eastern Region government, tabled a motion in the house accusing Dr Azikiwe of gross abuse of public office in that he allowed £2 million of public money to be invested in the African Continental Bank in which he had substantial personal interest and which at the time was running at a loss. The debate was refused by the Speaker since the matter was *sub judice* because of a libel action brought by Dr Azikiwe against Mr Eyo. Since the Premier would not accede to the Governor of the Region's suggestion that the matter be referred to an independent tribunal, the Colonial Secretary appointed a Commission of Inquiry under the Federal Chief Justice, Sir Stafford Foster-Sutton, which had the effect of delaying the resumed negotiations over the constitution.

Tales of corruption in public life were common in Nigeria at the time and concern over this was obviously one of Mr Lennox-Boyd's main reasons for establishing the Commission in such delicate circumstances. As far as Dr Azikiwe's supporters were concerned he was innocent even before he appeared before the tribunal, and the rather mild condemnation of the Commission that his conduct had 'fallen short of the expectations of honest reasonable people' seemed to confirm their view, especially since it was also conceded that Zik's primary motive 'was to make available an indigenous bank with the object of liberalizing credit for the people'.[5] This was not due merely to blind personal following, but to the fact that whatever the rather cold attitude of the British might have been towards the affair, it was felt that Dr Azikiwe had acted genuinely in the African interest by depositing government money in the African Continental Bank, especially as it was in danger of foundering. For them the bank represented an African achievement, and an attempt to rival the primacy of the British banks, one of which it was observed handled all government accounts. As Kalu Ezera points out, 'Zik's supporters generally believed that the whole affair was a conspiracy by the Colonial Office to descredit and "dethrone" him and to perpetuate British banking monopoly in the country.'[6]

West Africa wrote at the time very perceptively: 'The idea that a man who, like Dr Azikiwe, has built up a bank and a group of companies, however shaky their finances, should relinquish all control of them when he becomes a Minister, is not universally accepted in Nigeria, where the joint stock company finds unfertile soil.'[7] On the other hand the Commission of Inquiry had the salutary effect of regularizing the affairs of the bank, which, with the National Bank of Nigeria, supported mainly by the Western Region, represented a very considerable entrepreneurial achievement.

Immediately after the Commission's report, delivered on 16th January 1957, Dr Azikiwe transferred his interest to the Eastern Region government, and went to the country as a trial of strength. He won the election by a comfortable margin of 64 seats to 20 (U.N.I.P. 5, Action Group 13, Independents 2) and was thus in a strong position as chief representative of the N.C.N.C. and the Eastern Region government at the London Conference scheduled for May 1957. Likewise the Action Group had gone to the country in May 1956 so that in the words of Chief Awolowo it 'could go to the next Constitutional Conference fully armed with a mandate of the people in respect of all major issues which will be raised at the conference'.[8]

On 26th March 1957, the Federal House of Representatives, prior to the London conference and just after Ghana had achieved independence, passed a motion asking for independence in 1959. Once again it seemed at first that this might precipitate crisis, for the leader of the opposition, Chief Akintola, moving the motion, had originally asked for independence in 1957, although the North had already made it clear that she would not be hurried into regional self-government. However, the greatly improved relations between the parties were demonstrated clearly when Mr Jaja Wachuku of the N.C.N.C. asked Chief Akintola whether he would agree to change the date to 1959, which he did, whereupon the House voted it unanimously.

The 1957 conference itself was mainly concerned with the revision of the constitution of 1954 both in the light of experience in running it and in accordance with foreseen constitutional advance. It was agreed that both the West and the East should have self-government as soon as they wanted it. The Federal House was enlarged to 320 members, who were to be elected directly on the same basis nationally with the exception that suffrage would not be extended to women in the North, in accordance with that Region's Muslim susceptibilities. It was also agreed that there would be appointed a federal Prime Minister with a cabinet drawn from the House of Representatives or the proposed new Senate. The lack of a federal leader of government had hitherto been a major weakness of the constitution, but on the other hand until then it had been difficult to see how the various parties could agree on a Prime Minister, since the three national leaders were in the Regional Houses, and no one party commanded an overall majority. However, experience of working together and recognition of each others' talents made it possible for not only the N.C.N.C., which had been working in coalition with the N.P.C., but also the Action Group to form a national government under Alhaji Abubakar Tafawa Balewa, the former Minister of Transport and Deputy President of the N.P.C. This retiring, but extremely astute Northerner, had already impressed his colleagues as a minister, and in the House his great debating ability had gained him the respect of all legislators. Though in his early days as a national legislator he had talked in terms of Northern separatism, by 1957 he had become as convinced as anyone else of the necessity of national co-operation. In the sense that he was not associated with any of the major ethnic groups of Nigeria—unlike most of the Northern leaders he did not come from the Hausa Fulani aristocracy—and as a member of a small ethnic group he could in a way symbolize Nigeria as a whole and not one faction of it, though he was still perceived as a representative of the conservative Muslim North.

It might have seemed in 1957 that Nigeria was nearly ready for independence. The North had however refused to be rushed into self-government, on the grounds that Northern cadres were not ready to take over the Region's administration. With eighteen million people to govern and only a handful of university graduates, and probably no more than 2,000 holders of school certificate, the formation of a Northern administration would be dependent on expatriates or Southerners. Moreover, the Regional Premier, the Sardauna of Sokoto, scion of the royal house of Sokoto, fully realized that the tensions existing in the Region between the old forces of aristocracy as represented by the Emirs and their Native Authorities and the new forces of democracy as represented by the government in Kaduna must on no account clash.[9] The uncertain marriage between the two had to be handled with great care, and the N.P.C. seemed the only organization that could bridge the gap between them. The two Southern Regions had a head start as a result of their greater education, whilst the North, in which early agreements had excluded missionaries who had provided most of the schools in the South, had only just embarked on a large-scale education programme. Thus, before the 1957 conference, it seemed that the Northern reluctance for self-government might well hold up independence for the country as a whole, and it was with considerable relief that delegates heard the Sardauna of Sokoto announce that his Region would in fact become self-governing in 1959.

By far the most complex problem confronting the delegates was that of Nigeria's minority groups, and the demand for the creation of new states that had grown up amongst them. One of the main results of the accentuation of tribal politics in the years of the Macpherson constitution was the increase in the minority reaction against the major ethnic groups dominating the political life of the regions. This minority movement, always potentially existent because of historical and ethnic factors, took the form of political associations seeking the separation of so-called minority areas and the creation of new states. In the Northern Region some people in the predominantly non-Muslim and non-Hausa Middle Belt formed the United Middle Belt Congress. This new party demanded the creation of a separate state for the Middle Belt so that the people could escape from what its leaders alleged was the domination of the Fulani and Hausa. This had certain roots in history, for the areas claimed by this party were predominantly those which the cavalry of the Fulani had never conquered. In the Western Region, as a reaction against the allegedly Yoruba-dominated Action Group, the Mid-West State movement was started, supported largely by non-

Yoruba-speaking peoples and in particular the people of the old Benin
Empire. The N.C.N.C. also supported this movement on the grounds
that the only way to create a truly united Nigeria would be to create
more states, none of which would be large enough to dominate any of
the others. Curiously enough the Action Group itself gave its blessing
to this movement, partly because it was beginning to find the Mid-West
an electoral and economic liability and partly because it realized that if
it were to champion the creation of new states in the Eastern and
Northern Regions it could hardly object to the creation of one in the
Western Region itself.

In the East the Igbo formed a solid core of well over seven million, and
were surrounded by three provinces in which other groups pre-
dominated: Calabar, Ogoja and Rivers. The movement for the creation
of a separate state in the East was more complex. The main movement
was for the creation of the C.O.R. state or Calabar-Ogoja-Rivers state,
but there were subsidiary movements for the creation of an Ogoja state
and a Rivers state including Ijo from both Western and Eastern
Nigeria. But in all cases the movements were inspired by fear of the
dominant group, and by ethnic chauvinism.

The 1957 Conference referred this knotty matter to a special commission headed by Sir Henry Willink. Its tour of the country was
naturally the time for the most vocal outcry of minority groups, and in a
sense the whole problem became for a time wildly exaggerated, because
of the implicit opportunity the Commission gave to the voicing of all
sorts of grievances.

However, the Minorities Commission came out very strongly against
the creation of new states, because it felt that the fears and problems of
minority groups could be better solved within the existing political
framework.[10] In each case the Commission found that the cores of the
minority movements were too small compared with the area which
they claimed for their new state. For instance, they argued that in the
West, while most Edo wanted a Mid-West State, by no means all
Itsekiri and Ijo felt happy at the prospect of its creation.

Yet the Commission admitted that minority fears of ethnic domination and discrimination in development were real, and proposed that
minority areas be set up for both Calabar and the Mid-West. These
areas would have special councils, which could keep a watch on regional government activities and could also exercise delegated executive authority. For the Ijo areas of the Niger Delta the Commission
recommended the establishment of a special development board on
which the regional governments concerned and the Federal government would be represented. However, whilst the Commission gave
no truck to the creation of a Middle Belt state in the North, it did

recommend that a plebiscite be held there to determine whether Ilorin and Kabba wished to remain in the North or join up with the Western Region.

Otherwise the Commission felt that minority fears could be assuaged by the entrenchment of fundamental human rights in the constitution,

9. The various proposed political reorganizations of Nigeria, 1945–60

and by making any amendment to the constitution impossible without the virtual consent of the whole country and in particular the people most intimately affected. Finally, it insisted that the police should remain national rather than be regionalized as the N.P.C. and Action Group had requested.

At the 1958 conference the parties agreed with some reluctance to the acceptance of the minorities report. The Action Group was particularly anxious about the inclusion of the Ilorin and Kabba in the Western Region, and therefore the implementation of the plebiscite recommended by the Commission, but the North, which had agreed to take self-government on 15th March 1959, made it clear that it might be at the price of independence that this point be insisted upon. On the other hand both the Action Group and the N.P.C. had to compromise over the subject of the police. Both had wanted the regionalization of the police, but the N.C.N.C. and the British government, agreeing for once, saw in the regionalization of the police a danger to political freedom, particularly of minorities.

The agreement over the minorities report was, of course, largely influenced by the fact that none of the parties cared to stand out on the issue for fear of being branded as the one that held up independence. The problem still remained and was to colour Nigerian politics for some years to come. In retrospect it might seem that the Commission dodged the issue, especially since it was widely known that the British government would consider the creation of new states as instrumental in delaying the date for independence. But the lines on which the Commission was thinking were made clear by one of its members, Mr Philip Mason, in a series of articles in *West Africa*.[11] He argued that hopes of the continued unity of Nigeria and justice for individuals must rest initially on the grounds that none of the three major parties could dominate the other and that any party seeking to get such domination within the present political structure must seek support outside its regional stronghold, and therefore amongst the minority groups of the other regions. This fact, together with a police force independent of any regional government, and therefore any party, would be the best guarantee of minority rights.

The outcome of the federal elections of 1959 and the campaign that preceded them showed just how dominant a factor minorities remained and how anxious all the parties, including the N.P.C. with regard to its own minority area, were to gain their confidence. A comparison of the distribution of minorities and the strongholds of opposition in each region is very illuminating (see map on page 243). However, in a surprise election just before independence the Action Group retained control of the West, having made significant gains in the Mid-West as well as some losses in Yorubaland, suggesting that perhaps ethnic factors were receding in Nigerian politics.

The federal elections, as the table below shows, returned no party with a large enough majority to form a government by itself.[12] After a week of strenuous negotiations the N.P.C. and the N.C.N.C. agreed to form a coalition government, leaving the Action Group in opposition. During that week there had even been talk of an Action Group—N.C.N.C. alliance, which would have led to the unhappy situation of confronting South and North as Government and Opposition.

Party	North	East	West	Lagos	Total
N.P.C. and allies	135	1†	7‡	—	143
N.C.N.C./N.E.P.U. Alliance	8	58	21	2	89
Action Group	25	14	33	1	73
Independents	6*	—	1	—	7
	174	73	62	3	312

* Declared subsequently for N.P.C.
† Niger Delta Congress.
‡ Mabolaje Grand Alliance.

Alhaji Abubakar Tafawa Balewa, who was knighted in the New Year Honours, became Prime Minister and Dr Azikiwe, leader of the N.C.N.C., to the surprise of many, opted for the dignified but in itself politically uninfluential post of President of the newly formed Senate, which had an equal number of Senators nominated by each regional government. There was considerable speculation as to whether Dr Azikiwe would become Nigeria's first African Governor-General, or whether he was waiting for the post of Foreign Minister when Nigeria, on Independence, took over control of external affairs. As it turned out there were no major changes in the government on Independence and Dr Azikiwe, on the 16th November 1960, became Governor-General of the independent federation.

The rapid political developments that took place in the years from 1945–60 were paralleled by similar developments in the social and economic spheres. The social and economic changes of this period were of the same order as those experienced in the years 1906–12, prior to the amalgamation of Northern and Southern Nigeria. The period between the two world wars by contrast had been one of consolidation of changes already made rather than one of innovation. This was largely dictated by the fact that government revenue was barely sufficient to cover the cost of the general administration of the country. Indeed during the thirties, when world prices for Nigeria's agricultural exports fell to a disastrously low level, cuts in government services had to be made since the funds from which these were paid were in large part derived from duties on exports, and on the imports which the earnings from these exports allowed the country to buy. Yet this is not to minimize the importance of these years in the history of Nigeria, for it was during this period that the nationalistic movement grew up and the future leaders of Nigeria received their education. More important still, during these years was laid the basis of the social and economic transformation of the country that enabled the nationalists to convince the British in the fifties that they were ready for a self-government which the latter had only envisaged as taking place some time in a distant but unspecified future.

The stimulus for the rapid changes that took place between 1945 and 1960 was Nigeria's involvement in the Second World War. Just as the war had opened up new political horizons for the country, so it provided impetus for economic and social development. Most important of all was the new role assumed by the government in the direction of the country's economy. Hitherto the government had been largely a passive agent in the economic affairs of the country, being guided by the principles of laissez-faire. The economic exploitation of the country was almost entirely in the hands of large import-export companies, in particular the United Africa Company, and the government's main concern was to ensure that the interests of the indigenous population were safeguarded, as in the days when Lord Leverhulme had tried to introduce plantations into the country. Now, in time of war, the colonial administration had to ensure that the Metropolitan government was supplied with as much of the foodstuffs and raw materials produced by the country as possible, and that these should be at low prices. Thus price-controls and wage-ceilings were introduced and the government assumed responsibility for the export of most of Nigeria's agricultural products. Many of these measures hurt indigenous interests[13] but the fact of the government's active participation in the direction of the economy was to be of utmost importance for the post-war years. The government came increasingly to accept that it bore responsibility not only for the regulation of the national economy, but also for its stimulation.

The increased demand for Nigerian raw materials by the allies and the use of Nigeria as a staging-ground in the war effort had an immense economic impact on the country. Exports in the war years more than doubled in value from £10,300,000 to £24,000,000.[14] Associated with this dramatic increase in production was the rapid growth of urban centres like Enugu, Lagos, Kano and Port Harcourt. As far as future economic development was concerned one of the most important effects of the war was the release from military service of a large number of Nigerians who had learned special trades or skills.[15]

The economic expansion resulting from the war continued into the post-war period, not only because of the rising world demand for Nigeria's raw materials, but also because international concern with the morality of colonialism was forcing most colonial powers to pay more attention to the economic development of their colonies for the benefit of their indigenous inhabitants. Thus Britain, which had for long maintained as a cardinal point of colonial policy that her colonies should pay for their own services and provide their own development funds, now accepted, as we have seen, part of the cost of their economic and social development on to her metropolitan budget. In addition to the development funds received from Britain, the Nigerian administration was receiving increasing revenues from duties on imports and exports and thus had at its disposal for the first time the wherewithal to transform Nigeria from the 'colonial backwater' it had been in the thirties into a rapidly modernizing state able to take its place among the independent nations of the world. Yet in 1945 neither the nationalist leaders, who constantly demanded that the administration provide their people with the same services they provided the expatriates in their European reservations, nor the British government, more conscious of the need for social reform in the colonies now that it was under Labour control, could have envisaged that by 1960 all children of school age in Southern Nigeria would enjoy primary education, free in the Western Region and at a nominal charge in the Eastern Region.

The extent of the rapid economic changes that took place in the post-war period is brought out in the table on page 248.[16]

The basis of these rapid post-war economic changes was agriculture, which on the eve of independence still accounted for over 85 per cent of the country's exports.[17] This was the result not so much of the increase in agricultural production, which was considerable, but of the rise in world prices for the export crops produced by Nigeria. Until 1953 this rise was continuous. The balance of Nigeria's exports was accounted for mainly by tin and columbite mined on the Jos Plateau. Fortunately for the country as a whole the variety of primary products was sufficiently diverse to avoid the worst effects of the vagaries of the world market, especially after 1953. However, the Northern and Eastern Regions, which during this period still depended largely on one export crop, were more vulnerable than the West, which was producing palm-oil, rubber,

cocoa and timber for export. On average in the years 1956–8
groundnuts, coming exclusively from the North, earned some £30 million a year; palm products from the East and West £33 million; cotton
and linters, mainly from the North, £8 million; cocoa from the West,
£25 million; and rubber from the West, mainly from the area that is
now Bendel State, but with some also from the East, £7 million.[18]

Item	1947	1953	1958
Revenue of Governments (£thousands)	£14,193	£51,110	£81,288
Currency in circulation (£thousands)	£23,429	£51,365	£55,118
Bank deposits (£thousands)	£13,697	£31,238	£58,118
Exports (£thousands)	£44,314	£124,232	£135,690
Imports (£thousands)	£32,636	£108,290	£167,074
Railway freight tons (miles—1,000)	571,000	827,000	1,232,000
Cement imports and local manufacture (tons)	107,306	297,436	573,119

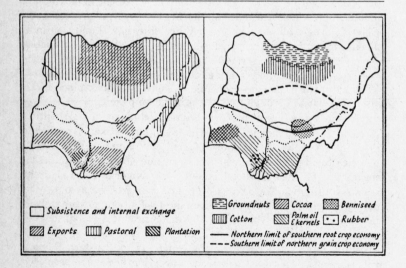

☐ Subsistence and internal exchange

▨ Exports   ⊞ Pastoral   ▧ Plantation

▤ Groundnuts   ▨ Cocoa   ▨ Benniseed
⊞ Cotton   ▨ Palm oil & kernels   ⠿ Rubber

—— Northern limit of southern root crop economy
--- Southern limit of northern grain crop economy

10. Nigeria's economy in 1960

All crops were bought up by the Statutory Marketing Board established in the immediate post-war years to ensure price stabilization. At the opening of the season, the Marketing Boards fixed the price for purchase of the crop for which they were responsible. If the world price fell below this price, then reserved funds accumulated in favourable years were used to buttress this up. Fortunately up till 1953 prices for all Nigeria's export crop rose steadily so that the Boards were able to accumulate substantial reserves for this purpose. The Marketing Boards so established were: the Nigerian Cocoa Marketing Board (1947), the Nigerian Groundnut Marketing Board (1949), the Nigerian Oil Palm Produce Marketing Board (1949) and the Nigerian Cotton Marketing Board. In the year 1954 these Boards, organized on a national basis and responsible each for the purchase and export of one crop, were dissolved and replaced by Regional Marketing Boards. Under the 1954 constitution agriculture became a regional concern, so that the purchase of agricultural produce had to be reorganized on a regional basis. The assets of the national Marketing Boards were divided among the new Regional Marketing Boards, which were responsible for the marketing of all export crops produced within their regions. However, since export was a federal concern under the new constitution, a Central Produce Marketing Board was established to export the crops purchased by the Regional Marketing Boards through their licensed agents.[19]

The large reserves built up by these Boards permitted the Nigerian-dominated governments of the regions formed in the five years before independence to indulge in a spate of investment spending that left imports exceeding exports by £31 million in 1958, that is only £2 million less than the total value of imports alone in 1947. Thus in the decade before independence imports quadrupled in value, whilst exports only little more than doubled, and remained almost constant in the second five years, a fact that was already giving economists cause for concern before independence.

This expansion in agricultural production was not associated with a significant growth in industry, though industrial centres were created in Lagos, Ikeja, Ibadan, Kano, Kaduna, Aba and Port Harcourt. Before independence the only heavy industries were coal- and tin-mining and two major cement works, one in the East and one in the West. Light industry included cigarette factories, breweries, a large textile mill in Kaduna, a huge plywood factory in Sapele and cotton ginneries in the North. Nevertheless in the years before independence the Federal and the Regional governments were giving top priority to industrial expansion in their development programmes, anxious one day to free Nigeria from her excessive dependence on agriculture for her export income.

One of the main hopes in this direction was the exploitation of large oil reserves in the Niger Delta. By 1960, Shell-B.P. had spent something in the range of £60 million on the search for oil and Nigeria was already beginning to export small quantities of crude oil.

Because of the importance of foreign exchange to Nigeria, there was a tendency to think of imports and exports as the sole gauge of her economic well-being. But in the post-war years there was also a remarkable expansion of her internal exchange economy. For instance Nigeria's national income in 1956–7 was estimated at just over £800 million, of which export crops accounted for only £84·4 million, whilst locally consumed foodstuffs were valued at £342·6 million.[20] Revenue from duties on export crops in 1957 only brought in just over 10 per cent of the total revenue earned by the Federal and Regional governments.

National income itself rose in the years 1950–1 from an estimated £593·4 million to £812·3 million in 1956–7. Taking into account the different methods used for these two National Income Surveys, and the rise of prices in the intervening years, the increase in National Income probably amounted to about £150 million, that is a growth of not less than 4 per cent a year. Per capita income was estimated at between £25 and £29 per year for 1956–7.[21]

As a result of this rapid economic expansion more and more Nigerians were drawn into participation in the new money economy. This was facilitated by the extension of the country's road system, particularly those roads that gave access to parts of the country far distant from either the railway, which still remained the main artery of the export trade, or from the Rivers Niger and Benue, on which a substantial part of Nigeria's trade was carried in the flood seasons. Some idea of the importance of the expansion of the road system is gained by a comparison of the mileages of road in Nigeria in 1946 and 1958. In the former year there were only 40,000 km. of road, with only 1,120 km. bitumenized. By the latter year 25,600 km. had been added of which well over 4,800 were bitumenized. Many of these roads led into parts of the country that had only been marginally affected by colonial occupation.[22] Communications were further facilitated by the development of the internal airlines and the great improvement of the posts and telecommunications system.

This new level of economic activity led to a great increase in employment opportunities. Since expatriate workers were extremely expensive to bring out to Nigeria, both the government and the commercial houses looked to educated Nigerians to fill these positions. But since educational opportunities for Africans, particularly at the secondary and university level, had been severely limited before the war, it was difficult to find Nigerians with the appropriate qualifications for these new jobs. Thus the government undertook a great expansion of educational facilities, particularly at the secondary level, and in 1948 the University College of Ibadan was established. At the same time scholarships were provided both by the government and commercial firms for Nigerians to study abroad. Usually Nigerians sent on these scholarships were bonded to work for their sponsors when their training was completed.

Despite this expansion of educational facilities, in 1955 Nigeria was only educating 800 undergraduates and 12,000 secondary school students a year,[23] and most of these came from Southern Nigeria. The need for more clerks, technicians, administrators and professionally qualified men like doctors and engineers, for employment both in government service and in commerce, was a constant problem in the post-war years and severely hampered the execution of governmental development plans. In its expansion of educational opportunities, the government was subjected to great pressure by the nationalists, who thought of education as a panacea for most of their country's ills. These nationalists, once they began to assume control of government policy, determined to ensure that there would be places in schools for all Nigerian children. Thus in the West, which in 1957 introduced Universal Free Primary Education, almost 50 per cent of the current budget was devoted to education. This concern with mass education inevitably reduced the amount of funds available for higher education, so much more expensive to provide. It also led to two major problems of the post-independence period, problems that were already manifest before independence. First was the problem of replacing the British civil servants, who, despite the Federal and Regional governments' declared policy of rapid Nigerianization,[24] in 1956 still occupied most of the technical positions in the government services. In that same year the Colonial Secretary, foreseeing the dangers of a mass exodus of British officials without sufficient Nigerians qualified to replace them, proposed a scheme whereby expatriate civil servants were guaranteed their pension rights by the British government and alternative employment overseas or in the United Kingdom if they should become redundant. Alternatively they could take their earned pension and a lump-sum compensation reaching a maximum of £10,000 according to service. Unfortunately large numbers of them opted for the second, and in 1958 a new scheme was introduced whereby they could draw 90 per cent of their lump-sum compensation in advance of their retirement as long as they agreed to give one year's notice. Nevertheless, large numbers of British civil servants left the country before independence.

The problem was further exacerbated by the fact that commercial houses, also under political pressure to Nigerianize their managerial staff, were anxious to secure the services of qualified Nigerians. And with the expansion of the economy, the number of posts to be filled was continuously increasing.

Lack of trained manpower was paralleled by an excess in supply of elementary school-leavers, possessing only a Primary VI school leaving certificate. Since the standard of education in many primary schools was poor because of the lack of qualified teachers, these Primary VI certificates often meant that while the possessor could read and write he only had a very rudimentary knowledge of the other subjects he had been taught, and was therefore not employable in clerical posts, even if these posts were available. The problem was becoming acute in the years immediately prior to independence when the first products of the universal primary education schemes in the West and East were coming on to the employment market. In 1959, the Ashby report estimated that just over 650,000 children entered primary schools,[25] and in the year of independence 180,000 children left school in Western Nigeria alone.[26] The problem would not have been grave if the primary school-leavers had been prepared to work on the farms as their fathers did. But they preferred to seek their fortunes in the towns where they could use their education to secure jobs as junior clerks, messengers or shop assistants. Thus a single advertisement for the post of messenger could attract upward of five thousand applicants. The problem was partly the result of an education system that was producing children with an elementary education at such a rate that not even the most booming economy in Africa could supply them with the jobs they sought and partly the result of an education system that did nothing to prepare them for a return to the farms where they might use newly acquired knowledge to improve a system of farming which otherwise seemed to them to hold no future. By independence an expert on the problem of school-leavers could write: 'No social and economic problem in Nigeria is so urgent as that of finding employment for the ever-increasing number of school-leavers.'[27]

Thus on the achievement of independence Nigeria was faced with the paradoxical situation that her rapid but uneven expansion of educational facilities had confronted her with two problems: on the one hand the governments had to decide what to do with the vast number of unemployed school-leavers, and on the other they had quickly to provide the higher level manpower—administrators, professional personnel, technicians, teachers, officers in the police and army and the judicial services—which had previously been supplied by the colonial power and without which they could not prosecute their ambitious development schemes.[28] To consider the latter problem the Ashby Commission on Higher Education was appointed in 1959 submitting its report in 1960,[29] in which it advocated an expansion of educational facilities at the secondary, technical and university level that would cost the Federal and Regional governments nearly 50 per cent of their recurrent budgets. Furthermore it insisted not only that the present primary educational system be maintained in the South, but that primary education be extended in the North, so that in fact there would result an even greater output of primary school-leavers seeking jobs that did not exist.

This improvement of educational facilities was accompanied by the important if less spectacular extension of other social services. Hospital places more than doubled in the post-war period. A teaching hospital was established at Ibadan, the most advanced in tropical Africa. It even had departments for the training of psychiatric and medical social workers. Water supplies were improved in rural areas as well as towns. In Lagos substantial, if not altogether successful, urban redevelopment was undertaken. This concern with the provision of social services was heightened with the accession of Nigerians to ministerial posts in the Central and Regional governments after 1951. Now was their opportunity to provide their people with those facilities which they had accused the British of reserving for the expatriate, even though the funds for them were provided by the Nigerian taxpayer.

The second major problem associated with the expansion of the economy in the post-war period was the rapid and often uncontrolled growth of the major urban centres. The problems of uncontrolled growth were most acute in Lagos,[30] but to a greater or lesser extent they were present in Port Harcourt, Enugu, Onitsha, Benin, Ibadan, and Kano. The growth in the population of the towns had been greatly stimulated by the influx of primary school-leavers in search of work. The most pressing problem became the provision of housing for the immigrants. People arrived at a rate faster than houses could be built to accommodate them. In these circumstances there was an open market for speculators who could build sub-standard houses for which they could charge vastly inflated rents. This increase in urban population led to a great strain on municipal services such as water supplies, drainage, and garbage collection, services which often could not be provided on an adequate scale without vast outlays of capital that even large municipalities like Lagos did not have at their disposal. Even a national service such as the Electricity Corporation of Nigeria (now Nigerian Electric Power Authority) was hard pressed to ensure a constant supply of electricity for domestic and industrial purposes in some of the major cities. The growth of the population of the major towns and the increase in the number of motor-cars showed how inadequate was the planning of cities that were either pre-colonial in origin

or designed by the British in the days when the motor-car was a luxury
not enjoyed in Nigeria and horses and bicycles were the common form
of transport for the colonial administrator.

It was in these urban centres that the loosening of the traditional
bonds which held Nigerian societies together became most marked. This
weakening of former ties in no way implied a breakdown in traditional
society. For even in the urban centres, where the image of the
melting-pot seems most appropriate, traditional ties have proved very
resilient. The so-called tribal unions, bringing together people from the
same ethnic group, or from the same town or village, remained one of
the most important forms of social contact in the cities.[31] They linked
the expatriated urban dweller with his people at home and exercised
considerable traditional discipline over him, as Chinua Achebe has
shown so clearly in his novel *No Longer at Ease*.[32] Even credit unions in
the towns were organized on an ethnic basis. It was difficult for the
Nigerian in towns to obtain credit from banks or from people other than
his own ethnic group, since it was only his own ethnic group that could
provide the social controls that would ensure that he would repay
money borrowed. Though the immigrant to the towns would meet girls
from other ethnic groups, he would rarely marry one of them. Inter-
ethnic marriages were unusual except among the new élite. Yet the
towns, particularly those that were important economic centres or
seats of government, served as the focus for many new contacts and
especially the formation of non-ethnic associations. Though traditional
allegiances did not break down, but rather were transformed to meet
the new situations presented by town life as exemplified in the credit
unions, the immigrants found many new ties of loyalty that cut across
ethnic barriers. The most obvious of these were membership in trade
unions, sporting associations, literary and debating societies, old boys'
clubs and political parties that were not organized on an ethnic basis.
Apart from membership of a political party, probably the most important cross-ethnic organizations in the towns were those sponsored by
the universalist religions.

The two universalist religions, Christianity and Islam, made their
greatest progress in the urban centres, particularly those of the South.
They also made great headway in the rural areas. In the East, Christianity remained unchallenged by Islam, whilst the converse was true
of the far North. In the Middle Belt and the Western Region, Islam
overtook Christianity despite the earlier initiative of the latter religion
in much of this area. Islam was particularly successful in Yorubaland,[33] where in some parts it had preceeded Christianity as an immigrant religion by several decades. Islam of course had the great advantage of not being identified with the colonial power and also of being an

almost exclusively African controlled religion.[34] Furthermore Islam in West Africa has generally been tolerant of the traditional beliefs and customs of the peoples it converted whereas the Christian missionaries insisted on a complete abandonment of traditional customs even where these were only remotely connected with traditional religion. Although the Anglican Church in Nigeria initially had as its ambition the creation of an African-run Church and had to this end appointed an African, Samuel Ajayi Crowther, as Bishop in 1864, it abandoned this policy in 1890 for one of a missionary church in which leadership would be in the hands of missionary clergy and Africans would only act as their assistants. This latter policy was until very recent years pursued by all the other major Christian churches in Nigeria, notably the Roman Catholics, the Methodists and the Baptists.

Reaction to the abandonment of the so-called 'native church' policy by the Church Missionary Society was swift. In the 1890s a large number of Anglicans broke with the parent church to form an African Church in which they would be governed by their own bishops. Their quarrel with the Church Missionary Society was not only political but also doctrinal, since many Africans felt that the rules and conduct of the Church should be adapted to the realities of Africa. Thus they argued for group baptism, tolerance of polygamy, particularly on the part of first generation converts who had already contracted poly-gamous marriages, or the use of traditional African music and dance in services. As J. Bertin Webster has shown in his study of the African Churches in Yorubaland, in its resentment of alien control and its quest for a church suited to the local situation, the African Church Movement was a precursor of the nationalist movement.[35] The African churches are still strong, accounting for a large number of Nigerian Christians, for it was not until the post-war period that the Christian Churches of foreign origin began to Africanize their leadership. Another important development in the Christian Church in Nigeria during the colonial period was the growth of syncretistic churches, notably the *aladura*, which sought to combine elements of traditional religion with those of Christianity.

By independence such was the success of the two universalist re-ligions that nearly two-thirds of the population, then estimated at 36 million, were either Muslim or Christian. Such an estimate is, how-ever, a little misleading for in many cases Islam and Christianity were but a veneer. Indeed traditional religion at least in the rural areas remains remarkably virile. Indigenous religions have of course been at a disadvantage because with rare exceptions none of them are mission-ary religions and they are confined to one particular ethnic group. Their strength depends on regular access to their shrines and priests, so that the emigrant is usually cut off from the life-blood of his religion. An obvious exception to this generalization is the Yoruba religion, which has not only survived in the New World among former Yoruba slaves, but has even gained adherents amongst whites. A Yoruba 'Temple' was opened in New York.

The new Nigerian élite is composed almost entirely of adherents of these two universalist religions. This is not surprising, given the historic role of Islam in the North and the fact that in the South most education was provided through the missions. For instance in the East primary education was largely in the hands of the Roman Catholic and Anglican churches. This élite has been variously defined,[36] but can for our purposes best be characterized as the group of Nigerians who have taken over the 'Senior service' jobs in government, commerce and industry, that is those posts hitherto reserved exclusively for Europeans, or their equivalents in earning power. Thus of course lawyers would be included in this group, though the law, like the medical profession, was not reserved exclusively to Europeans; so too would the trader or shopkeeper who has established himself independently of the European firms, and yet earned enough to live at the same level as the Nigerian now filling positions formerly held by Europeans.

The emergence of the élite was one of the most dramatic post-war phenomena and was the result not only of the programme of Africanization carried on after 1950, but also of the expansion of educational opportunities. This élite was characterized too by the fact that its earning power was the same as that of its European predecessor, and far above that of the average Nigerian, whether urban worker or peasant farmer.

To begin with this élite tended to accept British cultural norms as the desired ones. There was nothing very unusual about this since the majority of the élite had gained their education in Britain and even when they had obtained higher education in Nigeria the history they learnt was British, the books they read were by English authors. However, in the years before independence there was increasing demand for a return to African cultural values. Thus African history was introduced to the curriculum in the University College (now University) of Ibadan, the Nigerian Museum was founded, the Nigerian Society for the Promotion of Art and Culture was formed. Fortunately this awakening interest in African as distinct from European culture was paralleled by the emergence of a group of young Nigerian artists and writers who, as recent years have proved, were the precursors of the most virile modern culture in Tropical Africa. Nigeria's most striking achievements have been in the field of creative writing, with poets like Wole Soyinka and J. P. Clark, and novelists like Chinua Achebe and Cyprian Ekwensi already establishing their reputations before independence. In the field of painting and culture Ben Enwonwu had a long-standing reputation rivalled only by that of the sculptor Felix Idubor. But the really exciting work was coming from a group of young painters, the most notable of whom were Demas Nwoko, Y. Grillo, Jimoh Akolo and Uche Okeke.[37]

The most striking development of all in the post-war years was the rapid politicization of the masses. It is one thing to grant people the vote in what was then still a largely illiterate society, quite another to get them to the polls. Yet in the 1959 Federal Election, as K. J. W. Post has shown in the study he made of it, a remarkably high proportion of those eligible to vote actually went to the polls. In some constituencies voting was over 90 per cent of those eligible.[38]

This politicization came about as a result of a number of factors, the most obvious of which were the increased activity and sophistication of the political parties. Education clearly helped. So too did the radio, which though politically neutral, informed an increasingly large number of people about the political situation in their country. A similar role was played by the press whether it was identified with a party like *The West African Pilot* or *The Daily Service* (later *The Daily Express*), or independent like *The Daily Times*. Though circulation figures for these papers were comparatively small before independence, each copy was read by a large number of people and its contents conveyed by word of mouth to many more who were illiterate.

Another important factor in the politicization of the masses was the democratization of local government. Thus under the local government law of 1950 the Eastern Region established a system of local government similar to that of Britain, though this was subsequently considerably modified. County Councils, for instance, were abolished and District Officers were given greatly increased powers. In the West the local government law of 1953, whilst it retained traditional members on the councils, introduced effective elected majorities. In the North the Native Authority Ordinance of 1952 abolished the status of sole native authority enjoyed by some emirs, and in 1954 an amendment authorized the Governor to include a certain number of elected members on the councils, though they did not attain very much power on the councils. The development of local government in Nigeria was one of the most interesting features of the post-war years, particularly as there was an increasing devolvement of authority to them, especially in the field of development. Thus the Kano Native Authority, with an annual budget of over £1 million in this period, was responsible for a large number of development programmes. However, early optimism about the course of local government in the post-war years was not justified by events subsequent to independence, with regional governments finding it necessary to withdraw powers from local authorities and to increase supervision of their activities. Many councils were suspended. Nevertheless elections for local government authorities provided important training for participation in the political process.

The Federation of Nigeria, which became independent on 1st October 1960, was thus a country of great diversity and complexity. The long negotiations over the form independence should take, whilst they clearly exacerbated traditional antagonisms, seemed to indicate to outside obvservers that the foundations of independent Nigeria were as solidly built as those of any independent African state. Peoples of various groups had been brought into close contact with one another, learnt about common factors as well as differences, begun to think of themselves as Nigerians rather than Hausa, Igbo or Yoruba. Frustrating years of constitutional negotiation and the consequent delay of independence seemed to have had their reward in the formulation of a constitution freely negotiated by Nigerians themselves.

18 A Decade of Troubles

When Nigeria became an independent member of the international community there was considerable optimism about its future both within the country and outside, particularly among the Western powers. Independence had been achieved through patient negotiation between Nigerian leaders and their colonial masters, not by violent revolution. The three governing parties of the regions — the N.P.C. in the North, the N.C.N.C. in the East, and the Action Group in the West — all formally espoused Western-style parliamentary democracy. At the Federal level the N.P.C. and the N.C.N.C., despite the considerable differences in their political philosophies, had agreed to form a coalition government while the Action Group provided the 'loyal opposition'. Dr Nnamdi Azikiwe, the only politician with real popularity outside his region of origin, agreed to take on the purely ceremonial post of Governor-General and become 'Father of the Nation'. The Prime Minister, Sir Abubakar Tafawa Balewa, was well known for his political moderation, a factor which particularly appealed to the Western powers, with whose economies Nigeria was still closely integrated. Unlike the majority of African states Nigeria had a viable, diversified economy with great potential for development given the size of its market and the existence of substantial oil resources. Despite declarations of socialist intent, all three governing parties were committed to the capitalist economic system.

Even given the tensions that had preceded independence, Nigeria appeared in its first year of sovereign nationhood a sea of tranquillity compared with the Congo. Yet within less than seven years it was to be plunged into a thirty-month-long civil war. Civilian rule was to be discredited and military rule which replaced it was to prove unable to hold the country together.

At first, in the early years of independence, the constitution seemed, for all its limitations, able to contain the various strains to which it was subjected. As one Nigerian newspaper put it succinctly: 'Nigerians seemed to have perfected the art of walking to the brink of disaster without falling in'. Indeed it was only with the complete breakdown of law and order in the Western Region in late 1965 that the military finally overthrew the government and suspended the constitution.

Of the many factors over and above the historical, regional and ethnic differences that had proved stumbling blocks on Nigeria's path to independence, five stand out as contributing to the situation that made the military *coup d'état* of January 1966 a generally welcomed one. First, by the end of 1965 the politicians had earned almost universal contempt for their corruption, profligacy and lack of real concern for those they ruled and who had elected them. Secondly, the gap in wealth between the burgeoning middle classes and the growing wage-earning classes grew rapidly greater during the first five years of independence. The politicians, civil servants and employers both expatriate and Nigerian showed little concern for the plight of the worker who found it difficult to make ends meet in the face of rising food prices and increasing rents. Thirdly, the moderate, often seemingly slavish, pro-Western stand of the Balewa independence government alienated the educated élite as well as a substantial proportion of literate voters. Fourthly, and most important, was the cynical way in which politics were conducted during these years made it seem that no provision of the constitution was sacred. Fifthly, the imbalance in the constitution, whereby the Nothern Region, which the 1952–3 census had given a slight overall majority of the population in the country, was represented by more seats in the Federal House of Assembly than the south's two Regions, bedevilled politics in the years preceding the coup.

Discontent with the Balewa government first manifested itself over foreign policy, which came to be widely criticized among the educated population as too pro-Western and not sufficiently anti-colonial. There were many who had hoped that on achieving independence Nigeria, as the largest country in Africa, would give leadership in the anti-colonial struggle and take over championship of the Pan-African cause from Ghana. At first it seemed possible that this might be the case when in January 1961 Nigeria became the only country to break off diplomatic relations with France in protest against her testing of atomic bombs in the Sahara. But this did not prove to be so. Thereafter Balewa, who was his own Foreign Minister, pursued a consistently pro-Western policy. Non-Communist powers were given preferential treatment diplomatically over Communist ones; and Balewa did not even establish a mission in Moscow until 1962, while he permitted Portugal and the Central African Federation to set up missions in Lagos. Though he was party to the expulsion of South Africa from the Commonwealth, his representative at the United Nations, Jaja Wachuku, argued for the retention of Portugal and South Africa in the world body. And although subsequently Wachuku's stand was denounced by his government, Balewa took no remedial action. Balewa took up leadership of the Monrovia group of moderate African states, many of which were former French colonies still heavily dependent economically and politically on their former metropole. Even after he had effected the reconciliation of the Monrovia moderates with the radical Casablanca group, which included Ghana and Guinea, at the Lagos Conference in January 1962, thus promoting the establishment of the Organisation of African Unity, he pursued a consistently pro-Western policy within that Organisation. Throughout the Congo crisis he avoided alienation of those Western powers which were clearly involved in it for their own economic advantage. For instance Nigeria was one of the few African states to recognize Tshombe's government. Significantly, at the time of his assassination in January 1966 Balewa had just hosted the Commonwealth Prime Ministers' Conference in Lagos in which the Unilateral Declaration of Independence by a white minority régime in Rhodesia was the crucial issue. Yet the O.A.U. had unanimously resolved that if Britain had not crushed the Rhodesian rebellion by the 15th of December 1965, all member states of the O.A.U. should break off diplomatic relations with her.

The desire of many educated Nigerians for a more positive, independent and anti-colonialist policy was manifested in the press and made itself more than clear in the widespread criticism of the Anglo-Nigerian Defence Pact. Under the terms of this pact, signed by the leaders of the three major parties prior to independence, both governments agreed 'to afford each other such assistance as may be necessary for mutual defence and to consult together on the measures to be taken jointly or separately to ensure the fullest co-operation between them for this purpose'.[1]

In August 1961 the All Nigerian Peoples Conference, called by the Prime Minister himself, which brought together politicians of all parties and people from other walks of life, roundly condemned the Pact. But their condemnation evoked no response from the Federal government. Awolowo's criticisms of the Pact a month later only served to annoy the government, which was aware that he himself had been a signatory to the Pact and suspected that his new-found radicalism smacked of political opportunism rather than conviction. As it was, Awolowo's increasing identification with the international policies of Nkrumah reflected the opinions of many educated Nigerians, in particular students, who themselves staged violent demonstrations against the Pact. Eventually the Pact was withdrawn in January 1962, but only after it had served to demonstrate how great was the divide as to the best approach to international affairs between the government on the one hand and the press, the educated élite and even some government backbenchers on the other hand. The failure of the government to pursue a vigorous overtly anti-colonialist foreign policy alienated it from a substantial majority of the educated élite and partly accounts for the contempt in which many of them came to hold it.

It was, however, the failure of the politicians to respect both the letter and the spirit of the constitution that led to the chaos that precipitated the January 1966 coup.[2] In April 1961 the Federal House of Representatives passed a motion for the creation of a new Mid-West Region to be excised from the non-Yoruba areas of the Western Region and within a year its creation had been approved by the Northern and Eastern Region parliaments. In April 1962 the Western Region government began court proceedings to prevent its creation. Now the Action Group had always championed the creation of new states, including a Mid-West State. It did, however, object to the creation of a single new state on its own, believing that the North and the East, both of which contained important minorities clamorous for creation of new states, were using their dominant political position to dismember the Action-Group-dominated Western Region while leaving their own Regions intact. That their intention was to reduce the power of the opposition already seemed clear from the Enquiry ordered by the Federal government into the affairs of the Western Region (and therefore Action Group) supported National Bank. After an Enquiry was declared illegal by the Lagos High Court in May 1961, the Federal government set up a special Tribunal of Enquiry by Act of Parliament outside the jurisdiction of the Law Courts. However, in this case the Federal Supreme Court ruled the Federal government's action unconstitutional and the Enquiry was suspended. Nevertheless it seemed to indicate the direction the governing coalition was taking with regard to the Opposition.

This direction became only too clear in May 1962 when a state of emergency was declared in the Western Region and the Federal government took over its administration. In February 1962 the growing rift between Awolowo and his deputy and successor as Premier of the Western Region, Chief S. L. Akintola, came into the open at the Action Group Congress in Jos. Basically the rift concerned the future role of the party. Akintola and some of the party elders and business supporters advocated a return to the pre-1959 days when the Action Group had participated in the national government. In particular Action Group businessmen resented their exclusion from consideration for Federal contracts because of the opposition role of the party. Awolowo and many of the younger idealists in the party felt that advocating an increasingly socialist programme at home and a radical anti-colonial policy overseas would gain them sufficient national appeal to win the next Federal election. At the meeting of the Party Executive Awolowo and his supporters won the day and the removal of Akintola from the Premiership was approved on the grounds of 'maladministration, anti-party activities and gross indiscipline'.[3] To forestall his removal Akintola asked the Regional Governor, the Oni of Ife, to dissolve the Western House of Assembly so he could take his case to the people. The Governor refused his request and, on the receipt of a petition signed by a majority of members of the House of Assembly that he remove Akintola as Premier, did so. He then called on Awolowo's chief supporter in the Western House, Alhaji S. Adegbenro, to form a government. When Adegbenro tried to present his government to the House, Akintola's supporters and the N.C.N.C. opposition created such conditions of disorder that the House was suspended and Adegbenro was unable to prove that he had a majority in the House before the Federal government, with indecent haste, declared a state of emergency in the West. Despite Awolowo's protest that no state of emergency as defined by the Constitution existed such as to justify the Federal government's action, the Federal House of Representatives approved it.

Thereafter the Federal government seemed to set about crushing the Action Group systematically. A Commission of Enquiry was appointed in June to inquire into the affairs of six Western Nigeria Statutory Corporations. In July the Supreme Court dismissed the Western Region's motion against the creation of the Mid-West Region and soon after ruled that the Western Region Governor's dismissal of Akintola was unlawful. Thereupon Adegbenro appealed to the Judicial Committee of the Privy Council in London as permitted under the Constitution. In September Awolowo and the bulk of the leadership of the Action Group that remained loyal to him were arrested on charges of conspiring to overthrow the Federal Government.

The fortunes of the Action Group now seemed to be at their lowest ebb. But the Party still enjoyed some popular support. In October 1962 it won the elections to the Lagos City Council, ousting the N.C.N.C. This triumph was short-lived. On 1st January 1963 the end of the state of emergency in the West was proclaimed and Akintola and his faction of the Action Group, now named the United People's Party, formed a coalition with the N.C.N.C., thus placing the Action Group in opposition in its stronghold, the West. That same month Akintola was given further support when the Commission of Inquiry into the affairs of the six Statutory Corporations condemned Chief Awolowo's direction of the use of funds in the Region but exonerated him. In June 1963 the

Action Group's last hope of regaining power in the West was dashed when the Federal Parliament nullified the verdict of the Judicial Committee of the Privy Council that the Governor of the Western Region had acted within the Constitution in dismissing Akintola and calling on Adegbenro to form a government. The following August the Federal Parliament approved the establishment of an Interim Administration for the new Mid-West Region whose creation had been overwhelmingly approved by a referendum of those concerned. In September the final nail seemed to have been knocked in the Action Group's coffin: Chief Awolowo was jailed for treasonable felony, as were Chief Enahoro, extradited from Britain, and eighteen other leading Action Groupers.

On 1st October 1963 Nigeria became a Republic within the Commonwealth and Azikiwe, its first independent Governor-General, now became its first President. It did so against the background of a general strike that was called off only on the eve of the celebrations. The Joint Action Committee of all Trade Unions demanded higher wages, which at first the government refused to entertain. The strike was only ended when the government promised to establish a Wages Commission of Enquiry (Morgan Commission) which did not, however, report until nine months later. During the intervening months serious cracks in the N.P.C.-N.C.N.C. coalition began to appear: with the Action Group emasculated, the uncomfortable bedfellows, lacking a common opponent, began to turn on each other.

In December 1962 unofficial results of the census taken the previous May had indicated that the North had a larger population than the three Southern Regions combined. This implied that the South would forever be at the mercy of a Northern majority, whereas Southern politicians had been convinced that the census would reveal that the South was in fact more populous than the North. As a result of widespread doubts about the accuracy of the census the Prime Minister decided on a new one. This was held on 5th November 1963 and the preliminary results, announced on 24th February 1964, gave Nigeria a population of 55 million as against 31 million for the 1952–1953 census: the majority of the population was still in the north. The Eastern Region government, along with the Mid-West government (elections for which had recently been won by the N.C.N.C.), rejected the results. They were, of course, accepted by the N.P.C. in the North under the forceful leadership of the Sardauna of Sokoto and by his client in the West, Akintola, who had just formed a new party called the Nigerian National Democratic Party from his own U.P.P. and a faction of the Western N.C.N.C.

Against the background of mounting attacks on the census results by both the N.C.N.C. and the Action Group, the Eastern Region Solicitor-General took out a writ in the Federal Supreme Court to restrain the Federal government from using the figures. Both parties feared that the results would be used as the basis of delimitation of constituencies for the forthcoming Federal election, thus giving a greater number of seats to the Northern Region than the combined Southern Regions. But the Federal Supreme Court rejected the writ.

It was in the context of the census controversy and the fears that the South would forever be politically subjugated to the North that the N.C.N.C. and the Action Group announced that they would campaign jointly in the forthcoming Federal election. Shortly afterwards, the N.P.C. announced the formation of a Nigerian National Alliance consisting of itself, the N.N.D.P. and two southern minority parties. In September this alliance was cemented by the inclusion by Balewa of two N.N.D.P. ministers in the Federal Cabinet.

The final Census figures were published that same month:

		Millions		Millions	
North		29·8	1952–3 =	16·2	
East		12·4		= 7·2	
West	South =	10·2	}	= 8·1	} South =
Mid-West	25·76	2·5			15·65
Lagos		·66		= ·35	

It now appeared that the North had a population four million greater than that of the Southern Regions combined. Nevertheless the N.C.N.C. and its ally the Northern Elements Progressive Union, and the Action Group with its northern ally, the United Middle Belt Congress, felt sure that if they combined forces and the election was fairly conducted they could win a sufficient number of seats in the North to give them, in combination with those in the South, an overall majority. At the very least they would win all three Southern Regions, which would give them control of the Senate,[4] thereby enabling them to block legislation inimical to their interests. Accordingly in October these four parties formed the United Progressive Grand Alliance (U.P.G.A.).

While wrangling over the census had been taking place, the country had been plunged into a second general strike in June 1964. The strike was called on 1st June by the Joint Action Committee of the Trade Unions to protest at delays by the government in acting on the recommendations of the Morgan Wages Commission. On 3rd June the government issued a White Paper which rejected the proposed wage increases as economically prohibitive and put forward its own much lower scale of wages.

Examples of the proposed increases by Morgan and Government were:

Lagos (Highest Wage Area)

Morgan: £12 a month; Government: £9 2*s*. 6*d*.

North: Kabba (Lowest Wage Area)

Morgan: £6 10*s*. a month; Government: £4 15*s*.

The Joint Action Committee rejected the government's offer as derisory and stayed out on strike. On 8th June the Federal Minister of Labour declared that all government workers who stayed on strike would be 'dismissed with loss of all privileges' and in this he was followed by private enterprise. But the workers were not to be threatened by this 'national lock-out' and stayed on strike, indicating the extent of their economic plight. On 13th June, after the government had climbed down and talked with the Joint Action Committee, it was agreed that there would be a return to work if the government would negotiate with the J.A.C. on the basis of the Morgan recommendations. Eventually at the end of the month a compromise was reached on £10 a month minimum wage for Lagos and £5 15*s*. for Kabba. But the workers gained little: by the time their new wage scales were approved, market-women had raised food prices and landlords rents to such a level that the workers' increases in wages were negated.

As the country prepared for the forthcoming General Election the situation deteriorated rapidly. In the South there was general discontent with the census results. Workers were still disgruntled over their economic situation, and the educated élite was still exasperated by its government's pro-Western policies. In November for instance, the Federal government had not only failed to condemn the joint American-Belgian operation in Stanleyville (now Kisangani) to rescue their nationals, but Jaja Wachuku, the Nigerian representative at the U.N., had argued that as the operation had been authorized by the legal government of the Congo, 'it could not be regarded as foreign intervention'.[5]

Generally the tone of politics took a serious turn for the worse. In the North vicious attacks were launched on the 'Igbo opportunists' and in the South equally venomous attacks were made on Northerners in the Press. In Tiv country, where the United Middle Belt Congress enjoyed its greatest support, discontent with the N.P.C.-controlled regional government was such that it erupted into riots serious enough to disrupt train services on the Eastern Line from Enugu to Jos.

On 8th December the Federal Parliament was dissolved and the date for the Federal election was fixed for 30th December. The previous October a conference of the major parties had been called to discuss the election and had agreed to arrangements that it was believed would ensure it would be a fair one. But as soon as the date for closure of nominations had passed it became clear to the U.P.G.A. that they would not work. Sixty-one N.P.C. candidates were returned unopposed in the North despite the fact that an U.P.G.A. candidate had presented himself for nomination in each Northern constituency. The U.P.G.A. leaders were now convinced that the election would be rigged in the North and the West, making it impossible not only to gain an overall majority of seats but even to win all three Southern Regions. As a result of this and further evidence of planned election rigging, the U.P.G.A. called for a boycott of the elections which was almost totally effective in the East and largely effective in the West. The N.P.C. and its allies won an overwhelming victory.

Because of his own concern at the way the elections had been conducted President Azikiwe refused at first to call on Balewa to form a government. He was, however, after much pressure, and talk of an army take-over and secession, persuaded to call Balewa to form a government on certain conditions. The first was that it would be a Government of National Unity. But Balewa in the event did not include the Action Group in it. The second was that new elections would be held in those constituencies, notably in the East, where no effective election had taken place. These were subsequently held. The third was that any challenge as to the validity of the election should only be made through the courts. The fourth was that elections should be held for a new Western House of Assembly in the near future so that U.P.G.A. could demonstrate that it had the popular support in the Western Region which it claimed.

During the two days when Azikiwe tried to avoid calling on Balewa to form a government the country was on the verge of disintegration. As it was, his concession that he had no constitutional powers to do otherwise merely postponed disaster, which was precipitated by the election to the Western House.

The 1964 Federal election in retrospect seemed quite orderly compared with the 1965 Western election, in which barefaced rigging accompanied by threats, bribes, beatings, arson and even murder became the order of the day. As the election set for 11th October approached it was increasingly clear that law and order had broken down in the West. Yet the Federal government did not intervene and declare a state of emergency as it had once been so quick to do. Instead the mockery of an election went ahead with one result — an U.P.G.A. victory — announced over the Eastern Region radio, and another, made official — an N.N.D.P. victory — announced over the Federal radio. Thereafter, despite the presence of troops in Ibadan, the West became lawless. It was almost impossible to travel at night, and some main roads were unsafe by day. Political executions, beatings and arson became prevalent. It was in this context of apparent helplessness of the Federal government that on the night of 14th–15th January 1966 a group of young majors staged a coup in which the Federal Prime Minister, the Federal Minister of Finance, the Premiers of the Northern and Western Regions and a majority of officers above the rank of major were assassinated. Civilian rule had come to an end in ignominy. The experiment in military rule that followed was to fare little better.

The group of officers who staged the coup, led by Major Chukwuma Nzeogwu, gained control of Kaduna but were unable to impose their authority over the rest of the country. Instead, the surviving senior officers, led by the head of the army, Major-General Johnson Aguyi-Ironsi took over government with the acquiescence, however reluctant, of the remains of the Federal Cabinet. The Kaduna majors gave themselves up and were placed in detention. The new military régime of Ironsi was generally welcomed as a respite from the ills of civilian rule. Ironsi seemed to get off to a good start. He appointed military governors for each region, and his choice of Major Hassan Usman Katsina, son of the Emir of Katsina, for the North seemed particularly astute, assuaging as it did initial fears that the coup was an anti-Northern one since both the Federal Prime Minister, who was a Northerner, and the Northern Regional Premier, as well as all senior army officers of Northern origin had been murdered. An early return to civilian rule was promised, and Chief Rotimi-Williams, the distinguished lawyer, and Dr T. O. Elias, the legal scholar and former Attorney-General, were appointed to draft a new constitution. From the start Ironsi made it clear that he felt the direction the country should take should be away from the old regional structure towards a more unitary arrangement. In the honeymoon he enjoyed after assuming power the implications of this were not fully appreciated by educated Nigerians; neither were the implications of the way in which the coup had brought Ironsi, an Igbo, to power. Soon however, the fact that neither of the two Igbo Regional Premiers had been killed, that only one Igbo senior officer had been murdered, and that the majority of Nzeogwu's co-plotters were Igbo, became a subject of widespread discussion. In the North there was considerable resentment that Nzeogwu and his fellow plotters were not brought to trial for murder and mutiny, though here Ironsi was in a dilemma because many Southerners considered them heroes who had put an end to a régime that had been anathema to them.

Fears that the coup had been directed towards establishing an Igbo hegemony became increasingly widespread as Ironsi surrounded himself with a small clique of advisers who often by-passed both the civil service and the study groups he had set up to look into the future constitutional, judicial and economic arrangements for the country. The appointment of Francis Nwokedi, an Igbo, as sole commissioner to inquire 'into the unification of the regional public services' was particularly inept, given Northern sensitivities about domination by the better educated Southerners.

There was growing disenchantment with the nature of the revolution. The new military rulers moved into the palaces and drove the limousines of the civilians they had displaced. 'The more things changed the more they stayed the same.'[6]

On 24th May, without waiting for the report of his constitutional study group or submitting their report to the promised constituent assembly, Ironsi broadcast to the nation that a new constitution had been promulgated. 'The former Regions are abolished, and Nigeria grouped into a number of territorial areas called provinces. Nigeria ceases to be what is described as a Federation. It now becomes simply the Republic of Nigeria.'[7] The Regional and Federal public services were declared unified and 'every civil servant is now called upon to see his function in any part of Nigeria in which he is serving in the context of the whole country'.[8]

The reaction in the North was swift and violent. The new unitary constitution, and in particular its provision for a unitary civil service, was seen as giving the Igbo a special advantage: since they had a huge educated élite as compared with that of the North, Northerners could not compete on equal terms for posts in the civil service and would cease to be masters in their own home. Hundreds of Igbos were killed in riots in Northern towns the following weekend.

The situation was brought temporarily under control by promises that the old regions would continue to function as such though now called groups of provinces and that no new permanent constitution would be imposed on the country without being submitted to a referendum. But among Northern army officers there was still considerable bitterness that Nzeogwu and his fellow plotters had not been brought to justice for murdering their senior colleagues. As far as they were concerned the North, with a tiny educated élite, had been robbed of both its political and military leadership. In July Northern officers staged a coup in which Ironsi, on a visit to Ibadan, was killed, together with his host in Ibadan, Governor Fajuyi. Many Igbo officers and soldiers were also killed by Northern officers. For a while the country was without leadership. The senior surviving officer, Brigadier Ogundipe, was unable to assert his authority over the troops. Finally the Army Chief of Staff, Lt. Col. Yakubu Gowon, a Northerner from the Middle Belt, took over as Head of State.

Gowon's position as Head of the Armed Forces and thus as Head of State was never recognized by Lt. Col. Ojukwu, Military Governor of the Eastern Region. He argued that Gowon was not the most senior surviving officer and therefore had no right to the position. But *de facto*, Gowon was the only officer who at that time was able to exert control over the army. Despite his reservations about Gowon's position, Ojukwu did agree at first to treat with the new régime. At the start Gowon (like Ironsi) talked in terms of an early return to civilian rule and, after having declared that the country would return to the old regional structure, organized meetings of leaders of thought in each region to prepare the groundwork for an Ad Hoc Constitutional Review Conference which had its first meeting in Lagos on 12th September. At first the drift of the conference was towards a confederal arrangement with the right to secession by the constituent regions recognized. But as it progressed arguments began to gain ground in favour of a stronger central government than a confederal constitution would allow and of the creation of more states from the existing regions. Surprisingly, the Northern delegation, which at first had supported a confederal view, now argued in favour of this latter solution, which the Eastern delegates did not care for at all, since they were determined to maintain the integrity of their Region. The deliberations of this conference were abruptly ended by the news of new massacres of Igbos in the North, this time organized by both civilians and soldiers. Resentment of the dominant economic position of the Igbos in the North and of their control of so many administrative and clerical posts in the Region, that had been fired under the Ironsi régime, had not been assuaged by his murder. Thousands of Igbos were massacred and Igbos and other Southerners streamed south, where retaliatory action, particularly in the east, started a movement of Northerners back to their Region. Nigeria seemed finally on the verge of falling apart. The Eastern Region expelled all non-Easterners with the exception of Igbos from the Mid-West. Increasingly the Region acted as though it were independent of Lagos.

Ojukwu refused to attend any meetings in Lagos because of fears for his safety. He called for all Easterners to return home, and thousands poured out of Lagos which had once had almost as many Igbo inhabitants as indigenous Yorubas. There was now practically no communication between the Federal government and the Eastern Regional government.

Ojukwu did, however, agree to one last attempt to find a constitutional formula that would hold Nigeria together. This was held at Aburi, in Ghana, where Ojukwu would feel safe meeting with Gowon, his fellow regional governors and the heads of the armed services, and was hosted by the Ghanaian Head of State, Lt. General Ankrah. This last-minute attempt to stave off secession and maintain the unity of Nigeria was thwarted by the fact that no written agreement signed by all participants was produced at the end of the conference. The result was that although all participants left the conference believing that they had reached agreement on a formula that would maintain the integrity of the country, different versions of this formula were published by Enugu and Lagos. Effectively what Ojukwu claimed they had all agreed to — and he supported his claim with the publication of a transcript of the tapes that Lt. General Ankrah had suggested they make of their discussions[9] — was the loosest possible confederation between the regions. Each of them would have its own army, and each of them would be effectively sovereign, merely sharing some common services. Indeed the post of Supreme Military Commander would, under Ojukwu's interpretation, be reduced to that of a mere cipher, little more than President of a Common Services Commission. This interpretation proved unacceptable to Gowon. It is clear that at Aburi Gowon and his fellow participants representing the Lagos government had not fully appreciated the limitations of what they had apparently agreed to. While they were prepared to accept a formula that permitted the greatest possible degree of decentralization consistent with the maintenance of the Nigerian polity, they had not appreciated that the very formula they had agreed to would permit any region which so chose to interpret it thus, effective independence. Lagos now came up with a compromise, confederal formula which gave the regions virtual autonomy with veto powers over both the executive and legislative decisions of the Supreme Military Council and over any military appointments made in their respective regions. But this did not prove acceptable to Ojukwu, who now seemed clearly bent on secession.

Outside, the idea of regional autonomy, if not secession itself, was gaining ground. In the West there was little positive interest in the maintenance of a unified Nigeria, and there was deep resentment at the fact that because in the past few Yoruba had enlisted in the army troops stationed in Ibadan and Abeokuta were of predominantly Northern origin despite the agreement that only troops indigenous to a region should be stationed there. It seemed therefore that there would be little in Ojukwu's way if he did secede. He had the wherewithal to do so, for the major portion of Nigeria's oil resources was located in his region, though significantly mainly in the non-Igbo 'minority' areas. At this stage, many of the minority leaders, traumatized by the massacres in the North which had involved some of their own people as well as Igbos, and having no positive alternative option before them, supported Ojukwu.

In these circumstances Gowon's proclamation on 27th May 1967 that Nigeria was henceforth to be divided into twelve states was a masterstroke. The new constitutional arrangement had wide appeal. In the first place it divided the North into six states, at one and the same time satisfying minority interests there since they were at last given the status for which they had long been agitating, and, by breaking up the monolithic North, reducing Southern fears of Northern domination. The East was divided into three states, two of which represented minority interests in that region. The Ijo in the new Rivers State, and the Efik, Ibibio and other minority groups in the new South-Eastern State had long resented the political domination of their region by the Igbo and had agitated for separate states. The Federal government now offered them a positive focus for loyalty to the Federation rather than any secessionist ventures by Ojukwu. The Mid-West and West were left intact with the exception of the new Lagos State, excised from the latter.

Three days after Gowon's dramatic announcement, Ojukwu proclaimed the former Eastern Region as the sovereign Republic of Biafra. He had the almost full support of the Igbo population for this act, but the creation of the Rivers State and the South-Eastern State bit deep into his support from the minority areas, the majority of whose people became more interested in a future as members of states of a federation of Nigeria than in independence in a sovereign Biafra in which they feared they would be dominated by an Igbo majority.

The Federal government took no immediate action to suppress Ojukwu's rebellion. And even when Ojukwu's forces skirmished with Federal forces on the 'Biafra' border with the Benue-Plateau State, and the decision to invade the secessionist areas was taken, the suppression of the rebellion was described as a 'police operation'. The Federal government was confident that the rebellion would be quickly put down. But it reckoned without the fact that Ojukwu had a small but effective army consisting of the Igbo officers who had left the Federal army and who had been busy training up rank and file. Furthermore, Igbos had been the majority ethnic group in the Federal army's technical services so that the Biafran army was technically well provided for; and Ojukwu had been systematically stock-piling arms to prepare for secession. Even before his move the Federal army had been under 10,000 strong, had lost many key officers through assassination or desertion, and had very extended lines of communication. At first, however, the Federal forces seemed justified in their optimism that all that was necessary to crush the rebellion was a 'police operation'. Ogoja, on the northern border, was taken on 11th July and the university town of Nsukka, after a stiff battle, on the 15th. Eleven days later, on the 26th, the oil-terminal at Bonny was occupied by Federal forces in a joint military-naval operation which gave them a southern bridgehead and a base from which the navy could blockade the secessionist ports.

What had been seen as a police operation was turned into a full-scale war when the secessionist forces invaded the Mid-West State on 9th August.[10] The Mid-West, which marched with the western boundary of Biafra, was the soft underbelly of the Federation since the Western Igbos who lived in the eastern parts of that state were susceptible to Ojukwu's propaganda. Indeed it was with the connivance of some Mid-Western Igbo officers and government officials that secessionist forces invaded and occupied the area. In a swift sweep towards Lagos the secessionist forces reached Ore in the Western State on 21st August. An attempt to attack Lagos through the lagoon from Okitipupa was staved off by Federal forces, who finally drove the secessionists out of Ore on 29th August. It took them until 20th October to re-take the Mid-West.

The invasion of the Mid-West had made it clear to the Federal authorities that they were engaged in much more than a 'police operation'. Large-scale recruitment for the army was undertaken throughout the country, swelling it by the end of the war to nearly 250,000 men. From the liberation of the Mid-West in October 1967 to the final surrender of the secessionist forces on 12th January 1970 the Federal troops were engaged in a fierce town by town, village by village battle for control of the East-Central State, the Igbo heartland of Biafra. Its capital, which also served as the capital of the secessionist régime, did however fall to the Federal forces as early as 2nd October. Shortly afterwards, Mr Ukpabi Asika, Lecturer in Political Science at the University of Ibadan, was appointed Administrator of the East-Central State with the task of forming a government to run the areas taken by the Federal forces. The minority areas were returned to Federal control much more easily then the Igbo heartland, since the bulk of their population were in sympathy with the Federal cause. By March 1968 Federal control had been re-asserted over the major part of the South-East State and on 19th April Port Harcourt, the capital of the Rivers State, was lost by the secessionists.

The Igbo heartland, however, held out for another twenty-one months after the loss of their major port and airport. There is no space here to detail the long-drawn-out battles on three fronts which were fought with great bravery and under appalling conditions on both sides. A number of factors account for the length of the resistance by the secessionist forces. In the first place they firmly believed the propaganda so effectively disseminated by the Biafra government, and spread by overseas sympathizers, that the Federal troops were intent

11. The nineteen States, 1975

on genocide. They had, of course, the bitter experience of the massacres in the North to give conviction to them, so that they fought to the last ditch and with people starving for want of food supplies rather than come under Federal control. In the second place the Biafran army had a skilful core leadership from the deserters from the Federal army. Thirdly, Biafran propaganda overseas was highly effective in obtaining support in the form of arms, money and foodstuffs from overseas. In America, Britain, France and Germany many people firmly believed that Biafra was a victim of a Federal government bent on genocide and that the war was one between Northern Muslims and Biafran Christians, despite the fact that the Federal leader was, himself, a Christian. Fourthly, a number of countries that wished independent Africa no good fished in the troubled waters of the Nigerian Civil War: South Africa, Portugal and Rhodesia. France, still piqued at the Federal government's unilateral rupture of diplomatic relations in 1961, and eyeing the oil resources of the secessionist state, gave all but open support to Ojukwu. Finally, four members of the O.A.U., which tried on several occasions to mediate between the two sides, split the Organisation by recognizing Biafra as a sovereign state. These were Tanzania, Zambia, Ivory Coast and Gabon, the latter two of which acted as staging posts for arms and mercenaries for Biafra.

By mid 1969 it had become clear that it was only a matter of time before Biafra would fall to the Federal forces. But Ojukwu refused to concede defeat despite the very considerable suffering continued resistance was inflicting on his people. Only as the Federal troops closed in on his last strongholds in late December did Ojukwu begin to consider abandoning the fight. Finally on 11th January 1970 Ojukwu and his top advisers fled to the Ivory Coast, leaving the head of the secessionist army, Lt. Col. Philip Effiong, to broadcast the end of secession.

During the two and a half years of the war, the bulk of Nigeria's resources were devoted to its military effort. There were major shortages of consumer goods due to lack of foreign exchange, the bulk of which was devoted to the purchase of military equipment. Because of strict government controls the economy did not become overheated as a result of the war. Rather, the war had a major beneficial effect on the economy in that shortage of foreign exchange led to the encouragement of import substitution industries, with the result that after the war Nigeria was manufacturing a whole range of goods from its own raw materials which hitherto had been imported. The federally controlled areas of the country remained remarkably calm throughout the war, though there were some peasant disturbances over excessive taxation and inadequate amenities in the Western State. But Nigeria — with the exception of the East-Central State — was as united in those years as it had ever been. The new state structure was established remarkably smoothly, and civilians were associated closely with the military not only in pursuing the war, but also in developing the new administrative structure of the country. The Deputy Chairman of the Federal Executive Council was Chief Awolowo, and most of the Federal and State government commissioners (ministers) during the war were civilians. The re-integration of the secessionist areas took place much more easily than many outside observers had predicted. Once the secessionists, in particular the Igbo, came back under Federal control they realized that the Federal troops had not indulged in genocide as their leaders would have had them believe. At the end of the war a general amnesty was offered to all those who had fought against the Nigerian army; only some former officers of the Nigerian army were given prison sentences, and all of these are free today. No one was executed for his part in the rebellion and no reparations or indemnities were demanded. Many former rebels returned to the posts they had occupied in the Federal government before the secession.

With the war won, the difficult task of winning the peace began. The first problem facing the government was what to do with the huge army that had been recruited during the war. It would prove too dangerous for the social stability of the country to have thousands of demobilized soldiers thrown on to the employment market. So it was decided to maintain the army at its existing level, despite the drain on the Federal budget. The second problem was to put the economy, particularly that of the war-torn areas, back on its feet. This task was to be made relatively light because of the large revenues coming in from oil. The main problem of the peace was to give a new sense of direction to the country after a decade of troubles. On 1st October 1970, the tenth anniversary of the country's independence, the Head of State announced a coherent plan to return the country to civilian rule in 1976. Despite disappointment at the distance of the date set, civilians and in particular former politicians, had a target before them. The military argued that in the intervening years they could prepare a solid basis for the return to a civilian administration. They could restore the country's economy to its former prosperity, conduct a national census fairly so that there would be no basis for recrimination over the delimitation of constituencies, and establish additional new states if necessary. The prospects held out by the Gowon administration for Nigeria on that Independence Day, when in Lagos, troops and schoolchildren paraded joyfully in a torrential downpour before their Head of State, looked bright indeed. But on 29th July 1975, the anniversary of his accession to power, General Gowon was to be overthrown in a bloodless military coup for failing to realize that promise.

Postscript: 1970–1976

The most significant development of the post-war years has been Nigeria's emergence as a major producer of oil. By 1976 she had become the 7th largest producer in the world with a production of two million barrels a day accounting for over 90% of the value of exports. This new-found wealth had three major consequences for Gowon's peace-time administration. In the first place, it could envisage government services and development programmes on a scale the civilian régime could never have dared contemplate. In 1975 Federal revenue was 3,122 million Naira as compared with 368 million Naira for 1965.* Second, because oil revenues accrued to the Federal government, which redistributed them to the State partly on the basis of derivation, and partly on the basis of need, the latter became increasingly dependent on it economically. Thus the greater centralization Ironsi had sought to establish *de jure* now came about *de facto*. Thirdly, while the new prosperity from oil brought great wealth to the entrepreneurial classes and corrupt government officials, its by-product of inflation exacerbated by the 1972–74 drought and the world-wide inflation resulting from the steep rise in the price of petroleum products, made life increasingly difficult for the wage-earning and salaried classes. Furthermore, the peasants suffered as agricultural production fell because of the drought and prices for export crops did not rise *pari passu* with inflation. The resentment of the workers and those on fixed salaries at the new-found wealth of the entrepreneurial classes was increased by the profligacy and ostentation with which they spent it. Worse still the oil boom gave opportunities— quickly seized— for corruption on a scale by the side of which that of the civilian régime paled.

Much of the growing unpopularity of Gowon's peace-time régime can be attributed to its failure to adapt itself to the changed economic circumstances of the country. Yet at first it seemed to be getting down to business. The country's currency was decimalized. The difficult task of organizing the change over of the direction of traffic from the left-hand to the right-hand side of the road to conform with neighbouring African states was accomplished remarkably smoothly. The decree on indigenization of business ensured total indigenous control of some

* Converted at the old rate of ₦2.00 = £1.

categories of business, hitherto owned by expatriates, and majority or minority participation in others. A national census was held in December 1973, and a National Youth Service Corps established to enlist all students under thirty graduating from university in a year's service to government. The economy got back to a normal footing remarkably swiftly and at first the contrast between the deprivations suffered during the war years and the developmental activity of peace-time gave credit in the eyes of the people to the Federal and State governments. The government's emphasis on culture epitomized by its plans to host the second All-African and Black Festival of the Arts and Culture was to begin with highly popular.

Against this background of positive action many of the problems that had bedevilled the old civilian régime manifested themselves. As prices rose and the entrepreneurial classes prospered, the workers, whose wages remained static or did not rise in proportion to inflation, denied the right to strike, became increasingly disgrunted. The mili-tary governors became increasingly autocratic, and some of them were notoriously corrupt, evoking comparisons with the worst offenders of the civilian régime. Indeed some of them treated their states as though they were private estates to be administered and exploited as they wished. Despite their obvious unpopularity, and widespread demands for their replacement, Gowon took no action except to replace the Military Governor of the Western State. Indeed, despite the growing centralization of government services, it seemed that Gowon was unable to control his State governors. Disconcerting, too, was the way in which the six Northern governors operated as a bloc, through reg-ular meetings of the Interim Common Services Agency (I.C.S.A.) which was established to administer certain services of the former Northern Region such as Ahmadu Bello University, the Bank of the North and *The New Nigerian* newspaper. Fears grew of a revival of the old mono-lithic North, which the new state structure had been set up to supersede, as the far-from-interim I.C.S.A. seemed to be a disguise for the continuation of northern solidarity. In the East-Central State, the slow pace of reconstruction and rehabilitation compared with that in the Rivers and South-Eastern States, evoked fears among the Igbo that despite the Federal government's avowed intention of re-integrating them into national life, it was in fact discriminating against them. Within the states, various minority groups accused the majority group of exploiting government in their own interest, and were frustrated that their agitation for the creation of the new states Gowon had promised received no response from him. Ethnic politics once again became a common talking point, with proposals for quota systems, particularly for admission to universities, being proposed because of fears that some ethnic groups were advancing at the expense of others. Southern fears of continued Northern domination were revived by the preliminary results of the 1973 Census, which showed once again a majority of the population in the former north, this time by a much larger margin than the controversial 1963 Census. It seems clear that Gowon was particularly alarmed at the public outcry over the census results.

In mid 1974, then, the situation in Nigeria was all too uncomfortably reminiscent of that of a decade earlier. And it was in this context that on 1st October 1974, the anniversary of independence, Gowon announced that the proposed return to civilian rule in 1976 was indefinitely postponed. In his view the country still needed the firm rule that only the military could provide. Indeed the civilians, many of them former politicians who had been co-opted into the Federal government as Commissioners, would largely be replaced by military. In part this was a sop by Gowon to senior officers who were resentful that they had no share in government and who hoped that they might replace the military governors. These latter Gowon promised would be changed after April 1975 when they had introduced their 1975–80 state development plans. Likewise, new states would be created after that date.

The only real palliatives to the postponement of the return to civilian rule were the Government's announcements that it would introduce universal free Primary Education throughout the country by 1976 and that it would implement the recommendation of the Commission set up under Chief Udoji on the restructuring of the public services and the review of salaries in the light of inflation. It was however a palliative that turned sour and precipitated the situation which brought about the overthrow of the government.

The revision of salaries, known popularly as 'Udoji', was very generous. The basic minimum wage in the public sector was doubled, while no one in public service received less than a 30 per cent increase. Arrears back-dated to 1st April 1974 were paid to all in the public service, which included statutory corporations and universities.

The salaries review had two immediate consequences. The first was widespread strikes in the private sector on which the Udoji recommendations were not made binding. Despite the fact that strikes were illegal under military rule, the government was unable to force strikers to return to work, thus demonstrating its impotence. In the end the private sector had to concede not only the Udoji Commission's wage increases but also its generous pension terms to their employees by passing on the cost in increased prices to the consumer. The second consequence of the wage increases was a steep rise in the inflation they were designed to compensate. The increased price of consumer goods resulting from the granting of Udoji to employees in the private sector, coupled with the increase in rents and foodstuffs that have attended all over-the-line pay awards in Nigeria, resulted in galloping inflation that soon left the worker worse off in purchasing power than he had been prior to Udoji. The award of nine months arrears paid in one lump sum injected a huge amount of money suddenly into the economy, creating a scarcity of motor cars, television sets, radios, and motor-bicycles. The distributive trade could not cope with increased demand for goods and in particular petrol, which became desperately short in some parts of the country. The ports were not geared to the new level of demand for imports and Apapa was clogged with ships waiting to offload some two million tons of cement that had been ordered in mysterious circumstances by the Ministry of Defence. There was a general breakdown in services with shortages of essential commodities like milk and sugar.

April 1975 came and the new Federal Development Plan envisaging a total expenditure of over ₦30,000 million was introduced. The States followed with their own development plans based on the amount of money they could raise through local taxation and the allocations made them in the Federal plan. But the military governors were not changed. There was no news about the creation of new states. The controversial census results were still being checked, with each State represented by observers in the checking offices. Criticism of the Festival, which had already been twice postponed, grew as it became clear that despite the large sums devoted to infrastructure for it, Nigeria was unlikely to be able to hold it as planned in November without disgracing itself as host. But these criticisms seemed to make no impact on the government, which despite abundant evidence to the contrary insisted all would be ready on the day. The only positive development in an otherwise increasingly chaotic situation was the setting up of the Economic Community of West African States (E.C.O.W.A.S.) in Lagos largely on Nigeria's initiative.

By July 1975 the country seemed to be in a desperate situation with the Government apparently oblivious to it. In the circumstances the bloodless coup of 29th July which overthrew Gowon in his absence at the Kampala summit of the O.A.U. gave little surprise to the Nigerian public, except perhaps that it had not taken place before.

The new régime headed by Brigadier, later General, Murtala Ramat Mohammed, with Brigadier, later Lt. General, Olusegun Obasonjo as Chief of Staff quickly got down to business. The heads of armed services and the twelve state military governors were dismissed. A target date was set for the return to civilian rule in 1979.

Meanwhile, a number of Commissions of Inquiry were established
with precise reporting dates to undertake reforms considered as an
essential prelude to civilian rule. A constitutional drafting committee
was set up under the Chairmanship of Chief Rotimi Williams. Com-
mittees were established to make recommendations on the desirability
of establishing a new Federal capital given that Lagos, with its traffic
jams and location, was generally considered unsuitable; to make
recommendations on new states; to look into the assets of public officers; to inquire into the organization of the Festival, which was indefinitely postponed; to inquire into the cement scandal; and to make
recommendations on the future of I.C.S.A. and the Eastern States
Common Services Agency. The new government then proceeded to
retire public servants who were deemed corrupt, inefficient or
incapacitated on grounds of old age or ill-health. It promised to speed
up rehabilitation of the infrastructure in the East-Central State. Most
important of all, it decided to tackle the delicate question of reduction
in size of the army, an issue which Gowon had side-stepped. It was
considered essential to reduce the army from 250,000 to 100,000 so that
most of the defence budget and most officers' time could be spent on
training and equipment.

The Mohammed government also took new initiatives in the field of
foreign affairs. Gowon's foreign policy had been a moderate one
reminiscent of that of Tafawa Balewa's. Reconciliation had been
effected with the African states that had recognized the secessionist
régime. In the O.A.U. Nigeria had been a force for moderation, rarely
taking strong stands over issues relating to Portugal, Rhodesia and
South Africa. One of the first acts of the new régime in the international field was to back the M.P.L.A. government of Angola, thus
helping to swing the majority of the O.A.U. behind it. It was open in its
condemnation of apartheid in South Africa and of all those Western
powers that covertly assisted it. This new line in foreign policy coupled
with the régime's manifest determination to undertake reform at home
gave it an unprecedented popularity, particularly among intellectuals
and students who had been so critical of the previous régime, which was
consolidated by General Murtala's broadcast to the nation in January
1976. In this he confirmed that his régime really intended to implement its promised programme. He announced that Nigeria would now
comprise nineteen states, of which twelve were new. A new capital
would be built near Abuja. Ten of the twelve former state governors
were dismissed from their respective services with ignominy for abuse
of office. I.C.S.A. was dismantled, thus abolishing the last formal link
between the Northern states. It is in the context of its dynamism and
popularity that the widespread hostility towards the leaders of the

abortive coup against Murtala's régime on Friday 13th February 1976 must be seen. With the exception of those disinherited by the July coup and those subsequently retired from the public services, there was little antagonism towards the régime. Rather, Nigerians felt that at last they had a government which reflected their own hopes for the future of their country. The coup, led by Lt. Col. B. S. Dimka, head of the Army's Physical Training Corps, fortunately failed in its attempt to wipe out the leadership of Murtala's régime though they did assassinate Murtala himself. Nigeria had once again been led to the brink of disaster and the failure of the coup was widely welcomed by a nation which, having at last been set on a course of which the majority approved, suddenly saw how fragile its new-found unity and sense of direction were. It has been the difficult task of General Olusegun Obasanjo, and the Supreme Military Council, to try and retrieve the momentum of Murtala's régime and to secure Nigeria against the possibility of further attempts to wreck its new-found sense of purpose.

APPENDIX A Dynasty of the Shehus of Borno to 1974*

SAIFAWA DYNASTY
Mai Dunama Lafiami
k. 1817. Maintained on the Borno throne as titular ruler as was his successor Ibrahim. The latter was executed by Shehu Umar following his complicity in the Wadai invasion of 1846. His son Ali was killed fighting the troops of the Shehu at Minarge bringing an end to the 1,000-year rule of the Saifawa Dynasty. Shehu Umar then became ruler in name as well as in fact but retained the title of Shehu or Shaykh.

Mohammed el-Amin al Kanemi (1)
d. 1837

RABEH DYNASTY
Rabeh
1893–1900
(Conquers Borno in 1893 and installs himself as Amir)

Fadl Allah
1900–1
(does not seem to have held title of Amir)

Umar (2) 1837–81 — Abd al-Rahman (3)[a] 1853–4 — Abba Masta[b]

Bukar(4) 1881–4

Ibrahim (5) 1884–5

Hashim (6)[c] 1885–93/4

Kiyari (7)[d] 1893/4

Sanda Wudoroma (8)[e] 1893/4

Ibrahim Dikwa 1905–6

Sanda Mandarama Dikwa 1902–15

Umar Sanda Kura (9) (10)[f] Dikwa 1900–1 Borno 1922–37

Bukar Garba (11) Dikwa 1901–2 Borno 1902–22

Umar Sanda Kiyarimi (12) Dikwa 1927–37 Borno 1937–69

Masta Dikwa 1937–50

Yarima Dikwa 1954–

Masta Dikwa 1952–4

Umar (13) Baba Ya Mairami Borno 1969–74

Bukar Dikwa 1950–2

a. Abd al-Rahman seized the throne from his brother in 1853 but was overthrown within a year by Umar's supporters.
b. Abba Masta was chosen as Shehu but the decision of the electors was overruled by Ibrahim backed by the royal gunmen.
c. Hashim was killed on Abba Kiyari's orders following his attempt to come to terms with Rabeh.
d and e. Both Kiyari and his brother Sanda Wudoroma were captured and executed by Rabeh.
f. Umar Sanda Kura was appointed Shehu by the Foreau expedition in 1899 and deposed by the French authorities on his failure to produce an indemnity of $80,000.

Bukar Garbai also failed to collect the indemnity and was enticed to British Borno where he became the first Shehu thereafter. Until 1915 there were two Shehus, one in German Borno at Dikwa and one in British Borno. In recent years it has been customary to refer to the former as Emir of Dikwa.
* I am indebted to Mr J. E. Lavers for making available to me this dynasty of the Shehus of Borno in advance of the publication of his own work on Borno in the nineteenth century.

APPENDIX B The Sokoto Dynasty

* Usman dan Fodio held only the title of *Amir al-Mu'minin*. The additional title of Caliph or Sultan of Sokoto was taken by his son Bello and all his successors.

APPENDIX C Alafins of Oyo*

1. Oranyan (Oranmiyan)—Son or Grandson of Oduduwa and Founder of the present ruling dynasty of Benin.
2. Ajaka—dethroned.
3. Sango.
4. Ajaka—reinstalled.
5. Aganju.
6. Kori.
7. Oluaso.
8. Onigbogi—conducted evacuation of Oyo-Ile, probably early sixteenth century (Smith).†
9. Ofiran (Ofinran).
10. Eguguojo (Egunoju)—founder of Oyo-Igboho.
11. Orompoto—possibly a woman (Smith).
12. Ajiboyede.
13. Abipa.
14. Obalokun, c. 1614.
    Oluodo—said to have drowned in the Niger when pursued by the Nupe. Not buried in the Bara (royal burial ground)? Name suppressed. Personal communication from Robert Smith.
15. Ajagbo.
16. Odarawu.
17. Kanran.
18. Jayin.
    Interregnum.
19. Ayibi.
20. Osiyago.
21. Ojigi, was reigning in the 1730's (Dalzel).
22. Gberu.
23. Amuniwaiye.
24. Onisile, ?–1754.

* This list is based on the list in Johnson, *op. cit.* Appendix B, pp. 669–70. Datings, where given, have their source recorded in brackets. There are several versions of this King list, none of which can be treated as definitive.
† Smith 'The Alafin in Exile', *op. cit.*

25. Labisi, 1754, reigned less than a year (Akinjogbin).*
26. Awonbioju (Oduboye), reigned 130 days.
27. Agbolouje, 1754 (Akinjogbin).
28. Majeogbe, 1754–1770 (Akinjogbin).
29. Abiodun, *c.* 1770–89 (Akinjogbin).
30. Awole, *c.* 1789–96 (Akinjogbin).
31. Adebo ⎫
             ⎬ *c.* 1796/7†
32. Maku ⎭

   Interregnum, *c.* 1797–1802.†
33. Majotu, reigned in 1830 (Lander),‡ *c.* 1802–30–1.†
34. Amodo, *c.* 1830–i–*c.* 1833–4.†
35. Oluewu, *c.* 1833–4–*c.* 1835–6.†
36. Atiba, *c.* 1837–59 (Ajayi§). Founder of New Oyo.
37. Adelu, 1859–75.
38. Adeyemi, 1876–1905.
39. Lawani, 1905–11.
40. Ladigbolu I, 1911–44.
41. Adeniran, 1945–56 (deposed).
42. Ladigbolu II, 1956–69.
43. Lamidi Adeyemi II, 1971–   . (For two years the Western State
    government and the Oyo Kingmakers were in dispute as to who
    should succeed Ladigbolu II.)

* Akinjogbin 'Prelude to the Yoruba Civil Wars', *op. cit* and *Dahomey and its Neighbours 1708–1818*, London Ph.D. Thesis, 1963.
† Law, R.C.C. 'The Chronology of the Yoruba Wars of the Early Nineteenth Century: A Reconsideration' *Journal of the Historical Society of Nigeria*, V, 2, 1970.
‡ Lander cited in Ajayi and Smith, *op. cit.*, p. 9.
§ In Ajayi and Smith, *ibid.*

APPENDIX D British Governors of Nigeria, 1900-1960

Colony and Protectorate of Lagos
Governor
1899–1904: Sir William Macgregor
1904–6:   Sir Walter Egerton

Protectorate of Southern Nigeria
High Commissioner
1900–4: Sir Ralph Moor
1904–6: Sir Walter Egerton

Protectorate of Northern Nigeria
High Commissioner/Governor
1900–7:   Sir Frederick Lugard
1907–9:   Sir Percy Girouard*
1909–12: Sir Hesketh Bell
1912–14: Sir Frederick Lugard

Colony and Protectorate of Southern Nigeria
Governor
1906–12: Sir Walter Egerton
1912–14: Sir Frederick Lugard

Colony and Protectorate of Nigeria
Governor-General
1914–19: Sir Frederick Lugard
Governor
1919–25: Sir Hugh Clifford
1925–31: Sir Graeme Thomson
1931–5:   Sir Donald Cameron
1935–43: Sir Bernard Bourdillon
1943–8:   Sir Arthur Richards
1948–54:   Sir John Macpherson
Governor-General
1954: Sir John Macpherson
1954–60: Sir James Robertson

* Girouard's title was changed from High Commissioner to Governor in 1908.

APPENDIX E National Ministries to 1964

1951 CONSTITUTION: COUNCIL OF MINISTERS

Northern Region

M. Abubakar Tafawa Balewa, Minister of Works (N.P.C.).
M. Shettima Kashim, Minister of Social Services (N.P.C.).
M. Muhammadu Ribadu, Minister of Natural Resources (N.P.C.).
Alhaji Usuman Nagogo, Emir of Katsina, Minister without Portfolio (N.P.C.).

Eastern Region

Mr Okoi Arikpo, Minister of Lands, Survey and Development (N.C.N.C.).*
Mr Eni Njoku, Minister of Mines and Power (N.C.N.C.).
Mr A. C. Nwapa, Minister of Commerce and Industries (N.C.N.C.).

Western Region

H. H. Sir Adesoji Aderemi, Oni of Ife, Minister without Portfolio (A.G.).
Chief Arthur Prest, Minister of Communications (A.G.).
Chief Bode Thomas, Minister of Transport (A.G.).
Chief S. L. Akintola, Minister of Labour (A.G.).

Southern Cameroons

Dr E. M. L. Endeley, Minister without Portfolio (N.C.N.C.).*

Members Ex-Officio

The Governor (President of the Council).
The Chief Secretary to the Government.
The Lieutenant-Governors of the three Regions.
The Attorney-General.
The Financial Secretary.

* Joined N.I.P. on 23rd February 1953.

1954 CONSTITUTION: COUNCIL OF MINISTERS

Northern Region

Mallam Abubakar Tafawa Balewa, Minister of Transport (N.P.C.).
Alhaji Inuwa Wada, Federal Minister (N.P.C.).
Mallam Muhammadu Ribadu, Minister of Land, Mines and Power (N.P.C.).

Western Region

Alhaji Adegoke Adelabu, Minister of Natural Resources and Social Services (N.C.N.C.).
Chief Kola Balogun, Minister of Research and Information (N.C.N.C.).
Chief Festus Okotie-Eboh, Minister of Labour and Welfare (N.C.N.C.).

Eastern Region

Mr Raymond Njoku, Minister of Trade and Industry (N.C.N.C.).
Dr K. O. Mbadiwe, Minister of Communications and Aviation (N.C.N.C.).
Mr M. T. Mbu, Federal Minister (N.C.N.C.).

Southern Cameroons

Mr Victor Mukete, Federal Minister (N.C.N.C.).

Members Ex-Officio

Governor-General (President)
Chief Secretary
Financial Secretary
Attorney-General

1957 CONSTITUTION: NATIONAL GOVERNMENT

Alhaji Abubakar Tafawa Balewa, Prime Minister and Minister of Finance (N.P.C.).
N.P.C.
Mallam Bukar Dipcharima, Minister of State.
Alhaji Muhammadu Ribadu, Minister of Lagos Affairs, Mines and Power.
Alhaji Inuwa Wada, Minister of Works and Surveys.

N.C.N.C.
Chief Kola Balogun, Minister of Research and Information.
Mr J. M. Johnson, Minister of Internal Affairs.
Dr K. O. Mbadiwe, Minister of Commerce and Industry.
Mr R. A. Njoku, Minister of Transport.
Mr Aja Nwachuku, Minister of Education.
Chief Festus Okotie-Eboh, Minister of Labour and Welfare.

A.G.
Chief S. L. Akintola, Minister of Communications and Aviation.
Mr Ayo Rosiji, Minister of Health.

K.N.C. (*Kamerun National Congress*)
Mr Victor Mukete, Minister of State.

1960 INDEPENDENCE GOVERNMENT: N.P.C.–N.C.N.C. COALITION

Alhaji Sir Abubakar Tafawa Balewa, Prime Minister and Minister of Foreign Affairs (N.P.C.).
Mr T. O. S. Benson, Minister of Information (N.C.N.C.).
Mr Olu Akinfosile, Minister of Communications (N.C.N.C.).
Mallam Zanna Bukar Dipcharima, Minister of Commerce and Industry (N.P.C.).
Chief J. M. Johnson, Minister of Labour and Welfare (N.C.N.C.).
Mr Raymond Njoku, Minister of Transport and Aviation (N.C.N.C.).
Mr Aja Nwachuku, Minister of Education (N.C.N.C.).
Chief Festus Okotie-Eboh, Minister of Finance (N.C.N.C.).
Alhaji Muhammadu Ribadu, Minister of Defence (N.P.C.).
Mallam Usuman Sarki, Minister of Internal Affairs (N.P.C.).
Mallam Maitama Sule, Minister of Mines and Power (N.P.C.).
Mallam Musa Yaradua, Minister of Lagos Affairs (N.P.C.).
Mr Jaja Wachuku, Minister of Economic Development (N.C.N.C.).
Alhaji Inuwa Wada, Minister of Works and Surveys (N.P.C.).
Mallam Waziri Ibrahim, Minister of Health (N.P.C.).
Mallam Shehu Shagari, Minister of Pensions (N.P.C.).
Dr T. O. Elias, Attorney-General and Minister of Justice.
Dr M. A. Majekodunmi, Minister of State.
Dr E. A. Esin, Minister of State (N.C.N.C.).
Mallam Nuhu Bamali, Minister of State (N.P.C.).
Chief F. Omo-Osagie, Minister of State (N.C.N.C.).
Mr J. C. Obande, Minister of State (N.P.C.).

3rd September 1964

Chief Ayo Rosiji (N.N.D.P.) Minister without Portfolio.
Chief A. M. A. Akimloye (N.N.D.P.) Minister without Portfolio.

Since the publication of the Second Edition of *The Story of Nigeria* in 1966 a number of general histories of Nigeria have been published. By far the best is contained in Thomas Hodgkin's introduction to his second edition of *Nigerian Perspectives: An Historical Anthology*, London 1975. This provides a concise and stimulating summary of current thinking and research on the pre-colonial history of Nigeria. Walter Schwarz's *Nigeria*, London 1968 is very useful for the period after independence, which is treated only cursorily in this volume. His book provides incisive insights into the events which led up to the civil war.

Latest archaeological research in Nigeria is comprehensively treated in Thurstan Shaw's 'Archaeology in Nigeria' *Antiquity*, XLIII, 1969, which has a full bibliography. This should be read in conjunction with his essay on the prehistory of West Africa in J. F. A. Ajayi and Michael Crowder (eds), *History of West Africa*, vol. I, 2nd edn, London 1976, in which the prehistory of Nigeria can be seen in the context of that of West Africa as a whole. Frank Willett's essay on Nigeria in P. L. Shinnie (ed.), *The African Iron Age*, London 1971, is also a useful survey of the latest archaeological evidence for the Nigerian Iron Age.

A geographical setting for the study of Nigerian history is to be found in Akin L. Mabogunje's 'The Lands and Peoples of Nigeria' in Ajayi and Crowder (eds), *History of West Africa*, vol. I. W. B. Morgan and J. C. Pugh's *West Africa*, London 1969, provides a more detailed setting for the history of Nigeria generally. An excellent and provocative background to the study of the development of states in Nigeria is provided by Robin Horton in 'Stateless Societies in the History of West Africa' in the *History of West Africa*, vol. I.

For the early history of the savannah states Abdullahi Smith's essay on Hausaland and Borno before *c.* 1500 in Ajayi and Crowder (eds), *History of West Africa,* vol. I, is important. The same author has published an excellent detailed study of the early history of one Hausa state, Zazzau (Zaria), in M. J. Mortimore (ed.), *Zaria and its Regions: A Nigerian City and its Environs*, Zaria 1970. The sixteenth century in Hausaland and Borno is dealt with in the light of latest research by J. O. Hunwick in 'Hausaland, Bornu and Songhai' in Ajayi and Crow-

der (eds), *History of West Africa*, vol. I. Yusuf Bala Usman's thesis for
Ahmadu Bello University on Katsina in the nineteenth century
contains stimulating insights into the early history of Hausaland.

An important reassessment of the history of Borno during the seventeenth and eighteenth centuries is to be found in J. E. Lavers's 'Islam in
the Bornu Caliphate 1600–1800', *Odu*, new series, No. 5, 1970. Lavers
successfully dispels the traditional view that Borno was in decline
during this period.

The best introduction to the early history of Yorubaland is Robert
Smith's *Kingdoms of the Yoruba*, London 1969. This should be read in
conjunction with H. M. A. Obayemi's chapter on 'The Early History of
the Yoruba and Edo-Speaking peoples and their neighbours to *c*. 1600'
in Ajayi and Crowder (eds), *History of West Africa*, vol. I, 2nd edn, 1976,
which provides a provocative reassessment of the history of the Yoruba
and their neighbours. Frank Willett's *Ife in the History of West African
Sculpture*, London 1967, is a fine study of the place of Ife art in relation
to that of the rest of the Nigerian region. There is a concise survey of the
early history of Benin in Alan Ryder's *Benin and the Europeans
1485–1897*, London 1969. A recent important study of the early history
of Benin from the archaeological point of view is Graham Connah's
'Archaeology in Benin' *Journal of African History*, XIII, 1, 1972. See
also his 'New Light on the Benin City Walls' *Journal of the Historical
Society of Nigeria*, III, 4, 1967, and his recent monograph on *Benin
Archaeology*, London 1975. There are important contributions to early
Benin history in R. A. Bradbury (ed.), *Benin Studies*, London 1973.

The early history of the Niger Delta and the Igbo and Ibibio hinterland has been recently reassessed in E. J. Alagoa's 'The Niger-Delta
States and their Neighbours 1600–1800' in Ajayi and Crowder (eds),
History of West Africa, vol. I. For conflicting views of the rise of the
city-states of the Niger-Delta see Robin Hortons's 'From Fishing Village to City State' in Mary Douglas and Phyllis Kaberry (eds), *Man in
Africa* London 1969, and E. J. Alagoa's 'Long Distance Trade and
States in the Niger Delta' *Journal of African History*, XI, 3, 1970. See
also his 'Development of Institutions in the States of the Eastern Niger
Delta' *Journal of African History*, XII, 2, 1971. A. J. Latham's *Old
Calabar 1600–1891*, London 1973, is a valuable study of the early
history of this city-state. Thurstan Shaw's magisterial account of his
excavations, *Igbo-Ukwu*, London 1970, has to be taken into account by
any student of the early history of the Igbo. The early history of the
peoples of the Upper Benue Basin and the Bauchi Plateau is treated in
considerable detail by Sa'ad Abubakar in the Historical Society of
Nigeria's *The Groundwork of Nigerian History* (forthcoming). Likewise the pre-nineteenth-century history of the peoples of the Niger-

Benue valley is treated thoroughly in the same work by Ade Obayemi.

Any general overview of Nigeria's pre-nineteenth-century history has to take into account Philip Curtin's incisive study, *The African Slave Trade: A Census*, Madison, Wisconsin 1970. This book, together with Ryder's book on Benin and the Europeans, not only renders more precise but sensibly diminishes the importance of the European impact on Nigeria's history before the nineteenth century. Its figures have, however, recently been challenged by J. D. Inikori in his 'Curtin and Anstey on the Slave Trade: A Reassessment' *J.A.H.*, XVII, 3, 1976.

The study of the Jihad of Usman dan Fodio has been inestimably advanced by Murray Last's meticulous study, *The Sokoto Caliphate*, London 1967. A more general view of what was happening in northern Nigeria throughout the nineteenth century is given by R. A. Adeleye's *Power and Diplomacy in Northern Nigeria 1800–1906: The Sokoto Caliphate and its Enemies*, London 1971. See also H. A. S. Johnston's *The Fulani Empire of Sokoto*, London 1967.

Specific studies of the constituent emirates of the Caliphate are to be found in Sa'ad Abubakar's 'The Emirate of Fombina [Adamawa] 1809–1903', Ph.D. thesis, Ahmadu Bello University 1970; M. Mason's 'The Nupe Kindom in the 19th Century: A Political History', Ph.D. thesis, Birmingham 1970, and his article on 'The Jihad in the South: An Outline of the 19th-Century Nupe Hegemony in North-Eastern Yorubaland and Afenmai' *Journal of the Historical Society of Nigeria*, V, 2, 1970. Yauri, which was in a tributary (*jizya*) relationship to the Caliphate in the nineteenth century, has been studied in depth by Mahdi Adamu in 'A Hausa Government in Decline: Yauri in the 19th Century', M.A. thesis, Ahmadu Bello University 1968; Bello Alkali has made a study of Kebbi, Sokoto's enemy throughout the nineteenth century, in 'A Hausa Community in Crisis: Kebbi in the 19th century', M.A. thesis, Ahmadu Bello University 1969. Victor W. Low has made a meticulous study of the Emirates of Gombe, Katagum and Hadejia, supplemented with superb maps, in *Three Nigerian Emirates*, Northwestern 1972. For a detailed study of one aspect of trade in the Sokoto Caliphate, kola, see Paul E. Lovejoy's 'The Hausa Kola Trade to the Volta Basin 1700–1900: A Commercial System in the Long-Distance Exchange of West Africa', Ph.D. thesis, Wisconsin 1973. There is an excellent analysis of changes in the administrative systems of Hausaland in the nineteenth and twentieth centuries in Murray Last's 'Aspects of Administration and Dissent in Hausaland, 1800–1968' *Africa*, XL, 4, October 1970. A useful contribution to the study of late nineteenth-century history in Sokoto and Borno is M. A. Al-Hajj's 'Mahdism in the Western Sudan with special reference to Northern

Nigeria', Ph.D thesis, Ahmadu Bello University 1973. S. A. Balogun gives an account of the role of Gwandu in the Sokoto Caliphate in his 'The Gwandu Emirate and its dependencies', Ph.D. thesis, Ibadan 1972.

The nineteenth-century history of Borno has had much less attention paid to it than the Sokoto Caliphate. Perhaps the best study of the Shehus is contained in Louis Brenner's *The Shehus of Kukawa: A History of the Al-Kanemi Dynasty of Bornu*, Clarendon 1973. See also his joint chapter with Ronald Cohen in Ajayi and Crowder (eds), *History of West Africa*, vol. II.

An important contribution to the nineteenth-century history of the Middle Belt is M. Mason, 'Population Density and "Slave-Raiding"—The Case of the Middle Belt of Nigeria' *J.A.H.* X, 4, 1969, pp. 551–564. A. H. M. Kirk-Greene has provided some basic detailed material in his edited reprint of the *Gazetteers of the Northern Provinces*, London 1972, which can still be helpful in the study of the history of areas not drawn into the mainstream of historical movements in the area.

The eighteenth- and nineteenth-century history of Oyo has recently been reconsidered in detail. Among the most important reassessments are: R. S. Smith's 'Event and Portent: the fall of Old Oyo, a problem in historical explanation' *Africa*, XLI, 3, July 1971; P. Morton-Williams's 'The Yoruba Kingdom of Oyo' in Daryll Forde and Phyllis Kaberry (eds), *West African Kingdoms in the Nineteenth Century*, Oxford 1967; P. Morton-Williams's 'The Oyo Yoruba and the Atlantic Slave Trade 1670–1830' *Journal of the Historical Society of Nigeria*, III, 2, 1964; J. A. Atanda's 'The Fall of the Old Oyo Empire: A Re-Consideration of its Cause' *Journal of the Historical Society of Nigeria*, V, 4, 1971; P. Morton-Williams's 'The Influence of Habitat and Trade on the Politics of Oyo and Ashanti' in Mary Douglas and P. M. Kaberry (eds), *Man in Africa*, London 1969. I. A. Akinjogbin's *Dahomey and its Neighbours 1708–1818*, Cambridge 1967, is useful for a study of Oyo's relationship with its tributary state of Dahomey, though some historians are critical of his analysis of the interrelationship of the Yoruba-Aja states as expressed in his concept of the Ebi social theory. Robin Law, who has recently completed an important thesis on Oyo, has expressed reservations about Akinjogbin's interpretations in a long review of the book in the *Journal of the Historical Society of Nigeria*, IV, 2, June 1968, and two important articles, 'The Constitutional Struggles of Oyo in the Eighteenth Century' *Journal of African History*, XII, 1, 1971, and 'Oyo and its Northern Neighbours' *Kano Studies*, new series, I. 1, 1973.

The hitherto somewhat obscure seventeenth- and eighteenth-century history of Benin from 1600 to the time of the British occupation, has been dealt with in detail by Alan Ryder in his *Benin and the Europeans.*

Apart from the books and articles mentioned above relating to the nineteenth-century history of Nigeria, some important monographs and articles have appeared that have greatly helped our understanding of this period. Obaro Ikime's *Merchant Prince of the Niger Delta*, London 1968, apart from being a study of Nana Olumu, Governor of the Benin River, has valuable information on Itsekiri-Urhobo relations. An excellent study of the relations between the Eastern Yoruba and the Ibadan (Oyo) Empire is contained in S. A. Akintoye's *Revolution and Power Politics in Yorubaland: Ibadan Expansion and the Rise of the Ekiti Parapo*, London 1971. Akintoye has also published an important article on the relations between the Eastern Yoruba and Benin in 'The Eastern Yoruba and the Benin Kingdom' *Journal of the Historical Society of Nigeria*, IV, 4, 1969. See also his 'The Ondo Road Eastwards of Lagos' *Journal of African History*, X, 4, 1969. R. N. Henderson, *The King in Every Man*, London 1972, includes most interesting insights into the development of chieftaincy in Onitsha from the earliest times with some stimulating inferences about the relationship between Igbo, Bini and Igala political institutions, the last of which can be studied in depth in J. S. Boston's *The Igala Kingdom*, London 1968. Elizabeth Isichei has published two studies of the pre-colonial history of the Igbo: *The Ibo People and the Europeans,* London 1973, and *A History of the Igbo-Speaking Peoples*, London 1975, both of which help our understanding of this major Nigerian group.

The colonial period of Nigerian history has been comparatively well served in the past six years by microcosmic studies, particularly those concerning aspects of British administration: among these the most notable are Obaro Ikime's *Niger-Delta Rivalry: Itsekiri-Urhobo Relations and the European Presence 1884–1936*, London 1969; J. A. Atanda's *The New 'Oyo Empire': Indirect Rule and Change in Western Nigeria 1894–1934*, London 1973. A. E. Afigbo *The Warrant Chiefs: Indirect Rule in Southeastern Nigeria 1891–1929*, London 1973, is a major contribution to the understanding of British administration in Nigeria and African reaction to it. Philip Igbafe has written an important thesis on 'Benin under British Administration 1897–1938: A Study in Institutional Adaptation', Ph.D. thesis, Ibadan 1967. Some of his findings have been published in article form, e.g. 'The District Head System in Benin, 1914–1935' *Odu*, III, 2, and 'British Rule in Benin 1897–1920: Direct or Indirect?' *Journal of the Historical Society of Nigeria*, III, 4, 1967. See also his article on 'The Benin Water Rate Agitation 1937–39: An Example of Social Conflict' *Journal of the Historical Society of Nigeria*, IV, 3, 1969. Adamu Fika has written a penetrating study of the reaction of a Northern Nigerian emirate to British administration in 'The Political and Economic Re-orientation of Kano Emirate 1882–1940', Ph.D. thesis, London 1973.

The position of the chief under colonial rule is treated with reference to a number of Nigerian examples in Michael Crowder and Obaro Ikime (eds), *West African Chiefs: Their Changing Status Under Colonial Rule and Independence*, Ife 1971. Resistance to colonial occupation is considered in Michael Crowder (ed.), *West African Resistance: The Military Response to Colonial Occupation*, London 1971, in which there is a notable study of the Ijebu expedition of 1892 by R. S. Smith.

British administration in Nigeria has been studied in a provocative book by I. F. Nicholson, *The Administration of Nigeria 1900–1960: Men, Methods and Myths*, Oxford 1969, while the role of the British Political Officer in Northern Nigeria is dealt with on a broad scale by Robert F. Heussler in *The British in Northern Nigeria*, London 1968, and on a microcosmic scale by Michael Crowder in *Revolt in Bussa: A Study of British 'Native Administration' in Bussa, 1902–1935*, London 1973. There is a fascinating study of the problems faced by the British in administering the Tiv in David Dorward's 'Early British Administration Among the Tiv' *African Affairs*, 2, 1970. His doctoral thesis on this subject has been accepted by Birmingham.

Pioneering work on the study of Nigeria's economic history is contained in A. G. Hopkins's 'An Economic History of Lagos: 1880–1914', Ph.D. thesis, London 1964. Hopkins has published many invaluable articles, too numerous to list here. Examples are: 'Economic Aspects of Political Movements in Nigeria and the Gold Coast, 1919–1939' *Journal of African History*, I, 1966; 'The Currency Revolution in South West Nigeria in the late 19th Century' *Journal of the Historical Society of Nigeria*, III, 3, 1966; 'R. B. Blaize, Merchant Prince of West Africa' *Tarikh*, I, No. 2, and 'The Lagos Strike of 1897: An Exploration of Nigerian Labour History' *Past and Present*, No. 35, 1969. His *Economic History of West Africa*, London 1973, is indispensable for the study of all periods of Nigerian History.

An important contribution to our understanding of the recent economic history of Nigeria is R. J. Gavin's 'A History of Economic Development in Nigeria' in *The Groundwork of Nigerian History* (forthcoming). It has a very full bibliography of sources in its notes. Polly Hill's *Studies in Rural Capitalism in West Africa*, London 1970, and *Rural Hausa: A Village and a Setting*, London 1972, are vital for the understanding of economic change at the grassroots level over the past ninety years.

Among important recent contributions to the political history of Nigeria are G. O. Olusanya's *The Second World War and Nigerian*

Politics, London 1973, B. J. Dudley's *Parties and Politics in Northern Nigeria*, London 1968, and C. S. Whitaker's *The Politics of Tradition: Continuity and Change in Northern Nigeria 1946–1966*, Princeton 1970. Perhaps the best account among many published about the Nigerian civil war, most of which were highly *engagé*, is John de St Jorre's *The Nigerian Civil War*, London 1972.

Notes

Chapter 1 The Birth of Nigeria (between pages 11 and 23)

1 A. H. M. Kirk-Greene 'Who coined the name Nigeria?' *West Africa*, 22nd December 1956.

2 Several general histories of Nigeria have been published but so far no full-scale history has been written by a Nigerian. Wale Ademoyega's *The Federation of Nigeria*, London, 1962, is more a general description of the country's geography, politics and resources than a history. D. O. Okonkwo's *History of Nigeria in a New Setting*, Aba (Nigeria), 1961, is essentially designed for schools. The best introduction to Nigerian history is still Thomas Hodgkin's introductory essay *Nigerian Perspectives*, London, 1960. M. C. English's *An Outline of Nigerian History*, London, 1959, though intended for the junior classes of secondary schools provides a well-balanced introductory survey. Of the two full-length histories published so far, Sir Alan Burns's *History of Nigeria*, London, 1962 (6th edition), is essentially an administrative history that pays little attention to pre-European history or to the nationalist period. Sir Rex Niven's *Short History of Nigeria*, London, 1937, almost as long as that of Burns, shows more sympathy for the history of Nigerian peoples before contact with the Europeans. A shortened and substantially revised version of the present work, designed for school certificate candidates, entitled *Nigeria: A Modern History for Schools*, London, 1965, has been prepared by Rex Akpofure and the author. Two general surveys of Nigeria are recommended: K. M. Buchanan and J. C. Pugh *Land and People in Nigeria*, London, 1955, and *Nigeria: The Political and Economic Background*, London, 1960. Reference should also be made to R. J. Harrison Church *West Africa*, London, 1964 (2nd edition).

3 There was considerable controversy in Nigeria over the results for the 1962 census as well as those for 1963 (published in 1964). The figures for 1962 were never officially released, whilst those for 1963 gave a population for the country of 55,620,268. The controversy was not so much centred on the plausibility of a 20 million increase over the 1953 census figure of 31,168,000 (for it is generally agreed that that census was inadequately conducted) but over the distribution of population region by region. See Chapter 18.

4 Joseph H. Greenberg *Studies in African Linguistic Classification*, U.S.A., 1955. I have in fact followed in this edition the revised version of Greenberg's book published under the new title, *The Languages of Africa*, in 1963 as a supplement to *The International Journal of American Linguistics*, XXIX, 1 Pt 2, 1963.

5 *Ibid.* The author has changed his designation for certain African linguistic families from those used in his earlier work. In so far as Nigeria is concerned the changes are as follows:

1. Central-Saharan=Nilo-Saharan.
2. Niger-Congo = Congo-Kordofanian, though Niger-Congo still describes a major sub-family of this newly designated branch.
3. Chad-Afroasiatic=Afro-Asiatic.

6 G. P. Murdock *Africa—Its Peoples and their Culture History*, New York, 1959.

7 Thurstan Shaw 'Field Research in Nigerian Archaeology' *J.H.S.N.*, II, 4, 1963, pp. 449–64 provides a survey of the state of archaeological research in Nigeria up to independence. See also his *Archaeology and Nigeria*, Ibadan, 1964. Also *Preserving the Past—The Nigerian Museum and its Art Treasures*, Lagos, 1959.

8 Jan Vansina 'Recording the Oral History of the Bakuba—I: Methods' *J.A.H.*, I, 1, 1960, pp. 43–51. For general discussions of the problems confronting the historian of Africa today see J. Vansina, R. Mauny and L.-V. Thomas eds. *The Historian in Tropical Africa*, London, 1964, and K. Onwuka Diké 'The Study of African History' in *The Proceedings of the First International Congress of Africanists*, eds. Lalage Bown and Michael Crowder, London, 1964. Also Vincent Monteil 'La décolonisation de l'Histoire' Supplément au no 142 *Preuves*, December 1962.

9 Vansina 'Bakuba' *op. cit.*, p. 52. In this respect the section on oral history in Murdock *op. cit.*, p. 43 must be treated with extreme caution.

10 H. R. Palmer *The Bornu, Sahara and Sudan*, London, 1936. P. Amaury Talbot *The Peoples of Southern Nigeria*, 4 vols., London, 1926. C. K. Meek *A Sudanese Kingdom*, London, 1931.

11 Murdock *op. cit.*, pp. 64–70. See also Roland Portères 'Vieilles Agricultures de l'Afrique intertropicale' *L'Agronomie Tropicale*, V, 1950, pp. 489–507. A useful review article dealing with both Murdock's and Portères' hypotheses is J. D. Fage's 'Anthropology, Botany and History' *J.A.H.*, II, 2, 1961, pp. 299–309.

12 This section has been rewritten in the context of Thurstan Shaw 'The Prehistory of West Africa' in J. F. Ade Ajayi and Michael Crowder (eds), *History of West Africa*, vol. I, London 1971.

13 See Shaw 'Field Research' *op. cit.*, pp. 450–4.

14 B.E.B. Fagg 'Cave Paintings and Rock Gongs of Birnin Kudu' *Proceedings of the Third Pan-African Congress on Pre-History*, Lusaka, 1955.

15 J. Desmond Clark 'The Prehistoric Origins of African Culture' *J.A.H.*, V, 2, 1964. pp. 180–1.

16 Dating of the Nok culture has been achieved by the Carbon 14 process, but with present techniques its results can only be considered tentative. See *J.A.H.*, II, 1, 1960, pp. 137–9, 'Radio Carbon dates for Sub-Saharan Africa' where details of the various radio carbon dates for the Nok culture are given.

17 B. E. B. Fagg: 'The Nok terracottas in West African Art History' *Actes du 4e Congrès Pan-Africain de la prèhistoire et de l'étude du quaternaire* published by Musée Royal de l'Afrique Centrale, Tervuren, Belgium. Annales série IN—8°, sciences humaines, no. 40 1962, p. 447.

18 Daryll Forde 'The Culture Map of West Africa—successive adaptations to Tropical Forests and Grasslands' *Trans. New York Acad. Sci.* Ser. II, 15 April 1953, pp. 206–19, reprinted in Simon and Phoebe Ottenberg ed. *The Cultures of Africa*, New York, 1960, pp. 116–39.

Chapter 2 **Sudanese States** (between pages 24 and 36)

1 Roland Oliver and J. D. Fage *A Short History of Africa*, London, 1962, Chapter IV, 'The Sudanic Civilization', pp. 44–52.
    For a very useful discussion of the state-building process see Robert G. Armstrong *State Structures in Negro Africa* (unpublished Ph.D. dissertation, University of Chicago 1952, available on microfilm). See also his article 'The Development of Kingdoms in Negro Africa' *J.H.S.N.*, II, 1, December 1960, pp. 27–40. See also Robin Horton, 'Stateless Societies' in Ajayi and Crowder *op. cit.* vol. I.

2 In the first edition it was suggested that the Zaghawa were of Berber origin. Since then J. S. Trimingham has suggested that they were in fact a Negro people: *A History of Islam in West Africa*, London, 1962, pp. 104–5. Citing Al-Masu'di, Ibn Sa'īd, Ibn Khaldun and Al-Idrīsī he concluded, 'At any rate they were distinct from both Berbers and Sudan blacks, like the Teda of today who are probably their descendants.' One of the reasons for believing that the Zaghawa were not of Negro origin was the statement that Mai Selma (c. 1193–1210) was the first black ruler of Kanem. Yves Urvoy *L'Histoire de l'Empire de Bornou*, Dakar, 1949, p. 39.

3 Quoted in Yaqut *Mu'jam*, ii, 932–3.

4 H. R. Palmer *Sudanese Memoirs*, 3 vols., Lagos, 1928, and *The Bornu, Sahara and Sudan*, London 1936. Urvoy *op. cit.* Trimingham *op. cit.* has a good summary of the history of Kanem-Borno, and uses Arabic sources extensively. See also E. W. Bovill *The Golden Trade of the Moors*, London, 1955 and his earlier *Caravans of the Old Sahara*, London, 1933. Also: Heinrich Barth *Travels and Discoveries in Northern and Central Africa*, 5 vols., London, 1857–8; A. Schultze *The Sultanate of Bornu* (trans. P. A. Benton), London, 1913; and Annie M.-D. Lebeuf *Les Populations du Tchad*, Paris, 1959, pp. 33–46.

5 The map in *Sudanese Memoirs*, vol. II places it just to the north-east whilst the map in *Bornu, Sahara and Sudan* places it due east.

6 Urvoy *op. cit.*, p. 27.

7 I am indebted to Dr A. D. H. Bivar for this discussion of the location of Njimi. Subsequent to the appearance of the first edition of this book, Dr Bivar with P. L. Shinnie published a detailed account of the location in 'Old Kanuri Capitals', *J.A.H.*, II, 1, 1962, pp. 1–10.

8 Trimingham *op. cit.*, p. 115 suggests that Hume was the founder of a new dynasty.

9 Ibn Khaldun *Histoire des Berbères et des dynasties de l'Afrique septentroniale* tr. M. le Baron de Slane. Algiers, 1854, vol. II, p. 347.

10 *Ibid.*, vol. II, p. 109, described Kanem as dominating all the regions of the desert as far as Fezzan.

11 Ahmad ibn 'Abdullah al-Qualqashandi *Subh al-a'sha* written in 1387, Cairo edition 1913–19, viii, pp. 116–18, quoted in Hodgkin *op. cit.*, p. 77–8.

12 Palmer *Sudanese Memoirs*, vol. III, p. 109, *The Kano Chronicle* records that Abdullahi Burja 'was the first in Hausaland to give Bornu tsare or gaisuwa. He opened roads from Bornu to Gwanja' (i.e. Gonja in Central (Modern) Ghana).

13 Bivar and Shinnie *op. cit.*, p. 2, state that it was founded in *c.* 1470 which could mean that if we accept the usual dates given for Mai Ali Gaji's reign (1473–1501, by Trimingham *op. cit.*, Urvoy *op. cit.*) it could not have been founded by him. However, the authors do not give the source for their dating

of the foundation of N'gazargamu, nor do they attribute its foundation to Mai Ali Gaji. On the other hand Trimingham who places its foundation at *c.* 1481 does not give a source for this date either.

14 Palmer *Sudanese Memoirs*, vol. III, p. 133, where the Bayajidda legend is cited in *The Daura Girgam*. See also Alhaji Hassan and Mallam Shu'aibu Na'ibi *A Chronicle of Abuja* translated and arranged from the Hausa by Frank Heath (2nd edition), Lagos, 1962. Also M. G. Smith p. 340. Also M. G. Smith 'The Beginnings of Hausa Society' *The Historian in Tropical Africa*, London 1964, p. 340.

15 This discussion is based on Abdullahi Smith 'The Early States of the Central Sudan' in Ajayi and Crowder *op. cit.* vol. I.

16 In the first edition it was concluded that Islam reached Hausaland 'undoubtedly from Mali'. This is a view shared by a number of historians notably Oliver and Fage *op. cit.*, p. 86, and is based on *The Kano Chronicle.* 'Thus, for example, it was Mande merchants of the fifteenth century who introduced Islam into Hausaland.' However, Joseph H. Greenberg argues in 'Linguistic Evidence for the Influence of Kanuri on Hausa' *J.A.H.*, I, 2, 1960, that Islam first reached Hausaland from Borno. He cites as evidence the fact that certain Hausa words which must have come into use as a result of contact with Islam have Kanuri roots, rather than Arabic or even Mande roots. Thus the word 'write' is of Kanuri origin, and the word 'read', though of ultimate Arabic origin, has been borrowed via Kanuri.

17 Translated from the Arabic by T. H. Baldwin as *The Obligations of Princes*, Beirut, 1932.

18 *The Kano Chronicle op. cit.*

19 See J. O. Hunwick, 'Songhay, Bornu and Hausaland in the Sixteenth Century' in Ajayi and Crowder *op. cit.* vol. I.

20 Leo Africanus *History and Description of Africa*, 3 vols., London, 1896, trans. John Pory, ed. Robert Brown, III, p. 830.

21 There has been some confusion over the meaning of the word Kanta. Some authorities use it as the personal name of the man who led the Kebbi revolt against the Askia; others use it as the gubernatorial title of the Songhai governor of Kebbi; but consensus seems to favour the opinion that it was the kingly title of the rulers of Kebbi. It is so employed in this edition.

22 Imam Ahmed ibn Fartua *History of the First Twelve Years of the Reign of Mai Idris Alooma of Bornu 1571–1583*, translated from the Arabic by H. R. Palmer. Lagos, Government Printer, 1926. H. R. Palmer *Sudanese Memoirs*, vol. I, includes *The Kanem Wars of Mai Idris Alooma* by Imam Ahmed ibn Fartua.

23 Urvoy *op. cit.*, p. 78.

Chapter 3 **Kingdoms of the Forest** (between pages 37 and 47)

1 The problem of interpreting Yoruba myths of origin is raised by a number of authors. Probably the best summary is P. C. Lloyd 'Sacred Kingship and Government among the Yoruba' *Africa*, XXX, 3, 1960, pp. 221–37. See also P. C. Lloyd 'Yoruba myths—a sociologist's interpretation' *Odu*, 2, 1956, pp. 20–8; S. O. Biobaku *The Origin of the Yorubas*, Lagos, 1955; Ulli Beier and S. O. Biobaku 'The Use and Interpretation of Yoruba Myths' *Odu*, 1, 1955, pp. 12–25; Ulli Beier 'Before Oduduwa' *Odu*, 3, 1956, pp. 25–32; and E. Bolaji Idowu *Oludumare — God in Yoruba Belief*, London, 1962.

2 Versions of this myth vary in detail but not in substance. See Peter

Morton-Williams 'An Outline of the Cosmology and Cult Organisation of the Oyo Yoruba.' *Africa*, XXXIV, 3, July 1964, pp. 243–62 for a slightly different version of this myth and an interesting discussion of its significance.

3   Samuel Johnson *The History of the Yorubas*, Lagos, 1921, pp. 7–8. Much of the material for this chapter has been derived from Johnson's invaluable book whose main defect is its Oyo bias.

4   Jacob Egharevba *A Short History of Benin*, Ibadan, 1960 (2nd edition). For the history of Benin see also R. E. Bradbury and P. C. Lloyd *The Benin Kingdom and the Edo-speaking Peoples etc., plus the Itsekiri*, London, 1959 and R. E. Bradbury 'The historical uses of comparative ethnography with special reference to Benin and the Yoruba' *The Historian in Tropical Africa*, London, 1964, pp. 145–64.

5   The Ife bronzes are in fact brasses. See R. Mauny 'A possible source of copper for the oldest brass heads of Ife' *J.H.S.N.*, II, 3, December 1963, pp. 393–5.

6   Frank Willett in 'Ife and its Archaeology' *J.A.H.*, I, 2, 1960, pp. 231–48, gives a full account of the history of the discovery of the Ife bronzes and terracottas from the time of Leo Frobenius' visit to Ife in 1910 to his own more recent excavations.

7   See *An Introduction to the Art of Ife*, Lagos, 1955, for a general description of the Ife bronzes and terracottas, photographs of a number of which are reproduced in this pamphlet.

8   Thurstan Shaw 'Field Research in Nigerian Archaeology *op. cit.*, p. 457.

9   Unpublished. I owe this information to a personal communication by Mr Morton-Williams who kindly commented on this chapter before it went to press.

10   I have made a number of changes to this section in the early history of Oyo in the light of the Introduction in J. F. Ade Ajayi and Robert Smith *Yoruba Warfare in the Nineteenth Century*, Ibadan and London, 1964, pp. 1–5.

11   *Ibid.*, p. 3.

12   Before the nineteenth century there was no common term for the Yoruba-speaking peoples. They were designated such by European missionaries from the term Yoöba which the Oyo used to describe their dialect of the Yoruba language. Ajayi and Smith *op. cit.*, p. 2. Peter Morton-Williams in a personal communication has suggested that it may come from Yarba, the Hausa name for them.

13   Robert Smith 'The Alafin in Exile: A Study of the Igboho Period of Oyo History' *J.A.H.*, VI, 1, 1965, pp. 57–77. Mr Smith very kindly let me see a copy of this paper before it went to press.

14   *Ibid.*, p. 68; and Johnson *op. cit.*, p. 174.

15   Peter Morton-Williams has an excellent analysis of the 'constitution' of Oyo in his article 'The Yoruba Ogboni Cult in Oyo' *Africa*, XXX, 4, 1960, pp. 362–72.

16   See Frank Willett 'Investigations at Old Oyo, 1956–7: An Interim Report' *J.H.S.N.*, II, 1, December 1960, pp. 59–77, where Willett reports that the Afin, or palace, 'covers a very substantial area, probably something of the order of one square mile' (p. 67). The town itself was enclosed by walls the outer of which according to Clapperton was fifteen miles in circumference. (Hugh Clapperton, *Journal of a Second Expedition into the Interior of Africa from the Bight of Benin to Soccattoo*, London, 1829, p. 58.) The present Afin at Oyo is also enormous, and Robert Smith has suggested that it may in fact reproduce the ground plan and dimensions of that at Old Oyo (Oyo-Ile) (personal communication).

17 R. E. Bradbury 'The historical uses of comparative ethnography with special reference to Benin and the Yoruba' *op. cit.*, p. 145 ff.

18 P. C. Lloyd 'The traditional political system of the Yoruba' *The Southwestern Journal of Anthropology*, X, 4, Winter, 1954, pp. 366–84; also Lloyd 'Sacred Kingship . . .' *op. cit.*

19 Johnson's list of Alafin would make the present Alafin 43rd; Mr Robert Smith has compiled a list of 45 and in a personal communication with the author writes that in Oyo it is maintained that in all there have been seventy Alafin. See Appendix C.

20 Johnson *op. cit.*, p. 40.

21 S. F. Nadel *A Black Byzantium*, London 1942, Chapter VI and Appendix III. See also note 50 (p. 74) to Robert Smith's 'The Alafin in Exile' *op. cit.* for a discussion of the dating of Tsoede's reign.

22 Personal communication with the author.

23 Since the publication of the first edition of this book a very useful article has appeared on the origin of kingship in Idah by John Boston entitled 'Notes on the Origin of the Igala Kingship' *J.H.S.N.*, II, 3, December 1962.

24 Dennis Williams suggests (see: R. Smith, *op. cit.*, note 50, p. 74) that the famous Nupe bronzes may be of a considerably later date.

25 R. Smith *op. cit.*, for a full account of the sojourn at Igboho.

26 William Bosman *A New and Accurate Description of the Coast of Guinea*, London, 1705, p. 397.

27 See R. E. Bradbury 'Chronological Problems in the Study of Benin History' *J.H.S.N.*, I, 4, 1959, p. 285, where he suggests that Egharevba's date of 1200 for the beginning of the dynasty is too early (Egharevba *op. cit.*, pp. 85–6). If we accept Bradbury's suggested date of 'not later than 1300' for the foundation of the dynasty, then there is a considerable discrepancy between the suggested date for the foundation of Oyo (Morton-Williams between 1390 and 1440) and that of Benin's new dynasty that has to be resolved. Professor A.F.C. Ryder has cast doubt on the supposed Ife origin of the Benin dynasty in an article entitled 'The Ife-Benin relationship' *J.A.H.*, VI, 1, 1965, pp. 25–37.

28 In a paper read to the Department of History, University of Ibadan, seminar on 'Feudalism in Africa', Mr P. Igbafe suggested that though it is not certain when primogeniture was introduced to Benin, it was probably at the beginning of the eighteenth century.

29 R. E. Bradbury 'The Rituals of Divine Kingship in Benin' *Nigeria Magazine*, No. 59, 1959.

30 *Ibid.*

31 For this information I am indebted to Mr P. Igbafe's contribution cited above.

32 The best book available on Benin art is P. J. C. Dark *Benin Art*, London, 1961, with excellent photographs by W. and B. Forman.

33 See Graham Connah 'Archaeological Research in Benin City 1961–1964' *J.H.S.N.*, II, 4, December 1963, pp. 472–3 and map.

Chapter 4. **The Atlantic Slave Trade** (between pages 48 and 58)

1 For the early history of European trade with West Africa see J. W. Blake *European Beginnings in West Africa*, *1454–1578*, London, 1937, which should be read in conjunction with the same author's collection of documents covering this period, *Europeans in West Africa*, London, 1942, 2 vols. See also Bovill *The Golden Trade of the Moors*, pp. 111–20.

2 Ruy de Pina *Chronica del Rey Dom João II*, ch. 24, trans. in J. W. Blake *Europeans in West Africa*, I, 78–9, reprinted in Hodgkin *Nigerian Perspectives*, p. 97.

3 Richard Eden 'The Voyage of M. Thomas Windham to Guinea and the Kingdom of Benin, Anno 1553' in Richard Hakluyt *The Principal Navigations, Voyages, Traffiques and Discoveries of the English Nation*, Glasgow, 1904, vol. VI, p. 149, reprinted in Blake *Europeans in West Africa* II, pp. 314–20.

4 Letter from Duarte Pires to King Manuel of Portugal dated 20th October 1516, trans. in Blake *op. cit.* I, pp. 123–4.
   See also Hodgkin *op. cit.* pp. 99–100.

5 From the account of a 'Voyage from Lisbona to the island of San Tomé south of the Equator, described by a Portuguese pilot and sent to his magnificence Count Rimondo della Torre, gentleman of Verona, and translated from Portuguese into Italian', published in Giovanni Battista Ramusio *Navigazioni e Viaggi*, Venice, 1550. In Blake *op. cit.*, I, pp. 150–1 and Hodgkin *op. cit.*, pp. 100–1.

6 Eden: 'The Voyage of Thomas Windham, etc.' Blake *op. cit.*, I, pp. 148–50.

7 Most authorities agree that 15,000,000 must be treated only as a conservative figure. See Daniel Mannix in collaboration with Malcolm Cowley *Black Cargoes—a History of the Atlantic Slave Trade 1518–1865*, London, 1963, p. 287, and Basil Davidson *Black Mother*, London, 1961, pp. 87–8. The lack of reliable statistics for the trade — some have estimated that as many as 50 million slaves reached the Americas—means that all the figures used here must be treated as very tentative. G. I. Jones in 'European and African Tradition on the Rio Real' *J.A.H.*, IV, 3, 1963, p. 391, has pointed to the danger of uncritical acceptance of contemporary estimates of the extent of the slave trade.

8 For general accounts of the slave trade see: H. A. Wyndham *The Atlantic Slavery*, London, 1935; Elizabeth Donnan *Documents illustrative of the Slave Trade to America*, 4 vols., Washington, 1930–5; Davidson *op. cit.*; Mannix with Cowley *op. cit.*

9 James Welsh *A Voyage to Benin beyond the country of Guinea made by Master James Welsh who set foorth in the yeere 1588*, in Hakluyt *op. cit.*, VI, pp. 456–8.

10 James Barbot *An Abstract of a Voyage to New Calabar River or Rio Real in the year 1699*, trans. and pub. in Churchill *Collection of Voyages and Travels*, 3rd edition, 1744–6, V, p. 459.

11 G. I. Jones 'Native and Trade Currencies in Southern Nigeria during the 18th and 19th Centuries' *Africa*, XXVIII, 1, 1958.

12 Captain Hugh Crow *Memoirs of the late Capt. Hugh Crow*, Liverpool, 1830.

13 Source: personal communication from M. Pierre Verger.

14 I am indebted to M. Pierre Verger for advice on this section. M. Verger has prepared a thesis on the slave trade between Brazil and West Africa. He has, already published material relevant to this topic, notably: 'Nigeria, Brazil and Cuba' in Michael Crowder ed. *Nigeria 1960—A special Independence Issue of Nigeria Magazine*, 1960; and *Bahia and the West Coast Trade 1549–1851*, Ibadan, 1964.

15 Verger 'Nigeria, Brazil and Cuba' *ibid.*, p. 174.

Chapter 5   **The Niger Delta and its Hinterland**
(between pages 59 and 68)

1 I am greatly indebted to Mr Robin Horton for assistance in the preparation of material on the Ijo trading states. Since the publication of the first edition of this book there has appeared a work of major importance for the history of Nigeria which deals with the relationships between the Ijo and peoples of the Eastern hinterland; G. I. Jones *The Trading States of the Oil Rivers*, London, 1963. Where necessary I have revised or added to the text in the light of Jones's work.

2 E. J. Alagoa *The Small Brave City State: A History of Brass-Nembe in the Niger Delta*, Ibadan and Wisconsin, 1964, p. 57.

3 There is a very little primary source material for the history of Igboland before the nineteenth century. Some impressions of eighteenth-century Igboland may however be gained from *The Interesting Narrative of the Life of Olaudah Equiano, or Gustavus Vassa, the African, written by himself*, London, 1879, and cited in Thomas Hodgkin's *Nigerian Perspectives*, pp. 155–66. It appears however to refer to a Western Igbo society.

4 See C. Thurstan Shaw 'Research Note: Bronzes from Eastern Nigeria—Excavations at Igbo Ukwu' *J.H.S.N.*, II, 1, December 1960, pp. 162–5.

5 Personal communication with the author.

6 The pattern of trading in the hinterland was also altered by the demands of the slave trade. Where there had been no political organization that could offer security of trade throughout the hinterland prior to the slave trade, an oracular cult was founded in Aro Chukwu whose priests were able to use its authority throughout Igboland in order to conduct trade. See S. J. Ottenberg 'Ibo Oracles and Inter-group Relations' *Southwestern Journal of Anthropology*, XIV, 3, Autumn 1958, pp. 295–314.

7 G. I. Jones *op. cit.*, p. 177. 'The Kalabari, Bonny and Okrika people maintain that *amanyanabo* should be used to designate only the office of "king", that is, the chieftaincy of a community which was vested in a single dynasty. They contrast the office of the king with the former office of the village head, called *amadabo* by the Okrika which it replaced.' The *amanyanabo* are of course the kings of contemporary European visitors' reports.

8 Jones *ibid.*

9 P. C. Lloyd 'The Itsekiri Kingdom in the Nineteenth Century; an Outline Social History' *J.A.H.*, IV, 2, 1963, p. 217 writes, 'Itsekiri social structure differed rather markedly from that of the Ijoh towns of Brass, Bonny and Opobo; the term "house" was very little used.'

10 Daryll Forde ed. *Efik Traders of Old Calabar*, London, 1956, p. 141. Chapter by G. I. Jones on 'The Political Organization of Old Calabar', pp. 116–57.

11 Barbot *op. cit.*, V, p. 459.

12 Jones *op. cit.*, pp. 88–101.

13 Ottenberg *op. cit.*, also Jones *op. cit.*, various references. At present relatively little is known about the history of the Aro. However, Dr K. O. Diké, with Miss Felicia Ekejiuba, has been conducting research on the Aro trading settlements in eastern Nigeria.

14 Olfert Dapper *Descriptions de l'Afrique*, Amsterdam, 1686, cited in Hodgkin *op. cit.*, p. 127.

15 From a letter from David van Nyendael to William Bosman in 1702, published in William Bosman *A New and Accurate Description of the Coast of Guinea*, London, 1907 ed., p. 461. For a useful critical discussion of the whole

question of Benin's supposed decline in the eighteenth century see James D.
Graham 'The Slave Trade, Depopulation and Human Sacrifice in Benin
History: The General Approach' *Cahiers d'Etudes Africaines*, V, 2, 18, 1965,
pp. 317–34.

16 John Adams *Sketches taken during ten voyages to Africa between the years
1786 and 1800*, Liverpool, n.d., p. 32.

17 Olfert Dapper *op. cit.*, pp. 314–15, cited in Hodgkin *op. cit.*, pp. 130–1.

18 See P. C. Lloyd and A. F. C. Ryder 'Don Domingos, Prince of Warri', *Odu*, 4,
1957.

19 Father Jerome Merolla da Sorrento *A Voyage to the Congo and several other
countries in Southern Africk in the year 1682* cited in Hodgkin *op. cit.*, pp.
138–40.

20 Lloyd 'The Itsekiri . . .' *op. cit.*, p. 210.

21 John Adams *op. cit.*, p. 38. G. I. Jones has warned against the uncritical
acceptance of Adams's estimates 'European and African Tradition . . .' *op.
cit.*, p. 391.

22 W. R. G. Horton 'The Ohu system of slavery in a northern Ibo village-group'
Africa, XXIV, 4, October 1954, pp. 311–36.

Chapter 6   The Holy War of Usman dan Fodio (1804–30)
(between pages 69 and 83)

1 K. Krieger *Geschichte von Zamfara*, Berlin, 1959.

2 Bovill *op. cit.*, pp. 224–5.

3 Thus, in Usman dan Fodio's *Wathiqat ahl al-Sudan*, which may well have
been the proclamation of war in the Jihad, it is declared in paragraph xiv:
'And that to make war against the king who is an apostate—who has not
abandoned the religion of Islam so far as the professing of it is concerned, and
who mingles the observances of Islam with the observances of heathendom,
like the kings of Hausaland for the most part—is obligatory by assent, and
that to take the government from him by assent.' See A. D. H. Bivar 'Wathiqat ahl al-Sudan: Manifesto of the Fulani Jihad' *J.A.H.*, II, 2, 1961, pp.
235–43.

4 A full and excellent discussion of the Fulani Jihads is to be found in H. F. C.
Smith 'A Neglected Theme in West African History: the Islamic Revolutions
of the 19th Century' *J.H.S.N.*, II, 2, 1961. For general background studies of
the Fulani see Derek Stenning *Savannah Nomads*, London 1959, which
deals with the Wodaabe of Western Borno; and Edward Hopen *The Pastoral
Fulbe Family in Gwandu*, London, 1958. D. J. Stenning 'Transhumance,
Migratory Drift, Migration: Patterns of Pastoral Fulani Nomadism' *J. R.
Anthrop. Inst.*, 87, 1957, pp. 57–73. Further works dealing specifically with
the Jihad of Usman dan Fodio are: E. J. Arnett *The Rise of the Sokoto Fulani*
(paraphrase of *Infaku'l Maisur* of Sultan Bello Muhammad), Kano, 1922.
S. J. Hogben *The Muhammadan Emirates of Nigeria*, London, 1930. J.
Spencer Trimingham *A History of Islam in West Africa*, London, 1962.
Articles in journals are cited in subsequent footnotes.

The main problem confronting the historian of the Jihad is the lack of
information about the attitudes of the conquered peoples to the Fulani. No
Hausa records of the Jihad appear to have survived, whilst much of the
material written by the Fulani on which we now have to rely for want of an
alternative source is in the nature of war propaganda.

5 A. H. M. Kirk-Greene *Adamawa, Past and Present*, London, 1958, p. 153.

6 See Thomas Hodgkin "Uthman dan Fodio' in Michael Crowder (ed.) *Nigeria 1960—a special Independence Issue of Nigeria Magazine*, pp. 129–36. Also for a detailed account of his early life F. H. El Masri 'The Life of Shehu Usuman dan Fodio before the Jihad' *J.H.S.N.*, II, 4, December 1963, pp. 435–48.

7 H. F. C. Smith 'Muhammad Bello, Amir Al-mu'minin', *Ibadan*, 9, June 1960, p. 16.

8 M. Hiskett 'Material relating to the state of learning among the Fulani before their Jihad' *Bulletin of the School of Oriental and African Studies*, XIX 3, 1957.

9 M. G. Smith and M. Muntaka Kumasi *An Account of the Obligations of Withdrawal; being a translation of the 'Bayan Wujub al Hirja allal Ibad' of Shehu Usumanu dan Fodio*, 1959, unpublished, Part I, where Usman dan Fodio writes: '. . . but the countries of Bornu, Kano, Katsina, Songhai, and Malle, as Ahmed Baba shows . . . all these are heathen states without any doubt, since the chiefs . . . are heathen . . . although they practise the religion of Islam, because they are polytheists also. They have obstructed the way of Islam and have put worldly standards before the Faith. In the view of all the 'ulama all this is simply heathen.' See also Usman dan Fodio *Tanbih al-Ikhwan* and also Muhammad Bello *Infaq al Maysur*. The above references are taken from M. G. Smith's 'The Jihad of Shehu dan Fodio—Some Problems', a paper presented to the International African Institute Seminar on *Islam in Tropical Africa* held at Zaria, December 1963.

10 M. Hiskett 'Kitab al-Farq' *Bulletin of the School of Oriental and African Studies*, XXII, 3, 1960.

11 M. G. Smith and M. Muntaka Kumasi *op. cit.*, Section 13, cited from M. G. Smith 'The Jihad of Shehu dan Fodio' *op. cit.*

12 For an explanation of the significance of the Sunna see Reuben Levy *The Social Structure of Islam* (2nd edition), London, 1962, pp. 170–1.

13 H. R. Palmer 'An Early Fulani Conception of Islam' *J. Afr. Soc.*, XIII, 1914, pp. 407–14 and XIV, 1914, pp. 53–9, and XV, 1915, pp. 185–92, being a translation of Usman dan Fodio's *Tanbih al-Ikhwan* (The Admonition of the Brethren).

14 Hodgkin "Uthman dan Fodio' *op. cit.*, pp. 131–2.

15 Hiskett 'Material Relating to . . . the Jihad' *op. cit.*

16 See Trimingham *op. cit.*, in particular p. 200. Another argument brought forward by critics of the Jihad in support of their interpretation that it was largely racial in character is the fact that the Habe Hausa rulers were all replaced by Fulanis. However, H. F. C. Smith has shown that in the one case where a Habe ruler, Isiaka Jatau, Sarkin Zazzau, responded to the call of Usman dan Fodio for religious reform, he was allowed to keep his throne and reigned as first Emir of Zaria. 'The Dynastic Chronology of Fulani Zaria' *J.H.S.N.*, II, 2, December 1961, pp. 279–80.

17 This correspondence is printed in Hodgkin *Nigerian Perspectives*, pp. 198–205.

18 Nana, daughter of Usman dan Fodio, was to write:

> *Yunfa fled from bare-legged herdsmen.*
> *Who had neither mail nor horseman.*
> *We that had been chased like hares*
> *Can now live in houses.*

see F. Daniel 'Shehu dan Fodio' *J. Afr. Soc.*, XXV, 1926, p. 281.

19 Arnett *op. cit.*, p. 71.

20 F. W. de St. Croix *The Fulani of Northern Nigeria*, Lagos, 1945, p. 2.

21 H. F. C. Smith *op. cit.*

22 Alhaji Hassan and Mallam Shu'aibu Na'ibi *A Chronicle of Abuja op. cit.*, p. 4.
    There is no reference to the reign of Isiaka Jatau in the Chronicle, which records that the Shehu's forces 'fell upon the King of Zazzau, Muhammadu Makau on Saturday the tenth day of the month of Zulhaji in the year 1804 whilst he was at the prayer-ground of Idi outside the town' (p. 4). This would suggest that M. Makau was a true Muslim, which if it were so, would bring into question the legitimacy of the Jihad, since it was only lawful to attack those rulers who were by Koranic definition 'pagan'.

23 H. F. C. Smith *op. cit.*, p. 280.

24 Urvoy *op. cit.*, p. 103.

25 D. Denham, H. Clapperton, and W. Oudney *Narrative of Travels and Discoveries in Northern and Central Africa in the years 1822, 1823 and 1824*, London, 1826, cited in Hodgkin *Nigerian Perspectives*, pp. 205–8.

26 *Ibid.*, pp. 214–15, 244. There is an eye-witness account by Major Dixon Denham of the decisive defeat of the Bagirmi army by Borno in 1824. However, the year before Bagirmi had actually invaded Borno.

27 Isiaka Jatau, first Emir of Zaria, was not of course a flag-bearer. Nor was the Habe ruler of Daura who became a Muslim and accepted the authority of Sokoto. Yakubu is described as non-Fulani in Hogben *op. cit.*, p. 172; but Kirk-Greene *op. cit.*, p. 154 says that the Yakubu was a brother of Buba Yero of Gombe who was definitely Fulani!

28 For the Jihad in Adamawa Province see Kirk-Greene *op. cit.*

29 For the Jihad in Nupe see Hogben *op. cit.* and Nadel *op. cit.*

30 For the Jihad in Ilorin see H. B. Herman-Hodge *Gazetteer of Ilorin Province*, London, 1929, Hogben *op. cit.*, Johnson *op. cit.*

31 I have revised my earlier account of the Jihad in Ilorin in the light of J. F. Ade Ajayi's introduction to 'The Narrative of Samuel Ajayi Crowther' in a collection of African travellers' reports edited by Philip Curtin, *Africa Remembered*, Ibadan and Wisconsin 1969. See also B. G. Martin 'A new Arabic History of Ilorin' *Research Bulletin*, Institute of African Studies, University of Ibadan, Centre of Arabic Documentation, I, 2, January 1965, pp. 20–7.

32 Ajayi *ibid.*

33 Al-Hajj Sa'id *History of Sokoto* trans. C. E. J. Whitting, Kano, 1949, p. 37.
    W. E. N. Kensdale 'Field Notes on the Arabic Literature of the Western Sudan' *J. R. Asiatic Soc.*, 1955, 1956 and 1958 lists 83 works by Usman dan Fodio, 75 by Abdullahi dan Fodio, and 93 by Muhammad Bello.

34 Cited in Hodgkin *Nigerian Perspectives*, pp. 194–5.

Chapter 7   Yoruba Civil Wars (between pages 84 and 97)

1 Sir Alan Burns *History of Nigeria*, London, 1958, 5th edition, p. 26.

2 Personal communication from Mr Peter Morton-Williams.

3 I am indebted to Dr Akin Mabogunje for his advice on the construction of this map.

4 Lloyd 'The traditional political system of the Yoruba' *op. cit.*, pp. 366–84.

5 Ajayi and Smith *op. cit.*, p. 4.

6 Bosman *op. cit.*, pp. 397–8.

7 Archibald Dalzell *History of Dahomey an Inland Kingdom of Africa*, London, 1800, p. 15.

8 For an interesting discussion of the reasons behind Dahomey's conquest of these coastal states see 'Agaja and the conquest of the coastal Aja states' *J.H.S.N.*, II, 4, 1963, pp. 545–66.

9 R. Smith 'The Alafin in Exile' *op. cit.*, p. 73, citing I. A. Akinjogbin's Ph.D. thesis *Dahomey and its Neighbours 1708–1818*.

10 Dalzell *op. cit.*, p. 157.

11 Johnson *op. cit.*, p. 188.

12 I. A. Akinjogbin 'The Prelude to the Yoruba Civil Wars' *Odu*, new series, no. 2, p. 197.

13 Biobaku *op. cit.*, pp. 8–10.

14 Private communication with Mr Peter Morton-Williams.

15 Akinjogbin 'Prelude' *op. cit.* All subsequent references to Akinjogbin in this chapter are to this particular paper.

16 J. D. Fage *Introduction to the History of West Africa*, London, 1955, p. 91.

17 Ajayi and Smith *op. cit.*, p. 124.

18 The stress on the constitutional importance of the Oni of Ife is one of the more important points in Akinjogbin's paper *op. cit.*

19 Johnson *op. cit.*, p. 192.

20 See J. F. Ade Ajayi's introduction to 'The Narrative of Samuel Ajayi Crowther' *op. cit.*

21 Johnson *op. cit.*, pp. 206–7.

22 Johnson *op. cit.*, p. 189, Ajayi *op. cit.*

23 The date for the fall of Owu is usually given as *c.* 1825. However, Omer-Cooper has suggested that 1827 would be more accurate. See Robert Smith 'Ijaiye, the Western Palatinate of the Yoruba' *J.H.S.N.*, II, 3, December 1962, p. 331. It is now thought to have been around 1820.

24 Johnson *op. cit.*, p. 196.

25 C. W. Newbury *The Western Slave Coast and its Rulers*, Oxford 1961, p. 38.

26 R. Smith 'Ijaiye' *op. cit.*, p. 52.

27 Willett 'Investigations at Old Oyo' *op. cit.*

28 Ajayi and Smith *op. cit.*, p. 29.

29 See: Edouard Dunglas 'La première attaque des Dahoméennes contre Abeokuta' *Etudes Dahoméennes*, I, 1949, I.F.A.N. See also *Nigeria Magazine*, No. 64, March 1960 where extracts on this paper by Dunglas appear in English. Smith has a most useful analysis of the strategy of the battle of Abeokuta in Ajayi and Smith *op. cit.*, pp. 37–9. I have made a number of changes to the text in the light of Smith's account.

Chapter 8 · The Suppression of the Slave Trade
(between pages 98 and 105)

1 For detailed studies of the movement in Britain for the abolition of the slave trade see: Thomas J. Clarkson *History of the Rise, Progress and Accomplishment of the Abolition of the African Slave Trade*, 2 vols., London, 1808; Sir Reginald Coupland *The British Anti-Slavery Movement*, London, 1933.

2 Eric Williams *Capitalism and Slavery*, London, 1964.

3 A. Falconbridge *An Account of the Slave Trade on the Coast of Africa*, London, 1788. Among other important abolitionist works were: T. Clarkson *Essay on the Slavery and Commerce of the Human Species*, 1788; and J. Newton *Thoughts upon the African Slave Trade* (pamphlet), London, 1788.

4 See Diké *Trade and Politics in the Niger Delta*, pp. 11–14.
5 *Captain Canot, or Twenty Years of an African Slaver* ed. by Brantz Meyer, New York, 1854.
6 Lecky *History of England*.
7 The slave trade only became legal for Spaniards in 1789.
8 See Christopher Lloyd *The Navy and the Slave Trade*, London, 1949, on which I have relied heavily in this chapter. Also Mannix with Cowley *op. cit.*, Chapter 9, pp. 191–215; Sir Alan Burns *op cit.*; *Report of the House of Commons Select Committee on the Slave Trade*, London, 1842; C. W. Newbury *The Western Slave Coast and its Rulers*, Oxford, 1961, Chapter II, pp. 35–48.
9 Source not traced.
10 H. Crow *Memoirs*, London, 1830, p. 137.
11 Cited by Diké *op. cit.*, p. 48.
12 *Ibid.*, p. 67.
13 Burns *op. cit.*, p. 104; Diké *op. cit.*, p. 48.
14 Diké *op. cit.*, p. 53.
15 W. F. W. Owen *Narrative of a Voyage to Explore the Shores of Africa, Arabia and Madagascar*, New York, 1833.
16 Reprinted in Jones *op. cit.* Appendix B, pp. 221–2.
17 Cited in Christopher Lloyd *op. cit.*
18 See: E. J. Alagoa *op. cit.*, pp. 57–8.
19 Source not traced.

Chapter 9   **Explorers and Missionaries** (between pages 106 and 119)

1 See Appendix 'Mortality in West Africa' to Philip D. Curtin *The Image of Africa*, Wisconsin, 1964, pp. 483–7.
2 A. Adu Boahen *Britain, the Sahara and the Western Sudan 1788–1861*, London, 1964, Chapter I, pp. 1–28.
3 *Ibid.*, p. 3.
4 The Proceedings of the African Association have recently been published in a new edition by Robin Hallett ed.: *The Records of the African Association, 1788–1831*, London, 1964.
5 Boahen *op. cit.*, p. 12, shows that whilst the Niger problem was of great concern to the Association 'its solution was not, as is generally supposed, the first concern of the Association'.
6 Leo Africanus *op. cit.*, I, pp. 124–5, but see also III, p. 1096, for a more accurate translation of this vital passage.
7 *Travels of Mungo Park* ed. Ronald Miller, London, 1954, pp. 78–9.
8 *The Proceedings of the Association for Promoting the Discovery of the Interior Parts of Africa*, London, 1790.
9 Miller *op. cit.*, 149.
10 'Abstract of Mr. Park's account of his travels and discoveries abridged . . . by B. Edwards . . . also geographical illustrations of Mr. Park's journeys . . . by Major Rennell.' *Proceedings op. cit.*
11 Burns *op. cit.*, p. 78.
12 *Proceedings op. cit.*
13 Miller *op. cit.*, pp. 281–364. See also 'The Death of Mungo Park' *Nigeria Magazine*, No. 71, 1961.

14 James MacQueen *A Geographical and Commercial View of Northern Central Africa*, Edinburgh, 1821.

15 Denham, Clapperton and Oudney *op. cit.*, cited in Hodgkin *Nigerian Perspectives*, p. 211.

16 A. H. M. Kirk-Greene has a useful note in *Man*, nos. 219 and 220, November1963, on 'Some spears from Bornu, Northern Nigeria' which gives an idea of the weapons used by armies in Northern Nigeria at that period.

17 Denham, Clapperton and Oudney *op. cit.*, 'Captain Clapperton's Narrative', pp. 51–3, cited in Hodgkin *Nigerian Perspectives*, pp. 215–17.

18 *Ibid.*

19 H. Clapperton *Journal of a Second Expedition into the Interior of Africa from the Bight of Benin to Soccattoo*, London, 1829, pp. 196–8.

20 Richard and John Lander *Journals of an Expedition to Explore the Course and Termination of the Niger*, London, 1832.

21 Macgregor Laird and R. A. K. Oldfield *Narrative of an Expedition into the Interior of Africa*, 2 vols., London, 1837.

22 Sir Thomas Fowell Buxton *The African Slave Trade and its Remedy*, London, 1839. See also J. Gallagher 'Fowell Buxton and the New African Policy 1832–1842' *Cambridge Historical Journal*, X, 1, 1950, and C. C. Ifemesia 'The "Civilising" Mission of 1841: Aspects of an Episode in Anglo-Nigerian Relations', *J.H.S.N.*, II, 3, 1962, pp. 291–310.

23 Eugene Stock ed. *The History of the Church Missionary Society*, London, 1899, vol. I, p. 45, cited in James Coleman *Nigeria: Background to Nationalism*, 1958, p. 91.

24 Henri Brunschwig *L'Avènement de l'Afrique* Paris, 1964, p. 70; see also W. Simpson *A Private Journal kept during the Niger Expedition 1841–2 from May, 1841 to June, 1842*, London, 1843.

25 Robert Jamieson *An Appeal to the Government and People of Great Britain Against the Proposed Niger Expedition*, London, 1840.

26 J. F. Schön and S. A. Crowther *Journals of . . . the expedition up the Niger in 1841*, London, 1842. Also Simpson *op. cit.*

27 The best account of Crowther's role in the evangelization of Nigeria is contained in J. F. Ade Ajayi's thesis *Christian Missions and the Making of Nigeria* on which I have relied heavily for material for the second half of this chapter. This thesis has been published as *Christian Missions in Nigeria 1841–1891: The Making of an Educated Elite*, London, 1965.

28 In the first edition of this book the expedition was described conventionally as a 'disastrous' failure—see for instance J. D. Hargreaves *Prelude to the Partition of West Africa*, London, 1963, who also takes this position. However, subsequent to publication of the first edition there has appeared the important article by C. C. Ifemesia, cited above, in which he shows 'how near to success the expedition was at the time and how it set the pattern for subsequent ventures which eventually led to the British occupation of the entire country [Nigeria] at the turn of the twentieth century'.

29 J. F. Ade Ajayi 'Henry Venn and the Policy of Development' *J.H.S.N.*, I, 4, 1959.

30 Ifemesia *op. cit.*, p. 310.

31 J. F. Ade Ajayi 'The British Occupation of Lagos 1851–1861' *Nigeria Magazine* 69, August 1961, pp. 96–105.

32 Anna Hinderer *Seventeen Years in the Yoruba Country*, London, 1873.

33 Ajayi *Missions op. cit.*

34 Donald M. Macfarlane *Calabar and the Church of Scotland Mission*,

1846–1946, London, 1946; and Rev. Hugh Goldie *Calabar and its Mission*, London, 1890.

35 See K. Onwuka Diké *Origins of the Niger Mission 1841–1891*, Lagos, 1957; also S. A. Crowther and J. C. Taylor *The Gospel on the Banks of the Niger, Journals and notices of the native missionaries accompanying the Niger Expedition of 1857–9*, London, 1859; and S. A. Crowther, *Journal of an Expedition up the Niger and the Tshadda Rivers . . . in 1854*, London, 1855.

36 J. D. Hargreaves *op. cit.*, p. 4 and Boahen *op. cit.*, pp. 181–215, where there is a full discussion of the origins and achievements of the Central African Mission and its influence in the 1854 Mission.

37 Heinrich Barth *Travels and Discoveries in Northern and Central Africa*, 5 vols., London, 1857–8. A useful anthology of Barth's writings on Northern Nigeria is A. H. M. Kirk-Greene's *Barth's Travels in Northern Nigeria*, London, 1962.

38 Boahen *op. cit.*, p. 213.

39 W. B. Baikie *Narrative of an Exploring Voyage up the Rivers Kw'ora and Binue (commonly known as the Niger and Tshadda) in 1854*, London, 1856; also Michael Crowder 'Pioneer of the Niger—W. B. Baikie' *West African Review*, XXVI, 339, December 1955, pp. 1157–61.

40 The much discussed *Africa and the Victorians* by Ronald Robinson and John Gallagher with Alice Denny, London, 1961, which was published after the first edition of this book went to press, has a most useful chapter on 'The Spirit of Victorian Expansion', pp. 1–25, which gives a full account of the attitudes of the society from which these missionaries came to the outside world and Britain's role in it.

Chapter 10 **The Growth of Legitimate Trade**
(between pages 120 and 138)

1 This paragraph has been revised in view of the arguments of Robinson and Gallagher *op. cit.* See pp. 29–30 for particular reference to the Parliamentary Select Committee.

2 Diké *Trade and Politics in the Niger Delta*, p. 101.

3 R. Smith 'Ijaiye, the Western Palatinate of the Yoruba' *op. cit.*, p. 332.
      W. D. McIntyre in 'Commander Glover and the Colony of Lagos, 1861–73' *J.A.H.*, IV, 1, 1963 cites a passage from a Colonial Office minute which brings out the paradoxical position of the humanitarian very nicely: '. . . by encouraging legitimate commerce we may turn serfdom with its loose intermittent obligations, into that unrelenting methodised slavery which is inflicted by a master who sees his way to making a profit of every hour of his slaves' labour.' (Minute by Rogers, 14, XII, 1863, on Glover to Newcastle, 10, xi, 1863, C.O. 147/4.)

4 Diké *op. cit.*, p. 100–1.

5 G. I. Jones 'Native and Trade Currencies in Southern Nigeria during the 18th and 19th Centuries' *Africa* XXVIII, 1, 1958. See also A. H. M. Kirk-Greene 'The Major Currencies in Nigerian History' *J.H.S.N.*, II, 1, December 1960.

6 K. Onwuka Diké 'John Beecroft 1790–1854: Her Britannic Majesty's Consul to the Bights of Benin and Biafra 1849–54' *J.H.S.N.*, I, 1, December 1956, pp. 5–14.

7 *Ibid.*, p. 14.

8 For Beecroft's role in Bonny affairs I have relied heavily on Diké *Trade and Politics in the Niger Delta.*, Chapter VII.

9 Jones *Trading States op. cit.*, p. 14.

10 The text of this treaty is printed in Jones *ibid.*, Appendix B, pp. 222–5.

11 J. F. Ade Ajayi 'The British Occupation of Lagos 1851-61' *op. cit.* refutes this view.

12 Ajayi *Missions op. cit.*, p. 38.

13 Cited in Ajayi 'British Occupation of Lagos' *op. cit.*

14 Diké *op. cit.*, pp. 137–43. I have modified my original account, based on Diké, in view of Jones *Trading States op. cit.*, pp. 116–20.

15 See Jones *ibid.*, p. 119, where he shows that whilst most of the chiefs of Bonny were against Pepple, they hesitated to have him deported on three grounds: 'What was to happen about the king's debts? What would be the reaction of the Imo river oil markets? Was the deportation of a native of Bonny contrary to their customs and forbidden by their religion?'

16 *Ibid.*, pp. 119–20.

17 T. J. Hutchinson *Ten Years Wandering among the Ethiopians*, London, 1861, pp. 173–8.

18 See Baikie *op. cit.*

19 Diké *op. cit.*, p. 170.

20 Howard Pedrarza *The Story of Lokoja—the first British Settlement in Nigeria*, London, 1960.

21 Cited by Pedrarza *ibid.*, p. 55.

22 Diké *Origins of the Niger Mission, 1841–1891*, Lagos, 1957, pp. 10–11. See also S. Crowther and J. C. Taylor *The Gospel on the Banks of the Niger*, London, 1859.

23 The Crowther-Townsend dispute is given detailed treatment in Ajayi *Missions op. cit.*

For an interesting study of the forward-looking ideas of Venn on a large number of subjects relating to the European role in Africa see J. F. Ade Ajayi's 'Henry Venn and the Policy of Development' *op. cit.*

24 Biobaku *op. cit.*, p. 53.

25 I have revised my account of the causes and course of the Ijaye war in the light of Ajayi and Smith *op. cit.*, pp. 76–80, and Smith '*Ijaiye*' *op. cit.*, p. 340. The original version was based on Johnson's account in *History of the Yorubas op. cit.*, pp. 331–54.

26 For a detailed account of the course of the war see Ajayi and Smith *ibid.*, pp. 86–122.

27 Biobaku *op. cit.*, pp. 104–5.

In preparation for the secondment of this force to the Egba, a Captain A. T. Jones of the 2nd West India Regiment was sent to Abeokuta where he made a report on the military situation in that area, which is published as an appendix in Ajayi and Smith *op. cit.*, entitled 'Captain Jones's Report on the Egba Army in 1861', pp. 129–40.

28 Cited in Biobaku *op. cit.*, p. 68.

29 Burns *op. cit.*, p. 126.

30 Since the first edition of this book was published a very useful article on Glover has appeared. See W. D. McIntyre 'Commander Glover and ... Lagos' *op. cit.*

31 Ajayi *Missions op. cit.*, p. 201.

32 Biobaku *op. cit.*, p. 77.

Chapter 11   **Prelude to Alien Rule** (between pages 139 and 151)

1 I have relied heavily on Biobaku *op. cit.*, pp. 73–95 for my account of Glover's activities in Lagos and Yorubaland. See also McIntyre *op. cit.* Glover's wife wrote a full-length biography of her husband: Lady Glover *Life of Sir John Hawley Glover*, London, 1897.

2 Biobaku *op. cit.*, pp. 79–80.

3 *Ibid.*, Map No. 4. 'A Sketch showing Trade Routes to the Interior from Lagos' reproduced from Commander Glover's coloured plan in C.O. 147/21, 1872.

4 *Ibid.*, p. 95.

5 Johnson *op. cit.*, p. 416.

6 Notes as to source mislaid.

7 There is a full account of the early career of Jaja and his rise to power in Bonny in Diké *Trade and Politics op. cit.*, pp. 182–202. See also G. I. Jones *Trading States op. cit.*, pp. 127–32.

8 Jones *ibid.* suggests this date from a letter from Consul Richard Burton to the Foreign Office, p. 128.

9 *Ibid.*, pp. 128–9.

10 Cited in Diké *Trade and Politics op. cit.*, p. 194. F.O. 84/1326, No. 27, Granville to Livingstone, 3 Aug. 1870.

11 P. C. Lloyd 'The Itsekiri' *op. cit.*, pp. 212–23.

12 *Ibid.*, p. 224.

13 See Pedrarza *op. cit.*, pp. 67–74, also Burns *op.cit.*, p. 139.

14 Diké *Niger Mission op. cit.*, pp. 16–18.

15 Macfarlane *op. cit.*

16 See J. E. Flint *Sir George Goldie and the Making of Nigeria*, London, 1960, for a study of Goldie's career in Nigeria and for an excellent account of British policy in the Niger region. Unfortunately Goldie made it impossible for anyone to write a full-scale biography of him for he had a passionate hatred of any publicity about himself. However, something of the complexity of his character emerges in the pages of the book and also in Lady Dorothy Wellesley's impressionistic *Sir George Goldie—Founder of Nigeria*, London, 1934.

17 He was, however, not the first Englishman in Nigeria to have made this appreciation, for Baikie and Glover had both expressed concern over French ambitions to the Foreign Office as early as 1859. See McIntyre *op. cit.*, pp. 59–60.

18 *London Gazette*, 5th June 1885. See Burns *op. cit.*, p. 145.

Chapter 12   **Company and Consuls** (between pages 152 and 170)

1 The principal clauses of the Charter are reproduced in Burns *op. cit.*, pp. 152–3.

2 For the history of the Royal Niger Company's activities I have relied heavily on Flint *op. cit.* Also see A. N. Cook *British Enterprise in Nigeria*, 1943, Chapter III, pp. 79–114, and Burns *op. cit.*, Chapter XIII, pp. 151–64.

3 Burns *ibid.*, pp. 157–8.

4 Mary Kingsley *West African Studies*, London, 2nd edn. 1901, p. 308.

5 Cited in Wellesley *op. cit.*, p. 21.

6 See J. Lombard 'Un système politique traditionnel de type féodal: les Bariba

du Nord-Dahomey *Bulletin de l'I.F.A.N.*, XIX, sér. B, Nos, 3–4, 1957, pp. 464–506; and Michael Crowder *Revolt in Bussa*, London, 1973, Chapter I.

7 See *The Diaries of Lord Lugard, Vol. IV, Nigeria, 1894–5 and 1898* ed. Margery Perham and Mary Bull, London, 1963. Extracts of the diary are published in Herman-Hodge *Gazetteer of Ilorin Province op. cit.* There is a full account of the race to Nikki in the first volume of Margery Perham's biography of Lugard, *Lugard: The Years of Adventure 1855–1898*, London, 1956.

8 *Diaries of Lord Lugard*, IV, p. 143.

9 Perham *Lugard op. cit.* I, p. 537.

10 Cited in Cook *op. cit.*, p. 61.

11 The full text of the letter is reproduced in *Burns op. cit.*, p. 149.

12 The full text of this treaty is reproduced in *ibid.*, Appendix J, pp. 326–8.

13 Cook *op. cit.*, p. 66.

14 P. C. Lloyd 'The Itsekiri' *op. cit.*, p. 229.

15 Cook *op. cit.*, p. 72.

16 Flint *op. cit.*, Chapter 7, pp. 129–55, has a full account of Macdonald's investigation.

17 *Ibid.*, Chapter 9, pp. 187–215 has a full account of the war between Brass and the R.N.C.

18 Edun Akenzua 'The British Occupation of Benin' *Nigeria Magazine*, No. 59, 1960. See also James D. Graham 'The Slave Trade . . . in Benin History' *op. cit.*

19 H. Ling Roth *Great Benin—Its Customs, Art and Horrors*, Halifax, 1903. See also Alan Boisragon *The Benin Massacre*, London, 1897 and R. H. Bacon *Benin, the City of Blood*, London, 1897.

20 Cited in Johnson *op. cit.*, p. 547.

21 *Ibid.*, p. 593.

22 *Ibid.*, pp. 613–14.

23 *Ibid.*, p. 623.

24 *Ibid.*, p. 632.

Chapter 13   **Emirs and Maxims** (between pages 171 and 187)

1 Cited in Burns *op. cit.*, p. 162–3 from *Papers relating to the Surrender of the Charter of the Royal Niger Company, 1899* (C. 9372).

2 Wellesley *op. cit.*, pp. 98–9.

3 Perham *Lugard op. cit.*, II, p. 27.

4 See for example Lady Lugard *A Tropical Dependency*, London, 1905, in particular Chapter 43, pp. 399–407.

5 Cited by Burns *op. cit.*, p. 177, no source given.

6 *Annual Report for Northern Nigeria*, 1902, p. 43.

7 J. A. Burdon 'The Fulani Emirates of Northern Nigeria' *J. Roy. Geo. Soc.*, VI, December 1904, pp. 636–51.

8 *Ibid.*, p. 649.

9 Hiskett 'Kitab al-Farq' *op. cit.*

10 D. M. Last in a paper entitled 'Notes on a Muslim Caliphate, with special reference to Sokoto' presented to the Seminar on Feudalism in the Department of History, University of Ibadan, 26th October 1963.

11 Al-Hajj Sa'id *op. cit.*, p. 11.

12 For an excellent short biographical study of Sultan Bello, see H. F. C. Smith 'Muhammad Bello, Amir Al-mu'minin', *Ibadan*, 9, June 1960.

13 H. Clapperton *Journal of a Second Expedition into the Interior of Africa etc.*, London, 1829, pp. 196–8.

14 For instance Lady Lugard *op. cit.*, Trimingham *op. cit.*, p. 205 where he writes, ''Atīq (Bello's successor) a rigid puritan, attempted some reforms, but the religious enthusiasm of the Fulbe had ebbed, for only 'Uthmān and a few of his original followers were moved by genuine religious conviction. The fruits of power sapped the vital energies that had brought such success and the *jihād* degenerated into undisguised slave-raiding which, together with perpetual wars, ruined and depopulated vast areas. During the reign of 'Alī (1842–59) power passed completely into the hands of the provincial governors whose number 'Alī had increased, and as independent rulers they recognised only the religious authority of the ruler of Sokoto.' See also Lugard's *Reports on Northern Nigeria* for 1900, 1901, 1902.

15 Boahen *op. cit.*, Appendix IV, 'Political Conditions in the Western Sudan in the First Half of the Nineteenth Century', pp. 219–47.

16 M. G. Smith *Government in Zazzau* London 1960, pp. 163–6.

17 A. H. M. Kirk-Greene *Adamawa, Past and Present op. cit.*; pp. 125–65.

18 M. G. Smith *op. cit.*, pp. 159–64.

19 Barth *op. cit.* (New York, 1857 edition), III, p. 81.

20 *Ibid.*, II, pp. 186–7.

21 Kirk-Greene *op. cit.*, p. 140.

22 Boahen *op. cit.*, p. 241 (F.O. 101/34, Barth to F.O., 28, January 1853).

23 Barth *op. cit.*, I, pp. 510–15.

24 Kirk-Greene *op. cit.*, pp. 139–40.

25 Mary Smith *Baba of Karo*, London, 1954.

26 Cook *op. cit.*, p. 155. The 1885 Treaty between the Sultan of Sokoto (Umaru, 1881–91) and Joseph Thompson, on behalf of the National African Company is reproduced in Burns *op. cit.*, Appendix G, pp. 322–3.

27 For Lugard's conquest of Northern Nigeria I have relied mainly on Perham *Lugard op. cit.*, I, C. W. J. Orr *The Making of Northern Nigeria*, London, 1911, and Lugard's own Annual Reports.

28 Lugard *The Dual Mandate in Tropical Africa*, London, 1923. See also Perham *Lugard op. cit.*, II, pp. 138–73.

29 *Annual Report for Northern Nigeria 1901*. Report for period January 1901–March 1901, p. 15.

30 Cited in Perham *Lugard op. cit.*, II, p. 45.

31 See *Annual Report for Northern Nigeria 1901*, *op. cit.*, p. 15.

32 *Ibid.*, p. 7.

33 *Annual Report for Northern Nigeria 1902*, p. 10.

34 Saburi Biobaku and Mohammad Al-Hajj 'The Sudanese Mahidiyya and the Niger-Chad Region', p. 13. Paper presented to the Seminar on *Islam in Tropical Africa* (cited). The authors show how the Mahdi was in correspondence with Borno and Sokoto demanding both recognition and support.

35 For Rabeh's career see Urvoy *op. cit.*, Schultze *op. cit.*, and E. Gentil *La Chute de l'Empire de Rabeh*, Paris, 1902.

36 *Annual Report for Northern Nigeria, 1901*, p. 15.

37 *Ibid.*, p. 15.

38 D. J. M. Muffet in *Concerning Brave Captains*, London, 1964, pp. 34–51.

39 Lady Lugard *op. cit.*, p. 441.

40 Hilaire Belloc in *The Modern Traveller* cited in Perham *Lugard*, *op. cit.*, II, p. 45.
41 *Annual Report for Northern Nigeria 1902*, Appendix III, p. 105.
42 Muffet *op. cit.*, pp. 143–212.
43 *Ibid.*, p. 147.
44 *Ibid.*, p. 137.
45 *Annual Report for Northern Nigeria 1903*.
46 Biobaku and Al-Hajj *op. cit.*, p. 15.
47 Perham *Lugard op. cit.*, II, p. 252.
48 Cited *Ibid.*, p. 258, from Cmd. 3620, p. 19.
49 M. G. Smith *op. cit.*, pp. 205–6.

Chapter 14   The Unification of Nigeria (between pages 188 and 206)

1 J. C. Anene 'The Southern Nigeria Protectorate and the Aros, 1900–02' *J.H.S.N.*, I, 1, December 1956, pp. 20–6. Unfortunately in writing on the Aro in the first edition I missed this article. I have now revised my earlier account in view of this additional material.
2 *Ibid.*, p. 21.
3 *Ibid.*, p. 26.
4 See Burns *op. cit.*, p. 210. Also for a short passage on the pacification of Urhobo see 'The Establishment of British Administration in the Urhobo Country (1891–1913)' *J.H.S.N.*, I, 3, December 1958, pp. 198–200.
5 *Colonial Office Annual Reports for Southern Nigeria* for 1908 and 1910.
6 There is an excellent and very full account of the impact of Western economic forces on Nigerian society in James Coleman *Nigeria: Background to Nationalism*, 1958, pp. 63–90.
7 Direct taxation, which was unknown in most parts of Southern Nigeria, was conceived by Lugard and other British administrators, to be useful not so much for raising revenue for government (for this could always be obtained by duties on imports and exports), but because of its alleged 'moral benefits'. Taxation forced the African to work more than was necessary to satisfy his immediate wants. Since work was considered morally good, then taxation, which forced the African to work more, was morally beneficial. Of course it was also beneficial to the colonial power, anxious to exploit the country's economic resources, since in order to raise funds for the payment of taxes, the African had to grow cash crops which, like cocoa, were often of no use to him for personal consumption. See Lugard *The Dual Mandate in British Tropical Africa*, London, 1922, Chapter XII, pp. 230–55.
8 Captain J. F. J. Fitzpatrick 'Nigeria's Curse—The Native Administration' *National Review*, No. 502, December 1924, p. 618.
9 See Mary Bull 'Indirect Rule in Northern Nigeria, 1906–1911', in *Essays in Imperial Government* (presented to Margery Perham), ed. Kenneth Robinson and Frederick Madden, Oxford, 1963.
10 P. C. Lloyd 'Kings, Chiefs and Local Government' *West Africa*, 31st January 1953.
11 For a full length biography of Mary Slessor on which much of this section is based, see W. P. Livingstone *Mary Slessor of Calabar*, 4th edition, London, 1935. Also 'Mary Slessor' *Nigeria Magazine*, No. 58, 1958.
12 James S. Coleman *op. cit.*, p. 101. I am much in debt to Professor Coleman's

chapter on 'Christianity and Missionaries', pp. 91–112, for this section on
missionary impact on Nigeria; and also to discussions with Mr Robin Horton.

13 Ajayi *Missions op. cit.*, p. 225–6.

14 *Ibid.*, pp. 253–4.

15 See Coleman *op. cit.*, Chapter 5, 'Western Education', pp. 113–40 for a full
discussion of the impact of Western education on Nigerian societies.

16 For a full discussion of the economics and politics of 'amalgamation' see
Perham *Lugard op. cit.*, II, Chapter XX: 'The Creation of Nigeria', pp.
408–21. Also *Nigeria: Report by Sir F. D. Lugard on the Amalgamation of
Northern and Southern Nigeria and Administration, 1912–1919*, Cmd. 468,
London, 1920, and Cook *op. cit.*, pp. 190–211.

17 E. D. Morel *Nigeria, its Peoples and Problems*, 2nd edition, London, 1912, pp.
201–10.

18 See Perham *op. cit.*, p. 414.

19 *Ibid.*, Chapter XIX, pp. 377–407.

20 *Report on Amalgamation op. cit.*, p. 12.

21 Perham *op. cit.*, pp. 418–20.

22 Cited by Cook *op. cit.*, p. 207, no source given.

23 *Report on Amalgamation op. cit.*, 14–15.

24 Perham *op. cit.*, pp. 487–8.

25 Of course direct taxation was not altogether foreign to the Yoruba since it
was introduced to Ilorin by the Fulani after 1830.

26 This report is not a published one, existing only in typescript: 'Reports of a
Tour in the Southern Provinces in 1914 by H. R. Palmer', cited by Margery
Perham from the Lugard Papers. Perham *op. cit.*, p. 444.

27 *Ibid.*, pp. 445–7.

28 Lugard shared many of the prejudices against mixing with educated Africans current among the British at the time. (See Lugard *The Dual Mandate
op. cit.*, p. 87, where he cites an article he wrote in the *Edinburgh Review* of
April 1921: 'Here, then, is the true conception of the inter-relation of colour:
complete uniformity in ideals, absolute equality in the paths of knowledge
and culture, equal opportunity for those who strive, equal admiration for
those who achieve; in matters social and racial a separate path, each pursuing his own inherited traditions, preserving his own race-purity and
race-pride; equality in things spiritual, agreed divergence in the physical
and material.') However, he not only appointed Moore to this Commission of
Enquiry but also made Henry Carr Resident of Lagos. He was also a close
personal friend of Sir Kitoye Ajasa, publisher of the pro-Government
Nigerian Pioneer, see Coleman *op. cit.*, p. 185 and 453, n. 12.

29 See Burns *op. cit.*, p. 217 where the letters of the Shehu of Borno and the
Lamido of Adamawa to Lugard are printed. See also Burns for a detailed
account of the course of the war (pp. 216–24). Perham discusses Lugard's role
in the Nigerian war effort in Chapter XXVII of *Lugard op. cit.*, II. For the
conquest of the Cameroons and Nigeria's military role in it, see W. O.
Henderson *Studies in German Colonial History*, Chicago, 1962, Chapter
VIII, pp. 96–108. Also *Statistics of the Military Effort of the British Empire
during the Great War 1914–1920*, London, 1922.

30 'Les sénoussistes pendant la guerre 1914–1918' in *Les Troupes coloniales
pendant la guerre 1914–1918*, Paris, 1931, pp. 483–98.

31 Information supplied in a personal communication from Mr Robin Horton.

32 Cited by Burns *op. cit.*, p. 221. Source not given.

33 Letter dated 19th June 1918, cited by Perham *Lugard op. cit.*, II, p. 549.

Chapter 15 **The Rise of Nigerian Nationalism**
(between pages 207 and 223)

1 See Perham *Lugard op. cit.*, II, Chapter XIX: 'The Two Nigerias, 1912–1914', pp. 377–407.
2 I have relied heavily in this chapter on Coleman's admirable study of the growth of Nigerian nationalism, *op. cit.*
3 K. Onwuka Diké *100 Years of British Rule in Nigeria, 1851–1951*, Lagos, 1957, p. 35.
4 Coleman *ibid.*, pp. 188–92. For a biography of Garvey see E. D. Cronan *Black Moses—the story of Marcus Garvey and the Universal Negro Improvement Association*, Wisconsin, 1955.
5 Kalu Ezera *Constitutional Developments in Nigeria*, London, 1960, p. 24, cited from Martin Wight *The Gold Coast Legislative Council*, London, 1946, p. 27.
6 Address by the Governor *Nigerian Council* (Gvt. Records of Proceedings of Council, Lagos), 29th December 1920, p. 20.
7 Ezera *op. cit.*, pp. 26–7; Coleman *op. cit.*, p. 196-7. Coleman stresses that it will be impossible to assess the influence of nationalist agitation on Clifford's decision until we have access to the relevant official papers.
8 *Proceedings of the Nigerian Council*, 1923, p. 4, cited in Cook *op. cit.*, p. 247.
9 See Coleman *op. cit.*, for a more detailed account. Also J. F. Ade Ajayi *Milestones in Nigerian History*, Ibadan, 1962, pp. 28–38; Diké *100 Years of British Rule op. cit.*, pp. 33–42; Burns *op. cit.* for official attitudes to the nationalists; Perham *Lugard op. cit.*, II, Chapter XXIX, pp. 581–606; Raymond L. Buell *The Native Problem in Africa*, 2 vols., New York, 1928; Joan Wheare *Nigerian Legislative Council*, 1949; Obafemi Awolowo *The Path to Nigerian Freedom*, London, 1946; Nnamdi Azikiwe *Renascent Africa*, London, 1937.
10 Nigeria, *Annual Report* for 1920, p. 6.
11 Fitzpatrick 'Nigeria's Curse' *op. cit.*, p. 618.
12 Source not traced.
13 I have relied heavily on Margery Perham *Native Administration in Nigeria*, London, 1937, for my account of the working of indirect rule in Nigeria in the inter-war period. See also Lord Hailey *Native Administration in the British African Territories*, London, 1951, Pts. II and IV. Also L. P. Mair *Native Policies in Africa*, London, 1936.
14 *Report on the Eastern Provinces by the Secretary of Native Affairs*, Lagos, 1922.
15 *Report of a Commission of Enquiry appointed to inquire into certain incidents at Opobo, Abak and Utu-Etim-Ekpo in December, 1929*, Sessional Paper No. 12 of 1930, Lagos, 1930.
16 *Report of a Commission of Enquiry appointed to inquire into the Disturbances in the Calabar and Owerri Provinces, December, 1929*, Sessional Paper No. 28 of 1930, Lagos, 1930.
17 Perham *Native Administration op. cit.*, p. 215 (1962 edition).
18 Hailey *op. cit.*, pt. III, p. 160.
19 *Supplement to Gazette Extraordinary*, 6th March 1933, p. 17, cited in Perham *op. cit.*, p. 332.
20 *Principles of Native Administration and their Application*, Lagos, 1934.
21 *Annual Report for 1932*, Lagos.
22 See *Report of the Commission of Inquiry into the Administration of Justice in Kenya, Uganda, and the Tanganyika Territory, in Municipal Matters, May*

1933 and Correspondence arising out of the Report, Cmd. 4623, 1934, p. 134–5, cited in Perham *op. cit.*, p. 338.

23 Lugard *Dual Mandate op. cit.*, pp. 544–5.

24 *Nigerian Handbook*, 2nd edition, Lagos, 1953.

25 *West Africa*, 26th July 1924.

26 *Debate in House of Commons*, 29th July 1926, Hansard, 198, p. 2399, etc. See particularly speech of Mr Snell, who makes a strong attack on the plantation system in Africa.

27 Coleman *op. cit.*, p. 207.

28 For his own account of the history of the Nigerian Youth Movement see Obafemi Awolowo *Awo: The Autobiography of Chief Obafemi Awolowo*, London, 1960, pp. 113–59.

29 In the preparation of this section I am much indebted to Mr Richard Gleicher, who has been undertaking research on the memoirs and other writings of British officials who served in Nigeria from 1900–40.

30 Burns *op. cit.*, 258

31 Lugard *Dual Mandate op. cit.*, p. 87.

32 *Report on Amalgamation op. cit.*, p. 19.

33 Coleman *op. cit.*, p. 153.

34 J. F. Ade Ajayi *Milestones in Nigerian History*, Ibadan, 1962, p. 24.

35 Coleman *op. cit.*, p. 161.

36 Perham *Native Administration op. cit.*, p. 343.

37 Sir Bernard Bourdillon *The Future of the Colonial Empire*, London, 1945, p. 56.

38 Perham *op. cit.*, p. 361.

39 *Ibid.*, p. 362.

40 Obafemi Awolowo *Nigerian Freedom op. cit.*, p. 63. It is interesting to note that Lucy Mair had recognized this fact, though without enthusiasm, as early as 1936 in her *Native Policies in Africa op cit.*, pp. 283–6.

41 W. R. Crocker *Self-Government for the Colonies*, London, 1949, Chapter 6, pp. 43–62, where he cites some of the more virulent of the post-war nationalist abuses.

42 Meyer Fortes 'The impact of the war on British West Africa', *International Affairs*, XXI, 2 April, 1945, pp. 206–19.

43 *Life*, 10th October 1942, cited in Lord Hailey *An African Survey Revised, 1956*, London, 1957, p. 245.

44 *The Constitution of the N.C.N.C.*, Lagos, 1945, p. 1.

Chapter 16   **Three Constitutions** (between pages 224 and 236)

1 *Proposals for the Revision of the Constitution of Nigeria:* Cmd. 6599 (1945), p. 6.

2 K. Onwuka Diké *100 Years of British Rule in Nigeria 1851–1951*, Lagos, 1957, p. 43.

3 For a fuller discussion of the Richards Constitution, and the two constitutions that followed it in 1951 and 1954, see Ezera, *Constitutional Developments in Nigeria*, London, 1960, Coleman *op. cit.*, and Eme Awa, *Federal Government in Nigeria*, Berkeley and Los Angeles, 1964, pp. 17–24.

4 *N.C.N.C. Memorandum on the New Constitution of Nigeria*, Lagos, 1945.

5 Sir Bernard Bourdillon 'Nigeria's New Constitution' *United Empire*, XXXVI, 2, March-April, 1946, pp. 76–80.

6 Ezera *op. cit.*, p. 65; see also Sir Bernard Bourdillon *Memorandum on the Future Political Development in Nigeria*, Lagos, 1939.

7 Coleman *op. cit.*, p. 258.

8 See *A Ten Year Plan of Development and Welfare for Nigeria*, Lagos, 1946.

9 *Report of the Commission appointed by His Excellency the Governor to make recommendations about the recruitment and training of Nigerians for Senior Posts in the Government Service of Nigeria*, Lagos, 1948.

10 See David Apter *The Gold Coast in Transition*, Princeton (U.S.A.), 1955, pp. 169–74 or Apter *Ghana in Transition* (revised edition of the above), New York, 1963, pp. 169–74.

11 Ezera *op. cit.*, pp. 89–96. See also Coleman *op. cit.*, Chapter XVI 'The Ibo and Yoruba Strands in Nigerian Nationalism', pp. 332–52.

12 Cited by Ezera *op. cit.*, p. 91, from *The West African Pilot* of 8th July 1949.

13 Awolowo *Nigerian Freedom op. cit.*, p. 173.

14 Cited in Coleman *op. cit.*, p. 346.

15 *Ibid.*, pp. 344–5 from *The Constitution of the Egbe Omo Oduduwa*, Ijebu-Ode, 1948, pp. 5–6.

16 *Report of the Commission of Enquiry into the Disorders in the Eastern Provinces of Nigeria*, Lagos, 1950, and see Ezera *op. cit.*, pp. 97–100.

17 Ezera *op. cit.*, pp. 118–20.

18 For an admirable study of the development of political parties in Nigeria see Richard Sklar *Nigerian Political Parties—Power in an Emergent Nation*, Princeton (U.S.A.), 1963.

19 See Sir Ahmadu Bello, Sardauna of Sokoto, *My Life*, London, 1962, pp. 110–12.

20 *Nigeria (Constitution) Order-in-Council, 1951*, Section 162, p. 58.

21 Included in the four ministers elected from the East.

22 See the Sardauna of Sokoto's own account of the Northern position in his autobiography *op. cit.*, pp. 110–48.

23 *Ibid.*, pp. 135–6.

24 See for instance Ezera *op. cit.*, p. 171.

25 *Report on the Kano Disturbances, 16th, 17th, 18th and 19th May, 1953*, Lagos and Kaduna, 1953, p. 21.

26 For full details of the eight-point programme see Bello *op. cit.*, pp. 143–4.

27 Source not traced.

28 *Hansard* v. 515, p. 2263, 21st May 1953. Debate in House of Commons.

29 *Report by the Conference on the Nigerian Constitution held in London in July and August, 1953*, Cmd. 8934, London, 1953.

30 *Report by the Resumed Conference on the Nigerian Constitution held in Lagos in January and February, 1954*, Cmd. 9050, London, 1954.

31 *Report of the Fiscal Commissioner on the Financial Effects of the Proposed new constitutional arrangements*, Cmd. 9026, London, 1953.

Chapter 17 **Independence Achieved** (between pages 237 and 258)

1 The figures for the the results of the federal election in both the North and East are inaccurate in the first edition. I have revised these in the light of Richard Sklar *op. cit.*, p. 35. The actual figures are *North*: N.P.C.=79, Allies=5, Independents=4, Action Group=1, Middle Belt People's Party=1; *East*: N.C.N.C.=32, U.N.I.P.=4, Action Group=3, Independents=3; *West*: N.C.N.C.=23, Action Group=18, Commoners' Liberal Party=1; *Southern Cameroons*: K.N.C.=5; *Lagos*: N.C.N.C.=1, Action Group=1.

2 *West Africa* 'Sir John and Nigeria', 16th April 1955, pp. 337–8.

3 *West Africa* 'Eyes on Nigeria', 4th February 1956, p. 97.

4 *Self-Government for the Western Region.* Sessional Paper No. 3 of 1955, Ibadan, 1955.

5 *Proceedings of the Tribunal appointed to inquire into Allegations of improper conduct by the Premier of the Eastern Region of Nigeria in connection with the affairs of the African Continental Bank, Limited, and other relevant matters, August-November, 1956,* Lagos, 1957, also *Report of the Tribunal appointed to inquire into allegations reflecting on the Official Conduct of the Premier of, and certain persons holding Ministerial and other Public Offices in, the Eastern Region of Nigeria.* Cmd. 51, London, 1957, p. 42.

6 Ezera *op. cit.,* pp. 230–1.

7 *West Africa* 'The Bank Report' 19th January 1957, p. 49. Sklar *op. cit.,* pp. 143–89 has an excellent section on the N.C.N.C. and the African Continental Bank.

8 *West Africa* 'Polling in West Africa', 26th May 1956, p. 315.

9 Michael Crowder 'Political Tensions in Northern Nigeria' *West Africa,* 11th and 18th January 1958.

10 *Report of the Commission appointed to enquire into the fears of Minorities and the means of allaying them.* Cmd. 505, London, 1958.

11 Philip Mason *West Africa* 'Conference and Minorities Commission': I 'Prospects of Permanence' 22nd November 1958, p. 1115; II 'Safeguards for Citizens' 29th November 1958, p. 1135.

12 Revised figures. There was an inaccuracy in the table in the first edition. See Sklar *op. cit.,* pp. 36–7. Since the appearance of the first edition K. J. W. Post has published an excellent study, *The Nigerian Federal Election of 1959,* London 1963.

13 Coleman *op. cit.,* p. 252.

14 *The Economic Development of Nigeria* (International Bank for Reconstruction and Development), Baltimore, 1955, p. 666.

15 Coleman *op. cit.,* p. 254.

16 Adapted from the table 'Selected Indicators of Economic Growth' in *Economy Survey of Nigeria, 1959,* Lagos, 1959.

17 Material for this section is based on *The Economic Survey of Nigeria, op. cit.* and *Nigeria: The Political and Economic Background* (Royal Institute of International Affairs), London 1960. 'Nigeria Gets Ready for 1960' *New Commonwealth,* July 1959, pp. 434–7 and 'One Sixth of Africa's Market' *New Commonwealth,* July 1960, pp. 425–31.

18 *Economic Survey ibid,* p. 27.

19 For a full and critical discussion of national marketing boards see P. T. Bauer *West African Trade,* London, 1963, (2nd edition) in particular Part V, pp. 263–343.

20 *Economic Survey op. cit.,* p. 22.

21 *Ibid.,* p. 17.

22 For a study of the impact of the road on traditional societies, see Joyce Cary *Mister Johnson,* London, 1939.

23 Nigeria Works It Out' *Economist,* 7th July 1962, p. 42.

24 See Sir Sidney Phillipson and S. O. Adebo *Nigerianisation of the Civil Service: A Review of Policy and Machinery,* Lagos, 1954, and *Report of the Commission . . . to make recommendations about the recruitment and training of Nigerians for Senior Posts in the Government Service of Nigeria,* Lagos, 1948, and *Statement of Policy on the Nigerianisation of the Federal*

Public Service and the Higher Training of Nigerians, 1956–60, Lagos, 1956.

25 *Investment in Education: Report of the Commission on Higher Education in Nigeria* (Chairman: Sir Eric Ashby), Lagos, 1960.

26 Archibald Callaway 'School Leavers in the Developing Economy of Nigeria' in *The Nigerian Political Scene* ed. Taylor Cole and Robert Tilman, London, 1962.

27 Callaway *ibid.* For a treatment of the problem on a pan-African scale see the same author's 'Unemployment among African School Leavers' *Journal of Modern African Studies*, I, 3, 1965, pp. 351–71.

28 Fred J. Harbison 'Human Resources and Economic Development' in Cole and Tilman *op. cit.*, pp. 210–16.

29 Ashby *op. cit.*

30 For a study of urban problems in Lagos see Peter Marris *Family and Social Change in an African City*, London, 1961.

31 For studies of the role of voluntary associations in the modern cities see Kenneth Little 'West African Urbanization as a Social Process' in *Cahiers d'Etudes Africaines*, III, 1960, pp. 90–102, reprinted in W. J. Hanna *Independent Black Africa*, Chicago, 1964, pp. 137–48 and Immanuel Wallerstein 'Voluntary Associations' in Coleman and Rosberg *Political Parties and National Integration in Tropical Africa*, Berkeley and Los Angeles, 1964, pp. 413–43. For a comprehensive study of Credit Unions see Shirley Ardener 'The Comparative Study of Rotating Credit Unions' *Journal of the Royal Anthropological Institute*, vol. 94, Pt. II, 1964.

32 Chinua Achebe *No Longer at Ease*, London, 1960.

33 J. S. Trimingham, *Islam in West Africa* (report to the C.M.S. & Methodist Church Council), London, 1953.

34 J. S. Trimingham *Islam in West Africa*, London 1959, chapter 'The Process of Religious Change', pp. 24–40. The only exception was of course the Pakistani directed Ahmaddiyya movement in Yorubaland.

35 J. Bertin Webster, *The African Churches among the Yoruba*, London, 1964, p. 193.

36 See for instance the Introduction in Hugh H. Smythe and Mabel M. Smythe *The New Nigerian Elite*, Stanford, 1960.

37 See Michael Crowder 'New Nigerian Artists and Writers' in *Prospect*. Roger Bannister ed., Hutchinson, 1963, pp. 147–53.

38 Post *op. cit.*, tables on pp. 351, 353 and 355.

Chapter 18   **A Decade of Troubles** (between pages 259 and 277)

1 Sessional Paper No. 4 of 1960 quoted in Claude S. Phillips Jnr, *The Development of Nigerian Foreign Policy*, Evanston, 1964, p. 146.

2 It will be some time before these six years can be placed in the same historical perspective as the history of Nigeria before it gained its independence. There are, however, two books which give as balanced an account of the period as is possible to give at this time, though both of them required many pages to do it. Walter Schwarz in his *Nigeria* (London, 1968) covers the period from independence up to the secession of the Eastern Region at 2 a.m. on 30th May 1967 (pages 114–301), while John de St Jorre gives as impartial an account of the subsequent civil war as at present possible in his *The Nigerian Civil War* (London, 1972, 391 pages of text). Other books that can be

recommended as background to this period are: Martin Dent, *The Military and Political Process in Nigeria, 1966–68*, London 1973; A. H. M. Kirk-Greene, *Crisis and Conflict in Nigeria: A Documentary Sourcebook, 1966–1970*, 2 vols., London, 1971; Robin A. Luckham, *The Nigerian Military, 1960–1967:A Sociological Analysis of Authority and Revolt*, London, 1971; John P. Mackintosh, et al., *Nigerian Government and Politics*, London, 1966; N. J. Miners, *The Nigerian Army 1955–1966*, London, 1971; John Oyinbo, *Nigeria—Crisis and Beyond*, London, 1971; S. K. Panter-Brick (ed.), *Nigerian Politics and Military Rule: Prelude to Civil War*, London, 1970; Michael A. Samuels (ed.), *The Nigeria-Biafra Conflict*, Washington, D.C., 1969; Ralph Uwechue, *Reflections on the Nigerian Civil War* (revised edition). New York, 1971. For passionately pro-Biafra accounts, samples are: Frederick Forsyth, *The Biafra Story*, London, 1969; Auberon Waugh and Suzanne Cronje, *Biafra: Britain's Shame*, London, 1969. Samples of Nigerian equivalents of these are: Robert G. Armstrong, *Nigeria: The Issues at Stake*, Ibadan, 1967; S. O. O. Amali, *Ibos and their Fellow Nigerians*, Ibadan, 1967. Robert Collis, *Nigeria in Conflict*, London, 1970.

The most balanced reporting on the civil war is to be found in *West Africa*, which kept a War Diary, and in the *Financial Times*, particularly the reports and despatches of Bridget Bloom, formerly on the staff of *West Africa*; John de St Jorre has a very full list of Official Pamphlets relating to the war in his selected Bibliography.

3 *West Africa,* 17 February 1962.

4 While the Federal House of Representatives comprised members elected by constituencies allocated on the basis of population, members of the Senate were appointed by the government of each region on an equal basis irrespective of size. Thus, if the U.P.G.A. were to win control of all three Southern Regions it would have three-quarters of the membership of the Senate and would be able, with more than a two-thirds majority, to block legislation of a government relying on a Northern Region based majority.

5 *Yearbook of the United Nations,* 1964, cited by S. O. Osoba in his 'Independence and After: the Challenge to Statesmanship' *Groundwork of Nigerian History,* forthcoming. Osoba provides some particularly incisive insights into the attitude of the élite to the foreign policy of Balewa's government.

6 See Schwarz *op. cit.* p. 203.

7 Press release No. 723, Federal Ministry of Information, Lagos, 24 May 1966, cited in Schwarz, *op. cit.* p. 205.

8 *Ibid.*

9 The full transcript of the tapes was published by the Eastern Region government in *Eastern Daylight.*

10 For a detailed account of this operation and the rest of the war see St Jorre *op. cit.*

Bibliography

Ajayi, J. F. Ade *Milestones in Nigerian History*, Ibadan, 1962.

Ajayi, J. F. Ade *Christian Missions in Nigeria 1841–1891: The Making of an Educated Elite*, London, 1965.

Ajayi, J. F. Ade, and Smith, Robert *Yoruba Warfare in the Nineteenth Century*, Ibadan and London, 1964.

Alagoa, E. J. *The Small Brave City State: A History of Brass-Nembe in the Niger Delta*, Ibadan and Wisconsin, 1964.

Alimen, H. *The Prehistory of Africa*, London, 1957.

Armstrong, Robert G. *State Structures in Negro Africa*, unpublished Ph.D. dissertation, Chicago University 1952, available on microfilm.

Arnett, E. J. *The Rise of the Sokoto Fulani* (Paraphrase of *Infaku'l Maisur* of Sultan Bello Muhammad), Kano, 1922.

Austin, Dennis *West Africa and the Commonwealth*, London, 1957.

Awa, E. O. *Federal Government in Nigeria*, Berkeley and Los Angeles, 1964.

Awolowo, Obafemi *The Path to Nigerian Freedom*, London, 1947.

Awolowo, Obafemi *Awo: The Autobiography of Chief Obafemi Awolowo*, London, 1960.

Azikiwe, Nnamdi *Renascent Africa*, Lagos, 1937.

Azikiwe, Nnamdi *Zik*, London, 1961.

Baikie, William B. *Narrative of an Exploring Voyage up the Rivers Kw'ora and Binue (commonly known as the Niger and Tshadda) in 1854*, London, 1856.

Barth, Heinrich *Travels and Discoveries in Northern and Central Africa*, London, 5 vols., 1857–8.

Bauer, P. T. *West African Trade*, London, 1963 (2nd edition).

Bello, Sir Ahmadu, Sardauna of Sokoto *My Life*, London, 1962.

Biobaku, S. O. *The Egba and their Neighbours, 1832–1872*, London, 1957.

Biobaku, S. O. *The Origin of the Yorubas*, Lagos, 1955.

Blake, J. W. *Europeans in West Africa, 1450–1560*, 2 vols., London, 1942.

Blake, J. W. *European Beginnings in West Africa, 1454–1578*, London, 1937.

Boahen, Adu *Britain, the Sahara and the Western Sudan, 1788–1861*, London, 1964.

Bohannan, Laura and Paul, *The Tiv of Central Nigeria*, London, 1953.

Bosman, William *A New and Accurate Description of the Coast of Guinea*, London, 1705; reprinted 1907.

Bovill, E. W. *The Golden Trade of the Moors*, London, 1955.

Bovill, E. W. *Caravans of the Old Sahara*, London, 1933.

Bown, Lalage, and Crowder, Michael (ed.), *Proceedings of the First International Congress of Africanists*, London, 1964.

Bradbury, R. E., and Lloyd, Peter C. *The Benin Kingdom and Edo-speaking Peoples, etc., plus the Itsekiri*, London, 1959.

Buchanan, K. M. and Pugh, J. C. *Land and People in Nigeria*, London, 1955.

Buell, R. L. *The Native Problem in Africa*, 2 vols., New York, 1928

Burdon, J. A. *Historical Notes on Certain Emirates and Tribes (Nigeria, Northern Provinces)*, London, 1909.

Burns, Sir Alan C. *History of Nigeria*, London, 1956; 5th edn 1958; 6th edn 1962.

Buxton, T. F. *The African Slave Trade and its Remedy*, London, 1839.

Cameron, Donald *Principles of Native Administration and their Application*, Lagos, 1934.

Cary, Joyce *Britain and West Africa*, London, 1940.

Church, R. J. Harrison *West Africa*, London, 1957; 2nd edn 1964.

Clapperton, Hugh *Journal of a Second Expedition into the Interior of Africa, from the Bight of Benin to Soccattoo*, London, 1829.

Coleman, James *Nigeria: Background to Nationalism*, Berkeley and Los Angeles, 1958.

Cook, Arthur N. *British Enterprise in Nigeria*, New York, 1943.

Cowan, L. Gray *Local Government in West Africa*, New York, 1958.

Crocker, W. R. *Nigeria: A Critique of British Colonial Administration*, London, 1936.

Cronan, E. D. *Black Moses—the story of Marcus Garvey and the Universal Negro Improvement Association*, Wisconsin, 1955.

Crowther, S. A. *Journal of an Expedition up the Niger and the Tshadda Rivers, undertaken by Macgregor Laird Esq., in connection with the British Government, in 1854*, London, 1855.

Davidson, Basil *Old Africa Rediscovered*, London, 1959.

Davidson, Basil *Black Mother*, London, 1961.

Davidson, Basil, and Ademola, A. (eds) *The New West Africa*, London, 1953.

Davies, J. G. *The Biu Book*, Nigeria, 1956.

Denham, D., Clapperton, H., and Oudney, N., *Narrative of Travels and Discoveries in Northern and Central Africa in the Years 1822, 1823 and 1824*, London, 1826.

Diké, K. Onwuka *Trade and Politics in the Niger Delta, 1830–1885*, London, 1956.

Diké, K. Onwuka *100 Years of British Rule in Nigeria, 1851–1951*, Lagos, 1957.

Diké, K. Onwuka *Origins of the Niger Mission, 1841–1891*, Lagos 1957.

East, Rupert (ed.) *Akiga's Story*, London, 1939.

Egharevba, J. U. *A Short History of Benin*, Lagos, 1936; 2nd edn Ibadan 1960.

English, M. C. *An Outline of Nigerian History*, London, 1959.

Ezera, Kalu *Constitutional Developments in Nigeria*, London, 1960.

Fage, J. D. *An Introduction to the History of West Africa*, London, 1955.

Fartua, Imam Ahmed ibn *History of the First Twelve Years of the Reign of Mai Idris Alooma of Bornu 1571–1583*, trans. with Introduction and Notes by H. R. Palmer, Lagos, 1926.

Flint, J. E. *Sir George Goldie and the Making of Nigeria*, London, 1960.

Forde, Daryll *The Yoruba-Speaking Peoples of South-Western Nigeria*, London, 1951.

Forde, Daryll (ed.) *Efik Traders of Old Calabar*, London, 1956.

Forde, Daryll, and Jones, G. I. *The Ibo and Ibibio-Speaking Peoples of South-Eastern Nigeria*, London, 1950.

Forde, Daryll, and others *Peoples of the Niger-Benue Confluence*, London, 1955.

Fortes, Meyer, and Evans-Pritchard, E. E. *African Political Systems*, London, 1940.

Geary, William N. M. *Nigeria Under British Rule*, London, 1927.

Greenberg, Joseph *Studies in African Linguistic Classification*, U.S.A., 1955.

Greenberg, Joseph H. *The Languages of Africa*. Supplement to *The International Journal of American Linguistics*, XXIX, 1, Pt. 2, Jan. 1963, Bloomington, 1963.

Hailey, Lord *Native Administration in the British African Territories*, 5 vols., London, 1951.

Hailey, Lord *An African Survey*, London, 1938.

Hailey Lord *An African Survey Revised, 1956*, London, 1957.

Hancock, W. K. *Survey of British Commonwealth Affairs*, 2 vols., Oxford, 1942.

Hargreaves, J. D. *Prelude to the Partition of West Africa*, London, 1963.

Harris, John *Books about Nigeria* (4th edition), Ibadan, 1963.

Harris, Philip *Local Government in Southern Nigeria*, London 1957.

Hassan Alhaji, and Na'ibi, Mallam Shu'aibu (trans. F. Heath) *A Chronicle of Abuja*, Ibadan, 1952; 2nd edn, Lagos, 1962.

Herman-Hodge, H. B. *Gazetteer of Ilorin Province*, London, 1929.

Hodgkin, Thomas *Nationalism in Colonial Africa*, London, 1956.

Hodgkin, Thomas *Nigerian Perspectives*, London, 1960, 2nd edn 1975.

Hogben, S. J. *The Muhammadan Emirates of Nigeria*, London, 1930.

Hopen, Edward *The Pastoral Fulbe Family in Gwandu*, London, 1959.

Howard, C. and Plumb, J. H. *West African Explorers*, London, 1952.

Hutchinson, T. J. *Ten Years' Wandering among the Ethiopians*, London, 1861.

Ibn Battuta (trans. H. A. R. Gibb) *Travels in Asia and Africa, 1325–1354*, London, 1953.

Idowu, E. Bolaji *Oludomare—God in Yoruba Belief*, London, 1962.

International Bank for Reconstruction and Development *The Economic Development of Nigeria*, U.S.A., 1955.

Johnson, Samuel *The History of the Yorubas*, Lagos, 1937.

Jones, G. I. *The Trading States of the Oil Rivers*, London, 1963.

Kingsley, Mary *West African Studies*, London, 1901 (2nd edition).

Kirk-Greene, A. H. M. *Adamawa, Past and Present*, London, 1958.

Kirk-Greene, A. H. M. *Barth's Travels in Northern Nigeria*, London, 1962.

Krieger, K. *Geschichte von Zamfara*, Berlin, 1959.

Laird, Macgregor, and Oldfield, R. A. K. *Narrative of an Expedition into the Interior of Africa in 1832, 1833 and 1834*, 2 vols, London, 1837.

Lander, Richard and John *Journals of an Expedition to Explore the Course and Termination of the Niger, etc.*, London, 1832.

Langa Langa *Up Against it in Nigeria*, London, 1922.

Livingstone, W. P. *Mary Slessor of Calabar*, London, 1933, 4th edn 1935.

Lloyd, Christopher *The Navy and the Slave Trade*, London, 1949.

Lugard, F. D. *The Dual Mandate in British Tropical Africa*, Edinburgh, 1929.

Lugard, F. D. *Nigeria: Report on the Amalgamation of Northern and Southern Nigeria and Administration, 1912–1919*, Cmd. 468, London, 1920.

Lugard, F. D. *Political Memoranda*, London, 1906.

Lugard, Lady *A Tropical Dependency*, London, 1905.

Macfarlane, Donald M. *Calabar and the Church of Scotland Mission, 1846–1946*, London 1946.

McPhee, Allan, *The Economic Revolution in West Africa*, London, 1926.

Mair, L. P. *Native Policies in Africa*, London, 1936.

Mannix, Daniel P., with Cowley, Malcolm *Black Cargoes—A History of the Atlantic Slave Trade 1518–1865*, London, 1963.

Mauny, Raymond *Tableau Géographique de l'Ouest Africain au Moyen Age*, Dakar, 1961.

Meek, C. K. *Northern Tribes of Nigeria*, London, 1925.

Meek, C. K. *A Sudanese Kingdom*, London, 1931.
Mockler-Ferryman, A. F. *British Nigeria*, London, 1902.
Morel, E. D. *Nigeria: Its Peoples and Problems*, 2nd edn. London, 1912.
Muffet, D. J. M. *Concerning Brave Captains*, London, 1964.
Murdock, G. P. *Africa—Its Peoples and their Culture History*, New York, 1959; Dakar, 1961.
Nadel, S. F. *A Black Byzantium*, London, 1942.
Newbury, C. W. *The Western Slave Coast and its Rulers*, Oxford, 1961.
Nigeria, *The Nigeria Handbook*, London, 1953.
Niven, C. R. *A Short History of Nigeria*, London, 1937.
Niven, C. R. *A Short History of the Yoruba Peoples*, London, 1958.
Oliver, Roland *Sir Harry Johnston and the Scramble for Africa*, London, 1957.
Oliver, Roland, and Fage, J. D. *A Short History of Africa*, London, 1962.
Orikpo, Akoi *Who Are the Nigerians?* Lagos, 1958.
Orr, C. W. J. *The Making of Northern Nigeria*, London, 1911.
Palmer, H. R. *The Bornu, Sahara and Sudan*, London, 1936.
Palmer, H. R. *Sudanese Memoirs,* 3 vols., Lagos, 1928.
  see also Fartua.
Park, Mungo *Travels in the Interior Districts of Africa, in 1795, 1796 and 1797, etc.*, London, 1799.
Park, Mungo *Journal of a mission to the interior of Africa in the year 1805, etc.*, London, 1815.
Parrinder, Geoffrey *The Story of Ketu—An Ancient Yoruba Kingdom*, Ibadan, 1956.
Pedler, F. J. *West Africa*, London, 1951.
Pedrarza, Howard J. *Borioboola-Gha: The Story of Lokoja, the first British Settlement in Nigeria*, London, 1960.
Perham, Margery *The Native Economies of Nigeria*, London, 1946.
Perham, Margery *Native Administration in Nigeria*, London, 1937.
Perham, Margery (I) *Lugard: The Years of Adventure, 1858–1898*, London, 1956.
Perham, Margery (II) *Lugard: The Years of Authority, 1899–1945*, London, 1960.
Perham, Margery, and Bull, Mary *The Diaries of Lord Lugard*, Vol. IV, London, 1963.
Post, K. J. W. *The Nigerian Federal Election of 1959*, London, 1963.
Prest, A. R., and Stewart, I. A. *The National Income of Nigeria*, London, 1953.
Robinson, Ronald, and Gallagher, John, with Denny, Alice *Africa and the Victorians*, London, 1961.
Roth, H. Ling *Great Benin: its Customs, Art and Horrors*, Halifax, 1903.
Royal Institute of International Affairs *Nigeria: The Political and Economic Background*, London, 1960.
St Croix, F. W. de *The Fulani of Northern Nigeria*, Lagos, 1944.
Schön, Jacob F., and Crowther, S. A. *Journals of the Rev. J. F. Schön and Mr. Samuel Crowther, who with the sanction of Her Majesty's Government, accompanied the expedition up the Niger in 1841, on behalf of the Church Missionary Society,* London, 1842.
Schultze, A. (trans. P. A. Benton) *The Sultanate of Bornu*, London, 1913.
Shaw, Thurstan *Archaeology and Nigeria*, Ibadan, 1964.
Sklar, Richard *Nigerian Political Parties—Power in an Emergent Nation*, Princeton, 1963.
Smith, Mary *Baba of Karo*, London, 1954.

Smith, M. G. *Government in Zazzau*, London, 1960.

Stenning, Derek *Savannah Nomads*, London, 1959.

Talbot, P. Amaury *The Peoples of Southern Nigeria*, vol. I *Historical Notes*, London, 1926.

Temple, C. L. *Notes on the Tribes, Provinces, Emirates and States of Northern Nigeria*, Lagos, 1922.

Thorp, Ellen *Ladder of Bones*, London, 1959.

Trimingham, J. Spencer *Islam in West Africa*, London, 1959.

Trimingham, J. Spencer *A History of Islam in West Africa*, London, 1962.

Urvoy, Yves *L'Histoire de l'Empire de Bornou*, 1949, Dakar.

Vansina, J., Mauny, R. and Thomas, L.-V. *The Historian in Tropical Africa*, London, 1964.

Wellesley, Lady Dorothy *Sir George Goldie*—Founder of Nigeria, London, 1934.

Westermann, Diedrich, and Bryan, M. A. *Languages of West Africa*, London, 1952.

Wheare, Joan *The Nigerian Legislative Council*, London, 1950.

Whitting, C. E. (trans) *History of Sokoto* by Al-Hajj Sa'id, Kano, 1949.

ARTICLES

Ajayi, J. F. Ade 'Nineteenth Century Origins of Nigerian Nationalism' *J.H.S.N.*, II, 2, 1961. 'Henry Venn and the Policy of Development' *J.H.S.N.*, I, 4, 1959. 'The British Occupation of Lagos 1851–1861' *Nigeria Magazine*, No. 69, August, 1961.

Akinjogbin, I. A. 'The Prelude to the Yoruba Civil Wars of the Nineteenth Century', *Odu*, new series, no. 2.

Anene, J. C. 'The Southern Nigerian Protectorate and the Aros, 1900–02' *J.H.S.N.*, I, 1, 1956.

Armstrong, R. G. 'The Development of Kingdoms in Negro Africa' *J.H.S.N.*, II, 1, 1960.

Beier, Ulli 'Before Oduduwa' *Odu*, 3, 1956.

Beier, Ulli, and Biobaku, S. O. 'The Use and Interpretation of Yoruba Myths' *Odu*, 1, 1955.

Biobaku, S. O. 'The problem of traditional history with special reference to Yoruba traditions' *J.H.S.N.*, I, 1, 1956.

Bivar, A. D. H. 'Wathiqat ahl al-Sudan: A Manifesto of the Fulani Jihad' *J.A.H.*, II, 2, 1961.

Bivar, A. D. H., and Shinnie, P. L. 'Old Kanuri Capitals' *J.A.H.*, III, 1, 1962.

Boston, J. 'Notes on the Origin of the Igala Kingship' *J.H.S.N.*, II, 3, 1962.

Bourdillon, Bernard, 'Nigeria's New Constitution' *United Empire*, XXXVI, 2, March-April 1946.

Bradbury, R. E. 'Chronological Problems in the Study of Benin History' *J.H.S.N.*, I, 4, 1959.

Bradbury, R. E. 'The historical uses of comparative ethnography with special reference to Benin and the Yoruba' *The Historian in Tropical Africa*, London 1964.

Bull, Mary 'Indirect Rule in Northern Nigeria, 1906–1911' in *Essays in Imperial Government*, ed. Kenneth Robinson and Frederick Madden, Oxford, 1963.

Burdon, John A. 'Sokoto History: tables of dates and genealogy' *J. Afr. Soc.*, 6, 24th July 1907.

Clark, J. Desmond 'The Spread of Food Production in Sub-Saharan Africa'

J.A.H., III, 2, 1962. 'The Prehistoric Origins of African Culture' *J.A.H.*, V, 2, 1964.

Dunglas, E. 'La première attaque des Dahoméens contre Abeokuta, 1851' *Etudes Dahoméennes*, I, 1948 and XX, 1957.

Fagg, Bernard 'A life-size terra-cotta head from Nok' *Man* 95, 1956. 'The Nok culture' *West African Review*, December, 1956. 'The Nok Cultures in Prehistory' *J.H.S.N.*, I, 4, 1959.

Forde, Daryll 'The Culture Map of West Africa' *Trans. New York Acad. Sci.*, *Ser.* 2, 15 April 1953.

Fortes, M. 'The impact of the war on British West Africa' *International Affairs*, XXI, 21st April 1945.

Gertzel, C. 'Relations between African and European Traders in the Niger Delta, 1880–1896' *J.A.H.*, III, 2, 1962.

Graham, James D. 'The Slave Trade, Depopulation and Human Sacrifice in Benin History' *Cahiers d'Etudes Africaines*, V, 2, 18, 1965.

Greenberg, J. H. 'Linguistic Evidence for the Influence of Kanuri on Hausa' *J.A.H.*, I, 2, 1960.

Hambly, Wilfrid D. 'Culture areas of Nigeria' *Chicago: Field Museum of Natural History* (Anthropological Series XXXI, 3), 1953.

Hiskett, M. 'Material relating to the state of learning among the Fulani before their Jihad' *Bulletin of the School of Oriental and African Studies*, XIX, 3, 1957. 'The Kano Chronicle' *Journal of the Royal Asiatic Soc.* XXX, 1957. 'Kitab al-Farq' *Bulletin of the School of Oriental and African Studies*, XXII, 3, 1960.

Hodgkin, Thomas "Uthman dan Fodio' *Nigeria 1960—a Special Independence Issue of Nigeria Magazine*, October 1960.

Horton, W. R. G. 'The Ohu system of slavery in a northern Ibo village-group' *Africa*, XXIV, 3, 1954.

Iffemesia, C. C. 'The "Civilising" Mission of 1841' *J.H.S.N.*, II, 3, December 1962.

Jones, G. I. 'Native and Trade Currencies in Southern Nigeria during the 18th and 19th Centuries' *Africa*, XXVIII, 1, 1958. 'European and African Tradition on the Rio Real' *J.A.H.*, IV, 3, 1963.

Kirk-Greene, A. H. M. 'Who coined the name Nigeria?' *West Africa*, 22nd December 1956.

Lloyd, Peter C. 'The traditional political system of the Yoruba' *Southwestern Journal of Anthropology*, X, 4, Winter 1954. 'The Itsekiri Kingdom in the Nineteenth Century; an Outline Social History' *J.A.H.* IV, 2, 1963.

Lloyd, P. C., and Ryder, A. F. C. 'Don Domingos, Prince of Warri—Portuguese contact with the Itsekiri' *Odu*, 1954.

Lugard, Frederick D. 'Expedition to Borgu' *Geog. Journal*, 6, 1895.

Morton-Williams, P. 'Some Yoruba Kingdoms under Modern Conditions' *J. Afr. Admin.*, 7th October 1955. 'The Yoruba Ogboni Cult in Oyo' *Africa*, XXX, 4, 1960. 'An Outline of the Cosmology and Cult Organisation of the Oyo Yoruba' *Africa*, XXXIV, 3, July 1964.

Palmer, H. R. 'The Bornu Girgam' *J. Afr. Soc.* XII, 45, October 1912. 'An Early Fulani Conception of Islam' *J. Afr. Soc.* XIII, 52, July 1914; XIV, 53, October 1914; XV, 54, January 1915. 'The Kano Chronicle' *J. Roy. Anthrop. Inst.* XXXVIII, 1908. 'History of Katsina' *J. Afr. Soc.* XXVI, 103, 1927.

Perry, Ruth 'New Sources for research in Nigerian history' *Africa* XXV, 3, 1955.

Ryder, A. F. C. 'Missionary Activity in the Kingdom of Warri to the Early Nineteenth Century' *J.H.S.N.*, II, 1, 1960.

Shaw Thurstan 'Field Research in Nigerian Archaeology' *J.H.S.N.*, II, 4, 1963.
Smith, H. F. C. 'The Dynastic Chronology of Fulani Zaria' *J.H.S.N.*, II, 2, 1961. 'A Neglected Theme in West African History: the Islamic Revolutions of the Nineteenth Century' *J.H.S.N.*, II, 2, 1961. 'Muhammad Bello, Amir Al-mu'minin' *Ibadan*, 9, June 1960.
Smith, M. G. 'The Origins of Hausa Society' in *The Historian in Tropical Africa*, London 1964.
Smith, Robert 'Ijaiye, the Western Palatinate of the Yoruba' *J.H.S.N.*, II, 3, 1962. 'The Alafin in Exile: A Study of the Igboho Period of Oyo History' *J.A.H.*, VI, 2, 1965.
Urvoy, Yves 'Chronologie du Bornou' *J. Soc. Africanistes*, 11, 1941, 21–32.
Verger, Pierre 'Yoruba influences in Brazil' *Odu*, 2, 1955, 3–11. 'Nigeria, Brazil and Cuba' *Nigeria 1960*, special Independence Issue of *Nigeria Magazine*, October 1960.
Willett, F. 'Investigations at Old Oyo 1956–7: An Interim Report' *J.H.S.N.*, II, 1, 1960. 'Ife and its Archaeology' *J.A.H.*, I, 2, 1960.

GOVERNMENT PUBLICATIONS

Northern Nigeria
   Annual Reports: 1900–1 through to 1912.

Southern Nigeria
   Annual Reports: 1899–1900 through to 1913.

Nigeria/British Government 1914–1960
   Annual Reports: 1915 onwards.
Political Memoranda, Lagos, 1918.
   Report by Sir F. D. Lugard on the Amalgamation of Northern and Southern Nigeria and Administration, 1912–1919, Cmd. 468, London 1920.
   Report on a Tour of the Eastern Provinces by the Secretary for Native Affairs, Lagos, 1923.
   Report of a Commission of Enquiry appointed to enquire into certain incidents at Obopo, Abak and Utu-Etim-Ekpo in December, 1929. Sessional Paper No. 12 of 1930, Lagos, 1930.
   Report of the Commission of Enquiry appointed to enquire into the Disturbances in the Calabar and Owerri Provinces, December, 1929. Sessional Paper No. 28 of 1930, Lagos, 1930.
   The Principles of Native Administration and their Application, Lagos, 1934.
   Report of the Commission appointed to make recommendations about the recruitment and training of Nigerians for Senior Posts in the Government Service of Nigeria, Lagos, 1948.
   Report of the Commission of Enquiry into the Disorders in the Eastern Provinces of Nigeria, Lagos, 1950.
   Proceedings of the General Conference on Review of the Constitution, January, 1950, Lagos 1950.
   Report on the Kano Disturbances 16th, 17th, 18th and 19th May 1953, Lagos and Kaduna 1953.
   Sir Sidney Phillipson and S. O. Adebo *Nigerisation of the Civil Service*, Lagos, 1954.

Report by the Conference on the Nigerian Constitution held in London in July and August, 1953. Cmd. 8934, London, 1953.

Report by the Resumed Conference on the Nigerian Constitution held in Lagos in January and February, 1954. Cmd. 9050, London, 1954.

Report by the Nigerian Constitutional Conference held in London in May and June, 1957. Cmd. 207, London, 1957.

Report of the Tribunal appointed to inquire into allegations reflecting on the Official Conduct of the Premier of, and certain persons holding Ministerial and other Public Offices in, the Eastern Region of Nigeria. Cmd. 51, London, 1957.

Report of the Resumed Nigeria Constitutional Conference held in London in September and October, 1958. Lagos, 1958.

Report of the Commission appointed to enquire into the fears of Minorities and the means of allaying them. Cmd. 505, London, 1958.

JOURNALS, ETC.

Africa: International African Institute, London.
African Affairs: Royal African Society, London.
Bulletin of the School of Oriental and African Studies: University of London, London.
Journal of African Administration: H.M.S.O., London.
Journal of African History: Cambridge University Press.
Journal of the Historical Society of Nigeria: Ibadan University Press.
New Commonwealth: London.
Nigeria Magazine: Exhibition Centre, Lagos.
Odu: Ibadan.
West Africa: London.
West African Review (ceased publication) London.

Index

Note: Material in summary form at the end of the book is not indexed.